Leisure and Aging

Theory and Practice

EDITORS

Heather J. Gibson, PhD
University of Florida

Jerome F. Singleton, PhD
Dalhousie University

Human Kinetics

Library of Congress Cataloging-in-Publication Data

Leisure and aging : theory and practice / Heather J. Gibson and Jerome F. Singleton, editors.
  p. cm.
 Includes bibliographical references and index.
 ISBN-13: 978-0-7360-9463-4 (hard cover)
 ISBN-10: 0-7360-9463-6 (hard cover)
 1. Older people--Recreation. 2. Leisure--Social aspects. 3. Aging. I. Gibson, Heather J. (Heather Julie) II. Singleton, Jerome F., 1950-
 GV184.L44 2011
 796.084'6--dc23

2011021507

ISBN-10: 0-7360-9463-6 (print)
ISBN-13: 978-0-7360-9463-4 (print)

The web addresses cited in this text were current as of July 2011, unless otherwise noted.

Acquisitions Editor: Gayle Kassing, PhD; **Developmental Editor:** Jacqueline Eaton Blakley; **Assistant Editor:** Anne Rumery; **Copyeditor:** Alisha Jeddeloh; **Indexer:** Andrea Hepner; **Permissions Manager:** Dalene Reeder; **Graphic Designer:** Robert Reuther; **Graphic Artist:** Angela K. Snyder; **Cover Designer:** Keith Blomberg; **Photographer (interior):** © Human Kinetics, unless otherwise noted; **Art Manager:** Kelly Hendren; **Associate Art Manager:** Alan L. Wilborn; **Illustrations:** © Human Kinetics, Inc.; **Printer:** Sheridan Books

Printed in the United States of America

10 9 8 7 6 5 4 3 2 1

The paper in this book is certified under a sustainable forestry program.

Human Kinetics
Website: www.HumanKinetics.com

United States: Human Kinetics
P.O. Box 5076
Champaign, IL 61825-5076
800-747-4457
e-mail: humank@hkusa.com

Canada: Human Kinetics
475 Devonshire Road Unit 100
Windsor, ON N8Y 2L5
800-465-7301 (in Canada only)
e-mail: info@hkcanada.com

Europe: Human Kinetics
107 Bradford Road
Stanningley
Leeds LS28 6AT, United Kingdom
+44 (0) 113 255 5665
e-mail: hk@hkeurope.com

Australia: Human Kinetics
57A Price Avenue
Lower Mitcham, South Australia 5062
08 8372 0999
e-mail: info@hkaustralia.com

New Zealand: Human Kinetics
P.O. Box 80
Torrens Park, South Australia 5062
0800 222 062
e-mail: info@hknewzealand.com

E5155

Contents

Preface **vii**   Acknowledgments   **x**

Acknowledgments

We would like to thank a number of people who have been instrumental in bringing this book to fruition. First, our thanks go to Dr. Sherry Dupuis, University of Waterloo, who first envisioned this book and suggested many of the ideas for chapter content. We hope that we have successfully brought to life her vision for this book. Second, we would like to thank the staff at Human Kinetics, notably Gayle Kassing, who saw the potential for this book and has supported it throughout, and Jackie Blakley, our developmental editor. Third, and by no means the least, we thank all of the authors who contributed their intellectual capital and their time and effort to the completion of these chapters. Without you, this book would not have been possible. We hope you like the finished product, and we look forward to hearing how the book is received by your students and by leisure and aging scholars.

I (Heather Gibson) would like to thank Jerry Singleton for taking on the role of communications link between the contributors and us. We felt from the start that it would be less confusing for all of us if there was one main contact person, and Jerry took on this role.

I (Jerry Singleton) would like to thank Heather Gibson for her ability to keep me on task and for her insights related to editing the text as we worked together during the last year and half. This text is the result of a collaborative effort of scholars and resources provided by Human Kinetics.

Preface

As the population ages, it is likely that more people will be retired or working part time, and conceivably the role of leisure in their lives will become increasingly important. Although leisure is important at all stages in the life course, we know that the life dimensions of work, family, and leisure shift in their primacy in various life stages (Rapoport & Rapoport, 1975). Because one of the tasks of late adulthood is to establish new connections with society once the primary roles in the paid workforce or family have diminished or are given up entirely, leisure may become important in later life for establishing a new sense of self (Levinson, Darrow, Klein, Levinson, & McKee, 1978).

This book provides a range of perspectives and insights on leisure and aging, from theoretical foundations to empirical findings and the application of these to future practice. This text will primarily benefit people who are in school or are currently working in the leisure, recreation, sport, and tourism sectors and need to understand how leisure contributes to the health and well-being of people who are aging. Leisure and aging scholars sit at the intersection of two areas of study, gerontology and leisure studies. McGuire (2000) and Gibson (2006) provide critical reviews in understanding the tension for scholars who bridge these two areas of study. Gibson suggests that

> while we [leisure scholars] may argue that leisure is more than activity, gerontologists consistently study the relationship between activity and later life well-being. They generally find that meaningful activity is beneficial in later life and they reconfirm the tenets of activity theory, thereby not moving the body of knowledge further than we did in the 1970s. (p. 397)

The varying ways that these two fields define the term *leisure* provide a wide range of insights on the well-being of older adults. Gerontologists use activity as indicator of well-being while leisure scholars use leisure as more of an integrative construct (Kleiber, 2006, as cited in Gibson, 2006).

Gerontologists often use the phrase *activities of daily living* (ADLs), which encompasses all types of activity, including housework, which may not necessarily be thought of as pleasurable. Leisure scholars, on the other hand, want to know what the activity means to the person. Thus, leisure scholars define *leisure* as activity but in terms of experience, focusing on the social nature of the experience, the intrinsic satisfaction associated with the experience, and the freedom of choice associated with the experience. Thus, in contrast to many gerontologists and health professionals, to leisure scholars it is not what the activity *is* that's important but who people participate with and why, when, where, and how they participate in the experience. These provide the social construction of the experience that may change as people enter and leave various stages of the life course.

Recreation and leisure professionals also need to be flexible in order to meet the needs of an increasingly older and culturally diverse population with varying attitudes and assumptions about both aging and leisure. It is projected that by the year 2017, 20% of the Canadian population will be of racially and ethnically diverse background (Statistics Canada, 2007). Similar patterns of increased racial and ethnic diversity are evident in the United States (Shrestha & Heisler, 2011). The U.S. Census Bureau suggests that as the population ages, increased diversity in older age groups will mirror changes evident in the population more generally (Wan, Sengupta, Velkoff, & DeBarros, 2005). Discussing people over the age of 65, U.S. census data show that in 2003, non-Hispanic whites constituted almost 83% of the older population. Blacks accounted for 8%, followed by Hispanics (6%) and Asians (3%). By 2030, it is predicted that although non-Hispanic whites will remain the majority, their proportion will decrease to 72%, and ethnic minorities will increase proportionately, with older Hispanics predicted to make up 11% of the older population, followed by 10% black and 5% Asian. As our world changes, recreation and leisure professionals must consider cultural and cohort differences and divergent perceptions of aging and leisure.

This book is designed to provide insights about a range of perspectives used to understand leisure and aging. *Leisure* is defined broadly throughout the book and encompasses aging in relation to physical activity and sport as well as tourism. The chapters vary in their academic and practical focus. Some provide theoretical foundations to help students understand the biological, sociological, and psychological changes associated with aging, drawing on the latest empirical findings on various issues associated with leisure and aging. Other chapters are more focused on practice and potential career directions. The overall goal is to create informed future professionals who understand how theory relates to practice.

Throughout the book, learning aids and other special features invite active learning and encourage critical examination of the content. Each chapter begins with learning objectives that outline the desired outcomes from reading that chapter. Key terms are highlighted when discussed, then defined in a handy list at the end of the chapter. Throughout each chapter, sidebars illuminate challenges and issues related to aging populations all over the world. Each chapter closes with extensive learning aids: Review and discussion questions, learning activities, and critical-thinking activities are offered, and additional readings relevant to the material covered in the chapters are included.

Learning is further supplemented by online ancillaries that are made available to instructors who adopt the text. An instructor guide offers chapter summaries, the textbook's learning aids in Word format, as well as additional learning aids not found in the textbook. A test bank includes ready-to-use questions covering the major points of each chapter, and a PowerPoint presentation summarizes each chapter's major points for use in lectures.

The book is divided into five parts. Part I, Setting the Stage, includes chapter 1, where Richard MacNeil and David Gould discuss global perspectives on leisure and aging as they relate to the demography of aging. It also includes chapter 2, where Rylee Dionigi and Sean Horton outline the pervasive stereotypes associated with aging and suggest ways leisure may encourage older adults to resist or conform to these stereotypes.

Part II, Theoretical and Methodological Perspectives on Leisure and Aging, contains four chapters. Chapter 3, written by Douglas Kleiber and Rebecca Genoe, explains theories of aging and their application to leisure, helping to provide a theoretical foundation for students and encouraging them to think critically about theory. Chapter 4 follows with a reminder of the role of theory in the research process as Bryan Smale and Jennifer Gillies take students through research design from start to finish. Chapters 5 and 6 return to theoretical discussions about the need to view later life in terms of heterogeneity instead of homogeneity. In chapter 5, Galit Nimrod and Megan Janke address change and continuity in leisure over the life span, with a call to think critically about the idea that later life is not one homogenous stage. Chapter 6, written by Steven Mock, Susan Shaw, Erica Hummel, and Carissa Bakker, examines the influence of gender, race, ethnicity, and sexual orientation on services to older adults and the need to consider these issues in research and practice with them.

Part III, Leisure and Healthy Aging, begins with chapter 7 by Bevan Grant and Mary Ann Kluge, who examine the benefits of physical activity in later life. In chapter 8, Roger Mannell and Ryan Snelgrove address psychological well-being. Part III concludes with chapter 9, written by Paul Heintzman and Erin Patriquin, who examine leisure in relation to social and spiritual well-being.

Part IV, Community, Aging, and Leisure, takes us into various aspects of community and aging. In chapter 10, Richard Gitelson and Julie Freelove-Charton examine life and leisure in three types of communities for older adults: active adult communities, continuing-care communities, and naturally occurring communities. Chapter 11 continues the focus on independent older adults and examines travel and tourism. Ian Patterson and Shane Pegg suggest that for many older adults, travel has become an important part of retirement.

Part V, Leisure in Long-Term Care, examines the issues associated with aging people who can no longer live independently in the community. In chapter 12, Sherry Dupuis, Colleen Whyte, and Jennifer Carson take the reader inside long-term care communities. They provide an overview of what constitutes long-term care settings and discuss various philosophies and resulting cultures of long-term care models. Chapter 13, written by Elaine Wiersma and Stephanie Chesser, continues the theme of long-term care and discusses the transition process from independent community living.

This book provides a wealth of knowledge on various aspects of life for older people and the role of leisure in their lives. Students are challenged throughout the chapters to engage in critical thinking about a phase of life that often seems so remote from their own. They are provided with theory and current research findings and are shown through a variety of learning activities how academic knowledge might inform practice as many of them contemplate occupations that involve working with older adults. Reflecting on some of these issues, the book concludes with thoughts about future directions for research and practice in the realm of leisure and aging.

REFERENCES

Gibson, H.J. (2006). Leisure and later life: Past, present and future. *Leisure Studies*, *25*(4), 397-401.

Levinson, D., Darrow, C., Klein, E., Levinson, N., & McKee, B. (1978). *The seasons of a man's life*. New York: Knopf.

McGuire, F. (2000). What do we know? Not much: The state of leisure and aging research. *Journal of Leisure Research*, *32*, 97-100.

Rapoport, R., & Rapoport, R.N. (1975). *Leisure and the family life cycle*. London: Routledge.

Shrestha, L.B., & Heisler, J.E. (2011). The changing demographic profile of the United States. Congressional Research Service. Retrieved from www.fas.org/sgp/crs/misc/RL32701.pdf.

Statistics Canada. (2007). A portrait of seniors in Canada. Retrieved from www.statcan.ca/english/freepub/89-519-XIE/89-519-XIE2006001.htm.

Wan, H., Sengupta, M., Velkoff , V., & DeBarros, K. (2005). *65+ in the United States: 2005*. U.S. Census Bureau Current Population Reports. Washington, DC: U.S. GPO. Retrieved from www.census.gov/prod/2006pubs/p23-209.pdf.

Setting the Stage

Part I introduces trends associated with the aging of populations around the world. More specifically, it discusses ideas about leisure and some of the negative connotations associated with aging, particularly in the Western world.

In chapter 1, Richard MacNeil and David Gould discuss global perspectives on leisure and aging in the context of the demography of aging. They contrast leisure and aging in more developed countries (MDCs) and less developed countries (LDCs). Several sidebars provide examples of population aging and life expectancy in a variety of countries around the world, including an in-depth look at Japan as the country with the fastest-aging population. Mercedes Bern-Klug authored the sidebar on participation by older adults in *papelpicado*, a Mexican art form. The authors conclude by addressing the challenges associated with population aging and provide an overview of leisure opportunities for older adults in both MDCs and LDCs.

Part I concludes with chapter 2 by Rylee Dionigi and Sean Horton. They discuss the pervasive stereotypes associated with aging and how leisure may encourage older adults to resist or conform to these stereotypes. They point to the media as a major source of these stereotypes and also the role of older adults in accepting these ageist messages. Dionigi and Horton also examine participation in sport and physical activity by older adults as a site of both resistance and conformity to negative stereotypes. With the positive aging movement, physical activity has been promoted as a source of health and well-being in later life; however, scholars have begun to question whether participation in physical activity also promotes the quest for youth and staving off old age rather than helping people accept their aging bodies. As a continuation of this theme, Cassandra Phoenix provides a case study of an older male bodybuilder.

CHAPTER 1

Global Perspectives on Leisure and Aging

Richard D. MacNeil ■ **David L. Gould**

LEARNING OBJECTIVES

After reading this chapter, you will be able to

- identify and describe at least three variables associated with the study of the demography of aging,

- explain the four stages of the demographic transition theory,

- discuss both the current and future status of population aging and the differences that exist between developed and developing regions with regard to population aging,

- describe the World Health Organization's model of active aging,

- identify at least three broad categories of leisure opportunities commonly available to retirement-aged adults in the more developed regions of the world, and

- describe prerequisite conditions associated with the development of leisure opportunities for retirement-aged adults in developing areas of the world.

The world is experiencing a profound transformation in its demographic structure. This transformation may be understood in a single word: *aging*. Although human populations have been aging for centuries, over the past 100 years the more developed (industrialized) nations in particular have experienced dramatic growth in the percentage of their populations identified as old. However, while the older populations in more developed nations may be peaking over the next 20 to 40 years, less developed nations are just beginning to experience rapid growth in the older segments of their societies. The projected changes in the world demographic structure are dramatic and their implications are profound. It is the purpose of this chapter to review population aging trends at the global level and to explore potential implications of the changing demographics for leisure in later adulthood.

The chapter is divided into three sections. The first section introduces the field of demography as it applies to the study of population aging. Variables associated with the demographic study of aging and older people are examined. The demographic transition theory, the idea that population aging can be explained by a decline in both birthrates and death rates following industrialization, is also discussed in this section.

The second part of the chapter uses the previously introduced demographic variables to highlight the current status and future projections of aging populations in two types of world regions, the more developed areas and the developing areas. Comparisons of selected variables that drive age-related growth are examined to project future changes in the world's age structure in these regions. This section also identifies some of the challenges posed by the growth of aging populations in more developed and developing countries.

The final section of the chapter focuses on leisure and its implications for global aging. The World Health Organization's (WHO's) active aging model is presented as a theoretical framework to discuss the potential contributions of leisure to the dignity and quality of life for seniors. The experience of leisure in the postretirement years in more developed nations is contrasted with that experienced in developing nations. Finally, a new conceptual model is introduced that explains the conditions needed to produce meaningful leisure experiences in later adulthood.

Demography and Population Aging

Demography is the statistical study of human populations, with particular reference to size, density, and distribution. The **demography of aging** studies older people in a population and the impact of **population aging** on society.

Demographic Variables

Demographers use a number of variables and measures to define and describe population aging.

- **Fertility rate** is "the average number of children that would be born to a woman by the time she had ended childbearing if she were to pass through all her childbearing years conforming to the age-specific fertility rates for a given year" (Haupt & Kane, 1998, p. 15h). The fertility rate is determined by dividing the number of live births in an area in a given year by 1,000. Fertility rates are inversely related to population aging—the higher the fertility rate, the greater the proportion of younger people in the population. Fertility rates have been declining in most areas of the world over the past several decades, but they generally remain considerably higher in developing rather than developed regions.

- A second variable that influences population aging is **life expectancy**, or "the length of time a person born in a particular year can expect to live" (Matcha, 2007, p. 83). The significance of this variable is that as life expectancy increases, a greater percentage of adults within a cohort survive for a longer period of years, thus increasing the proportion of older people within a society. Historically, life expectancy has gradually increased throughout the twentieth century. For example, the life expectancy at birth in the United States rose from about 49 years in 1900 to almost 76 years in 2000.

- **Median age** refers to the age at which half the population is older and half younger. An increase in median age is a clear reflection of an aging population. The median age of developed nations is consistently higher than what is found in developing countries.

- The **absolute number of older people** is used to study population change within a society over time. Not unexpectedly, the absolute number of older people worldwide has been steadily increasing. For instance, in 2008 there were an estimated 506 million people aged 65 and older worldwide, and this number is projected to increase to about 1.3 billion by 2040 (Kinsella & He, 2009).

■ **Proportion of older people** is a measure that shows the relationship between the older population and the rest of society. An increase in the proportion of older people means a decrease in other age groups, which is reflective of population aging. Japan, which had the world's greatest percentage of a population aged 65 and over in 2008 (21.6%), is the oldest nation in the world by this standard (Hooyman & Kiyak, 2008).

An awareness of these five variables helps to frame a perspective for understanding the phenomenon of population aging and appreciating its potential consequences. However, these variables alone cannot explain the historic rise in the number of older adults that has occurred worldwide over the past several centuries. This rise may be better understood by reviewing what has become known as the demographic transition theory.

Demographic Transition Theory

The **demographic transition theory** refers to the movement within a society from a condition of high birthrates and death rates to one of low birthrates and death rates. The term *demographic transition* describes a pattern of population change that has taken place in industrialized nations over the past 250 years. It is a transitional pattern that will likely be repeated by today's developing nations; in fact, some (e.g., China) have already started this process. The process will be described using the United States as an example.

The seminal work on this topic is David H. Fischer's 1978 publication, *Growing Old in America*. According to Fischer, during the first stages of the transition (1600s to early 1700s), the median age in the United States was between 15 and 17 years. Due to high infant mortality rates and inadequate birth control, fertility rates were high. At the same time, **mortality rates** (the rate of death by a percentage of a population) were also high due to factors such as harsh living conditions, lack of medical care, and inadequate public

health practices. Thus, life expectancy was only about 30 years and the number of older adults was relatively small. For instance, the 1790 census, the first to be conducted in the United States, reported only about 50,000 older people, who made up 2% of the total population.

The second stage of the transition occurred between the mid-1700s and early 1820s. During this time mortality rates began to fall and life expectancy began to rise. Better public health measures, improved diets, and decreased virulence of disease led to decreases in infant mortality. Whereas only about 12% of Americans lived to age 60 in the 1700s, Fischer (1978) reported that more than one-third of people born in 1830 survived to age 60. Consequently, the proportion of older adults in the population began to rise.

The third stage of the transition occurred between 1820 and 1960. By the middle of the nineteenth century, the birthrate began to decline. The average number of children in a marriage dropped from 7.04 in 1800 to 3.56 in 1900. Fischer (1978) has written that the fall in birthrates in the early part of the twentieth century accounts for about 80% of population aging at the time. The declining birthrate shaped population aging in the United States for the next 150 years.

A gradual decline in an agricultural-based economy and an increase in an industrial economy along with rising opportunities for women to engage in paid work further influenced the decrease in birthrates and the process of population aging during this stage. An important consequence of these factors was a rise in the median age in the United States, which rose steadily from 16.7 years in 1820 to 25.3 years in 1920. This trend was reflective of a society that was growing older.

The United States entered the fourth stage of the transition in the 1960s, when it reached the point at which it had a much lower birthrate and death rate than at any time in the past. At over 35 million, the older population is now larger than it has ever been. The median age hit 36 in 2008, also a record. In addition, the U.S. population will continue to age as the baby boom generation (a cohort of 76 million people born between 1946 and 1964) advance through the life cycle. The first of the baby boomers reached age 65 in the year 2011, and barring any rapid change in the birthrate or death rate, older adults will continue to increase as a proportion of the total population for several more decades. The aging of the boomers is expected to raise the median age of the country to 39 by 2040 and increase the percentage of older adults to over 20% (Kinsella & He, 2009). Most industrialized nations of the world have experienced a similar pattern of transition over the past 100 to 200 years.

As more nations experience demographic transition, new challenges related to the growth of an increasingly older population will become prevalent. With the baby boomers ready to enter the stage of later adulthood, the United States is already beginning to confront some of these issues. Debates about the future of health care and the sustainability of age-based social programs such as Social Security and Medicare are becoming increasingly contentious in the United States as well as in other developed countries. The challenges now being faced in developed nations will eventually spread to developing nations as they continue to grow older over the course of the next half century.

Dealing with challenges presented by population aging is unexplored territory; the world has never before faced this problem. How these challenges might be resolved remains uncertain. What is certain, however, is that the phenomenon of population aging will have profound effects on the social, financial, and political fabric of nations around the world over the next several decades.

Global Aging: Current and Future Status

The world grows older every day. In 2000, over 421 million people worldwide were aged 65 and over. This number was three times higher than it was in 1950, and according to projections by the United Nations, it will triple again to one and a half billion people by the year 2050 (United Nations, 2005). By 2050, it has been predicted that over 16% of the world's people will be aged 65 or over, compared with just 7% in 2005 (Hayutin, 2007), and the absolute number of people over age 65 will be larger than the population of children aged 0 to 14 years. This will be the first such occurrence in human history.

However dramatic these worldwide population figures appear, they do not reflect a vital piece of information: The phenomenon of global aging will be marked by tremendous variation across countries and regions of the globe. In an effort to examine this variation, it is helpful to distinguish between two broad categories of nations: the **more**

developed countries (MDCs) of the world and **less developed or developing countries (LDCs)**. MDCs are nations that have undergone the previously described demographic transition and are, for the most part, politically and financially stable and highly industrialized. In contrast, LDCs tend to be rural-agrarian nations with high fertility rates, low life expectancies, and a lack of basic public services such as health care infrastructure. The United Nations classifies less developed regions of the world as Asia (excluding Japan), Africa, and Latin America and the Caribbean. More developed regions include Europe, North America, Japan, Australia, and New Zealand (United Nations, 2005).

Hayutin (2007) projects that the percentage of people aged 65 and older in MDCs will slowly grow from about 15% of their total population in 2005 to about 26% by 2050. At that point the percentage of the old in MDCs is expected to begin to decline.

In contrast, among LDCs, population aging is expected to explode during the next half century. Reflecting the impact of fertility declines that began in LDCs in the 1960s and 1970s, as well as improving public health measures, better diet and medical care, and growing economic conditions consistent with the demographic transition, population aging in these countries will sharply accelerate after 2015. Hayutin predicts that the percentage of old people in LDCs will grow from about 5% in 2005 to over 15% by 2050. Considering that three-quarters of all people already reside in LDCs, it is clear that the rapid worldwide increase in older people will be largely fueled by growth in the number of seniors in the less developed regions of the world.

Figure 1.1 displays the contrast between population aging in LDCs and MDCs. The six

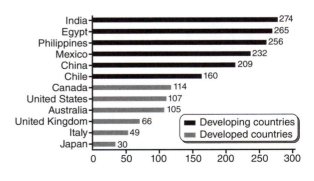

Figure 1.1   Percent increase in population aged 65 and over for selected nations: 2008 to 2040.

countries listed on the top of the vertical axis (i.e., India, Egypt, the Philippines, Mexico, China, and Chile) are all LDCs, while the six listed toward the bottom (i.e., Canada, the United States, Australia, the United Kingdom, Italy, and Japan) are all MDCs. As is readily apparent, the expected increase in people aged 65 and over in LDCs dwarfs the growth expected in MDCs.

In the year 2000, over 250 million (59%) people aged 65 or older resided in LDCs, in contrast to about 171 million (41%) in MDCs. Given the disproportionate number of people who currently reside in less developed regions, this difference between MDCs and LDCs in absolute numbers of elderly may not be surprising. Projecting ahead to 2025, there is expected to be a 52% increase (from 171 million to 260.3 million) in the number of old in MDCs but a 127% increase (from 250.3 million to 571.8 million) in LDCs. By 2050, it is projected that 78% of the world's older population will be found in less developed regions of the world (United Nations, 2005).

Between 2000 and 2025, Asia is expected to gain over a quarter billion older people. China alone will have a projected 322 million people aged 65 and over by 2050 (Hooyman & Kiyak, 2008). Very rapid growth in older populations is also projected for the developing nations of Africa and Latin America and the Caribbean, whereas much more modest growth is anticipated for Europe, North America, and Oceania (United Nations, 2005).

Demographic Variables and Global Aging

In the late 1990s, the world's **total population** (the total number of people in all age groups) reached 6 billion. Over the course of the next half century it will continue to grow but at a relatively slower rate than in past decades. Projections by the United Nations (2005) forecast the addition of another 2.7 billion humans by 2050.

As previously discussed, the rate of increase in total population varies among regions and nations. The growth rate of the total population in MDCs is expected to remain largely stable at around 1.2 billion over the next 50 years. By 2050, declines in the overall population are expected in many MDCs, including Japan and Germany. In contrast, a much more vigorous rate of growth is expected in the developing regions of the world. Of the expected 2.7 billion humans to be added, Asian nations will account for about 50% of the increase and African nations for about 40%.

What might be some reasons for the differences in total population growth rates of MDCs and LDCs? One reason has to do with the nature of human population growth. Human population growth is an example of **exponential growth**, a type of increase wherein an entity grows by a proportion of itself. Thus, the larger the initial size of the entity, the faster its potential rate of growth. (Think in terms of an interest-bearing bank account versus putting a set amount of money in a tin can.) In the year 2000, over 75% of the total human population resided in LDCs, compared with slightly over 22% in MDCs. Given these huge differences in population size, it should not be surprising that the fastest growth rates will occur in the developing regions of the world. By 2050, it is projected that 57.3% of the world's total population will be from Asia, almost 22% will be from Africa, and 8.4% will be from Latin American and Caribbean nations. In contrast, only about 7.2% of the world's people will be found in Europe, less than 5% in North America, and just 0.5% in Oceania (Hayutin, 2007).

Another reason for variation in growth rates is differences in fertility rates. Fertility rates have been declining worldwide since the late 1950s. In 1955, the world average fertility rate was 5.0. By 2005, the average had decreased to 2.7. As a basis for comparison, the **replacement rate**, which is 2.1, is the rate at which births and deaths would offset each other and would eventually result in zero population growth.

As we have seen, however, global rates are deceiving; patterns of fertility decline show significant variation around the globe. For instance, the fertility rate in MDCs fell from 2.8 in 1955 to 1.6 in 2005. Among the developed countries that experienced a rapid decline in fertility rates between 1950 and 2000 were Canada (3.73 to 1.51), Japan (2.75 to 1.33), Poland (3.62 to 1.26), and Italy (2.32 to 1.21). The primary demographic consequence of fertility decline, especially combined with increases in life expectancy, is population aging. This is evidenced by the fact that in MDCs, children accounted for 27% of the total population in 1950 versus only 12% for seniors, but by 2005 the proportion of seniors had grown to 20% while children had decreased to 17% (United Nations, 2005).

Fertility rates also began to decline in the 1950s in LDCs (from 6.2 in 1950 to 2.9 in 2005), but they remained well above the rates in MDCs. As a result, the rate of population aging in LDCs was much slower than in MDCs. Between 1950 and 2005, the proportion of children in LDCs had declined from 38% to 31%, while the proportion of older people had only increased from 6% to 8%. Because of continued declines in fertility rates over the past half century, however, a period of more rapid population aging lies ahead in developing regions. The United Nations' *World Population Prospects* (2005) projects that by 2050, the proportion of older people in these regions is expected to rise to 20%, whereas the proportion of children is expected to decline to 21%.

Fertility rates vary greatly among countries. In some of the youngest and poorest nations the fertility rate remains high. In the year 2000, five nations (i.e., Niger, Democratic Republic of Timor-Leste, Afghanistan, Guinea-Bissau, and Uganda) all had fertility rates of 7 or higher (United Nations, 2005). In many LDCs, the absolute number of women in or entering their childbearing years often offsets declines in fertility rates, thus slowing population aging.

It is clear that the timing and pacing of fertility declines will largely determine the pace of population aging. China experienced perhaps the most dramatic change in fertility rates, dropping from 6.22 in 1950 to 1.8 in 2008 (Kinsella & He, 2009). This decline was due to China's adoption of the one-child-per-family policy in the 1970s. The dramatic drop has had a minimal impact thus far upon the percentage of old people in Chinese society; however, having sustained a low fertility rate for several generations, a rapid acceleration in the proportion of old will occur between 2015 (8%) and 2035 (20%). According to Kinsella and He, in absolute numbers China currently has 106 million people aged 65 and older, the largest number in the world. By 2050, this number is expected to reach 322 million (Hooyman & Kiyak, 2008).

Life expectancy at birth is another demographic variable that is beneficial in understanding global aging. Increases in life expectancy, especially in combination with declines in fertility rates, are indicative of population aging. Life expectancy has been steadily increasing around the globe over the past half century. In 1955 the global life expectancy was 46 years, by 2005 it had grown to 66 years, and it is expected to be 75 years or so by 2050. In 2008, Japan had the highest life expectancy in the world at 82.1 years, while Zambia had one of the lowest at 38.6 years (Kinsella & He, 2009).

As with other demographic measures, regional variations exist. There are two ways to demon-strate these differences. First, when comparing the *specific age* of life expectancy, developed regions have usually had an 8- to 12-year advantage over developing regions. In 2005, for instance, residents of MDCs had a life expectancy of 76 years as compared with 64 in LDCs. By 2050, MDCs are expected to have an 8-year advantage, 82 years to 74 (Hayutin, 2007; United Nations, 2005). Differences in specific age reflect a number of demographic factors, including fertility rates and the current stage of demographic transition.

A second variation concerns the *rate of growth* in life expectancy. Among MDCs, life expectancy has continued to increase, but the rate of growth is slower than the increase seen in LDCs (e.g., from 76 years in 2005 to a projected 82 years in 2050 in MDCs versus an increase from 64 to 74 years in LDCs) (Hayutin, 2007). Why the difference in rates of growth? It is generally believed that developing regions are nearing the biological limits of longevity, and as they approach these limits, the rate of growth slows as the number of people reaching (or exceeding) the maximum age diminishes. In addition, many developing regions are in the early stages of the demographic transition and are just beginning to experience certain advantageous conditions that affect life expectancy, such as a growing economy, improved public health infrastructure, and better access to medical care.

A final demographic measure of population aging is median age. Increases in the median age of a nation reflect societal aging. Worldwide, the median age is rapidly increasing; it was 28 in 2005, and it is expected to climb to 38 by 2050 (United Nations, 2005). The trend identified in the previous paragraph is evident in median age as well. In MDCs where societal aging has slowed, the growth in median age will be gradual, with an average gain of about 7 years from 2005 until 2050. For example, between 2008 and 2040, Australia is expected to see an increase in median age of about 6 years, from age 37 to age 43; the United Kingdom is expected to see an increase of 5 years, from 39 to 44; and the United States is expected to see an increase of 3 years, from 36 to 39 (Kinsella & He, 2009).

In opposite fashion, by 2050 many developing regions will face steep increases in median age, largely due to their delayed declines in fertility rates. A 12.6-year rise in median age from 25.9 to 38.5 years is expected to occur in Latin America and the Caribbean, an 11.3 year increase is expected in Asia, and a 7.2 rise is anticipated in Africa (Sanderson & Scherbov, 2008). Mexico

Life Expectancy at Birth in Selected Nations

ife expectancy is defined as the average length of time that a birth cohort (i.e., people born in the same year) can expect to live. As shown in table 1.1, in 2008, the worldwide life expectancy at birth was 67.2 years (65.0 years for men and 69.5 years for women). However, as the table clearly reflects, life expectancy varies greatly among nations. This is because life expectancy is closely related to the severity of the living environment; the harsher the environment, the lower the life expectancy.

Changes associated with the demographic transition usually result in increased life expectancy. Thus, it is not surprising to find that more developed nations generally have higher life expectancies than less developed nations. Many of the countries with the lowest life expectancies have inadequate public health standards, insufficient medical care, and rampant malnutrition.

Sex differences in life expectancy occur all over the globe. Worldwide, females typically have life expectancies that are three to eight years longer than those of males. The reasons for these differences are not fully understood; however, some combination of genetic and social factors is likely the cause.

It is important to distinguish between life expectancy and **maximum life span**. Whereas life expectancy is a probability estimate based on environmental conditions such as disease and health care, maximum life span is the maximum number of years that a given species could expect to live if environmental hazards were eliminated. For humans, the maximum life span is estimated to be about 120 years.

■ TABLE 1.1

Life Expectancy at Birth in Selected Nations

	Overall	Male	Female
Japan	82.1	78.8	85.6
Australia	81.6	79.2	84.1
Canada	81.2	78.7	83.9
Israel	80.7	78.6	82.9
Italy	80.2	77.3	83.3
United Kingdom	79.0	76.5	81.6
United States	78.1	75.6	80.7
China	73.5	71.6	75.5
World average	67.2	65.0	69.5
Pakistan	65.2	63.5	67.1
Haiti	60.8	59.1	62.5
Ethiopia	55.4	53.0	58.0
Swaziland	47.8	47.8	47.8
Nigeria	46.9	46.1	47.7
Zambia	38.6	38.5	38.7

Reprinted from Central Intelligence Agency, 2008, *The world factbook*.

will age rapidly, largely due to a projected 30% decline in the number of children over the next half century. By 2050, half of Mexico's population will be over 43, an 18-year increase in median age from 2005. Thanks to the one-child mandate in the 1970s, China has a current median age of 33, about 7 years older than that of other developing countries (Hayutin, 2007). In contrast, developing nations that have not begun a demographic transition will see little change in median age over the next 50 years. Uganda, for instance, is projected to experience only a 1-year rise in median age, from age 15 in 2008 to age 16 in 2040 (Kinsella & He, 2009).

Challenges of Population Aging in MDCs

Population aging will affect different societies in different ways. More than one-quarter of populations in developed countries will be 65 years old or older by 2025. In the case of Japan, almost 40% of the population will be 65 or older by 2050. Increased numbers of older adults in MDCs will create growing competition between age groups for limited societal resources.

At the heart of the issue is the impact of population aging on a nation's **dependency ratio**, or the ratio of current workers to retirees. It is important to consider this ratio because most public assistance programs for seniors are funded by taxes, a large proportion of which is paid by current workers. A reduction in the working-age population combined with an increase in retirees will result in a growing dependency ratio. This decline in workers per retiree will increasingly strain the national budgets of MDCs (Hayutin, 2007).

Two main categories of senior-oriented assistance programs are found in MDCs. One is pension programs designed to help ensure income maintenance for older citizens and protect against financial risk. Though the financing of pension programs varies by nation, most countries require some form of mandatory contributions paid by workers and their employers during the working years. Once employees meet specific criteria (i.e., usually some combination of chronological age and number of years of contributions), they become eligible to receive pension funds. Representative of such programs are the National Insurance program in the United Kingdom, the Old Age Security program in Canada, the Old Age Pension in Japan, the Age Pension in Australia, and the Social Security system in the United States.

A common misconception about the funding of public pension programs is that retirees are merely being paid back, with interest, the contributions they made during their careers. Instead, most pension programs are supported by general tax revenues or, in some cases (e.g., the United States), by specific taxes paid by the current workforce. It is for this reason that the dependency ratio is so important.

The second category of public assistance commonly provided to seniors in MDCs is health care or health insurance programs. Moderating health care costs for seniors is particularly important given the fact that most retirees live on a fixed income and are also more likely to require a greater proportion of health services compared with younger members of society. Most European nations as well as countries such as Canada and Japan offer publically funded, universal health care to their entire population. In these countries health care is financed by the government through a system of national health insurance.

In the United States, publically funded health care for older adults is provided through the Medicare program. Medicare legislation was passed in 1965 with the intent of providing financial protection against the cost of medical care for people aged 65 and older. Medicare mainly provides health insurance to seniors who are typically retired and lack access to employer-provided group insurance plans.

Just as population aging is presenting many challenges in terms of funding for old-age pension programs, it is increasing the cost of publically funded health care. Costs are rising not only due to an increase in the absolute number of seniors in MDCs but also because of the relationship between health care services and rising life expectancies. As life expectancy has increased, people are surviving to older ages and reentering the health care system over and over. It has been reported that the 13% of the American population aged 65 and over accounts for more than 30% of the annual federal health care expenditure (Hooyman & Kiyak, 2008). In fact, the average expenditure for health services for adults aged 65 and over is nearly four times the cost for those under age 65. More importantly, expenditures increase even more among the oldest old, those over age 85, who are the fastest growing segment of the senior population (Hooyman & Kiyak, 2008). In 2007, Medicare was the fourth largest federal expenditure of the U.S. government, and it is projected to grow by 10% per year over the next decade (Lee, 2007). The Trustees of the Federal Hospital Insurance Trust Fund have projected that

Population Aging in Japan

apan is the most mature nation in the world in terms of population aging. As reflected in table 1.2, almost one-quarter of the total population in Japan is currently aged 65 or older. Perhaps more impressively, over the next four decades the proportion of older adults in Japan is projected to rise until it reaches just under 40% of the total population.

There are two primary reasons for this trend in Japan. First, people are living longer there than anywhere else in the world. Average life expectancies at birth have increased from slightly over 52 years in 1950 to 82.1 years in 2008. Japan currently has more **centenarians** (people who have lived to at least 100 years of age) than any other nation in the world. Second, the number of children born in Japan has declined dramatically. The total fertility rate dropped from 5.24 in 1920 to 1.26 in 2006.

Japan, as well as most other developed nations, has committed significant societal resources to its older citizens via publically sponsored pension programs and health care benefits. What challenges might Japan and these other nations face as the percentage of older adults continues to grow? At the most basic level, concerns about the affordability and sustainability of public pension plans and national health services are shared by governments around the world. These concerns are magnified as dependency ratios between workers and nonworkers grow, further contributing to the burdens to be faced by nations worldwide.

Japan and other countries are currently exploring strategies to meet such challenges. Among the more common proposals under consideration are reducing old-age pensions, raising the age of eligibility for pensions, increasing taxes to help fund assistance programs, and restructuring health care systems to emphasize the provision of noninstitutional and preventative care.

■ TABLE 1.2

Population Aging in Japan

Year	Population (1,000)	AGE COMPOSITION (%)		
		0-14 years	15-64 years	65 and older
1940	71,933	36.7	58.5	4.8
1960	94,302	30.2	64.1	5.7
1980	117,060	23.5	67.3	9.1
2000	126,926	14.6	67.9	17.3
PROJECTION				
2010	127,176	13.0	63.9	23.1
2020	122,735	10.8	60.0	29.2
2030	115,224	9.7	58.5	31.8
2040	105,695	9.3	54.2	36.5
2050	95,152	8.6	51.8	39.6

Reprinted from Statistics Bureau, Japan, 2009, *Statistics handbook of Japan.*

Medicare will become insolvent by 2019 unless a balance between incomes and spending can be restored (Kaiser Family Foundation, 2004).

As the percentage of older adults continues to rise over the next several decades, MDCs are actively pursuing strategies to preserve the commitments they made to their older citizens in a time before population aging became a reality. In terms of modifications to pension plans, much of the efforts to revise these programs are focused on changing existing eligibility standards. In Germany, for instance, the eligibility age for a full state pension is gradually being raised from 65 to 67. Similarly, Australia, which currently grants a retirement pension to men at age 65 and to women at 62.5, will initially raise the eligibility age of women to 65. Then, starting in 2017, it will raise the required age for both sexes by six months every 2 years, reaching age 67 in 2023. Portugal has recently placed restrictions on early retirement and the calculation of benefits in an effort to encourage workers to postpone retirement. Other countries, such as France and Italy, are considering legislation to require additional years of employment to be eligible for full state pensions. Some MDCs are debating the possibility of permitting increased immigration of young workers from developing countries to help reduce the dependency ratio in future years. Not surprisingly, government efforts to change retirement laws to protect pension plans are usually met by stiff resistance from labor unions (United Nations, 2009; Zaidi, 2010).

A different set of challenges is faced in managing the rising health care costs that are associated with population aging. Specific plans to help preserve publically funded health care for seniors remain vague and controversial. Most existing proposals call for increases in taxes, reductions in services, or a combination of both. As MDCs debate how best to meet the health care challenges of the future, the number of older adults continues to increase.

Challenges of Population Aging in LDCs

In contrast to MDCs, LDCs will continue to be dominated by younger populations in the short term. Despite the rapid growth of the aged population, less developed nations will continue to have relatively small proportions of older people. For example, on average only a little over 4% of the populations of African nations will be aged 65 or older in 2025, and developing regions as a whole will average only about 8% that year (United Nations, 2005). The proportion of people who are young (who have not yet or are just entering their prime reproductive years) and high fertility rates will keep the proportion of older people relatively low in these regions for the next quarter of a century.

Although the percentage of old may remain small in LDCs, these nations will experience explosive growth in the absolute number of older people. The total number of older adults in LDCs in 2005 was 300 million; by 2040 they will reach 1.3 billion (Kinsella & He, 2009). The rapid pace of change will require these nations to quickly adjust to societal aging. The sheer size of the old population will make such adjustments challenging.

Older people in many LDCs already face hardships owing to a lack of basic services (e.g., health care, economic supports) and social infrastructure designed to assist those in need. In South Africa, for instance, Gist (1994) found that only 47% of urban, black, older people and 15% of rural, black, older people had access to conveniences like running water and electricity. Few older people in the southern African nations of Botswana, Swaziland, and Zimbabwe were receiving pensions (Martin & Kinsella, 1994).

In many developing regions, younger family members have traditionally provided the support needed for the well-being of older relatives. However, societal forces such as growing urbanization, movement of young people to find jobs, weakening of traditional values, and deaths due to AIDS have left older people increasingly vulnerable. In addition, poor economies in many developing nations mean that older people have little work and few support services. According to Novak (2009), "Some of the poorest countries will see the most rapid increases in older people, but they have the least ability to respond to older people's needs" (p. 62).

China will face a unique problem in the next several decades. The policy of one child per couple that was adopted in the 1970s means that a young couple will be sandwiched between four aging parents and one young offspring. It also means that the single child will someday have sole responsibility for both parents. In a society that has traditionally depended heavily upon the family to support its elders, these changing social dynamics will present many challenges.

Just as the consequences of population aging are increasingly being felt in developed nations around the globe, it is predictable that less developed regions will experience similar challenges in the foreseeable future. However, demography is not destiny. Developing nations that already have social programs and pension plans in place will likely need to adapt and expand these programs to serve growing numbers of seniors. The many LDCs that have made no preparations for the demographic shift that will transpire during the next 40 to 60 years could probably learn much by following the events that unfold in the next 20 to 40 years in MDCs.

Leisure and Quality of Life in Older Adulthood

Throughout most of human history, life has been an experience wracked by illness and short on years. Past generations lived just long enough to reproduce. In 1974, the rapidly changing age distributions in industrialized societies moved renowned gerontologist Bernice Neugarten to draw a distinction between young-old and old-old adults. Young-old adults were 55- to 75-year-olds who had the potential to be "the first age group to reach the society of the future"; good health, education, purchasing power, free time, and political involvement would be their attributes (Neugarten, 1974, pp. 187-198). According to clinical psychologist Mary Pipher, the divide that separated the young-old from the old-old adults was the arrival of poor health. "The old-old," Pipher writes, "are less sanguine. They walk a road filled with potholes of pain, low energy, poor appetite, and inadequate sleep. They lead lives filled with loss of friends and family, of habits and pleasures, and of autonomy" (Pipher, 1999,

p. 30). As gerontologist Robert Butler (2008) has suggested, longevity is only desirable if it is connected to a high quality of life.

Determining what constitutes quality of life has proven difficult. On March 18, 1968, U.S. Senator Robert F. Kennedy addressed the issue of happiness and well-being in a unique political speech at the University of Kansas. Mere economic progress and worldly goods, Kennedy proclaimed, were not enough. The gross national product, he surmised, "measures everything, in short, except that which makes life worthwhile."

Responding to these perceived broken promises about gross national product, the Himalayan kingdom of Bhutan embarked on a public policy of a radically different kind—gross national happiness. Four pillars of a happy person, broken into nine domains and analyzed by 72 indicators, became the complex model of well-being that the government created in an attempt to accurately measure whether their efforts to improve the quality of life in Bhutan were working (Mydens, 2009).

Bhutan is far from the only country where happiness has vaulted into the national discourse. In February 2008, French president Nicolas Sarkozy organized a commission led by Nobel Prize economists Joseph Stiglitz and Amartya Sen to reexamine how France measures progress. Instead of focusing on the economic measure of gross domestic product (GDP), the commission's report, titled "The Measurement of Economic Performance and Social Progress Revisited," stressed indicators such as health, family cohesion, and leisure time. "GDP has increasingly become used as a measure of societal well-being, and changes in the structure of the economy and our society have made it an

Legacy Letter Project

In January 2007, David Gould, a faculty member in the leisure studies program at the University of Iowa, began soliciting letters from older people for his undergraduate students. Seniors were asked to address the question, "What do you know now that you wished you would have known in your 20s?" The seniors were also invited to include a photo of themselves when they were college-aged. The letters have arrived from around the world in the form of poems, short stories, eulogies, and more. They share the wisdom gained from raising a child with Down syndrome, surviving domestic violence, surviving breast cancer, and so on. Between the lines, they give glimpses into the changes that have taken place over the years from a time when undergraduate girls were required to pass a swimming test to graduate, when the marching band was made up of only men, and when a 1964 ivy green Mustang cost only $2,400. A consistent theme in many of the letters has been that the choices we make when we are young play a paramount role in our well-being as we age. The campaign is ongoing and has come to be known as the *Legacy Letter Project*. (See www.legacyletterproject.com.)

increasingly poor one," Stiglitz said. "It is time for our statistics system to put more emphasis on measuring the well-being of the population than on economic production" (Aldrik, 2009).

In 2008, the new economics foundation (nef) was commissioned by the UK government's Foresight Project on Mental Capital and Wellbeing to review the interdisciplinary work of over 400 scientists worldwide. The nef report identified five evidence-based ways to achieve well-being: Connect, be active, take notice, keep learning, and give (Aked, Marks, & Cordon, 2008).

According to behavioral geneticist Matthew McGue, trying to obtain both longevity and quality of life requires more than simply good genes. Drawing from his study of the Danish Twin Registry, McGue and Christensen (2001) calculated that just 15% to 30% of life span is genetically determined. Though chance factors certainly play a role in longevity, the importance of lifestyle cannot be understated when calculating the formula for a long life.

What lifestyles support not only longer but better lives? Explorer and author Dan Buettner (2008) set out to find the answer to this question by studying longevity cultures. His research identified five places where people live measurably longer, healthier lives: Sardinia, Italy; Okinawa, Japan; Loma Linda, California; Nicoya Peninsula, Costa Rica; and Icaria, Greece. These longevity hot spots are called *Blue Zones*. Buettner distilled the lessons of these cultures into the Power 9, nine common denominators that can be implemented by anyone. Five of the factors relate specifically to leisure: performing regular, low-intensity activity; living a purposeful life; slowing down; having a sense of belonging to a broader community; and investing deeply in one's family life. These factors are evidence of the potential of leisure to lengthen and improve the quality of our lives.

Active Aging

According to the WHO, quality of life "is a broad-ranging concept incorporating in a complex way a person's physical health, psychological state, level of independence, social relationships, personal beliefs and relationship to salient features in the environment" (WHO, 2002, p. 13). This

Leisure has the potential to contribute to longevity and quality of life.

conceptualization forms the basis of **active aging**, a widely accepted perspective on the process of "optimizing opportunities for health, participation, and security in order to enhance the quality of life as people age" (p. 1). Implicit in the term *active aging* is the notion that older adults should have the chance to realize their potential for physical, social, and mental well-being by continuing to participate in society according to their needs, desires, and capacities. *Active aging* conveys a more inclusive message than *healthy aging* because it emphasizes the maintenance of autonomy and independence as people grow older.

The WHO model of active aging contains six sets of determinants of health that influence people throughout their lives and affect their quality of life in the later years. The six sets include determinants related to the following (WHO, 2002):

1. Personal factors (e.g., cognitive and psychological health)
2. Social environment (e.g., social support, loneliness)
3. Behavioral factors (e.g., healthy lifestyle)
4. Access to health and social services (e.g., preventative and acute care)
5. Physical environment (e.g., safe housing, clean water)
6. Economic conditions

The WHO has also identified characteristics of the six categories. In reviewing these characteristics, one is struck by the repeated references to terms such as *personal choice, independence, participation, physical activity, self-efficacy, social engagement and support*, and *community involvement*. For the WHO, these characteristics reflect quality-of-life standards for older adults. They are also characteristics commonly associated with the leisure experience.

Leisure in Later Life in MDCs

By the end of the twentieth century, retirement had become an expected life event in most developed nations of the world. In retirement, leisure usually replaces work as a vehicle for finding meaning in one's life. Far from being simply diversions or leftover time, leisure in later life often evolves into a multidimensional aspect of life different from paid employment, household maintenance, and other instrumental activities. Aristotle described leisure as a realm in which human beings gain freedom for self-development when the necessities of life have been taken care of.

In a speech at the Eighth Annual National Wellness Conference, Kenneth Pelletier described a study conducted in Canada involving 4,000 people aged 65 or older (Pelletier, 1984). The researchers did extensive medical and psychological testing of the subjects at age 65 and then tested them again five years later. One purpose of the study was to identify factors that were most predictive of the subjects being alive and healthy at age 70. It turned out that neither the medical nor psychological parameters were particularly predictive. The most predictive factor turned out to be a simple, open-ended question, "What do you think your life is going to be like in the next five years?" Those who were optimistic, were involved in many recreational activities, and looked forward to the future were more likely to be healthy and alive five years later. This was the case even if they already had clearly debilitating, supposedly terminal medical conditions.

This study holds many implications for people nearing retirement. One of the most important of these involves retirees' expectations regarding leisure and the unobligated time usually associated with retirement. It would seem that health and well-being are enhanced by a perception that the true challenge in retirement is not simply finding experiences to fill time but finding personally fulfilling experiences.

Basic to this notion is the acceptance of the idea that leisure is not synonymous with idleness or diversion and that it is not the inevitable result of spare time, a holiday, or retirement. Instead, the leisure state results from concentration, stimulation, and active involvement in personally meaningful experiences. Being at leisure means that retirees are involved in experiences that give meaning to their lives.

The potential benefits of leisure involvement by older adults have been widely reviewed in recent years (see Cordes & Ibrahim, 2003; Edginton, DeGraff, Dieser, & Edginton, 2008). The general conclusion reached by researchers suggests that leisure is a critical component affecting life satisfaction and quality of life for retirement-aged adults.

Fortunately for many retirees in MDCs, opportunities to engage in quality leisure experiences are readily available. Informal, home-centered activities form the largest part of the leisure repertoire of most retirees; however, it appears

Leisure activities are more than idle diversion; they involve people in experiences that give meaning to their lives.

that participation in recreational activities that require extensive expenditures of time, money, and physical energy outside of the home have grown in popularity in recent decades. The following is a brief summary of some categories of leisure opportunities that have become increasingly popular for seniors in MDCs.

Educational Experiences

As the average level of education among seniors slowly rose in MDCs over the past century, so did the popularity of educational leisure experiences for retirees. A recent AARP (American Association of Retired Persons) study (Williams, Fries, Koppen, & Prisuta, 2010) reported that 29% of midlife and older Americans identified that they were either somewhat or very involved with educational activities.

One of the best known educational programs focused on adults is Road Scholar. Road Scholar is a program developed by Elderhostel, a not-for-profit leader in lifelong learning and educational travel for seniors. In Road Scholar programs older learners attend educational sessions on campuses and affiliated locations throughout the world. Road Scholar offers more than 8,000 learning adventures every year in all 50 states of the United States and in over 90 countries around the globe. Interest has steadily grown as over 160,000 older learners from all over the world enroll in these programs on a yearly basis (www.roadscholar.org).

Less formal opportunities for senior learning are developing at the local level. Sponsors of such programs often include senior centers, libraries, educational institutions, and hospitals. In addition, development of the World Wide Web has increased in-home educational experiences for all age groups. Programs such as SeniorNet are increasingly available to teach computer skills to seniors unfamiliar with computers.

Travel and Tourism

Over the last half century, leisure travel by older populations has become an increasingly important part of the recreation industry in MDCs. In the United States alone more than 81 million baby boomers and older adults traveled for pleasure in 2006, spending an estimated $126 billion on their travels (Focalyst, 2007). The tourism industry has understandably begun to aggressively market to this population, especially to young retirees who often have adequate incomes along with available time for travel (see chapter 11).

Volunteerism and Community Service

A recent AARP survey in the United States (Williams et al., 2010) found that 51% of respondents reported volunteering through an organization in the previous year. The same survey reported that 57% of respondents engaged in informal volunteering (volunteering on one's own). On average, adults who volunteered spent about 6 to 10 hours per month in service.

Seniors in other MDCs volunteer at rates similar to what has been reported in the U.S. In Canada, for instance, 36% of individuals age 65 and older are volunteers. They average about 218 hours per individual per year (Statistics Canada, 2007). Among persons aged 65-74 in England, 35% report engaging in informal volunteering and 31% in formal efforts (Low, Butt, Ellis-Paine, & Smith, 2007). Moreover, according to a 2006 Australian Bureau of Labor Statistics survey, 19.9% of people aged 55 years contributed over one quarter of the total annual volunteer hours (170.3 million hours) provided in the nation (Australian Bureau of Labor Statistics, 2008).

Volunteering is widely accepted as a primary component of active aging and healthy communities. Studies suggest that older volunteers generally experience a wide range of benefits such as improved self-rated health, greater life satisfaction, feelings of usefulness, and lower rates of disability and depression (Hooyman & Kiyak, 2008). At the same time, many organizations and institutions would be severely impaired without the services provided by volunteers.

The U.S. government sponsors a variety of volunteer service programs in which older citizens may participate. A few of the most popular programs include the Retired and Senior Volunteer Program (RSVP), Foster Grandparents, Senior Companionship Program, Volunteers-In-Parks (VIP), and Service Corps of Retired Executives (SCORE). In Canada, promoting volunteerism and coordinating the efforts of volunteer centers and provincial and territorial volunteer associations is the responsibility of the national organization, Volunteer Canada. Similarly, uVolunteer (http://uvolunteer.org) is an international volunteer program based in England. The organization has ongoing community development projects in many countries, including India, Peru, Costa Rica, Nepal, and Thailand.

Exercise, Fitness Activities, and Sport

In 1935, the year that Social Security legislation was passed in the United States, the typical 65-year-old could expect to live approximately 4.5 more years. By the year 2000, the average American male could expect to live another 14.5 years, the typical female another 19 years. The dramatic increase in the life expectancy of older adults is attributable to two main factors. First, advancements in public health, medicine, and the health sciences have significantly improved the chances of surviving into later adulthood. Second, Americans of all ages have accepted greater personal responsibility for their health and have increasingly taken proactive steps to improve it.

One such step has been becoming involved with exercise and fitness. A large body of literature reports on the positive effects of exercise and fitness activities in later life. The American College of Sports Medicine (ACSM) (as cited in Plonczynski, 2003) has said that physical activity can lead to more fitness, greater endurance, increased strength, and improved flexibility even at later stages of the life cycle. Despite these benefits, past generations of older people tended to avoid exercise and were less likely to engage in physical activities and sports than younger people (see chapter 2).

The leisure opportunities discussed previously have become increasingly popular among retirees in MDCs; however, the list is far from inclusive. Retirees are certainly not a homogeneous group. Individual leisure patterns are heavily influenced by variables such as age, gender, educational level, personal health, wealth, personal experiences, and cultural differences, to name a few. Moreover, it is generally accepted that leisure patterns displayed in younger adulthood are usually more predictive of leisure patterns in retirement than is the simple passage of chronological time.

One may wonder about population aging and its implications for the leisure behavior of retirement-aged adults. As has been previously discussed, most MDCs will experience a dramatic growth in the numbers of older citizens over the next 20 to 40 years. The sheer numbers of retirees will place more demands on the existing leisure infrastructure of these countries. Also, future retirees will tend to be healthier, wealthier, and

The Japanese Game of Gateball

Modeled off the European game of croquet, Eiji Suzuki created gateball in 1947 as an easy, low-cost amusement for Japanese children. After the 1964 Tokyo Olympics, however, the increased interest in sport prompted a home for the elderly in Kumamoto Prefecture to promote gateball to its residents. Requiring minimal physical strength and emphasizing teamwork, the game quickly became a favorite among older people and swept throughout Japan.

Gateball is played on a rectangular court 20 to 25 meters long and 15 to 20 meters wide with three gates (hoops) and a goal pole (center peg). Courts are commonly grass, gravel, clay, or concrete. Two teams (white and red), each consisting of five players, use mallets and balls similar to those in croquet. Each player has a numbered ball

Photo courtesy of John W. Traphagan.

that matches the playing order. Even-numbered balls are white; odd-numbered balls are red. Strategic thinking is an integral part of the game. Players work as a team to move through the gates while trying to prevent their opponents from accomplishing the same feat. Teams score 1 point for hitting their ball through the gate and 2 points for hitting the goal pole. Shots must be made within 10 seconds and games last 30 minutes. The winner is the team with the most points in the end.

In addition to providing social interaction and strategic thinking, older Japanese also play gateball to help prevent a mental condition known as *boke*. Considered by the Japanese as similar to Alzheimer's disease and dementia, boke is viewed as a soft form of senility that activity can control or perhaps even prevent. In this context, older people see gateball as a means to maintain their mental and physical abilities (Traphagan, 1998).

*Traphagan, J. W. (1998). Reasons for gateball participation among older Japanese. *Journal of Cross-Cultural Gerontology*, *13*, 159-175.

more educated than today's retirees (MacNeil, 2001). These differences will likely influence their leisure interests and behaviors in ways that are yet unimaginable. Nevertheless, based on the experiences of the past half century, it is reasonable to assume that most citizens of MDCs will have the opportunity to experience a retirement that is enhanced by meaningful and satisfying leisure.

Leisure in Later Life in LDCs

The information discussed in the preceding pages suggests that the expectation of retirement as an enjoyable and fulfilling time of life is reasonable for most people in MDCs. In contrast, this image of retirement is totally inappropriate for most people who reside in less developed areas of

the world. Robert Butler, a noted gerontologist, has commented, "I am very much struck by the absence of leisure in the developing world. [In the book *The Longevity Revolution*], I use the term *shortgevity* to define 32 countries in the world, most in Africa, that only enjoy two-thirds of the life expectancy that we in the North enjoy. They average 50 years of average life expectancy and 40 years or less of disability-free life expectancy. It is hard for me to think of leisure in their context" (personal correspondence, February 1, 2010).

The following model was developed in an effort to examine why the leisure experiences of retirement may be significantly different in MDCs and LDCs (see figure 1.2 on page 20). Before reviewing the model, a few assumptions will be considered.

Papelpicado

Mercedes Bern-Klug*

Featherlight and full of color, *papelpicado* remains a popular decorative art form in Mexico. *Papel* is the Spanish word for "paper" and *picado* means "punched" or "perforated." Rectangular sheets of tissue-thin paper are stacked and then the artist uses sharp chisels to cut images of flowers, animals, or geometric shapes though the stack. The result is a big, brightly colored paper doily of sorts. The sheets of tissue paper are typically squares or rectangles that are about 30 centimeters tall and 46 centimeters wide, although sizes can vary. After being punched through with a chisel, awl, or sharp blade, individual sheets of paper are separated from the stack. They are then lined up side by side with the tops of the papers attached to a string and hung across a room or a patio.

When a person cuts the sheets of tissue with a pair of scissors, it is called *papelcortado* (cut paper). To make the geometric shapes, the sheet of paper is folded multiple times. A snip of the scissors removes a small wedge of the brightly colored paper. Unfolding the paper is like unfolding a hand-cut paper snowflake. Papelcortado decorations require only paper, scissors, and a bit of imagination. It is an activity for people aged 4 to 104, and it can be done in solitude or in groups. Grandparents and grandchildren can work together. Though this activity requires no special talent, years of experience can result in elaborate designs.

The beautifully cut, brightly colored sheets of strung tissue paper are used in the home for a variety of occasions, including birthdays, anniversaries, and holidays. Papelpicado is often included as part of the decorations for Day of the Dead altars, where photos and cherished items of departed family members are displayed to commemorate the Christian All Souls' Day in early November as well as pre-Christian traditions that honor the deceased.

Señora Herminia Albarrán Romero is an older Mexican artist, now living in California, who received a National Heritage Fellowship from the National Endowment for the Arts in 2005 to continue creating her beautiful paper decorations and to teach others to do the same.

For more information about Señora Albarrán, visit

http://en.wikipedia.org/wiki/Herminia_Albarr%C3%A1n_Romero.

For more information about the Mexican Day of the Dead, see

www.mexconnect.com/articles/3099-mexico-s-day-of-the-dead-resource-page.

Photo by Chris Simon, 2001. Courtesy of the Alliance for California Traditional Arts.

Papelpicado artist and altarista (altar artist) Herminia Albarrán Romero.

*Mercedes Bern-Klug, PhD, MSW, is an assistant professor in the School of Social Work at the University of Iowa.

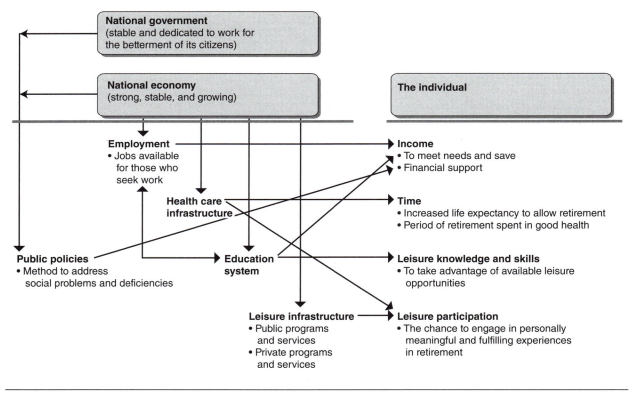

Figure 1.2   Model of prerequisites for meaningful leisure.

- The model assumes that having the opportunity to retire and to spend one's later adult years in a personally satisfying and meaningful manner is a quality-of-life issue. As such, the model depicts the interaction of variables that contribute to this event.

- It is assumed that in LDCs, the retirement experience for members of the higher socioeconomic classes is likely to be similar to the experiences of most people who reside in MDCs, so the model reflects what would be needed for members of other socioeconomic classes (i.e., the nonwealthy) to experience retirement in a fashion similar to their peers in MDCs.

- The model largely reflects characteristics associated with nations in the later stages of the demographic transition (i.e., MDCs).

- A noted limitation of the model is the presumption that developing nations will seek to follow a political and economic path similar to that followed by MDCs. This may not be the case. However, in support of this presumption, at least three currently developing nations (China, India, and Mexico) seem well on their way to repeating a developmental pattern similar to that which occurred in MDCs.

The model is divided into two sets of variables. On the left side are variables associated with the society as a whole, and variables associated with individual members of society are on the right side. The model suggests that the foundation needed for the advancement of quality-of-life issues is a stable *national government*. In the absence of a prevailing form of a central government, anarchy and chaos will prevent the development of the structures and resources required to promote quality of life among citizens. (It is understood that in some nations a strong central political structure may exist that represses, rather than enhances, quality of life. Although true, the point of the model is to suggest that societal advancement is improbable without a stable central governing body).

A stable central governing structure fosters the development of a *nation's economy*. The ability of a country to help its older citizens largely depends on its economy. Nations with strong economies can make more resources available for their old. The demographic transition model reflects the fact that as a nation's economy grows, its financial base moves from an agrarian focus to an industrial one. Industrial economies tend to produce more jobs and increase opportunities to acquire wealth compared with agrarian economies. The more jobs, the more people will have the chance to work and earn *income* to meet their immediate needs as well as save money for other uses. A comfortable retirement is feasible only with a certain degree of wealth. From a historical standpoint, widespread retirement first became possible in the United States when the industrial economy was productive enough to support sizable numbers of nonworking adults.

Moreover, the more robust an economy is, the greater the likelihood for the development of *government policies and programs* designed to address social problems and deficiencies faced by many older adults. For example, consider the development of the Social Security system in the United States. Social Security was established as a system of income maintenance for older adults to protect against financial risk. When Social Security legislation was proposed in 1935, the country was still dealing with the effects of the Great Depression. One reason Social Security received widespread support was because it was seen as a possible answer to a major social problem: unemployment. Governments, corporations, labor unions, and older workers all favored standardized retirement, because the exit of older workers opened job opportunities for younger workers and provided older workers the chance to spend their later years in a manner of their own choice. Social Security remains the single largest source of income for the average American retiree. Without the financial support provided by this government policy, retirement would be far less accessible for many older workers.

A growing economy also helps support a nation's *health care infrastructure.* Health care infrastructure includes medical personnel, hospitals and treatment centers, medical technology and equipment, and public health and safety standards. By any measure of comparison, the health care systems in developed nations are far more effective in reducing illness and increasing life expectancy compared with those in developing countries. Better health care increases the *absolute amount of time* (life expectancy) that the average person may have to spend in retirement. Statistics cited earlier in this chapter clearly demonstrate differences between life expectancies in MDCs and LDCs.

Perhaps more important than just an increase in life expectancy, effective health care systems can affect the *time in retirement spent in good health.* Chronic conditions can limit activity. Good health

increases both the total amount of activity options available and the potential amount of time that a retiree can engage in desired activities. This is significant because the greater the perceived options and ability to participate, the higher the life satisfaction in retirement.

Another common by-product of a stable economy is the development of a nation's *education system.* An education system may affect retirement in a number of ways. The higher the level of education a person receives, the more opportunities are available to secure a higher-paying job. Higher wages provide the opportunity to save more of one's income for retirement, and the more money saved, the more options are available in deciding when to retire and what activities to engage in during retirement. In addition, a sizable body of evidence supports the positive effects of education on the ability to *develop knowledge about leisure and leisure skills* that increase perceived life satisfaction (MacNeil, 1998). Moreover, Searle and Mahon (1990) found that older adults can expand their range of recreational involvement and consequently their sense of enjoyment through leisure education.

The development of a *leisure infrastructure* is another characteristic common in developed nations but largely missing in developing countries. In-home, informal activities form the largest component of most retirees' *leisure participation.* These activities, however, are often supplemented by programs, services, and facilities provided by either public or private sponsors. Public sponsors, usually government entities, provide a wide array of leisure opportunities in the form of recreation programs, parks, swimming pools, athletic fields, recreation centers, museums, and so on. The public leisure infrastructure is often supplemented by private and commercial sponsors. The private infrastructure includes much of the entertainment industry (e.g., amusement parks, movie theaters, concerts, professional sport), the hospitality industry (e.g., restaurants, hotels), and the travel and tourism industry (e.g., cruises, escorted tours, adventure travel). It stands to reason that the larger the leisure infrastructure within a nation, the greater the opportunity for retirees to find leisure experiences that are meaningful and fulfilling.

In summary, our discussion of leisure in later life in LDCs has been admittedly vague, largely because the phenomenon of retirement remains virtually nonexistent in developing regions of the world. A combination of factors such as political and economic instability, poverty, low life expectancy, poor health care services, little education, and the absence of a leisure infrastructure makes any conversation about the importance of leisure for older adults in developing countries irrelevant. If, however, LDCs follow a developmental pattern similar to what has already occurred in MDCs, it is likely that retirement will become an increasingly common life event and a conversation about the significance of leisure in later life will become meaningful.

Conclusion

Demographically speaking, the world is rapidly changing. Nations across the globe are experiencing the aging of their populations. One reason for this occurrence is the steady rise in the average number of years one can expect to live. In fewer than 100 years, human beings made greater gains in life expectancy than in the preceding 50 centuries. This has resulted in a steady increase in the absolute number of older people all over the world. At the same time, worldwide declines in fertility rates have resulted in increases in median age and the gradual rise in the proportion of older adults as a percentage of the total population.

In an ideal world, all adults would have the opportunity to retire from the labor force during their later years and to live the remaining years of their lives safely, comfortably, and peacefully. As discussed in this chapter, an important contributor to an older adulthood marked by dignity and quality is the experience of leisure. Our perception of leisure is not one of leftover time or diversional activities but instead one of freedom to pursue experiences that are personally meaningful and satisfying. In essence, leisure becomes the opportunity to pursue experiences that bring us pleasure, promote self-development, enhance our self-esteem, and allow us to engage in activities we are passionate about.

Will the opportunity to experience leisure in the later years, already enjoyed by many citizens of MDCs, ever become possible for adults in LDCs? In an effort to answer this question, a model outlining the conditions necessary to achieve this goal was presented. The model may work as theory, but are its prerequisites truly achievable? At present, there is too little evidence to know. However, the ideal of giving all people the choice to retire from work and to fill their later years with meaningful leisure experiences is a noble goal and a dream worth pursuing.

KEY TERMS

absolute number of older people—The total number of people aged 65 and older within a given population.

active aging—Optimizing opportunities for health, participation, and security in order to enhance quality of life as people age.

centenarians—People age 100 and over.

demography—The statistical study of human populations with particular reference to size, density, and distribution.

demography of aging—The study of older people in a population and the impact of population aging on society.

demographic transition theory—Refers to the movement in a society from high to low birthrates and death rates.

dependency ratio—The ratio of current workers to retirees.

exponential growth—A type of increase wherein an entity grows by a proportion of itself.

fertility rate—The average number of children that would be born to a woman by the time she had ended childbearing.

less developed or developing countries (LDCs)—Nations that tend to be rural-agrarian societies with high fertility rates, low life expectancies, and a lack of basic public services such as health care infrastructure.

life expectancy—The length of time a member of a birth cohort (i.e., people born in a specific year) can expect to live.

life expectancy at birth—The average length of time from birth that people in a given society, as well as in subgroups defined by gender, race, and ethnicity, are expected to live.

maximum life span—Biologically programmed maximum number of years that a species can expect to live.

median age—The age at which half the population is older and half is younger.

more developed countries (MDCs)—Nations that have undergone the demographic transition and are, for the most part, politically and financially stable and highly industrialized.

mortality rate—The rate of death by a percentage of a population.

population aging—The phenomenon in which older adults make up an increasingly larger proportion of a given population.

proportion of older people—A measure that shows the relationship between the size of the older population and the rest of society.

replacement rate—The rate at which births and deaths offset each other, eventually resulting in zero population growth.

total population—The absolute number of people in all age groups.

REVIEW AND DISCUSSION QUESTIONS

1. Define each of the following terms: *fertility rate*, *life expectancy*, and *median age*. Explain how demographers use each one to describe population aging.

2. Explain demographic transition theory and identify the four transformational stages described in this theory. Explain how the theory might be used to discuss the process of population aging within a country. Do you think this theory is applicable to developing nations of the world?

3. Review figure 1.1 on page 6. What do the data suggest about the future of population aging around the globe? Predict the regions of the world that will experience the most growth in older adults over the next 50 years, and explain some of the reasons for your predictions.

4. What do you feel are the major challenges that population aging presents to MDCs? To LDCs? Explain your answer.

5. Can leisure experiences contribute to the quality of life of retirement-aged adults? Be sure to provide specific examples to support your view.

6. Identify some ways in which population aging will affect the provision of leisure services in MDCs in future decades. Based on what you know about the baby boom generation, what types of leisure activities are likely to increase or decrease in popularity as baby boomers retire?

7. Review figure 1.2 on page 20. Explain the relationships between the societal variables listed on the left side of the figure and the individual variables listed on the right side of the figure.

LEARNING ACTIVITIES

1. The cultural system of any society includes all its historically created designs and expectations that are used as potential guides for behavior. It is culture that gives meaning to both actions and objects within a society. Recreational activities are an obvious by-product of a culture. Group activities of one culture may be cooperative and peaceful and those of another aggressive and competitive. The explanations for behavior in recreational settings are learned and follow culturally bound standards. Consequently, leisure is not a transcendent state of being; rather, it is thoroughly embedded in the particular culture in which it exists.

As described in the sidebar on page 19, papelpicado is a recreational activity unique to Mexican culture. To learn more about culturally based leisure experiences, select three nations on three continents to research, focusing on the identification of recreational experiences that are unique to the particular nations explored. Try to identify forms of leisure that older adults actively participate in. For each nation selected, write a short essay describing the identified activities.

2. Select at least two MDCs and two LDCs from around the globe. Research the main demographic structures in all four countries, looking at recent trends in fertility rates, life expectancy at birth, and median age. Using your findings, compare and contrast the future of population aging in all four countries.

3. Compare and contrast the challenges likely to be presented by population aging in both MDCs and LDCs. Explain why MDCs and LDCs are likely to face different challenges with respect to population aging. Suggest some strategies that might help both types of countries to deal with the challenges that they are likely to face.

4. Do you think retirement eventually will become an expected life event for older adults in LDCs? What would need to happen for this to occur?

5. Critically analyze the WHO's model of active aging (see page 15). Review each of the determinants presented in the model and discuss their relevance to the notion of active aging. Are there other determinants that might be added to improve the model? Could any of the present determinants be removed? Explain your answer.

6. Interview at least three people who are retired and are at least 65 years of age. Develop a set of questions to ask them about leisure

experiences during their retirement years. Ask them about their participation patterns and their involvement in the four categories of leisure opportunities (e.g., education, travel, volunteering, and fitness activity and sport) discussed in the chapter. Ask them their opinions about the importance of leisure experiences during their retirement years.

7. The authors of this chapter have argued that leisure experiences can help improve the quality of life among retirement-aged adults. What is your view of this claim? Develop a short essay summarizing your agreement or disagreement with the author's claims. Be sure to present specific information to support your views.

8. Critically analyze figure 1.2 on page 20. Identify what you believe to be the strengths and the weaknesses of this model. Can you think of other variables that you would add to the model to improve it? Explain your answer.

9. The Bhutanese government has determined that there are four pillars to a happy society: economy, culture, environment, and good governance. These pillars are further divided into nine domains: psychological well-being, ecology, health, education, culture, living standards, time use, community vitality, and good governance. If you were given the task of identifying the components of a happy civilization, what would they be? What role does leisure play in your list?

10. George Washington Carver proclaimed, "How far you go in life depends on your being tender with the young, compassionate with the aged, sympathetic with the striving, and tolerant of the weak and strong. Because someday in life you will have been all of these" (Pozgar, 2005, p. ix). Comparing the disparity between the more developed and less developed nations, do you consider longevity and quality of life to be human rights issues? What role can more developed nations take in ensuring better conditions around the world? How do MacNeil's prerequisites for meaningful leisure in retirement (see figure 1.2 on page 20) help conceptualize what needs to be done?

CRITICAL-THINKING ACTIVITY

A growing number of scientists are convinced that they are close to understanding the biologi-

cal processes involved with human aging. Moreover, many of these researchers are confident that once we understand why humans age, we will, for the first time in history, be able to increase the human life span. Though we will not become immortal, speculation is that we might reasonably project a life expectancy in the range of 200 to 400 years. Such a scenario obviously raises many questions.

For purposes of this exercise, assume that scientists have created an antiaging pill. Let us further assume that regular use of this pill will increase human life expectancy to 200 years. Based on this assumption, you are asked to critically analyze some implications of this scenario. First, consider some of the practical implications for a society with an average life expectancy of 200 years. What impact might it have upon family and family life; work, leisure, and retirement; education and religion; population growth and population dynamics; and politics and public policy?

Second, discuss the implications of a 200-year life expectancy for MDCs and LDCs. What are some of the societal challenges that might result from a doubling of human life expectancy? In what ways would the challenges faced by MDCs and LDCs be the same? How might they be different?

Third, based on the implications that you have already discussed, write a two-page essay in response to the following proposition: Further scientific investigations directed toward increasing human life span should or should not be continued at the present time. Use the essay to explain the reasoning behind the position you support.

SUGGESTED READING

Butler, R.N. (2008). *The longevity revolution.* New York: Public Affairs.

Dychtwald, K. (1999). *Age power: How the 21st century will be ruled by the new old.* New York: Jeremy P. Tarcher/Putnam.

Hayutin, A.M. (2007). Graying of the global population. *Public Policy and Aging Report, 17*(4), 12-18.

Kinsella, K., & He, W. (2009). *U.S. Census Bureau, International Population Reports, P95/09-1. An aging world: 2008.* Washington, DC: U.S. GPO.

MacNeil, R.D. (2001). Bob Dylan and the baby boom generation: The times they are a-changin'—again. *Activities, Adaptation and Aging, 25*(3/4), 45-58.

World Health Organization (WHO). (2002). *Active ageing: A policy framework.* Geneva: Author.

REFERENCES

Aked, J., Marks, N., & Cordon, C. (2008). *Five ways to well-being: The evidence.* London: NEF and the Foresight Commission.

Aldrik, P. (2009, September 14). Nicolas Sarkozy wants well-being measure to replace GDP. Retrieved from www.telegraph.co.uk/finance/economics/6189582/Nicolas-Sarkozy-wants-well-being-measure-to-replace-GDP.html.

Australian Bureau of Labor Statistics. (2008). *Australian Social Trends.* Retrieved from www.abs.gov.au/AUSSTATS/abs@.nsf/Lookup/4102.0Chapter4102008.

Buettner, D. (2008). *The Blue Zones.* Washington, DC: National Geographic Society.

Butler, R.N. (2008). *The longevity revolution.* New York: Public Affairs.

Central Intelligence Agency (CIA). (2008). The world factbook. Retrieved from www.cia.gov/library/publications/theworldfactbook/rankorder.

Cordes, K.A., & Ibrahim, H.M. (2003). *Applications in recreation and leisure* (3rd ed.). New York: McGraw-Hill.

Edginton, C.R., DeGraff, D.G., Dieser, R.B., & Edginton, S.R. (2008). *Leisure and life satisfaction: Foundational perspectives* (4th ed.). New York: McGraw-Hill.

Fischer, D.H. (1978). *Growing old in America.* Oxford, England: Oxford University Press.

Focalyst. (2007, June 30). The sky's the limit: Travel trends among the baby boom generation and beyond. Retrieved from http://assets.aarp.org/rgcenter/general/travel_trends_1.pdf.

Gist, Y.J. (1994). Aging trends—southern Africa. *Journal of Cross-Cultural Gerontology, 9,* 255-276.

Haupt, A., & Kane, T. (1998). *Population handbook* (4th ed.). Washington, DC: Population Reference Bureau.

Hayutin, A.M. (2007). Graying of the global population. *Public Policy and Aging Report, 17*(4), 12-18.

Hooyman, N.R., & Kiyak, H.A. (2008). *Social gerontology: A multidisciplinary perspective* (8th ed.). Boston: Pearson.

Kaiser Family Foundation. (2004). *Medicare chartbook: Financing Medicare.* Washington, DC: Author.

Kennedy, R.F. (1968, May 18). Speech presented at the University of Kansas.

Kinsella, K., & He, W. (2009). *An aging world: 2008.* Washington, DC: U.S. Census Bureau.

Lee, C. (2007). *Social security, medicare panel adjusts forecast.* Washington Post, April 24, 2007; A9.

Low, N., Butt, S., Ellis-Paine, A., & Smith, J. (2007). Helping Out: A National Survey of Volunteering and Charitable Giving. Institute for Volunteering Research. Retrieved from http://volunteering.org.uk/NR/rdonlyres/BFC9C41E-7636-48FB-843C-A89D2E93F277/0/OTS_Helping_Out.pdf.

MacNeil, R.D. (2001). Bob Dylan and the baby boom generation: The times they are a-changin'—again. *Activities, Adaptation & Aging, 25*(3/4), 45-58.

MacNeil, R.D. (1998). Leisure, lifelong learning and older adults: A conceptual overview. *Leisure Today, 69*(2), 26-28.

Martin, L.G., & Kinsella, K. (1994). Research on the demography of aging in developing countries. In L.G. Martin &

S.H. Preston (Eds.), *Demography of aging* (pp. 356-397). Washington, DC: National Academy Press.

Matcha, D.A. (2007). *The sociology of aging: An international perspective.* Cornwall-on-Hudson, NY: Sloan.

Mydens, S. (2009, May 7). Recalculating happiness in a Himalayan kingdom. *New York Times,* p. A8.

McGue, M., & Christensen, K. (2001). The heritability in cognitive functioning in very old adults: Evidence from Danish twins aged 75 years and older. *Psychology and Aging, 16*(2), 272-280.

Neugarten, B.L. (1974). Age groups in American society and the rise of the young-old. *ANNALS of the American Academy of Political and Social Science, 415,* 187-198.

Novak, M. (2009). *Issues in aging* (2nd ed.). Boston: Pearson Education.

Pelletier, K. (1984). Longevity: Fulfilling our biological potential. In J. Opatz (Ed.), *Wellness promotion strategies* (pp. 46-61). Dubuque, IA: Kendall/Hunt.

Pipher, M. (1999). *In another country.* New York: Penguin Putnam.

Plonczynski, D.J. (2003). Physical activity determinants of older women: What influences activity? *Medical Surgical Nursing, 12*(4), 213-223.

Pogzar, G. (2005). *Legal and ethical issues for health professionals.* Boston: Jones & Bartlett Publishers.

Road Scholar (2010). Adventures in lifelong learning. Retrieved from www.roadscholar.org.

Sanderson, W., & Scherbov, S. (2008). Population bulletin: Rethinking age and aging. *Population Reference Bureau, 63*(4), 1-16.

Searle, M.S., & Mahon, M.J. (1990). *Leisure education in a day hospital: The effects of selected social-psychological variables among older adults.* Paper presented at the 1990 National Recreation and Parks Association Leisure Research Symposium, Baltimore.

Statistics Bureau of Japan. (2009). *Statistics handbook of Japan, 2009.* Retrieved from www.stat.go.jp/english/data/handbook/index.htm.

Statistics Canada. (2007). Canada survey of giving, volunteering and participating. Retrieved from www.givingandvolunteering.ca.

United Nations Secretariat. (2005). *World population prospects: The 2004 revision.* New York: Population Division of the Department of Economic and Social Affairs of the United Nations Secretariat.

United Nations. (2009). *World population ageing 2009.* New York: Department of Economic and Social Affairs/Population Division, United Nations.

Williams, A., Fries, J., Koppen, J. & Prisuta, R. (2010). *Connecting and giving: a report on how mid-life and older Americans spend their time, make connections and build communities.* Washington, D.C.: AARP. Retrieved from www.aarp.org/giving-back/volunteering/info-01-2010/connecting_giving.html.

World Health Organization (WHO). (2002). *Active ageing: A policy framework.* Geneva: WHO.

Zaidi, A. (2010). *Fiscal and pension sustainability: Present and future issues in EU countries.* Vienna: The European Centre for Social Welfare Policy and Research.

CHAPTER 2

The Influence of Leisure on Discourses of Aging

Rylee A. Dionigi ■ **Sean Horton**

LEARNING OBJECTIVES

After reading this chapter, you will be able to

- recognize and describe stereotypes of old age and opposing discourses of aging in Western society;

- explain ageism and discuss how stereotypes can influence the way older adults are treated by society, the way they are understood by society, and their access to leisure;

- explain how cultural stereotypes can affect how older adults see themselves;

- explain how stereotypes can influence older people's decisions to engage in leisure, the type of activities in which they engage, and how they perform in such activities; and

- explain the role of leisure in resisting and perpetuating stereotypes of being old and aging, especially in the context of sport and physical activity.

This chapter discusses the influence of leisure on discourses of aging. In particular, it focuses on stereotypes of being old and aging in Western society and examines the role of leisure, especially sport and physical activity, in perpetuating and resisting stereotypes. First, the dominant negative discourse on aging is examined. The influence of the media in shaping this discourse is discussed, along with how this negative discourse has played a key role in shaping appropriate leisure activities for older people, affecting the behavior and expectations of older adults through self-stereotyping, influencing how young people understand older age, and perpetuating cultural stereotypes of being old. Second, a counterdiscourse of positive aging is presented. As part of this discourse, leisure, including physical activity, is being promoted by governments, academics, and health professionals as an effective means of maintaining individual and population health. Therefore, the chapter demonstrates how leisure provides space for older people to simultaneously resist and reinforce negative and positive discourses of aging.

Negative Aging Discourse

Aging is a complex biological, psychological, sociological, and universal process that everybody goes through; however, the process is unique for everybody. Despite these truths about aging, it is commonly viewed as a negative process. Older people have often been perceived as a homogenous group rather than as individuals with varying needs and experiences. The majority of knowledge about older people and aging is based on denigrating **stereotypes**, or unchallenged myths that are widespread and well entrenched in Western societies (McGuire, Boyd, & Tedrick, 2009; Ory, Hoffman, Hawkins, Sanner, & Mockenhaupt, 2003). In 1607, Shakespeare outlined the seven ages of man in *As You Like It*. He described the seventh and final stage as a reversion to childhood and ultimately complete oblivion, "sans teeth, sans eyes, sans taste, sans everything." This **aging as decline** discourse persists 400 years on, emphasizing ill health, idleness, disengagement, dependency, and deterioration as the inevitable processes of aging (Blaikie, 1999; Wearing, 1995).

An important ramification of this negative discourse is widespread ageism in society. The word **ageism** was introduced by Robert Butler (1969). It refers to a complex form of social oppression based on age, similar to prejudice based on race or gender (Bytheway, 1995). Ageism can be defined

as "a set of social relations that discriminate against older people and set them apart as being different by defining and understanding them in an oversimplified, generalised way" (Minichiello, Brown, & Kendig, 2000, p. 253). Therefore, ageism refers in part to making assumptions (or stereotypes) about how older people behave and what issues they are likely to encounter. These taken-for-granted notions of aging are disseminated through everyday language, humor, literature, media, public attitudes, social policy, and research, affecting how older age is understood at the cultural, interpersonal, and individual levels (Wearing, 1995).

Negative stereotyping of aging affects what is expected of older people, contributes to the establishment of age-appropriate norms, and highlights the value of youthfulness over older age. In recent surveys, more than 80% of North American seniors reported at least one incident of ageism, and more than half reported multiple incidents (Ory et al., 2003). Therefore, stereotyping can contribute to the social oppression or marginalization of older adults (Biggs, 1993). Generally speaking, Western cultures idolize youthfulness, competitiveness, achievement, health, autonomy, and independence and are anxious about factors commonly associated with aging (for example, graying hair, wrinkly skin, ill health, disability, dependency, loneliness, inactivity, and institutionalization) (Blaikie, 1999).

Considerable effort has gone into understanding why aging stereotypes are predominantly negative in Western society and how early these negative perceptions develop within individuals. Sociocultural structures (e.g., the rise of capitalism and the establishment of aged-care homes), traditional theories of aging (e.g., disengagement theory), and the medicalization of aging through fields of knowledge on aging (e.g., traditional gerontology and geriatrics) have all contributed to stereotypes of what it means to be old (Blaikie, 1999; Dionigi, 2008; Wearing, 1995). The focus here, however, is on the influence of the media.

Media Influence

The media have been singled out because they are a key source of negative stereotyping and because they have great influence on young people. *Media* is used here to collectively refer to television shows, commercials, and news broadcasts; movies; novels; magazines; websites; and birthday cards. In their review of representations of seniors on television, Montepare and Zebrowitz

(2002) noted that older adults are more likely to be portrayed in comical roles that reflect stereotypes about physical and cognitive decline and sexual impotence. In Australia, Wearing (1995) found that older people are depicted in novels, movies, and television as frail, disabled, dependent, withdrawn, widowed, forgetful, senile, or cranky. Roles beyond these common stereotypes are scarce; older adults, and women in particular, are notably underrepresented in movies, television shows, and commercials. Bazzini and colleagues' examination of movies covering half a century showed that, over the age of 35, 80% of the available roles go to men, with just 20% going to women (Bazzini, McIntosh, Smith, Cook, & Harris, 1997). Evidence suggests that this imbalance has recently started to change, albeit modestly, but a large percentage of female roles continue to depict aging in a negative light (Robinson, Callister, Magoffin, & Moore, 2007).

Moreover, fears about old age are reinforced through the media. For example, news broadcasts often highlight the so-called social and economic crisis of the aging population, which positions older people as a burden on society (see chapter 7). Various commercials, popular magazines, and websites promote antiaging remedies, contributing to the fear of the aging process (Gilleard & Higgs, 2000). Derogatory stereotypes of aging are also evident in birthday cards that joke about physiological losses and age concealment (Wearing, 1995).

These negative portrayals in the media influence the manner in which young people view older people. By the time children enter elementary school, negative impressions of seniors have already been established (Isaacs & Bearison, 1986), and there appears to be a distinct relationship between the amount of television watched and how negatively children view the aging process (Gerbner, Gross, Morgan, Signorelli, & Shanahan, 2002). These negative attitudes toward aging that are adopted at a young age tend to persist throughout adulthood. When people reach their senior years, they have spent the vast majority of their lives expressing and internalizing negative stereotypes of old age (Levy & Banaji, 2002). Thus, perhaps it is not surprising that the stereotypes older people hold regarding their own social group are not dramatically different from those held by the rest of society. Montepare and Zebrowitz (2002) noted that older adults view members of their own age group as "lower in status, less likeable, unhappier, more dependent, and less goal oriented than younger adults" (p. 90).

Self-Stereotyping Among Older Adults

Perhaps the most startling example of older adults' tendency to negatively self-stereotype comes from the Implicit Association Test (IAT), which attempts to measure subconscious attitudes and biases. The IAT pairs a social group (i.e., young–old) with an evaluative dimension (i.e., good–bad). The *response latency*, or the speed at which pairings are made, measures the strength of the implicit attitude. In addition to the measurement of implicit stereotypes, participants are also asked questions to determine their explicit, or consciously held, attitudes toward these social groups (Nosek, Banaji, & Greenwald, 2002).

Over a three-year period, slightly more than 68,000 responses specific to the age stereotype task were collected. The age of respondents ranged from 8 to 71 years. As expected, young people's explicit and implicit attitudes toward seniors were negative. As the age of the respondents increased, explicit (or conscious) attitudes toward older people gradually became more positive. Implicit (unconscious) attitudes, however, remained consistently and overwhelmingly negative; in fact, implicit attitudes toward the old were as negative among seniors as among the young. The authors noted that members of other groups tested (i.e., race, gender) generally show more positive implicit attitudes toward their own group compared with nongroup members, but older people are an exception to this trend. The results from the IAT show that seniors' subconscious stereotypes about their own social group are as negative as those held by the rest of society. As Levy and Banaji (2002) remarked about this tendency of seniors, with friends like oneself, who needs enemies?

A key consequence of the negative discourse of aging is the potential for stereotypes to become self-stereotypes as people age. The combination of negative stereotypes and ageism can result in a self-fulfilling prophecy in which older people buy into these negative views, affecting a host of leisure and exercise-related behaviors, as well as how older people make sense of themselves. Evidence suggests that internalized negative self-stereotypes among seniors can affect their performance in a number of physical and cognitive tasks, influence activities in which they engage, and have implications for long-term health and well-being.

Effects on Task Performance

A number of studies have examined the performance implications of stereotypes. While the

IAT test measures attitudes held at a subconscious level, social psychologist Becca Levy and colleagues (e.g., 1996, 1999) have conducted a number of studies to determine whether manipulating the subconscious can affect seniors' performance in a variety of physical and cognitive tasks. In a typical experiment, participants are seated at a computer, ostensibly playing a computer game. During this game, words are flashed on the computer screen at a speed that is too fast for the conscious mind to process, but they are detectable at a subconscious level. Levy (1996) found that priming participants with positive words of aging (i.e., *wise*, *sage*) resulted in improved performance on a subsequent memory task, while negative words (i.e., *decrepit*, *Alzheimer's*) worsened memory performance. Similarly, Hausdorff, Levy, and Wei (1999) found that a positive prime delivered subconsciously to seniors resulted in faster walking speed.

In addition to the subtle manner in which implicit stereotyping affects the performance of older adults, explicit stereotypes that are directly and consciously perceived have similar effects. These studies fit within the framework of **stereotype threat** and manipulate participants' conscious perceptions of the task they are undertaking (Steele & Aronson, 1995). For example, Desrichard and Kopetz (2005) subjected two groups of older adults to an identical memory task, part of which involved memorizing a route on a city map. The only difference in the two conditions was how the task was framed. Those who were told that the task measured their memory performance performed significantly worse than those who were told that it measured their orientation abilities. The authors speculated that the notion of memory triggers negative stereotypes of aging and failing memory, and simply eliciting this negative stereotype is enough to impair performance among older people.

Both types of studies (implicit and explicit, subconscious and conscious) demonstrate that typical stereotypes can affect the performance of older people on various cognitive and physical measures, primarily due to the fact that many older adults buy into negative stereotypes about their own social group. In other words, the stereotypes embedded in the negative discourse of aging have effectively disempowered many older people, making them feel that they cannot or should not do certain things (Gilleard & Higgs, 2000; Wearing, 1995). This conforming behavior tends to apply to involvement in various sport and leisure activities.

Activity Involvement

Traditionally, involvement in certain activities, competitive sport in particular, has been considered the exclusive domain of young people. Older adults were typically not expected to be capable of or interested in striving to score a goal in field sports, winning a medal in the pool or on the track, running marathons, or outsmarting opponents in racket sports. For most of the twentieth century, rest and disengagement from the productive spheres of society were the expected norm in later life (Blaikie, 1999; Grant, 2001). Therefore, more passive activities such as lawn bowling, gardening, bingo, crafts, watching television, and playing card games have become stereotypical leisure activities for the old. Vigorous sport and physical exercise has frequently been seen as inappropriate or even dangerous for older people (Dionigi, 2008; Grant, 2001).

Older people who buy into these stereotypes tend to be involved in more passive rather than active leisure pursuits, regardless of their ability or health status (Grant, 2002). This is particularly the case for older women, many of whom grew up in a time that discouraged physical activity for females of all ages (Vertinsky, 1995). As a result, many older women struggle with the notion of exercise, often have strong fears of physical activity, and therefore tend to avoid it (O'Brien Cousins, 2000). Older people who are active on a regular basis remain the minority among their age cohort. For more discussion on how stereotypes affect activity involvement, refer to chapter 7 by Grant and Kluge, as well as the section in this chapter titled Leisure as Reinforcement of Ageism (page 35).

Health Implications

As one might expect, the reluctance to engage in physically active leisure has long-term health implications for individuals and society, and self-stereotypes of aging seem to be an integral part of the equation. Levy and Myers (2004) noted that seniors with more positive opinions of their own aging took better care of their health, which included getting more exercise, eating a healthier diet, and visiting their family doctor more regularly. Longitudinal studies of the connection between stereotypes and health indicate that people with positive self-perceptions even tend to live up to 7.5 years longer than those with more negative self-perceptions of aging (Levy, Slade, Kunkel, & Kasl, 2002). Given the impact of a growing aging population on a nation's health

"I Want to Win"

In 2001 I met Edward* after he won a cycling race at the Australian Masters Games in Newcastle. He was 81 years old. He told me that he was not a competitive athlete in his youth (he began cycling at age 66 as a health precaution after he had a minor brain haemorrhage). The Masters Games are a multisport event for mature athletes (usually 30 years and over) (Dionigi, 2008), and age, not ability, is the qualifier for participation (Weir, Baker, & Horton, 2010). When I interviewed Edward in 2002 (see Dionigi, 2008, p. 129), he was working full time in the building industry, caring for his disabled wife, and maintaining his house and yard. He said the following about competing in cycling:

> Oh, at the Masters Games it's everything. Oh, my word. I mean I want the lot! I'm greedy . . . when I go into, say, events like in a Masters Games, it is competitive—*extremely*—I want to win . . . I want to be better than the chaps who are with me, right. I know then that, "OK, I have trained right." . . . Oh well, [if I lose] I can shake their hand off because they're better than what I am. I've done something wrong, or, no matter what I done I couldn't have beaten that certain person.

Edward regularly travels overseas to race in veterans cycling tournaments, and he has bike equipment in his home in order to adhere to a strict training regime:

> Each night I do a minimum of an hour and a half on an indoor cycle trainer . . . here in my own house. I've got two forms of that [a bike that he balances on rollers as he rides and a stationary bike] . . . then I would do 15 minutes of stretching, and I just love doing it. It's no chore and I don't say I have to do it . . . I've got the ability to do it, in the first place and . . . I don't have to be driven to it.

At age 89, Edward is still competing in cycling. Despite undergoing triple heart bypass surgery in 2008, he won a gold medal at the 2009 World Masters Games in Sydney.

As remarkable as Edward's story is, research on older athletes has found that many participants of masters events are highly competitive and have overcome personal challenges to maintain sport involvement. The expanding older population has resulted in more opportunities for involvement in various leisure activities, including a wide range of sports. The recent 2009 World Masters Games in Australia exemplifies this explosion in both interest and opportunity. Approximately 28,000 athletes representing 95 countries gathered in Sydney to partake in 28 sports. To put the size of this event in perspective, the 2008 Beijing Olympic Games had 10,500 athletes competing (Shephard, 2010). Since the inaugural World Masters event in Toronto in 1985, the number of participants has increased almost fourfold (Weir et al., 2010).

Notably, the majority of participants interviewed at the 2009 World Masters Games said they lived with a chronic condition, such as arthritis, asthma, osteoporosis, or diabetes, or had experienced surgery such as a hip or knee replacement, yet they learned how to manage and adapt to their circumstances so they could continue competing in sport (Dionigi, Horton, & Baker, 2010). One particularly noteworthy example from this study, Barb Boyer (pictured), had osteopenia prior to beginning Olympic weightlifting in her late 50s. Six years later her bone-density readings had improved to the point where they were equivalent to that of a 25-year-old (personal communication, October 18, 2009). Now in her late 60s, Barb prepares for competition by training six days a week, one to two hours per day. In Barb's case, the initiation of and continued involvement in competitive sport resulted in a profound improvement in her overall health. Maintaining sport performance despite age-related diseases and disabilities provides a sense of empowerment and demonstrates flexibility, acceptance, and determination in later life.

*"Edward" is a pseudonym.

Barb Boyer.

Photo courtesy of Paul Chen.

care budget, it is perhaps not surprising that there has been a shift in the discourse on aging in recent years. Negative stereotypes of old age and aging are being challenged. In particular, the health and fitness movement is encouraging older people to engage regularly in physically active leisure pursuits (see chapter 7).

Positive Aging Discourse

A counterdiscourse of **positive aging**, or aging well, emerged in the 1970s to celebrate later life as a time for enjoyment, leisure, activity, challenge, growth, and exploration (Featherstone & Hepworth, 1995). Also called *healthy aging, successful aging*, and *optimal aging*, this way of thinking about aging has emerged in academic research associated with gerontology and health care, exercise promotion, and leisure studies (Dupuis, 2002). Such approaches to understanding aging, as well as the health and fitness movement they underpin, have opened up opportunities for older people to participate in a range of physically active leisure activities. According to Grant (2002), "Older adults can live vital, independent, and active lives, and a leisure renaissance is seen as playing a positive part in this process" (p. 285).

Positive aging discourses include multiple messages about autonomy for older people, alternative ways of thinking about aging, self-responsibility for health, and advice on leisure, lifestyle, and physical activity (Grant & Stothart, 1999). These discourses are optimistic that many of the advantages of youth can be partly preserved into older age (Hayles, 2005). Such understandings highlight the potential for health, self-fulfillment, and personal empowerment in older age. They typically provide an interpretation of older adults as people who are enjoying an independent and active life, or a life of acceptance and contentment, despite growing older. Generally speaking, today's older population (particularly the baby boom generation) is considered to be more active, affluent, educated, assertive, and healthier than its predecessors (Gilleard & Higgs, 2000, 2002; MacNeil, 2001; McPherson, 2004).

Regular physical activity is now deemed an appropriate means to maintain health, resist the aging body, and postpone deep old age (i.e., prevent or delay disease and disability) (Gilleard & Higgs, 2000, 2002). This change in attitude helps explain the growth in masters sport participation that was outlined in the sidebar titled, "I Want to Win." Other healthy leisure practices (e.g., continued mental stimulation, socializing with

peers) are also promoted through positive aging discourses. On a broader level, encouraging older people to be physically, mentally, and socially active through leisure has become a key strategy for managing and reducing the potential economic and social burden commonly associated with the aging population. As Hargreaves (1994) noted

> Keeping the ageing body moving and functioning has become one way of dealing with what has been characterized as the 'problem of ageing populations'. Neglect of the physical body can be expensive in terms of medical care and welfare support, and exercise and sports can reduce health costs. (p. 265)

In addition, the changing viewpoints and images associated with aging not only challenge traditional negative understandings of older age at a societal level, but they also provide space for older people to resist ageist attitudes and feel empowered (Wearing, 1995). Leisure is one context where there is potential for such resistance.

Leisure as Resistance to Ageism

Sociologist and feminist theorist Betsy Wearing (1995) argues that the contradiction between the dominant negative discourse of aging and the liberating aspect of the emerging leisure (or positive aging) discourse provides space for older people to resist the stereotypical degenerative view of aging. Wearing believes that "leisure presents the potential to challenge ageism and the self-fulfilling prophesy of underuse of physical and mental abilities in old age" (p. 263). She argues that leisure highlights personal choice (albeit within sociocultural and individual constraints) and what older people "*can* do rather than what they are no longer physically capable of doing" (p. 272). Resistance through leisure can be individual or collective, intentional or unintentional, and it has the potential for personal empowerment and collective social change (Shaw, 2001, 2006). Resistance requires making "a space for oneself within the constraints of the powerful" (Wearing, 1995, p. 273). Therefore, from this poststructural standpoint it is argued that personal and cultural practices and understandings of leisure are linked to power relations, and through leisure older people can resist, negotiate, and perpetuate discourses of aging and stereotypes of old age.

Qualitative research reveals stories of older people who exemplify resistance to ageism through their involvement in traditional leisure activities, such as gardening and crafts (Wearing, 1995), as well as resistance through nontraditional leisure activities, such as competitive masters sport (Dionigi, 2008; Dionigi et al., 2010). Wearing's (1995) literature review provides examples of older people resisting the dominant negative discourse of aging through physical, mental, and social stimulation; a positive attitude toward life; and the ability to find immense enjoyment and satisfaction in leisure despite physical and financial constraints. One woman in her 70s was involved in the community; attended music concerts; took poetry and writing classes; enjoyed floral art, gardening, and sewing; and regularly hosted friends and relatives. All of these activities extended beyond her household duties and resisted notions of loneliness, decline, and disengagement in later life. Another woman in her 80s, despite suffering a severe stroke and having limited financial resources, kept busy by taking weekly bus trips to senior centers, reading, watching television, and chatting daily with visitors. Wearing argued that this woman "resists in the sense of carving out a space for herself [within her physical and material constraints], which gives her satisfaction" (p. 276).

Qualitative data on older athletes reveal that many older people are not only resisting stereotypes of aging but are also attempting to resist the physically aging body through sport performance and training. Dionigi's (2008) examples of older Australian Masters Games athletes provide a powerful, vital, determined, resilient, and highly active portrayal of older people, which is in stark contrast to the passive, dependent, and sedentary image of old age projected through the negative discourse of aging. Many of the participants in this research recognised this differentiation and were proud of the idea that they were challenging age-appropriate norms. For example, some women said:

It's sort of a feeling of POWER [squints her eyes and really emphasizes this word] . . . when my grandsons can go to school and say, "My grandma runs half marathons" and everybody else says, "Oh no, my grandma's in a nursing home" . . . I like that kind of feeling. (73-year-old runner and swimmer, p. 143)

I ride a bike and I swim and I run. I don't worry about trivial things, which happens very often when people get very old . . . I'm too busy to worry about that. (73-year-old triathlete, p. 142)

I can still do it! I'm not too old, I'll never be too old. . . . It's perception whether you are too old or not [to play competitive softball]. (60-year-old softball player, p. 156)

These women experienced a sense of personal empowerment and self-worth as well as managed their athletic identity through their involvement in sport. Likewise, some men commented:

I'm 65 and I'm still running around here with [men] 15 years younger than me. I'm proud of it . . . while I'm still moving and still playing a competitive sport, I feel good. (touch-football player, p. 155)

I think we are probably quite proud of the fact that at 65 we're playing such a young person's game. . . . I mean, the conditions on the surface that you play are very, very hard for old people . . . I doubt that there are that many people at 65 that could do what we're doing . . . we get a lot of satisfaction also beating the young ones too, and I suppose that there comes some kind of pride to the fact that even at this age we can do it . . . you're physically able to do it. (beach volleyball player, p. 156)

I just like to be able to . . . think that I can still do something. That I am still capable of throwing my body around and pulling it and twisting it, turning it and being able to put it where I want to put it and, of course, keep fit at the same time. (71-year-old gymnast, p. 151)

The men and women in this research said they were attempting to delay the physiological decline typically associated with aging by keeping highly active through sport participation, training, and other healthy practices such as eating well, stimulating their minds, and being involved in the community. Recent research by Dionigi et al. (2010) on the practices and experiences of older 2009 World Masters Games participants provides further support for these findings. This engagement with leisure can certainly have empowering outcomes at the personal and societal levels, particularly in regard to notions of aging.

At the same time, however, there are potentially problematic consequences associated with such leisure practices. When older people engage in meaningful leisure pursuits of their choosing, the potential exists for personal empowerment and resistance to the negative discourse of aging. On the other hand, the desire of these older people to keep active, busy, and engaged well into older age demonstrates conformity to positive aging discourses that promote self-responsibility for health (Katz, 2000). Somewhat ironically, these practices have the potential to establish new stereotypes of older people as healthy, wealthy, and active. Considerable debate has emerged in regard to the effectiveness of health promotion and positive aging approaches as strategies to empowerment given the many individual and sociocultural determinants of health, and the inequality of opportunities and access to health care and leisure (Jolanki, 2004).

Cassandra Phoenix*

Like many schoolboys, Bill grew up playing football (soccer). This was his first love and something he would be involved with into his adult years. However, after a succession of injuries, at the age of 43 Bill played his last competitive football match and decided instead to focus on the other (noncontact) form of exercise in his life: training with free weights. Describing this turning point, Bill said, "I decided, right, at least if I'm not playing football, I've got bodybuilding to fall back on because I wanted a physical challenge. I loved physical challenges and I knew bodybuilding could fill that gap." Asked why it was so important to him to feel physically challenged, Bill replied:

Photo courtesy of Cassandra Phoenix.

> It's a personal thing. I love the physical challenge of lifting those weights, of pushing my body as hard as it's safe to push it to get ready for competition. When you go to the gym, every workout is a challenge to you, to push a bit harder. You don't always do it, but at least you can try. You've got to take your age into consideration, too. Obviously, you're not lifting as heavy weights now as you were years ago, but you're still getting the same pleasure from it and you're still challenging your body.

Along with providing a physical challenge, the level of discipline demanded by competition in natural bodybuilding also appealed to Bill:

> I love going to the gym. It's a very simple discipline for me. I enjoy getting up every other morning at around 7 o'clock, having a bite to eat, getting down to the gym, and doing what I have to do. When I know a competition is coming up, I really train properly, taking the proper rest periods, and eating the proper foods, which are going to help my training. I think the disciplined lifestyle is what probably puts a lot of people off. I often have people asking me when I'm going to stop doing it.

Certainly, one needs a degree of self-discipline if planning to enter into a competition, yet Bill is aware that this disciplined lifestyle is commonly exaggerated and subsequently perceived as being obsessive. A further misconception regularly encountered by Bill is the confusion between powerlifting and bodybuilding. "Powerlifting," he said, "is just lifting as heavy a weight as you can. Bodybuilding is working different parts of your body in a controlled manner with a lighter weight to try to develop it. No one body part takes preference over the other; you want to be the best shape that you can be." Such misconceptions are important because they can inadvertently direct people away from the activity.

As a well-recognized (and for some, inspirational) character in his hometown and the natural bodybuilding community, I asked Bill what it is that people always want to know. "How I keep my enthusiasm!" he replied. The answer to that question resonates with the stories told by many other adults involved in serious physical leisure:

> If somebody had said to me 30 or 40 years ago that I'd still be doing this at 70 then I wouldn't have believed them. But over the years I've discovered the benefits that I've got, the feel-good factor, so I've kept doing it . . . I know that if I stop my training, I won't have that feel-good factor. It's not as

though it's a massive chore. I spend no longer than three hours a week in the gym. That's all it takes. If competitions come along, it's a bonus. It's a focus, but they are not what it's all about for me. Training, lifting those weights, I don't ever see myself not doing it while I can.

Bill is currently 73 years old, and he continues to train and compete in natural bodybuilding. His previous titles include Mr. Universe 2006 and Mr. Olympia 2007.

Acknowledgments

My sincere thanks go to Bill for sharing his stories with me. These data are taken from a project funded by the Nuffield Foundation titled, *Understanding Experiences and Expectations of Ageing Through Old and Young Bodies: A Narrative Study.* Publications resulting from this study include the following:

Phoenix, C. (2011). Young bodies, old bodies, and stories of the athletic self. In G. Kenyon, E. Bohlmeijer, & W. Randall (Eds.), *Storying later life: Issues, investigations, and interventions in narrative gerontology* (pp. 111-125). Open University Press: Buckinghamshire.

Phoenix, C. (2010). Auto-photography in aging studies: Exploring issues of identity construction in mature bodybuilders. *Journal of Aging Studies, 24*(3), 167-180.

*Cassandra Phoenix, PhD, teaches at the University of Exeter, UK.

Although older people who participate in nontraditional leisure activities such as sport are resisting stereotypes of old age and the discourse of aging as decline, some of the previous statements made by older athletes indicate that they are also accepting and reinforcing negative stereotypes of old age by setting themselves apart from most older people. These contradictory findings raise questions about the role of leisure in both resisting and perpetuating stereotypes of old age and aging, such as the following:

■ Are older people redefining what it means to grow old through their leisure practices, or are they perpetuating the undesirability of old age in Western society?

■ Is the push for self-responsibility as a means to age well problematic for older people who do not have the ability, access, means, or desire to lead an active, leisured lifestyle?

Leisure as Reinforcement of Ageism

Leisure can be a site for perpetuating stereotypes of old age and the negative discourse of aging. One argument is that stereotypes are upheld when older people limit their leisure involvement to sedentary or moderately active leisure pursuits due to negative self-stereotyping and the idea of age-appropriate activities. As mentioned previously in this chapter under the section titled Activity Involvement (page 30), if people have internalized the stereotypes that the older body is not capable of vigorous activity, they consider it too risky to play sport or push their bodies to the limit. Grant (2002) argued that many older people accept socially constructed norms that physical activity is inappropriate and consider it legitimate to be sedentary.

For example, O'Brien Cousins (2000) surveyed 143 women, all 70 years of age and older, on the perceived risks and the benefits of a number of physical activities, including brisk walking, aquacise, and biking or cycling, along with gentle strength and flexibility exercises. Although women tended to recognize general health benefits associated with physical activity, their responses were striking in the extent to which they often felt that the dangers outweighed the benefits. A number of women listed heart attacks, palpitations, and angina as risks associated with brisk walking. Similarly, many women felt that gentle stretching could throw their backs out. Clearly, a percentage of older women feel vulnerable at the prospect of even a modest level of exertion, which can result in inactivity and lead to further declines in physical and mental abilities. The high level of inactivity or sedentary leisure activities among many older people can perpetuate negative stereotypes of old and discourses of aging as decline (Grant, 2001).

Another way stereotypes and ageism are reinforced through leisure is when policies and health professionals, such as general practitioners or health care workers, recommend or restrict people's involvement to certain activities based on age. For example, a doctor may not encourage physical activity to an older person who might benefit from it because the doctor believes the person should be taking a well-earned rest (Ory et al., 2003). Furthermore, aged-care organizations have often been criticized for planning repetitive activities that lack meaning, self-expression, and self-direction for older adults (Godbey, 2008).

On the other hand, the discourses, images, and practices of highly active older people have the potential to perpetuate negative stereotypes of old age and create new stereotypes and unattainable images of older people as healthy, active, and wealthy, which can unwittingly contribute to ageism. When older people invest in positive aging discourses through leisure practices, they have the potential to establish a heightened denial or fear of ill health in old age at the individual and cultural levels (Blaikie, 1999; Gilleard & Higgs, 2000).

For instance, the talk and practices of older people in masters sport may, in part, perpetuate ageism in society by promoting values of youthfulness, competition, fitness, and ability and by positioning the aging body as a problem that needs to be fixed or ill health as something to be avoided (Dionigi, 2008). As argued by Gilleard and Higgs (2000), "Age-resisting fitness regimes promote a positive self-image of non-agedness that further reinforces the undesirability and fear of old age" (p. 81). Furthermore, our research on older athletes has found that, through their words and actions, many older people perpetuate negative stereotypes by expressing negative views toward disengagement and decline, presenting negative depictions of old age, and conveying the desire to feel young, stay healthy, and remain active (Dionigi, 2008; Dionigi et al., 2010). The quotations from older adults presented previously in this chapter exemplify this point, in addition to the following quotes from Dionigi (2008):

> I just suppose, the thing is you don't want to get *old*. You want to keep moving, keep mobile, active [and] . . . playing sport against [younger people] . . . old is when I can't move around properly, I suppose [she chuckles]. I don't want to be one of those persons, like you see in a nursing home that are just—[she demonstrates what she means by sitting limp with her head down]. (66-year-old female netball player, p. 167)

> If you've got good health, you've got to *use it* and *keep*, keep fit. Just to sit around . . . your muscles

go . . . as I say, keep going . . . if I was to sit around . . . I'd get rusty . . . like a lot of old people do . . . they're sitting at home getting around in their pyjamas. I know one fellow . . . he retired . . . he'd just given everything away . . . he didn't last very long. (89-year-old male runner and walker, p. 171)

These findings also point to the idea of ill health in old age as both a matter of choice *and* inevitable (Jolanki, 2004).

Coleman, Bond, and Peace (1993) argued that the philosophies of aging well or positive aging are an understandable reaction in the midst of an ageist society, but they are rather escapist in that they ignore the eventuality of deep old age (i.e., ill health and disability will come to most of us who live long enough to experience it). Although the promotion of a physically active lifestyle through leisure sounds promising, it puts the onus on individuals in terms of maintaining their health. This approach tends to ignore social constraints, and it assumes that everyone has the ability, desire, access, and resources to lead such a lifestyle. "The reality is that not all older people have the freedom or resources to opt for a healthier lifestyle" (Grant, 2002, p. 290).

Also, discourses of positive aging and the rising number of texts on active living through leisure have been criticized for being too prescriptive and suggesting quick-fix solutions to the aging process (Grant & Stothart, 1999). Such literature implies that there is an appropriate way for people to age successfully, which suggests a misunderstanding of the heterogeneity of the aging population and a failure to recognize that satisfying leisure participation derives from self-directedness and self-expressiveness (Biggs, 1993; Grant & Stothart). As Vertinsky (1995) warns, "Freeing individuals from stereotypical preconceptions should not, at the same time, require them to make the professionally prescribed choices in regard to healthy exercise" (p. 233). Furthermore, positive aging discourses provide a strong message that a healthy population is more about reducing government costs than addressing the varying needs of a wide range of older people (McCormack, 2000).

Therefore, these positive aging discourses (and the leisure practices they promote) imply that keeping physically, mentally, and socially active is necessary for the good health and well-being of older people *and* for the good of society. This message emphasizes that aging well is primarily a matter of civic duty, individual effort, and personal choice (Katz, 2000). This way of thinking about aging has the potential to position older people who cannot or do not keep active through leisure as lazy, immoral, or a burden on society. Such imperatives perpetuate negative stereotypes and the fear of ill health in old age and highlight the increasing value of activity, health, youthfulness, and bodily performance in Western culture (Gilleard & Higgs, 2000).

Positive aging discourses and associated practices also privilege and speak to those older (usually white, middle- or upper-class) people who have the means, desire, opportunity, access, and ability to enjoy an active, leisured lifestyle. Such discourses have the potential to further marginalize people who do not fit this description (Blaikie, 1999) as well as restrict other ways of knowing and experiencing aging. Clearly, advocating individual responsibility for health through leisure can be empowering for some, but it is potentially problematic for those who fall ill, are disabled, lack financial resources or education, are from different cultural backgrounds, or do not want to be active in their leisure time.

Conclusion

The circulation of traditional and contemporary aging discourses and stereotypes means that ill health in old age can simultaneously be seen as expected, pathological, a sign of poor willpower, and the result of leading the wrong lifestyle. In other words, one's state of health in later life is paradoxically seen as both naturally determined *and* a matter of personal choice (Jolanki, 2004). Understandings and stereotypes of old age and aging are continually changing. The role of leisure in resisting and perpetuating these contradictory ideas of what it means to grow old is complex and ongoing.

KEY TERMS

ageism—A complex form of social oppression based on age, similar to prejudice based on race or gender (Bytheway, 1995). It is "a set of social relations that discriminate against older people and set them apart as being different by defining and understanding them in an oversimplified, generalised way" (Minichiello et al., 2000, p. 253).

aging as decline—The dominant biological discourse of aging that positions older people as being in a state of constant decline and deterioration. This view of aging emphasizes ill health, idleness, disengagement, and dependency as inevitable processes of aging.

positive aging—A counterdiscourse to aging as decline that celebrates later life as a time for enjoyment, leisure, activity, challenge, growth, and exploration. It has also been called *healthy aging, successful aging, productive aging,* and *optimal aging.*

stereotypes—Unchallenged myths that are widespread and well entrenched in society. Stereotyping can involve making assumptions and generalizations about how people behave and what they are likely to experience without regard for individual differences or unique circumstances. Therefore, stereotyping can contribute to the social oppression or marginalization of older people (Biggs, 1993).

stereotype threat—A decline in performance due to the threat of being viewed through the lens of a negative stereotype or the fear of doing something that would inadvertently confirm a negative stereotype about one's social group. This concept has been examined in various contexts, including age, race, and gender.

REVIEW AND DISCUSSION QUESTIONS

1. Describe some common positive and negative stereotypes of old age and explain why neither extreme is an adequate reflection of the experiences of many older people.

2. Discuss two key discourses of aging in Western culture and explain how they have shaped and continue to shape leisure practices of older people.

3. What is ageism, and how can it affect older people?

4. Explain the process of self-stereotyping and the effects it can have on older people's performance, attitude, and behavior.

5. Explain how leisure can be a site of resistance for older people and give specific examples of resistance from research findings on the topic.

6. Explain how positive and negative stereotypes of old and aging can be perpetuated through leisure.

LEARNING ACTIVITIES

1. Write the first five words that come to mind when you hear the term *old.* Discuss how this reflects both your attitudes toward aging and societal views of getting older.

2. Describe a common myth of aging and discuss evidence that debunks it.

3. Go to the following Project Implicit website to take the Age IAT to measure your subconscious bias toward older people: https://implicit.harvard.edu/implicit/demo/takeatest.html.

4. Find a newspaper article or news segment about a person over the age of 60 and analyze the extent to which discourses of aging and stereotypes of old age are reproduced or challenged through the story.

5. Find a partner. One of you takes the view that your state of health in later life is naturally determined. The other makes the argument that your state of health in later life is a matter of choice. Have a debate.

6. The cultural emphasis on aging well (and the practices this discourse promotes) can be empowering for older people who have the means and ability to enjoy leisure activities of their choice, but it can further marginalize older people who do not have this choice (i.e., due to socioeconomic status, disability, disease, cultural background). Discuss this argument within groups of three to five people. Everyone in the group should discuss an implication that this idea may have for various older people (either someone they know or someone hypothetical).

7. Read the sidebar about Bill by Cassandra Phoenix (pages 34-35). People often ask Bill, "When are you going to give up the bodybuilding?" What does this question show about social expectations concerning older adults and serious physical activity? What implications might this have for Bill, for other active or inactive older adults, and for young people?

8. Bill refers to physical challenge as being especially important to him. How else might older adults be challenged through leisure? Provide examples and justify them.

SUGGESTED READING

Baker, J., Horton, S., & Weir, P. (2010). *The masters athlete: Understanding the role of sport and exercise in optimizing aging*. London: Routledge.

Bergquist, L. (2009). *Second wind: The rise of the ageless athlete*. Champaign, IL: Human Kinetics.

Dionigi, R.A. (2008). *Competing for life: Older people, sport and ageing*. Saarbrüecken, Germany: Verlag Dr. Müller.

Gawande, A. (2007). The way we age now. *New Yorker*. Retrieved from www.newyorker.com/reporting/2007/04/30/070430fa_fact_gawande.

Lee, M., Carpenter, B., & Meyers, L.S. (2007). Representations of older adults in television advertisements. *Journal of Aging Studies, 21*, 23-30.

Oeppen, J., & Vaupel, J.W. (2002). Broken limits to life expectancy. *Science, 296*, 1029-1031.

Phoenix, C., & Sparkes, A. (2009). Being Fred: Big stories, small stories and the accomplishment of a positive aging identity. *Qualitative Research, 9*(2), 219-236.

Tulle, E. (2007). Running to run: Embodiment, structure and agency amongst veteran elite runners. *Sociology, 41*(2), 329-346.

REFERENCES

Bazzini, D., McIntosh, W., Smith, S., Cook, S., & Harris, C. (1997). The aging woman in popular film: Underrepresented, unattractive, unfriendly, and unintelligent. *Sex Roles, 36*(7/8), 531-543.

Biggs, S. (1993). *Understanding ageing: Images, attitudes and professional practice*. Buckingham: Open University Press.

Blaikie, A. (1999). *Ageing and popular culture*. Cambridge, UK: Cambridge University Press.

Butler, R. (1969). Ageism: Another form of bigotry. *Gerontologist, 9*, 243-246.

Bytheway, B. (1995). *Ageism*. Buckingham: Open University Press.

Coleman, P., Bond, J., & Peace, S. (1993). Ageing in the twentieth century. In J. Bond, P. Coleman, & S. Peace (Eds.), *Ageing in society: An introduction to social gerontology* (2nd ed., pp. 1-18). London: Sage.

Desrichard, O., & Kopetz, C. (2005). A threat in the elder: The impact of task instructions, self-efficacy and performance expectations on memory performance in the elderly. *European Journal of Social Psychology, 35*, 537-552.

Dionigi, R.A. (2008). *Competing for life: Older people, sport and ageing*. Saarbrüecken, Germany: Verlag Dr. Müller.

Dionigi, R.A., Horton, S., & Baker, J. (2010). Seniors in sport: The experiences and practices of older World Masters Games competitors. *International Journal of Sport & Society, 1*(1), 55-68.

Dupuis, S.L. (2002). In celebration of later life. *Society and Leisure, 25*(2), 251-255.

Featherstone, M., & Hepworth, M. (1995). Images of positive aging: A case study of *Retirement Choice* magazine. In M. Featherstone & A. Wernick (Eds.), *Images of aging: Cultural representation of later life* (pp. 29-60). London: Routledge.

Gerbner, G., Gross, L., Morgan, M., Signorelli, N., & Shanahan, J. (2002). Growing up with television: Cultivation processes. In J. Bryant & D. Zillmann (Eds.), *Media effects: Advances in theory and research* (2nd ed., pp. 43-67). Hillsdale, NJ: Erlbaum.

Gilleard, C., & Higgs, P. (2000). *Cultures of ageing: Self, citizen and the body*. Harlow, UK: Prentice Hall.

Gilleard, C., & Higgs, P. (2002). The Third Age: Class, cohort or generation? *Ageing and Society*, *22*(3), 369-382.

Godbey, G. (2008). *Leisure in your life: New perspectives.* State College, PA: Venture.

Grant, B.C. (2001). "You're never too old": Beliefs about physical activity and playing sport in later life. *Ageing and Society*, *21*(6), 777-798.

Grant, B.C. (2002). Physical activity: Not a popular leisure choice in later life. *Society and Leisure*, *25*(2), 285-302.

Grant, B.C., & Stothart, B. (1999). Ageing, leisure and active living. *ACHPER Healthy Lifestyles Journal*, *46*(2/3), 29-32.

Hargreaves, J. (1994). *Sporting females: Critical issues in the history and sociology of women's sports.* London: Routledge.

Hausdorff, J.M., Levy, B.R., & Wei, J.Y. (1999). The power of ageism on physical function of older persons: Reversibility of age-related gait changes. *Journal of the American Geriatrics Society*, *47*, 1346-1349.

Hayles, C. (2005). Governmentality and sport in later life. Unpublished doctoral dissertation, University of Queensland, Australia.

Isaacs, L.W., & Bearison, D.J. (1986). The development of children's prejudice against the aged. *International Journal of Aging & Human Development*, *23*(3), 175-194.

Jolanki, O. (2004). Moral argumentation in talk about health and old age. *Health*, *8*(4), 483-503.

Katz, S. (2000). Busy bodies: Activity, aging, and the management of everyday life. *Journal of Aging Studies*, *14*(2), 135-152.

Levy, B.R. (1996). Improving memory in old age through implicit self-stereotyping. *Journal of Personality and Social Psychology*, *71*, 1092-1107.

Levy, B.R., & Banaji, M.R. (2002). Implicit ageism. In T.D. Nelson (Ed.), *Ageism: Stereotyping and prejudice against older persons* (pp. 27-48). Cambridge, MA: MIT Press.

Levy, B.R., & Myers, L.M. (2004). Preventive health behaviors influenced by self-perceptions of aging. *Preventive Medicine*, *39*, 625-629.

Levy, B.R., Slade, M.D., Kunkel, S.R., & Kasl, S.V. (2002). Longevity increased by positive self-perceptions of aging. *Journal of Personality and Social Psychology*, *83*, 261-270.

MacNeil, R. D. (2001). Bob Dylan and the Baby Boom generation: The times they are a-changin' - again. *Activities, Adaptation and Aging*, *25*(3/4), 45-58.

McCormack, J. (2000). Looking back and moving forward? Ageing in Australia 2000. *Ageing and Society*, *20*(5), 623-631.

McGuire, F., Boyd, R., & Tedrick, R. (2009). *Leisure and aging: Ulyssean living in later life* (4th ed.). Champaign, IL: Sagamore.

McPherson, B. (2004). *Aging as a social process: Canadian perspectives* (4th ed.). Don Mills, ON: Oxford University Press.

Minichiello, V., Brown, J., & Kendig, H. (2000). Perceptions and consequences of ageism: Views of older people. *Ageing and Society*, *20*(3), 253-278.

Montepare, J.M., & Zebrowitz, L.A. (2002). A social-developmental view of ageism. In T.D. Nelson (Ed.), *Ageism: Stereotyping and prejudice against older persons* (pp. 77-125). Cambridge, MA: MIT Press.

Nosek, B., Banaji, M.R., & Greenwald, A. (2002). Harvesting implicit group attitudes and beliefs from a demonstration web site. *Group Dynamics*, *6*, 101-115.

O'Brien Cousins, S. (2000). "My heart couldn't take it": Older women's beliefs about exercise benefits and risks. *Journal of Gerontology: Psychological Sciences*, *55B*, 283-294.

Ory, M., Hoffman, M.K., Hawkins, M., Sanner, B., & Mockenhaupt, R. (2003). Challenging aging stereotypes: Strategies for creating a more active society. *American Journal of Preventive Medicine*, *25*, 164-171.

Robinson, T., Callister, M., Magoffin, D., & Moore, J., (2007). The portrayal of older characters in Disney animated films. *Journal of Aging Studies*, *21*, 203-213.

Shaw, S.M. (2001). Conceptualizing resistance: Women's leisure as political practice. *Journal of Leisure Research*, *33*(2), 186-201.

Shaw, S.M. (2006). Resistance. In C. Rojek, S.M. Shaw, & A.J. Veal (Eds.), *A handbook of leisure studies* (pp. 533-545). New York: Palgrave, Macmillan.

Shephard, R.J. (2010). The future of Masters Games: Implications for policy and research. In J. Baker, S. Horton, & P. Weir (Eds.), *The masters athlete: Understanding the role of sport and exercise in optimizing aging* (pp. 186-193). London: Routledge.

Steele, C.M., & Aronson, J. (1995). Stereotype threat and the intellectual test performance of African Americans. *Journal of Personality and Social Psychology*, *69*(5), 797-811.

Vertinsky, P. (1995). Stereotypes of aging women and exercise: A historical perspective. *Journal of Aging and Physical Activity*, *3*, 223-237.

Wearing, B. (1995). Leisure and resistance in an ageing society. *Leisure Studies*, *14*(4), 263-279.

Weir, P., Baker, J., & Horton, S. (2010). The emergence of masters sport: Participatory trends and historical developments. In J. Baker, S. Horton, & P. Weir. (Eds.), *The masters athlete: Understanding the role of sport and exercise in optimizing aging* (pp. 7-14). London: Routledge.

Chapter 2
Acknowledgments

The authors would like to acknowledge the funding support provided by the Centre for Inland Health; Charles Sturt University, Australia; and the Social Sciences and Humanities Research Council of Canada. We would like to thank all of the participants for their insights and contributions, especially Barb Boyer.

Theoretical and Methodological Perspectives on Leisure and Aging

Part II provides a theoretical and methodological foundation for readers. The goal is that they will become knowledgeable about both classic and current theories and be able to engage with empirical research in leisure and aging.

Part II comprises four chapters. Chapter 3, by Douglas Kleiber and Rebecca Genoe, reviews classic and current theories of aging. They begin by addressing the question, what is a theory of aging? They then discuss the contributions and limitations of cross-sectional and longitudinal research designs. The authors suggest that the themes of continuity and change summarize the patterns of leisure as people age. Kleiber and Genoe divide their journey through the various theories into psychological and sociological theories. Under psychological theories, selective optimization theory, socioemotional selectivity theory, stage theories, and theories of self-identity are covered. The sociological theories include the three classic theories of aging, activity theory, disengagement theory, and continuity theory. The authors then cover some of the more recent developments in postmodernism and the growing use of ecological systems theory. They end their chapter by encouraging students to think critically about their use of theory. Chapter 3 includes two international sidebars, written by Lars Tornstam and Ricca Edmondson.

Chapter 4 provides students with an understanding of the link between theory and research. Bryan Smale and Jennifer Gillies provide a comprehensive yet concise overview of research design. The authors begin with a discussion about epistemology and how this guides the choice of method before introducing the two basic approaches to research, quantitative and qualitative. They start with an overview of the quantitative approach by addressing conceptualization and operationalization, levels of measurement, validity and reliability, and sampling. Next they discuss survey research, questionnaire design, and the increased use of experimental designs, and they finish this section with a discussion on data analysis. Qualitative approaches follow with a discussion of grounded theory, phenomenology, and ethnography as the three primary qualitative approaches used in our field, followed by descriptions of several methods. The authors conclude their chapter with the ethics associated with research.

The last two chapters in part II return to theoretical discussions about the need to view later life as heterogeneous instead of homogeneous. In chapter 5, Galit Nimrod and Megan Janke examine change and continuity in leisure over the life span. The authors suggest there are at least four patterns in people's leisure as they age: general decline, active to passive, outdoor to indoor, and a decline in novelty seeking. Nimrod and Janke address the influence of life transitions such as widowhood and retirement on leisure, and they raise concerns about the lack of leisure in the lives of older adults. Sigal Naim contributes an international sidebar that discusses the issue of early retirement, and Donald Roberson discusses the life of older adults in the Czech Republic.

Chapter 6 addresses the need to consider the influence of gender, race, ethnicity, and sexual orientation in our research and practice with later-life adults. Steven Mock, Susan Shaw, Erica Hummel, and Carissa Bakker introduce students to critical gerontology, which examines the influence of social structure and power in shaping the experiences of older adults. The authors discuss the influence of race and ethnicity, gender, and sexual orientation and suggest how leisure might provide these individuals with a site for resistance and the chance to renegotiate their identities.

CHAPTER 3

The Relevance of Leisure in Theories of Aging

Douglas A. Kleiber ■ **M. Rebecca Genoe**

LEARNING OBJECTIVES

After reading this chapter, you will be able to

- explain the relevance of aging theory in leisure research and practice,
- identify and explain several psychological theories of aging,
- identify and explain several sociological theories of aging,
- explain how aging theories have developed over time, and
- discuss prominent critiques of theories of aging.

What do theories of aging have to do with leisure services for older adults? The way leisure professionals design, implement, and evaluate leisure services, whether community based or institutional, is influenced by our perceptions of later life and how older adults adapt to the changes that aging brings. A recreation programmer who believes that older adults are better off if they disengage from society will provide different programs than one who believes that activity in later life is essential for aging well. Providers of leisure services must understand a variety of theories of aging in order to provide meaningful services for older adults.

In this chapter, we explore some of the many theories of aging that attempt to explain behavior in later life. There are many views of what it means to age well, a topic taken up in other chapters of this text. Contrary to what might be assumed, however, the various theories of aging per se are often equally debatable. This is partly due to the limited applicability of theories that have been advanced in the past. Indeed, theories about the so-called truth of aging are often criticized for being biased in one way or another (see, for discussion, Bengtson, Rice, & Johnson, 1999), a point to which we will return. Nevertheless, we present some of those theories that have withstood the test of close scrutiny as interpretations of aging that apply widely.

Recognizing that the biology of aging—confined by a finite end to the life span that is the result of ultimate cellular degeneration and system failure—is an essential underpinning for any attempt to characterize aging in general, in this chapter we nevertheless stay within the realm of social sciences, considering psychological and sociological perspectives in **social gerontology**. Degeneration and system failure can, of course, be hastened by the insults associated with aging, the illnesses and injuries that accumulate over time in what is sometimes called **secondary aging** (Whitbourne, 2001). We consider these to some extent, but we mostly seek to characterize the normal (primary) aging processes that everyone experiences with age, even those who have been fortunate and have stayed relatively healthy. We leave to other chapters the question of optimizing later life and avoiding life-compromising conditions; however, our general view of normal aging must address the human condition of aging and the normal problems of aging. Recognizing that decline is not failure and that accommodation and adaptation are not signs of weakness is an important first step in treating older people more appropriately, effectively, and humanely. If we understand how older adults normally and effectively manage the challenges that confront them with age, we can provide leisure opportunities that contribute to aging well.

Our task is narrowed, then, to a consideration of theories that recognize aging as a process of adaptation rather than one of lost youth and as a process that involves refined understanding as well as adjustment in ways that distinguish older ages from younger ones. Because there are countless theories that aim to understand aging (there are over 300 theories of biological aging alone [Medvedev, 1990]), we will also narrow our scope to those theories for which leisure is particularly relevant. Still, this gives us plenty of theoretical range: As a context of freedom of expression, leisure is relevant to all perspectives on aging that see people as self-determining and self-expressive given time and some degree of freedom.

Leisure as a Context for Continuity and Change

Generally we recognize that the losses that accompany aging also lead to losses of leisure, or at

What Is a Theory of Aging?

Theories are systematic explanations of phenomena based on observations. They may be appropriate at one time and then reinterpreted later on. Theoretical models are systematic and disclose presuppositions and evidence, they are always subject to criticism, and we develop them when we try to explain to others what causes something to occur (Kelly, 1987a). In general, then, theories of aging are important for explaining how and why things happen the way they do. Theories of aging are used to guide both leisure and aging research and practice.

least to changes in leisure activity, particularly when there is secondary aging. For example, as strength and agility decline with age, strenuous activity may become more challenging. More complicated activities may also become increasingly difficult in cases of diminished cognitive capacity. Nevertheless, aging may actually afford *more* leisure—there may be more time available as work and family roles become less demanding. These changes, which will be explored further in the discussion of sociological theories of aging, may also coincide with the abandonment of less meaningful activities. Furthermore, aging typically warrants changes in activity priorities and the development of compensatory strategies to maintain more meaningful activities. Finally, choices for involvement in free time may well be responses to the specific tasks and challenges common to a given age.

What does the existing evidence suggest about these assertions? Other chapters of this volume (particularly chapter 5 by Nimrod and Janke) provide more detail on specific changes in leisure behavior associated with aging, but, anticipating our review of specific theories of aging, we can make several general points about the evidence on later-life leisure. First, in support of popular assumptions and stereotypes, overall activity involvement appears to decrease with age (e.g., Agahi, Ahacic, & Parker, 2006; Cutler & Hendricks, 1990; Gordon, Gaitz, & Scott, 1976; Kelly, 1987a) (see figure 3.1). There are exceptions, of course; after declining from adolescence to adulthood, television watching increases again in old age, and older men cook for enjoyment more than younger men do, but most activities show a downward trend. When is disengagement a matter of choice, and when is it a consequence of primary or secondary aging?

Cross-sectional research, which compares groups of people from different generations or cohorts, may limit our interpretation of such declines. Are older women less likely to participate in physical activity as a reflection of age, or have the particular older women studied always been less likely to engage in physical activity across the life span? Do older adults read less than younger adults (see Gordon et al., 1976) as a result of educational level, or is it truly an age-related phenomenon? Similarly, does the political conservatism of older age groups reflect long-held values, or is it simply the product of aging? Cross-sectional research is limited in its ability to answer such questions since people from different

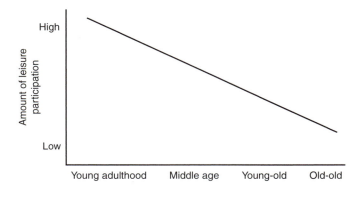

Figure 3.1 In general, activity involvement decreases with age.
Data from Gordon, Gaitz, and Scott 1976.

generations may have different opportunities and expectations over the course of their lives.

Longitudinal research helps with the problem of interpreting change to some extent by following the same people over a long time, but it still leaves us with a cohort problem if we do not consider multiple cohorts (age groups) at the same time. Even if a cohort has changed in a consistent way, the changes may not apply to a cohort that has had a dramatically different life history from other cohorts. Wars and economic depressions, for example, have clearly had an effect on the cohorts who have endured them. People who survived the Depression in the late 1920s and early 1930s have been less willing to abandon themselves to immediate gratification and self-indulgence than those who grew up with relative economic security (Elder, 1974). More than any other in recent history, that cohort has been oriented toward staying busy and being productive in the later phases of life. Other leisure-related cohort effects include an interest in music and dancing among those who grew up in the 1920s and an interest in fitness among those whose formative years included the 1960s and 1970s (McPherson, 1990). These interests have characterized these cohorts throughout their lives to some extent. (More is said about longitudinal and cross-sectional research in chapter 5.)

More sophisticated studies that follow several age groups over time would offer clearer indications of the relative influence of age and history on leisure activity, but even then we would still be left with the problem of interpreting the meaning of the changes observed. Changes in overt activity can mean different things to different people. A decline in involvement in stock-car racing, for example, might signal the end of interest in the activity for one person, while for another person interest is simply transferred to some other aspect of the activity, such as teaching others to drive. Or it may be that the meanings that were sought in the activity, such as testing one's skills in a competitive context, are found in another activity, such as coaching a youth basketball team.

Leisure researchers concern themselves primarily with changes in overt activity, but leisure interests, values, and orientations may also be influenced by developmental change (Kelly, 1987b; Kleiber, 1999). For example, interest in change itself varies substantially over the life course. Experimentalism and orientation to change are much more common among youth than their elders. Taking an evolutionary perspective, younger cohorts require flexibility to adapt to change and to move into new niches, while older generations are responsible for providing stability and security in the environment to afford the young a context in which to explore, experiment, and survive (Brent, 1978). The well-known generation gap between newer and older cohorts is partly attributable to this phenomenon. Seppo Iso-Ahola (1980) offered a hypothetical profile of the relative strength of preferences for novel versus familiar leisure forms over the life course, as depicted in figure 3.2. It is noteworthy that, if these preferences are correct, older people are more like young children than young adults in their greater preference for familiarity. On the other hand, generational change suggests something different for the future. If younger cohorts have grown up being more experimental, as

has been suggested of boomers and some of the cohorts following, there may be greater interest in change well into later life. For example, Nimrod and Kleiber (2007) found a readiness for innovation in an in-depth study of recent retirees.

In more recent years, the evidence has been stronger for maintaining activities in later life rather than for abandoning them or adopting new ones (Iso-Ahola, Jackson, & Dunn, 1994; McGuire, Dottavio, & O'Leary, 1987). The prevailing evidence suggests continuity of interests rather than change (Cutler & Hendricks, 1990; Iwasaki & Smale, 1998; Lee & King, 2003; Lounsbury & Hoopes, 1988; Palmore, 1981; Scott & Willits, 1989; Singleton, Forbes, & Agwani, 1993).

Of course, a picture of continuity of interest and activity may obscure rather different dynamics. Is continuity the result of the enduring influence of childhood experience or the relative lack of development in adult leisure? Does one continue with an activity because of a strong commitment to the activity or as a source of personal identity and self-consistency, as Robert Atchley (1989, 1993, 1999) suggests? Or is an activity maintained primarily as a familiar pattern, a buffer against stress and a source of stability? Perhaps all of these apply to varying degrees in various cases. Alternatively, does change in activities reflect a response to other developmental changes, or is it a failure to find activities that are sufficiently meaningful to support commitment and enduring involvement? In any case, studies of activity choice or consistency rarely do justice to the changes in meaning that occur across the life span. For a clearer picture, it is necessary to take a closer look at the develop-

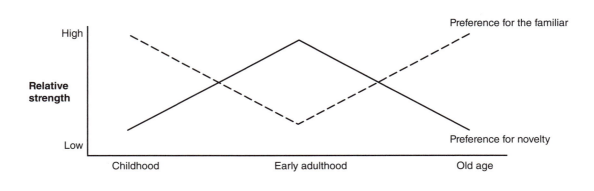

Figure 3.2   Hypothetical profile of the relative strength of preferences for novel versus familiar leisure forms over the life course.
Data from Iso-Ahola 1980.

ment of successive periods of the life course. We begin with psychological theories of aging and then turn to sociological theories.

Psychological Theories of Aging

In this section, we present a number of psychological theories of aging, including theories of control and dependence and theories of identity and self. Control and independence theories include the substitution or environmental fit model, selective optimization with compensation, socioemotional selectivity, and psychosocial stage theory. Theories of self and identity include the innovation

theory of successful aging, identity process theory, and multiple threshold perspective.

Theories of Control and Dependence

Loss of independence and control are often considered to be symptoms of aging, the inevitable consequences of deteriorating capacity and reliance on external resources. This view plays directly into the negative stereotypes of aging, especially common in the West, where older people are assumed to be helpless relatively soon after they retire. However, only the oldest old (those over 80) typically experience significant threats to control. Although the need for control

The Theory of Gerotranscendence

Lars Tornstam*

Beginning in 1989, I created the theory of gerotranscendence in order to address the mismatch between existing theories and reality (Tornstam, 2005). The theory captures observed changes in the way older adults often come to see the world and how they experience increased life satisfaction. It departs from other popular theories in describing successful aging as a forward or outward direction of development, including a redefinition of reality, in contrast to the more past-oriented integration process suggested by others (e.g., Erikson, 1959, 1963). The essential changes common to this redefinition of life are reflected in three dimensions.

The *cosmic dimension* incorporates changes in the definitions of time, where a transcendence of the borders between past and present occurs together with an ability to experience all previous ages at the same time. This includes the return to and transfiguration of childhood and other phases in life. It also includes an increased attachment to earlier generations, with a change in perspective from link to chain. The stream of life (chain) becomes more important than the individual life (link). The fear of death disappears and a new, relaxed comprehension of life and death results. The mystery of life is accepted, and cause for rejoicing changes from grand events to subtle experiences, such as those related simply to being in nature.

The *self dimension* includes a self-confrontation with the discovery of hidden aspects of the self, both good and bad, though a decrease of self-centeredness eventually occurs. A new body transcendence implies taking good care of the body but without obsession. The pieces of life's jigsaw puzzle form a new wholeness, which may be a delicate state, demanding tranquility and solitude.

Changes in the *dimension of social and personal relations* include more selectiveness and less interest in superficial relations, with an increasing need for periods of solitude. An understanding of the difference between self and role takes place, sometimes resulting in an urge to abandon roles or a new understanding of the necessity of roles in life. In a pattern of emancipated innocence, a new capacity to transcend needless social conventions in a playful, childlike way is born. At the same time, a reluctance to superficially separate right from wrong appears; thus it becomes more common to withhold judgments and advice. Transcendence of the right–wrong duality is accompanied by increased open-mindedness and tolerance and a willingness to relinquish control as necessary.

*Lars Tornstam, PhD, is professor emeritus at Uppsala University in Uppsala, Sweden.

appears to remain the same with age, the capacity for control and the nature of dependence change. Indeed, understanding where control must be shared and dependence accommodated can be recognized as a matter of wisdom (Baltes & Staudinger, 1993, 2000; Tornstam, 2005). Tornstam's theory of **gerotranscendence** includes, among other things, relinquishing the need for control as part of the acceptance of one's mortality.

Nevertheless, the desire to have control over one's interactions with the environment is generally recognized as fundamental to human social motivation (e.g., Fiske, 2004). Control is associated with the basic needs of competence and autonomy that are seen as fundamental to intrinsic motivation (Ryan & Deci, 2000). It takes on new forms in later life (Heckhausen, 1997; Heckhausen & Schultz, 1995); with age-related losses and fewer developmental gains, people make adjustments to maintain control. The most important adjustment involves less reliance on **primary control**, where one asserts one's own priorities and goals in an individualistic way, and more reliance on **secondary control**, which necessitates adjusting goals to fit the circumstances and having interpretive control by accepting and understanding that over which one has little influence (Rothbaum, Weisz, & Snyder, 1982; see also Kleiber, 1985).

For example, a person would assert primary control by finding a way to get the preferred cereal box on the top shelf at a grocery store. The same person would assert secondary control by choosing something similar on a lower shelf (Whitbourne, 2001). Leisure theorists refer to such responses—where a slightly less desirable activity is adopted in place of one that has become inaccessible—as **substitution** (e.g., Brunson & Shelby, 1993; Iso-Ahola, 1986; Kelly, Steinkamp, & Kelly, 1987). In any case, age-related changes in cognitive, physical, and social capacity attune one to the process of secondary control. Through secondary control, older people avoid frustration and a sense of inadequacy and instead channel their energies into more achievable goals. Failure to make this adjustment in perspective, insisting on primary control (with stubborn independence) in cases of relative incapacity, may be problematic and even pathological. Adoption of secondary control is not inevitably associated with optimal or successful aging, however; it is just more common in later life.

Accordingly, dependence should not be seen only, or even mostly, as a sign of decline and something to be resisted. It is clear that independence is a value and autonomy is a fundamental human need; however, the fact that this need is less important relative to belonging and connectedness in many non-Western cultures (Markus & Kitayama, 1991) should be a clue as to its social construction. Becoming interdependent and codependent is not only characteristic of other cultures, it is more common in later life where diminished capacities cause one to rely on other resources, both technological and human, to meet needs and achieve goals.

Margaret Baltes (1995) speaks of this kind of dependence as instrumental and distinguishes it from the dependence discussed by Seligman (1975) as a kind of learned helplessness based on non-contingency, a condition associated with depression. **Instrumental dependence** is a common and effective use of resources to compensate for limitations in later life. Although it may not be regarded as a sign of success, it is a sign of competence rather than failure. On the other hand, the assertion of independence at such times may be associated with social incompetence, isolation, and neglect. Independence is the cultural script, especially in the West, but instrumental dependence is the natural course of aging in response to one's biological limits and is a sign of wisdom and effective adaptation as well as secondary control. Of course, dependency can be promoted to a fault by others, thus undermining existing capacities to be independent. Service providers, including leisure service providers, must keep this in mind while recognizing that some dependence may be instrumental and healthy rather than pathological. For example, pairing older people with partners who are slightly younger in a game might be more effective than trying to get everyone to play independently.

In a practical sense, of course, environments can overprotect older people, thereby neglecting personal reserves and strengths. This may result in decreased competence and accelerated decline. However, selective instrumental dependence and secondary control allow people to sustain independence by maintaining abilities in high-priority areas. Selecting dependency to compensate for real or expected losses allows one to give up those less important goals that are hindered by losses, compensate for losses by activating latent reserves (those personal strengths and abilities that may not have been called on in the past), and become dependent in selected areas to free up strengths and energies for other areas. Dependency is thus used principally in two situations: when high-priority goals are endangered and reserves are lacking, and when lower-priority goals cannot be given up because they are necessary for survival. The bottom line is that dependency is associated with efficacy rather than incompetence in either case (Baltes & Carstensen, 1999).

Selective Optimization With Compensation Model

The **selective optimization with compensation** (SOC) model (Baltes & Baltes, 1990, 1998; Baltes & Carstensen, 1996; Freund & Baltes, 1998, 2002) takes account of how older adults adapt to age-related losses to maintain and enhance quality of life. The SOC model, which is compatible with the control and dependence theories just reviewed, argues that it is adaptive and healthy to respond to the limiting factors in the environment, especially as they mount with the losses accompanying aging, by being selective about activities of choice, abandoning those that are less personally meaningful, and compensating in whatever way necessary to optimize the more restricted number of alternatives. Baltes and Carstensen (1996) point out that "in their orchestration," these three processes "generate and regulate development and aging" (p. 218).

Selection is the process of reducing the number of activity domains to those that are most important. Abandoning activities may be accompanied by some regret, but it allows for a reprioritization of other activities, usually along a continuum of what is most personally meaningful. This process demonstrates some value in the controversial idea of disengagement, as long as it is voluntary and selective. (More will be said about disengagement when we turn to sociological theories.) Even when disengagement is involuntary, as with a physically disabling illness, the cognitive reappraisal that takes place may be ultimately liberating. Furthermore, selection may involve the identification of new possibilities, thereby encouraging personal growth.

Finally, *compensation* is a process that preserves involvement in a preferred activity in spite of emerging constraints. For example, to preserve effective engagement in tennis, one might eliminate other strenuous physical activities, use a larger racket face, and learn shot-placement strategies that do not require as much power in order to compensate for declining mobility and strength (Lang, Rieckmann, & Baltes, 2002).

In summarizing their analysis of the SOC model, Baltes and Baltes (1998) note, "By careful selection, optimization, and compensation we are able to minimize the negative consequences from losses that occur with old age and to work on aspects of growth and new peaks of success, albeit in a more restricted range" (p. 17). In addition, "making smaller territories of life larger and more beautiful is at the core of savoir vivre in old age" (p. 19). All three SOC processes are commonly reflected in the leisure choices made in retirement and later life. They are more common with age because they are stimulated by losses and limitations (Baltes & Baltes, 1990).

Considering SOC processes with respect to leisure, we may be guided in part by some general observations and practices of others. Selection is about discrimination, or deciding which interests and activities are worthy of deeper investment. It is reflected in the practice of interest identification, value clarification, option identification, and decision making, which are also some of the more central components of leisure education (e.g., Dattilo, 2008). Discrimination is also a leisure value emphasized by Goodale and Godbey (1988), who note the excesses and costs of a consumptive mentality. Indeed, a case can be made that leisure experience is well served when one relinquishes less meaningful activities and gives attention more completely to others.

Optimization involves taking an activity seriously (cf. Stebbins, 1992), committing to it, and becoming more psychologically involved in it (e.g., Havitz & Mannell, 2005; Mannell, 1993), leading perhaps to the optimal experience of flow (Csikszentmihalyi, 1990; Csikszentmihalyi & Csikszentmihalyi, 1988). Even the characteristic of perseverance that is associated with optimization can be found in some leisure involvements (Stebbins, 1992). In addition, optimization is served in leisure by specialization (Bryan, 2000; Scott & Schaefer, 2001), where the development and refinement of skills applied in an activity and the deepening commitment of enduring involvement bring out optimal performance and experience.

Compensation occurs in later life in response to losses and limitations well as to a gradual decrease in physical capacity and energy. The creative use of assistive technology and the ability to martial human resources to help maintain involvement (instrumental dependence) are compensatory tools, and much of the sociability of later life is based on the mutual support that shared activities provide for maintaining interest and involvement (Baltes, 1995). Finally, allowing more time for tasks and operations is also compensatory in maintaining desired involvement.

As noted earlier, **substitution** (or substitutability) theory is common in leisure research (Iso-Ahola, 1986) and describes conditions under which one activity may replace another to the same or similar effect. When a preferred activity is dropped and another activity takes its place, both secondary control and compensation occur. It would also be considered a constraint negotiation strategy from the perspective of some leisure researchers, but it begs a question of the very idea of constraint negotiation. Choosing another activity appears to be giving in to the constraint rather than negotiating it, but this only applies if the activity itself is important. If the activity is merely a means to an end—walking versus jogging as a means of exercise, for example—then is abandoning jogging a failure to negotiate the constraint to jogging, or is it a successful negotiation of the constraint to exercise? A constraint that results in the abandonment of some activities or triggers a turn in other directions is more about selection and reprioritization than constraint negotiation. It is true that giving up some activities is effectively a time management strategy that serves the realization of other interests, but SOC processes seem to be more applicable than constraint negotiation processes in explaining such cases.

In the case of substitution, when an activity is more of a means to an end—say, social involvement or exercise—then finding a substitute activity that leads to those goals would accurately be regarded as a compensatory strategy. Alternatively, if the constraint leads to a selection of new and more meaningful activities, then the constraint should be regarded as benign and not in need of negotiation. Also, leisure constraints may lead to the discovery of new interests (Kleiber, Hutchinson, & Williamson, 2002; Kleiber, McGuire, Aybar-Damali, & Norman, 2008; Kleiber & Nimrod, 2009). Heart problems may limit horseback riding, for example, but being presented with the opportunity to learn to fly over the same terrain may open up new interests compatible with the old. This is what SOC researchers call *loss-based selection*. Even though the activity is new, it is still selected to approximate what has been lost or in some cases to find some aspect of self that may have gone unexpressed. Indeed, instances of exploration and self-discovery may have facilitated the discovery of previously-unattended capacities, a general theme of innovation in later life (Nimrod & Kleiber, 2007). Thus, although most of the evidence supports a tendency toward continuation of activities in later life and the value of continued engagement, disengagement

from activities should not be seen as regrettable in most cases. Not only does it allow for a focus on more available and more meaningful activities, it also may lead to new opportunities. Constraints to activity such as a disability or the loss of a spouse may even bring about beneficial changes (Kleiber et al., 2008).

Socioemotional Selectivity Theory

It is generally accepted that even the normal circumstances of later life require some adaptation, and the SOC model describes the processes of selection, optimization, and compensation that most people use to make life more manageable, enjoyable, and meaningful. However, Leah Carstensen (1993) and colleagues (Carstensen, Fung, & Charles, 2003; Carstensen, Isaacowitz, & Charles, 1999) have gone even further in specifying what people in later life tend to do differently than younger people, and perhaps more importantly, what they avoid. With a greater awareness of limited time left to live (see also Neugarten,1979), older people are inclined toward positive feelings and tend to interact with familiar people rather than seeking new relationships that might be unpredictable and perhaps unpleasant. This positivity bias causes older people to seek out satisfaction in the present instead of the future. In contrast, younger people are more likely to be future oriented, acquiring new information and relationships that may be beneficial in the future.

Socioemotional selectivity (SES) theory notes that the reduction in number of contacts is often motivated by the need to redistribute resources in keeping with SOC processes. Older adults may choose more meaningful and pleasant activities, reflecting an active selection process intended to maintain emotionally close relationships. Regardless of age, people manage social worlds proactively in accordance with two goals: information seeking and emotional regulation (for meaning and attachment). Limited time left in life leads older people to favor the latter. Younger people behave similarly when faced with time restrictions. They may spend more time with close friends when approaching graduation and losing contact with close friends. Perceived time available is thus critical to other goals—if time is relatively unlimited, long-term achievement goals promote exploration and information acquisition. Limited time favors short-term goals, often related to how one feels (emotional gratification). From this perspective, it makes sense that the social leisure of younger people tends to be associated

Older adults may choose more meaningful and pleasant activities, reflecting an active selection process intended to maintain emotionally close relationships.

with making new contacts and having new experiences while that of older people is more likely to involve familiar friends and activities.

As noted, the SOC model presents aging as adaptation and thus emphasizes process rather than outcome, distinguishing it from other interpretations that see aging as a status achieved with certain characteristics. As such, the SOC model may be more appropriate not only for people who do not enjoy favorable circumstances but also for the vast range of value and cultural differences in the ideal outcomes of aging. Some of the more normative and ethnocentric views associated with successful aging have been roundly criticized. Nevertheless, adaptation is never value neutral, and goals do indeed reflect cultural values toward which selection, optimization, and compensation are directed. And, cultural variations notwithstanding, some of the most general goals can be identified (though their universality, priority, and specific applications can of course be questioned). Psychosocial stage theory attempts to do just that.

Psychosocial Stage Theory

It is generally accepted that the ideologies of independence, growth, connectedness, contribu-

tion to the future, and peace have a strong hold on the decisions and adjustments made in later life, regardless of circumstances. For Erik Erikson (1959, 1963), perhaps the best-known Western theorist of changes in orientation over the life span, these ideologies are best viewed in terms of the motives of **generativity** and **ego integrity**, purposes that he asserted to be common in all cultures (though gender differences in the timing and manner of expression have led to criticisms of the male bias in his original formulation [e.g., Miller-McLemore, 2004]).

Generativity involves contributing to the well-being of successive generations. It is expressed in parenting as well as "through various kinds of activities and enterprises in churches, schools, neighborhoods, communities, organizations and society writ large" (McAdams & Logan, 2004, p. 16). Mentoring, teaching, volunteer work, charitable activity, and religious and political involvement provide roles for "promoting society's traditions [and] taking on the responsibilities of good citizenship" (p. 16). It is common to find adults who take such roles with children, other younger people, or society as a whole; however, generativity is not inevitable in the course of aging. It may occur in private as well, as in tending to one's own family or estate and financial legacy. It is also reflected in creativity, as in seeking to leave a mark with a book of poems or photographs, which may have little impact on one's immediate community (see also Kleiber & Nimrod, 2008).

Generativity may be reflected in other contrasting ways. Efforts at social change are intentionally generative, as are efforts to protect the status quo through conservation and nurturance of tradition. Generativity can be both selfless and selfish. It is linked to one's desire for immortality in terms of work that will outlast oneself (Kotre, 1984), yet it can also be selfless, as in sacrificing self-interest for children or even community. Generativity can have aspects of both agency and communion (cf. Bakan, 1966)—agency in self-expansion, self-expression, self-development, and self-protection (i.e., in promoting individual self-interest) and communion in sharing oneself with others, merging self with community, and giving up of self for greater purposes. According to McAdams and Logan (2004), "Generativity challenges adults to be highly agentic and communal at the same time" (p. 18), but they can sometimes be in conflict.

Erikson saw generativity as being of greatest concern in the middle adult years. Although signs of generativity can be found in younger people (e.g., Stewart & Vandewater, 1998), full actualization does not typically occur before middle age. This is consistent with research on motivation for volunteering, which tends to have other purposes in early adulthood (e.g., making connections, building résumés). In contrast, according to Erikson, stagnation and self-preoccupation can begin to be liabilities in middle age. This issue may well persist as a developmental task into the latest period of the life course, where one's legacy becomes part of the life review process. Whether generativity is universally applicable has also been debated (cf. Stewart & Vandewater, 1998). Even within Western cultures, variations may be expected as a function of personal resources available. Although generativity appears to be of concern across socioeconomic levels, poverty may be a limiting factor.

Erikson moves from the issue of generativity versus stagnation to ego integrity versus despair, but others argue for intermediate stages. With due appreciation to Erikson for his life-span framework, several theorists (Antonovsky & Sagy, 1990; Vaillant, 2002) insist that there is an early aging transition that differs in character from the issues of advanced age. People are living longer, healthier lives than when Erikson advanced his life-span model (Agahi & Parker, 2005). Also, the attitudes of baby boomers, who are approaching retirement, reflect a higher priority on growth and change, which will ensure differences in later life for years to come (Dychtwald & Flower, 1990; Dychtwald & Kadlec, 1999; Freedman, 1999). Although the age of retirement has shifted in both directions for social and economic reasons, there appear to be some important tasks facing members of most industrialized societies around this time (ages 60-75). According to Antonovsky and Sagy (1990), the early period of later life, or the third age, asks that a person consider four questions:

1. What is to be done? (question of engagement)
2. What is personally worth doing? (reevaluation of life satisfaction)
3. What do I still believe about my world? (reevaluation of worldview with concern for coherence of purpose and approach to life)
4. How can I stay healthy enough to do what I want? (account of one's health vulnerability)

Though he shares this view of the young-old period as one of activity, Vaillant (2002) puts more emphasis on play, creativity, and satisfying social interaction as a consequence of retirement, noting that retirement is only a problem when it is involuntary or unplanned, there is no other means of support besides salary, home life is unhappy, or it is precipitated by preexisting bad health. When those do not apply, most people look for intrinsic satisfaction in their activities, replacing coworkers with other social networks, rediscovering how to play, exercising creativity, continuing to learn, and serving others in ways that are personally satisfying. Vaillant's views may be more ideal for aging well than what is normally expected, especially among those with more limited resources and in poorer health, but he does assert that a period of activity generally precedes a period of more passive contemplation around issues of integrity that Erikson associated with the final stage of life.

With respect to integrity versus despair, Erikson asserts that despair will likely occur if people do not come to terms with their past and present in later life in a way that provides a sense of wholeness and continuity. Understanding and accepting ourselves is an important part of the process. Thus, one would expect a greater tendency in later life to reminisce about the past as time permits. Reminiscence, whether done alone as a life review or more casually in groups, can reinforce continuity and contribute to a sense of integrity (Parker, 1995). The process of ego integration is not only reflected in passive activities, however; hobbies and expressive patterns of various kinds that connect one to the past and provide a sense of continuity are typically preferred over new activities (Lefrançois, Leclerc, & Poulin, 1998).

Psychosocial stage theory has long been criticized as being androcentric (i.e., applying only to males) and ethnocentric (i.e., applying only to dominant groups in North American societies). For example, girls and women are likely to be more consistently involved in matters of intimacy and nurturing throughout their lives than simply in early and middle adulthood. As noted before, intimacy and caregiving are also likely to be more directly related to identity formation in women (see Gilligan, 1982).

Many of the changes that occur over the life course are predictable but not inevitable (see also Agahi & Parker, 2005; Adams, 2004). There is considerable variance across cultures (Gauthier & Smeeding, 2003) and among segments of society. For example, there is evidence that in working-class communities, the experience of distinct stages and transitions is less common than in segments of the population with more education (Giele, 1980). The rates of participation in leisure activities discussed earlier are likely to have as much to do with the expectations of others as with the inevitable course of aging (Cutler & Hendricks, 1990; Lawton, 1994). Older people may feel uncomfortable in certain recreational contexts, such as outdoor concerts, where everyone else is younger and where youth is the target market. Miller (1965) once wrote of the so-called portent of embarrassment in describing what keeps older people from active involvement. Trying new activities or even drawing on old skills often evokes the self-consciousness that comes with declining competence and the appearance of being old. The prevailing evidence is that older people can learn new activities about as well (though perhaps more slowly) as younger people (Schaie & Geiwitz, 1982), but the expectation that you can't teach an old dog new tricks often keeps an older person from trying and may lead leisure service providers to prefer other clients. Nevertheless, times have changed and a fair bit of later life, particularly the earlier periods, includes some degree of self-reinvention through new activities (e.g., Adams, 2004; Nimrod & Kleiber, 2007; Vaillant, 2002; Yarnal, Chick, & Kerstetter, 2008).

Theories of Self and Identity in Later Life

The self is a function of attributes, roles, and actions at any age. It is simultaneously a social construction—a product of the views of others as well as of oneself—and an active constructor of meaning, "selecting among various imperatives; claiming, elaborating and personalizing some of them while ignoring, contesting, or rearranging others . . . continually involved in fashioning everyday experience" (Herzog & Markus, 1999, p. 228). Herzog and Markus note that, as with personality in general, the self may not change dramatically through the life course. Nevertheless, it can take on a different character in later life and obviously has more to make sense of as time goes by.

As with socioemotional selectivity, a time perspective plays into self-schemas. Research on so-called possible selves by Markus and colleagues (e.g., Markus & Nurius, 1986) demonstrates the power of consideration of future possibilities in current conceptions of self. In later life, with a more limited future, possible selves are not as compelling or common as past selves (Cross & Markus, 1991; Herzog, Franks, Markus, & Holmberg, 1996), which supports continuity of interests and activities rather than change and the adoption of new activities (Atchley, 1989, 1993) and also supports the greater likelihood of reminiscence in the leisure of older people.

On the other hand, dramatic changes in later life, particularly retirement (e.g., Nimrod, Janke, & Kleiber, 2009) and the death of a spouse (Janke, Nimrod, & Kleiber, 2008; Lopata, 1993) often precede changes and innovations that contribute to new self-concepts. Indeed, an **innovation theory of successful aging** (Nimrod, 2008; Nimrod & Kleiber, 2007) has been proposed that characterizes innovation in terms of both *self-preservation*, where aspects of self from the past are reconstructed in new ways, and *self-reinvention*, where changes in leisure behavior appear unrelated to the past, processes that are increasingly common in at least the third age. Though this theory is more explicitly a theory of successful aging, it is nevertheless more descriptive of general patterns of aging than had been previously suggested. Apparently you *can* teach an old dog new tricks; in fact, old dogs often want to learn. This is reflected in the tremendously expanded interest of older adults in Internet technology (Pew Internet and American Life, 2004). There is certainly a digital divide with respect to comfort and facility with technology, but seniors have taken to technological innovation in large numbers. It may be to connect more effectively with grandchildren or to answer health care questions, but learning is occurring.

Nevertheless, the aging self is more clearly confronted with the threat to a sense of competence and usefulness as capacities diminish. To some extent this is associated with the rolelessness of later life, the relinquishing of jobs and childrearing responsibilities, which will be examined further in the section on sociological theories, but it also is reflected in loss of leisure skills. But learning remains to the extent that **plasticity** remains, allowing for the development of new skills, and application of SOC principles continues to put a priority on competence in preferred and available activities (cf. Atchley, 1993; Mannell, 1993). As Herzog and Markus (1999) note, "Through their experiential, developmental and social qualities [leisure activities] may contribute to the social as well as the competent self schemas. Our own research (Herzog et al., in press) confirms this hypothesis" (p. 244).

Another approach to understanding the self in later life comes from Whitbourne's **identity process theory** (Whitbourne, 1986, 1996, 2001). Relying to some extent on Erikson's model of psychosocial development that we referred to previously, as well as Piaget's (1962) concepts of assimilation and accommodation, Whitbourne (2001) sees adult identity as the "composite of the individual's self-representation in a variety of substantive areas" (p. 45). These include physical appearance and capacity, cognitive functioning, personality traits, relationships with others, and social roles. Identity assimilation occurs when one interprets information about oneself in a favorable light with respect to maintaining a desirable self-conception. Identity accommodation, on the other hand, asks people to modify views of themselves in line with new, discrepant, and sometimes unflattering information.

The **multiple threshold perspective** (Whitbourne & Collins, 1998) proposes that personal recognition of aging occurs in a stepwise fashion across the years of adulthood in various physical, social, and cognitive domains. Identity is more threatened in areas of higher salience— the diminished ability to run for someone who has been a runner, for example—while giving up activities of less importance may have little impact. "At the point of crossing a threshold in a domain, the individual is stimulated to recognize the reality of aging" (p. 47); examples in the realm of appearance include balding, becoming gray haired, or having new facial wrinkles. As another example, recognition of so-called senior moments of failing memory, though often dismissed casually, is usually central to a person's sense of aging self (Whitbourne, 2001).

Social interaction in leisure settings could potentially exacerbate this awareness about oneself. Participating in some leisure activities, on the other hand, may protect an identity that resists a sense of aging, reflecting identity assimilation to a greater extent, and may thus be used to avoid a sense of age-related decline. However, a recognition of the "use it or lose it" axiom also reflects accommodation to the atrophy of neglected capacities that may imply advanced aging unnecessarily. Identity accommodation is precipitated by changes in life circumstances that disrupt one's personal narrative, and beginning a new or neglected activity reflects the inclination to innovate.

As noted, psychological theories such as those just described are often criticized for being ethnocentric (applying to some cultures more than others) or androcentric (biased toward males) and for failing to address influential variations in social context. There are many other ways to view later life (see, for example, Dr. Ricca Edmonson's discussion of wisdom from a humanistic perspective in the accompanying sidebar). Clearly age is socially constructed and contextually bound in a variety of ways that should be taken into account. Sociological theories are arguably more effective at addressing this particular critique.

Sociological Theories of Aging

Whereas psychological theories of aging focus on individual adaptation in later life, sociological theories consider broader social factors in relation to aging. In this section, we explore three of the classical sociological theories on aging: activity theory, disengagement theory, and continuity theory. Then we address postmodern perspectives on aging that critique those theories and others.

Activity Theory

Activity theory (Havigurst & Albrecht, 1953; Lemon, Bengston, & Peterson, 1972; Longino & Kart, 1982) is a theory of successful aging (and is thus a premise for some of the other chapters

Wisdom and Aging From a Humanistic Perspective

Ricca Edmondson*

Many of today's theorists of aging debate whether and in what ways later life can be regarded as a period of decline. But throughout recorded history, the idea of wisdom has been opposed to the idea that major human capacities must all grow weaker as people age. In terms of understanding other human beings or debating the best course of action in complex predicaments, the idea has been that people can grow more practiced and more competent as they age. In other words, they can grow wiser.

The idea of wisdom in this sense has been thought crucial to understanding the human condition. What is wisdom, and who possesses it? Is it something that can be achieved only by outstanding people? Humanistic approaches to wisdom and age see moving toward wisdom as a lifetime process that is carried out jointly with other people. From this point of view, people renowned for wisdom, from Solomon onward, offer insights into what wisdom might be. They do not preside over special insights that others could never attain; rather, they show aspects of a human capacity that everyone can aim for, although there is no guarantee that everyone can attain wisdom equally.

In the humanistic tradition, wisdom is strongly connected with communication and social interaction when both are used together to work for the common good. Psychologists exploring wisdom more recently, such as Baltes and Staudinger (2000) and Sternberg (1990), stress how wisdom is oriented to practical, empathetic understanding of other people but also to weighing the best courses of action in ethical terms. These are capacities that people with a potential for wisdom can develop as their lives progress. Adding to this from a philosophical and sociological point of view, we can trace how wise processes arise among people in inner-city tenements or among farmers in the countryside (Edmondson, 2009) as they converse, work, and relax together. Leisure and sporting activities can also be key locations where people make crucial decisions and debate what sort of person they should be. Since humans are embodied beings, not just minds, wisdom plays an important role here as elsewhere.

A humanistic approach to aging explores how people bestow meaning on their lives as they grow older, and the development of wisdom has a central role to play here. This approach draws on critical gerontology, which stresses that to understand aging, we must also take into account the large- and small-scale pressures that affect older people's material lives and their chances to influence what happens to them (Moody, 1992; Phillipson, 1998). This perspective underlines, too, the need for older people's lives to contain meaning in a way that is significant to them and others (Woerner & Edmondson, 2009). Older people should not be expected simply to grow wiser all by themselves, whatever their circumstances. The way society regards older citizens can support them as full contributors to society, valuing their wisdom, or it can do the opposite.

*Ricca Edmondson, PhD, is senior lecturer in the School of Political Science and Sociology at the National University of Ireland in Galway, Ireland.

in this volume), but it is often considered to be a general theory of aging as well. Activity theory postulates that older adults who are engaged in a variety of social activities have greater life satisfaction than those who do not (Lemon et al., 1972). It suggests that as people age, they replace lost roles (such as work roles), since remaining engaged in life and contributing to society is related to aging well (Chapman, 2005). Lemon and colleagues (1972) indicate that life satisfaction depends on having a number of role identities. When people frequently engage in a wide variety of activities, they receive enough role support to reaffirm their various identities, leading to positive self-regard. Informal social activities are the most effective for life satisfaction, while engagement in solitary activities is the least effective (Lemon et al., 1972; Longino & Kart, 1982). Indeed, Havigurst and Albrecht's (1953) research revealed that people who were more active adjusted better to later life. Though a minority of older adults might be content with a passive later life, the authors suggested that most older adults are better off when actively engaged in life.

There is evidence in the leisure literature that active engagement in a variety of activities does lead to higher levels of life satisfaction (e.g., Kelly et al., 1987; Nimrod, 2007; Nimrod & Adoni, 2006). Researchers have found a link between activity engagement and increased happiness, better functioning, and reduced mortality in later life (Menec, 2003). Leisure activity is a strong factor in explaining life satisfaction among recently retired adults (Nimrod, 2007). Recent retirees benefit from leisure engagement and experience improved well-being, supporting the claim that involvement in many activities leads to successful aging. Furthermore, the preference for activity also often leads to civic engagement, thus maintaining social integration while serving the needs of the community as well.

Although activity theory provides us with an optimistic view of aging, it too has been criticized. Activity theory may be too simplistic to capture the realities of later life (Bowling, 2007; Utz, Carr, Nesse, & Wortman, 2002). Additionally, it does not consider the resources that older adults may or may not have available in order to remain actively engaged in later life. Since most of the evidence is correlational, tests of the theory often fail to acknowledge the possibility that people with better circumstances, including health, wealth, and happiness, are in a better position to be active. Its emphasis on social activities also contradicts research that suggests solitary activities are beneficial for older adults (Burnett-Wolle & Godbey, 2005, 2007).

Activity theory may serve to justify recreation and leisure programs and interventions for older adults because it assumes that most of them want and need high levels of activity (Passuth & Bengtson, 1995). However, the evidence in its support is equivocal; despite all the positive associations found between activity and life satisfaction, some research has found no connection at all (Reitzes, Mutran, & Verril, 1995). Activity theory also offers only a limited view of leisure in attributing health and well-being to activity participation, failing to examine the mental health effects of more passive, informal, and contemplative leisure activities. Finally, the theory is arguably more prescriptive than descriptive since, as we noted earlier, older people are more likely to give up activities than start new ones.

Civic Engagement in Later Life

Notions of civic engagement in later life have emerged along with concepts of successful and active aging. Civic engagement emphasizes continued involvement in life through volunteering, paid work, or other contributions to community (Martinson & Minkler, 2006), which provides possibilities for optimistic perspectives on later life (Hinterlong, Morrow-Howell, & Sherraden, 2001) and serves the need for generativity as well (McAdams & Logan, 2004).

Still other benefits of civic engagement have been reported. Older volunteers experience both physical and mental challenges (Gottlieb & Gillespie, 2008) as well as feelings of purpose, personal growth, and learning (Bradley, 1999; Lund & Engelsrud, 2008). Research exploring civic engagement in later life reveals that older adults who contribute to their communities tend to be healthier and more active than those who do not (Kaskie, Imhoff, Cavanaugh, & Culp, 2008; Lund & Engelsrud, 2008). Some older adults construct their leisure as work in order to make a contribution to the community and to avoid being perceived as a burden on society (Mansvelt, 1997). Others resist retirement by serving their communities and maintaining active lives because of the association of retirement with aging, increased dependence, and disengagement from society (Gibson, Ashton-Schaeffer, Green, & Corbin, 2002).

Civic engagement may play an important role in identity creation and maintenance for older adults. Having opportunities to volunteer or contribute to community in other ways may provide new or continuously meaningful roles that have an impact on older adults' identities.

Despite the benefits of civic engagement for older adults, the movement has also received criticism. We must be careful to avoid devaluing those older adults who may not be able or who choose not to participate in civic engagement. Furthermore, little is understood about how different people and communities experience civic engagement (Martinson & Minkler, 2006). Civic engagement may be vital for some older adults' identities, but for others, emphasis on civic participation may limit possible selves by restricting opportunities to embrace all possibilities of aging (Martinson & Minkler, 2006).

Disengagement Theory

Disengagement theory is the second classic sociological theory of aging, emerging roughly 50 years ago (Cumming & Henry, 1961) as a response to activity theory. It asserts that it is reasonable to predict mutual withdrawal between the individual and society as death draws nearer. Described as the process in which relationships between society and the individual are disconnected (Cumming & Henry, 1961) the theory was introduced with the awareness that people often choose to withdraw from active role involvement as personal and social power and resources decline. At the same time, society recognizes this decline and turns to younger people for both. However, the theory has been largely discredited for two important reasons: It provides a rationale for the neglect of older people as if they want to be left alone; and it fails to distinguish those who disengage voluntarily from those who disengage unwillingly due to a lack of support and resources.

Nevertheless, the validity of some aspects of disengagement theory has been reconsidered (e.g., Achenbaum & Bengtson, 1994). In particular, the tenet of the theory that "a reduction in the number or variety of interactions leads to an increased freedom from the control of norms governing everyday behavior" (p. 757) recognizes the value of selection among various goals based on priorities. Selective disengagement, in other words, is an adaptive process that still allows for full and meaningful participation in life along the lines of selection and optimization in the SOC model referred to earlier. Disengagement from less meaningful aspects of life may lead to greater investment in others and more satisfaction as a result. Still, the second part of the theoretical relationship—that society in turn separates from the individual—reflects ageism rather than being part of a normal process. Accordingly, there has been great progress in combating such attitudes in recent decades.

Continuity Theory

Continuity theory emerged from the early 1970s to the mid-1980s as the most significant and compelling of the three classic sociological theories of aging (Bengston, Putney, & Johnson, 2005, Chapman, 2005). The theory developed as a response to both activity and disengagement theories, which were no longer adequate for explaining how people adjust to later life (Neugarten, Havigurst, & Tobin, 1968). In continuity theory, the focus shifts from the number of activities one participates in toward adjustment and adaptation to later life (Bowling, 2007). The theory suggests that over time, older adults continue to adapt to new situations following the same patterns they developed earlier in life. Personality remains relatively consistent as one ages (Atchley, 1999; Breytspraak, 1984). These aspects persist in later life, and people aim for continuity in roles as they age. Continuity theory does allow for change over time, but it occurs within a basic structure of familiarity and consistency (Atchley, 1989, 1999). Older adults continue to make decisions based on long-established needs (Neugarten et al., 1968), and as a result, changes can be integrated into one's life without upheaval (Atchley, 1989).

In continuity theory, people can be themselves instead of adopting a prescribed method of adjustment, such as disengaging or maintaining involvement in social activity (Matras, 1990). Someone who enjoys privacy and solitude in earlier life will likely continue this pattern in later life. Similarly, a person who is active and engages in many activities in early life will continue to do so in later life. However, Atchley (1989) suggests that one can have too much, too little, or just enough continuity. With too much continuity, people may feel as though they are in a rut, and there is not enough change for enrichment. When there is too little continuity, life may feel too unpredictable. When there is just enough continuity, or optimal continuity, the pace and degree of change matches one's personal preferences.

Leisure research often supports continuity theory, suggesting that older adults continue to pursue many of the same leisure activities in later life that they pursued earlier in life. A study exploring older men's leisure across the life span revealed that they tend to maintain their leisure interests from childhood through to later life and engage in similar activities (Genoe & Singleton, 2006). For example, one research participant engaged in playing music as a child and teenager, started a band as an older adult, and continued to play music to entertain other older adults living in long-term care long after retirement. Continuity is more difficult to maintain with advanced age, however (Strain, Grabusic, Searle, & Dunn, 2002); Agahi et al. (2006) found that in some cases older adults maintained continuity in their leisure participation for over 34 years, but others had added and dropped activities due to changes in status and functional ability.

Continuity theory provides an alternative to disengagement and activity theories by suggesting that there is more than one way that people age. However, it has also been criticized for its failure to fully consider the context of aging and the impact of social structure on continuity. The theory fails to adequately acknowledge that the multitude of changes that occur in later life may make continuity difficult (Matras, 1990; Utz et al., 2002). Despite criticism, Utz et al. argue that continuity theory may be more applicable to a wider range of older adults than activity or disengagement theories based on the findings that various types of older adults (i.e., married and widowed older adults) maintain their levels of social participation across the life span.

Postmodernism

More recently, gerontologists have considered aging from a postmodern perspective. **Postmodernism** challenges theories of aging, particularly for their emphasis on freedom, rationality, progress, and the power of science to improve the human condition. Postmodernists critique the process of building theory, reject the canons of science, and challenge the relevance of any theory (Bengtson et al., 1999, 2005). They aim to highlight that which is missing from the conversation on aging. Postmodern gerontologists argue that labels such as *old* that are ascribed to people in later life do not represent individuals, and no one actually embodies the abstraction (Katz, 1996).

Postmodern perspectives on aging result in positive images of aging that emphasize creativity, vitality, empowerment, and resourcefulness (Katz, 2005), creating "new avenues for self-care and self-definition in later life, thus empowering elders to innovate resourceful roles and ways of life" (Katz, 2001, p. 28). Leisure can play an important role in self-definition in later life and provides new roles and ways of life after retirement. However, postmodern society also emphasizes youth and antiaging consumer culture (Katz, 2001), further perpetuating myths and stereotypes of aging. When leisure service providers market their services as youthful, they also emphasize an antiaging attitude that can have negative implications for older adults.

As with the other theories of aging discussed in this chapter, postmodernism has its critics. It is often attacked for its antitheoretical stance and inability to replace or improve existing theory (Bengtson et al., 2005). The postmodern life course is characterized by a blurring of traditional boundaries that separate life stages, such as childhood, adolescence, and middle age (Katz, 2005), but as

with some other theories, the postmodernist focus on positive aging and antiaging effectively denies the realities of aging.

Ecological Systems Model

The ecological systems model integrates psychological and sociological theories of aging, combining some of the various perspectives in an ecological perspective, as has been done with a focus on children in the past (Bronfenbrenner, 1979), while also accommodating criticisms of postmodernism. By looking at multiple levels of influence, from individual differences, to family dynamics, to community health services, to the political climate, one can get a clearer picture of aging (see figure 3.3). Janke (personal communication, January 20, 2010) describes the model and offers a vision of how the ecological model may be applied to aging:

> Bronfenbrenner's ecological systems theory highlights the structures and systems in developing people's environments that shape their growth and experiences. These are portrayed as interrelated levels and include the microsystem, mesosystem, exosystem, and macrosystem (see figure 3.3). The microsystem relates to the immediate environment; for older adults this could include their family, the neighborhood in which they reside, their workplace, and so on. Mesosystems include connections between two or more microsystems. It suggests that a change in one microsystem can affect one's behavior or interactions in another microsystem. For example, retiring from work can affect conjugal relationships. The exosystem is an external environmental system that indirectly affects a person's development, such as community services or extended family. Finally, the macrosystem relates to the cultural context in which people develop, such as the customs and cultures that influence their environment, the political climate and events that occur, and the historical events (i.e., state of the economy, technology) that they are experiencing.

Without attention to such diverse influences, other theories of aging are simple abstractions that may not be very useful in their explanatory power.

Conclusion

Leisure researchers draw upon both psychological and sociological theories of aging to understand leisure in later life. As is evident in this chapter, theories of aging are highly debatable, but each can contribute something of value to discussions around leisure and aging well. Psychological theories of aging provide insight into how older

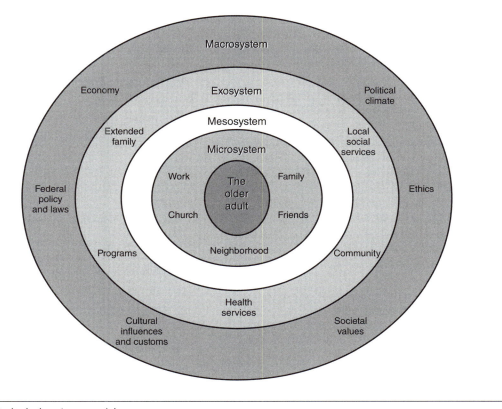

Figure 3.3 Ecological systems model.
Reprinted, by permission, from M. Janke.

adults may personally adjust to change and loss associated with later life, while sociological theories consider the impact of broader social factors on aging. All of these theories tell us something about older adults' leisure-related decisions in later life, and they may help us to consider how we can best support older adults in their leisure endeavors.

KEY TERMS

activity theory—The view that older adults age successfully when they replace lost roles with new roles in later life (Havigurst & Albrecht, 1953; Lemon et al., 1972; Longino & Kart, 1982).

continuity theory—The view that life patterns developed in earlier life are maintained in later life (Atchley, 1989, 1993).

cross-sectional research—Comparisons of various cohorts of society, such as age groups.

disengagement theory—The view that older adults withdraw from relationships and activities in later life to make way for younger people and prepare for death (Cumming & Henry, 1961).

ego integrity— The best result of the last of Erikson's developmental issues in which the adult comes to accept his or her life as it was lived (Erikson, 1963).

generativity—The best result of the penultimate of Erikson's developmental issues in which the adult comes to recognize his or her contributions to the well-being of successive generations (Erikson, 1963; McAdams & Logan, 2004).

gerotranscendence—A theory of aging that suggests that as people age, material things and productivity become less important and intergenerational relationships, life review, and altruism become more important (Tornstam, 2005).

innovation theory of successful aging—A theory postulating that older adults seek out new leisure activities in order to both re-create aspects of self and to invent new aspects (Nimrod, 2008; Nimrod & Kleiber, 2007).

instrumental dependence—The common and effective use of available social resources to compensate for limitations in later life.

longitudinal research—Research that follows people over time (also referred to as *prospective research*).

multiple threshold perspective—Proposes that people recognize aging across adulthood in various physical, social, and cognitive domains (Whitbourne & Collins, 1998).

plasticity—The capacity of neural pathways and synapses of the brain and nervous system for alteration in response to experience or injury.

primary control—Occurs when people assert their own priorities and goals in an individualistic way (Rothbaum et al., 1982).

postmodernism—Perspective that recognizes various and changing influences on life and that challenges the essentialism in existing theories of aging and the idea of theory building itself (Katz, 2005).

secondary aging—Illnesses and injuries that occur over time, that are not necessarily due to aging itself.

secondary control—Occurs when people adjust goals to fit their circumstances and accept aspects of life where they have little influence (Rothbaum et al., 1982).

selective optimization with compensation—Older adults choose among activities, relinquishing some while optimizing their abilities in others, using both technological and human resources to compensate for changes in order to continue participating in the chosen activities (Baltes & Baltes, 1990).

social gerontology—The social and psychological aspects of aging studies.

socioemotional selectivity—The view that older people choose to interact with familiar people to afford positive feelings and avoid unfamiliar relationships that may lead in unpredictable and unpleasant directions (Carstensen, 1993).

substitution—Adopting a less desirable activity in place of one that has become inaccessible (e.g., Brunson & Shelby, 1993; Iso-Ahola, 1986; Kelly et al., 1987).

REVIEW AND DISCUSSION QUESTIONS

1. What are the arguments for continuity and change in leisure activities in later life?

2. What are the limitations of both cross-sectional and longitudinal research in exploring changes in leisure with increased age?

3. What is the difference between primary and secondary control with respect to later life, and what are the implications for older adults' leisure engagement?

4. What is gerotranscendence?

5. When are constraints to leisure valuable in later life?

6. How does Lawton's environment fit model compare with Csikszentmihalyi's notion of flow?

7. What is the nature of selection, optimization, and compensation in the SOC model developed by Baltes, Baltes, and their colleagues?

8. What impact could SES theory have on older adults and their leisure?

9. What is Erikson's concept of generativity, and how does it relate to leisure in later life?

10. How have changing demographics affected the developmental tasks of later life?

11. What is the innovation theory of successful aging?

12. How does wisdom fit in theories of aging?

13. What are the characteristics of the three classical sociological theories of aging, and which theory has the greatest support?

14. How do postmodernists critique theories of aging?

LEARNING ACTIVITIES

1. Which theory (or theories) of aging fits best with your understanding of older adults? Do you know any older adults who fit one or more of these theories?

2. Make a list of your current leisure activities. Which of these activities do you think you will participate in after you retire? Will you drop activities or add activities to your repertoire?

3. Postmodernists argue that theory is not useful for understanding later life. Do you agree or disagree? Explain.

4. Interview an older adult about her leisure participation and engagement in life. Consider her responses to determine which theories her experiences reflect. Does the older adult fit into just one theory, more than one theory, or none of the theories?

CRITICAL-THINKING ACTIVITIES

1. Make a list of pros and cons for each theory discussed in this chapter. Based on the list, which theory do you think is most appropriate for leisure service providers?

2. Consider each theory individually. What are its implications for leisure practice? That is,

if you adopt a particular theory, how will that theory affect your service delivery?

3. Compare and contrast selective optimization with compensation and continuity theories as explanations of leisure choices in later life. How can each theory be used to explain various leisure activity patterns?

4. Identify someone in your community who provides leisure services to older adults. Prepare an interview guide (a list of interview questions) and ask questions about how the interviewee's service relates to theories of aging.

5. Find a partner or small group. Choose one theory and assign sides to debate the pros and cons of the theory. In your arguments, consider whether the theory perpetuates or negates ageist stereotypes and whether the theory is useful for practice. Alternatively, choose two theories and debate which theory is most appropriate for understanding leisure and later life.

SUGGESTED READING

Agahi, N., Ahacic, K., & Parker, M. (2006). Continuity of leisure participation from middle age to old age. *Journal of Gerontology: Social Sciences, 61B*(6), S340-S346.

Bowling, A. (2007). Aspirations for older age in the 21st century: What is successful aging? *International Journal of Aging and Human Development, 64*(3), 263-297.

Burnett-Wolle, S., & Godbey, G. (2005). Active aging 101. *Parks and Recreation*, March, 31-40.

Carstensen, L.L., Fung, H.H., & Charles, S.T. (2003). Socioemotional selectivity theory and the regulation of emotion in the second half of life. *Motivation and Emotion, 27*, 103-123.

Chapman, S.A. (2005). Theorizing about aging well: Constructing a narrative. *Canadian Journal on Aging, 24*(1), 9-18.

Edmonson, R., & Von Kondratowitz, H.J. (2009). *Valuing older people: A humanist approach to ageing*. Bristol: Policy Press.

Kleiber, D., & Nimrod, G. (2009). "I can't be very sad": Constraints and adaptations in the leisure of a 'learning in retirement' group. *Leisure Studies, 28*, 67-83.

Lynott, R.L., & Lynott, P.P. (1996). Tracing the course of theoretical development in the sociology of aging. *Gerontologist, 36*(6), 749-760.

Menec, V. (2003). The relationship between everyday activities and successful aging: A 6-year longitudinal study. *Journal of Gerontology: Psychological Sciences, 58*, P74-P82.

Nimrod, G. (2007). Expanding, reducing, concentrating and diffusing: Post-retirement leisure behavior and life satisfaction. *Leisure Sciences, 29*, 91-111.

REFERENCES

Achenbaum, W.A., & Bengtson, V.L. (1994). Re-engaging the disengagement theory: On the history and assessment of theory development in gerontology. *Gerontologist, 34*, 756-763.

Adams, K.B. (2004). Changing investment in activities and interests in elders' lives: Theory and measurement. *International Journal of Aging and Human Development, 58*, 87-108.

Agahi, N., Ahacic, K., & Parker, M. (2006). Continuity of leisure participation from middle age to old age. *Journal of Gerontology: Social Sciences, 61B*(6), S340-S346.

Agahi, N., & Parker, M.G. (2005). Are today's older people more active than their predecessors? Participation in leisure-time activities in Sweden in 1992 and 2002. *Aging and Society, 25*, 925-941.

Antonovsky, A., & Sagy, S. (1990). Confronting developmental tasks in the retirement transition. *Gerontologist, 30*, 362-368.

Atchley, R.C. (1989). A continuity theory of normal aging. *Gerontologist, 29*(2), 183-190.

Atchley, R.C. (1993). Continuity theory and the evolution of activity in later adulthood. In J.R. Kelly (Ed.), *Activity and aging: Staying involved in later life* (pp. 5-16). Newbury Park, CA: Sage.

Atchley, R.C. (1999). *Continuity and adaptation in aging: Creating positive experiences*. Baltimore: Johns Hopkins University Press.

Bakan, D. (1966). *The duality of human existence: Isolation and communion in Western man*. Boston: Beacon Press.

Baltes, M.M. (1995) Dependency in old age: Gains and losses. *Current Directions in Psychological Science, 4*, 14-19.

Baltes, P.B., & Baltes, M.M. (1990). Psychological perspectives on successful aging: The model of selective optimization with compensation. In P. Baltes & M. Baltes (Eds.), *Successful aging: Perspectives from the behavioral sciences* (pp. 1-34). New York: Cambridge University Press.

Baltes, P.B., & Baltes, M.M. (1998). Savior vivre in old age: How to master the shifting balance between gains and losses. *National Forum, 78*(2), 13-18.

Baltes, M.M., & Carstensen, L.L. (1996). The process of successful aging. *Aging and Society, 16*, 397-422.

Baltes, M.M., & Carstensen, L.L. (1999). Social-psychological theories and their applications to aging: From individual to collective. In V.L. Bengston & K.W. Schaie (Eds.), *Handbook of theories of aging* (pp. 209-226). New York: Springer.

Baltes, P.B., & Staudinger, U.M. (1993). The search for a psychology of wisdom. *Current Directions in Psychological Science, 2*, 75-80.

Baltes, P.B., & Staudinger, U.M. (2000). Wisdom: A meta-heuristic (pragmatic) to orchestrate mind and virtue toward excellence. *American Psychologist, 55*, 122-136.

Bengtson, V., Rice, C., & Johnston, M. (1999). Are theories important? Models and explanations in gerontology at the turn of the century. In V. Bengtson & K.W. Schaie (Eds.), *Handbook of theories of aging* (pp. 3-20). New York: Springer.

Bengtson, V., Putney, N., & Johnson, M. (2005). The problem of theory in gerontology today. In M. Johnson (Ed.), *The Cambridge handbook of age and ageing* (pp. 3-20). New York: Cambridge University Press.

Bowling, A. (2007). Aspirations for older age in the 21st century: What is successful aging? *International Journal of Aging and Human Development, 64*(3), 263-297.

Bradley, D. (1999). A reason to rise each morning: The meaning of volunteering in the lives of older adults. *Generations, 23*(4), 45-50.

Brent, S. (1978). Individual specialization, collective adaptation and rate of environmental change. *Human Development, 21*, 21-33.

Breytspraak, L. (1984). *The development of self in later life.* Boston: Little, Brown.

Bronfenbrenner, U. (1979). *The ecology of human development.* Cambridge, MA: Harvard University Press.

Brunson, M.W., & Shelby, B. (1993). Recreation substitutability: A research agenda. *Leisure Sciences, 15*, 67-74.

Bryan, H. (2000). Recreation specialization revisited. *Journal of Leisure Research, 32*, 18-21.

Burnett-Wolle, S., & Godbey, G. (2007) Refining research on older adults' leisure: Implications of selection, optimization and compensation and socioemotional selectivity theories. *Journal of Leisure Research, 39*, 498-513.

Burnett-Wolle, S., & Godbey, G. (2005). Active aging 101. *Parks and Recreation*, March, 31-40.

Carstensen, L.L. (1993). Motivation for social contact across the life span: A theory of socioemotional selectivity. In J.E. Jacobs (Ed.), *Developmental perspectives on motivation: Nebraska Symposium on Motivation* (Vol. 40, pp. 2090-2254). Lincoln, NE: University of Nebraska Press.

Carstensen, L.L., Fung, H.H., & Charles, S.T. (2003). Socioemotional selectivity theory and the regulation of emotion in the second half of life. *Motivation and Emotion, 27*, 103-123.

Carstensen, L.L., Isaacowitz, D.M., & Charles, S.T. (1999). Taking time seriously: A theory of socioemotional selectivity. *American Psychologist, 54*, 165-181.

Chapman, S.A. (2005). Theorizing about aging well: Constructing a narrative. *Canadian Journal on Aging, 24*(1), 9-18.

Cross, S.P., & Markus, H. (1991). Possible selves across the lifespan. *Human Development, 34*, 726-742.

Csikszentmihalyi, M. (1990). *Flow: The psychology of optimal experience.* New York: Harper Perennial.

Csikszentmihalyi, M., & Csikszentmihalyi, I. (Eds.). (1988). *Optimal experience: Psychological studies of flow in consciousness.* New York: Cambridge University Press.

Cumming, E., & Henry, W. (1961). *Growing old.* New York: Basic Books.

Cutler, S.J., & Hendricks, J. (1990). Leisure and time use across the life course. In R.H. Binstock & L.K. George (Eds.), *Handbook of aging and the social sciences* (pp. 169-185). New York: Academic Press.

Dattilo, J. (2008). *Leisure education program planning: A systematic approach.* State College, PA: Venture Press.

Dychtwald, K., & Flower, J. (1990). *Age wave: How the most important trend of our time will change your future.* New York: Bantam Books.

Dychtwald, K., & Kadlec, D. (1999). *Power years: A user's guide to the rest of your life.* New York: Wiley.

Edmondson, R. (2009). Wisdom: A humanist approach to valuing older people. In R. Edmondson & H.-J. von Kondratowitz (Eds.), *Valuing older people: A humanist approach to ageing* (pp. 201-216). Bristol: Policy Press.

Elder, G. (1974). *Children of the Great Depression.* Chicago: University of Chicago Press.

Erikson, E. (1959). *Identity and the life cycle.* New York: Norton.

Erikson, E. (1963). *Childhood and society.* New York: Norton.

Fiske, S.T. (2004). *Social beings: A core motives approach to social psychology.* New York: Wiley.

Freedman, M. (1999). *Prime time: How baby boomers will revolutionize retirement and transform America.* Cambridge, MA: Perseus.

Freund, A.M., & Baltes, P.B. (1998). Selection, optimization, and compensation as strategies of life management: Correlations with subjective indicators of successful aging. *Psychology and Aging, 13*, 531-543.

Freund, A.M., & Baltes, P.B. (2002). Life-management strategies of selection, optimization and compensation: Measurement by self-report and construct validity. *Journal of Personality and Social Psychology, 82*, 642-662.

Gauthier, A.H., & Smeeding, T.M. (2003). Time use at older ages: Cross-national differences. *Research on Aging, 25*, 247-274.

Genoe, M.R., & Singleton, J.F. (2006). Older men's leisure experiences across their lifespan. *Topics in Geriatric Rehabilitation, 22*(4), 348-356.

Gibson, H., Ashton-Shaeffer, C., Green, J., & Corbin, J. (2002). Leisure and retirement: Women's stories. *Loisir & Societe-Society and Leisure, 25*(2), 257-284.

Giele, J. (1980). Adulthood as a transcendence of age and sex. In T. Sinclair & E. Erikson (Eds.), *Themes of work and love in adulthood* (pp. 151-173). Cambridge, MA: Harvard University Press.

Gilligan, C. (1982). *In a different voice: Psychological theory and women's development.* Cambridge, MA: Harvard University Press.

Goodale, T.L., & Godbey, G. (1988). *The evolution of leisure.* State College, PA: Venture.

Gordon, C., Gaitz, C.M., & Scott, J. (1976). Leisure and lives: Personal expressivity across the life span. In R. Binstock & E. Shanas (Eds.), *Handbook of aging and the social sciences* (pp. 310-341). New York: Van Nostrand Reinhold.

Gottlieb, B., & Gillespie, A. (2008). Volunteerism, health, and civic engagement among older adults. *Canadian Journal on Aging, 27*(4), 399-406.

Havigurst, R.J., & Albrecht, R. (1953). *Older people*. New York: Longmans, Green and Co.

Havitz, M.E., & Mannell, R.C. (2005). Enduring involvement, situational involvement, and flow in leisure and non-leisure activities. *Journal of Leisure Research, 37*, 152-177.

Heckhausen, J. (1997). Developmental regulation across adulthood: Primary and secondary control of age-related challenges. *Developmental Psychology, 33*, 176-187.

Heckhausen, J., & Schultz, R. (1995). A life-span theory of control. *Psychological Review, 102*, 284-304.

Herzog, A.R., Franks, M.M., Markus, H.R., & Holmberg, D. (1998). Activities and well-being in older age: Effects of self-concept and educational attainment. *Psychology and Aging, 13*, 179-185.

Herzog, A.R., & Markus, H. (1999). Self-concept in life-span, aging research. In V.L. Bengtson & K.W. Schaie (Eds.), *Handbook of theories of aging* (pp. 227-252). New York: Springer.

Hinterlong, J., Morrow-Howell, N., & Sherraden, M. (2001). Productive aging: Principles and perspectives. In N. Morrow-Howell, J. Hinterlong, & M. Sherradan (Eds.), *Productive aging: Concepts and challenges* (pp. 3-18). Baltimore: Johns Hopkins University Press.

Iso-Ahola, S.E. (1980). *The social psychology of leisure and recreation*. Dubuque, IA: Brown.

Iso-Ahola, S.E. (1986). A theory of substitutability of leisure behavior. *Leisure Sciences, 8*, 367-389.

Iso-Ahola, S.E., Jackson, E., & Dunn, E. (1994). Starting, ceasing and replacing leisure activities over the life-span. *Journal of Leisure Research, 26*, 227-249.

Iwasaki, Y., & Smale, B.J.A. (1998). Longitudinal analyses of the relationships among life transitions, chronic health problems, leisure and psychological well-being. *Leisure Science, 20*, 25-52.

Janke, M., Nimrod, G., & Kleiber, D.A. (2008). Leisure patterns and health among recently widowed adults. *Activities, Adaptation and Aging, 32*, 19-39.

Kaskie, B., Imhof, S., Cavanaugh, J., & Culp, K. (2008). Civic engagement as a retirement role for aging Americans. *Gerontologist, 48*(3), 368-377.

Katz, S. (1996). *Disciplining old age: The formation of gerontological knowledge*. Charlottesville, VA: University Press of Virginia.

Katz, S. (2001). Growing older without aging? Positive aging, anti-ageism, and anti-aging. *Generations, 25*(4), 27-32.

Katz, S. (2005). Imagining the lifespan: From premodern miracles to postmodern fantasies. In S. Katz (Ed.), *Cultural aging: Lifecourse, lifestyle, and senior worlds* (pp. 23-36). Peterborough, ON: Broadview Press.

Kelly, J.R. (1987a). *Freedom to be: A new sociology of leisure*. New York: MacMillan.

Kelly, J.R. (1987b). *Peoria winter: Styles and resources in later life*. Lexington, MA: Heath.

Kelly, J.R., Steinkamp, M.W., & Kelly, J.R. (1987). Later-life satisfaction: Does leisure contribute? *Leisure Sciences, 9*, 189-200.

Kleiber, D. (1985). Motivational reorientation in adulthood and the resource of leisure. *Advances in Motivation and Achievement, 4*, 217-250.

Kleiber, D. (1999). *Leisure experience and human development*. New York: Basic Books.

Kleiber, D., Hutchinson, S., & Williamson, R. (2002). Leisure as a resource in transcending negative life events: Self-protection, self restoration and personal transformation. *Leisure Sciences, 24*, 219-235. Kleiber, D., McGuire, F., Aybar-Damali, B., & Norman, W. (2008). Having more by doing less: The paradox of leisure constraints in later life. *Journal of Leisure Research, 40*, 343-359.

Kleiber, D., & Nimrod, G. (2008). Expressions of generativity and civic engagement in a ,learning in retirement' group. *Journal of Adult Development, 15*, 76-86.

Kleiber, D., & Nimrod, G. (2009). "I can't be very sad": Constraints and adaptations in the leisure of a 'learning in retirement' group. *Leisure Studies, 28*, 67-83.

Kotre, J.N. (1984). *Outliving the self: Generativity and the interpretation of lives*. New York: Norton.

Lang, F.R., Rieckmann, N., & Baltes, M.M. (2002). Adapting to aging losses: Do resources facilitate strategies of selection, compensation, and optimization in everyday functioning? *Journal of Gerontology: Psychological Sciences, 57B*, 501-509.

Lawton, M.P. (1994). Personality and affective correlates of leisure activity participation by older people. *Journal of Leisure Research, 26*(2), 138-157.

Lee, R.E., & King, A.C. (2003). Discretionary time among older adults: How do physical activity promotion interventions affect sedentary and active behaviors? *Annual in Behavioral Medicine, 25*, 112-119.

Lefrançois, R., Leclerc, G., & Poulin, N. (1998). Predictors of activity involvement among older adults. *Activities, Adaptation & Aging, 22*, 15-29.

Lemon, B.W., Bengtson, V.L., & Peterson, J. (1972). Exploration of the activity theory of aging: Activity types and life satisfaction among in-movers to a retirement community. *Journal of Gerontology, 27*(4), 511-523.

Longino, C.F., & Kart, C.S. (1982). Explicating activity theory: A formal replication. *Journal of Gerontology, 37*(6), 713-722.

Lopata, H.Z. (1993). Widows: Social integration and activity. In J.R. Kelly (Ed.), *Activity and Aging* (pp. 99-105). Newbury Park, CA: Sage.

Lounsbury, J.W., & Hoopes, L.L. (1988). Five-year stability of leisure activity and motivation factors. *Journal of Leisure Research, 20*, 118-134.

Lund, A., & Engelsrud, G. (2008). 'I am not that old': Interpersonal experience of thriving and threats at a senior centre. *Aging & Society, 28*, 657-692.

Mannell, R.C. (1993). High investment activity and life satisfaction among older adults: Committed, serious leisure and flow activities. In J.R. Kelly (Ed.), *Activity and aging* (pp. 125-145). Newbury Park, CA: Sage.

Mansvelt, J. (1997). Working at leisure: Critical geographies of ageing. *Area, 29*(4), 289-298.

Markus, H.R., & Kitiyama, S. (1991). Culture and the self: Implications for cognition, emotion and motivation. *Psychological Review, 98*, 224-253.

Markus, H.R., & Nurius, P. (1986). Possible selves. *American Psychologist, 41*, 954-969.

Martinson, M., & Minkler, M. (2006). Civic engagement and older adults: A critical perspective. *Gerontologist, 46*(3), 318-324.

Matras, J. (1990). *Dependency, obligations, and entitlements: A new sociology of aging, life course, and the elderly.* Englewood Cliffs, NJ: Prentice Hall.

McAdams, D.P., & Logan, R.L. (2004). What is generativity? In E. de St.Aubin, D.P. McAdams, & T.-C. Kim (Eds.), *The generative society* (pp. 15-31). Washington, DC: American Psychological Association.

McGuire, F.A., Dottavio, F.D., & O'Leary, J.T. (1987). The relationship of early life experiences to later life leisure involvement. *Leisure Sciences, 9*, 251-257.

McPherson, B.D. (1990). *Aging as a social process.* Toronto: Butterworth.

Medvedev, Z.A. (1990). An attempt at rational classification of theories of aging. *Biological Science, 65*, 375-398.

Menec, V. (2003). The relationship between everyday activities and successful aging: A 6-year longitudinal study. *Journal of Gerontology: Psychological Sciences, 58*, P74-P82.

Miller, S.J. (1965). The social dilemma of the aging leisure participant. In A.M. Rose & W. Peterson (Eds.), *Older people and their social worlds* (pp. 77-92). Philadelphia: Davis.

Miller-McLemore, B.J. (2004). Generativity and gender: The politics of care. In E. de St.Aubin, D.P. McAdams, & T.-C. Kim (Eds.), *The generative society* (pp. 175-194). Washington, DC: American Psychological Association.

Moody, H.R. (1992). Gerontology and critical theory. *Gerontologist, 32*(3): 294-295.

Neugarten, B.L. (1979). Time, aging and the life cycle. *American Journal of Psychiatry, 136*, 887-893.

Neugarten, B., Havigurst, R., & Tobin, S. (1968). Personality and patterns of aging. In B. Neugarten (Ed.), *Middle age and aging: A reader in social psychology* (pp. 173-177). Chicago: University of Chicago Press.

Nimrod, G. (2007). Retirees' leisure: Activities, benefits, and their contribution to life satisfaction. *Leisure Studies, 26*(1), 65-80.

Nimrod, G. (2008). In support of innovation theory: Innovation in activity patterns and life satisfaction among recently retired individuals. *Aging & Society, 28*, 831-846.

Nimrod G., & Adoni, H. (2006). Leisure styles and life satisfaction among recent retirees in Israel. *Aging and Society, 26*, 607-630.

Nimrod, G., Janke, M.C., & Kleiber, D.A. (2009). Expanding, reducing, concentrating and diffusing: Activity patterns of recent retirees in the U.S. *Leisure Sciences, 31*, 37-52.

Nimrod, G., & Kleiber, D. (2007). Reconsidering change and continuity in later life: Toward an innovation theory of successful aging. *International Journal of Aging and Human Development, 65*, 1-22.

Palmore, E. (1981). *Social patterns in normal aging.* Durham, NC: Duke University Press.

Parker, R.G. (1995). Reminiscence: A continuity theory framework. *Gerontologist, 35*, 515-525.

Passuth, P., & Bengston, V. (1995). Sociological theories of aging: Current perspectives and future directions. In J. Quadagno & D. Street (Eds.), *Aging for the 21st century: Readings in social gerontology* (pp. 12-30). New York: St. Martin's Press.

Pew Internet and American Life. (2004). *Older Americans and the Internet.* Retrieved from www.pewinternet.org/Reports/2004/Older-Americans-and-the-Internet.aspx.

Phillipson, C. (1998). *Reconstructing old age.* London: Sage.

Piaget, J. (1962). *The construction of reality in the child.* New York: Basic Books.

Reitzes, D., Mutran, E., & Verrill, L. (1995). Activities and self-esteem: Continuing the development of activity theory. *Research on Aging, 17*(3), 260-277.

Rothbaum, F., Weisz, J.R., & Snyder, S.S. (1982). Changing the world and changing the self: A two-process model of perceived control. *Journal of Personality and Social Psychology, 42*, 5-37.

Rowe, J.W., & Kahn, R.L. (1998). *Successful aging.* New York: Pantheon Books.

Ryan, R., & Deci, E. (2000). Self-determination theory and the facilitation of intrinsic motivation, social development, and well-being. *American Psychologist, 55*, 68-78.

Schaie, K.W., & Geiwitz, J. (1982). *Adult development and aging.* Boston: Little, Brown.

Scott, D., & Shafer, C.S. (2001). Recreational specialization: A critical look at the construct. *Journal of Leisure Research, 33*, 319-343.

Scott, D., & Willits, F.K. (1989). Adolescent and adult leisure patterns: A 37-year follow-up study. *Leisure Sciences, 11*, 323-335.

Seligman, M. (1975). *Helplessness: On depression, development, and death.* San Francisco: Freeman.

Singleton, J.F., Forbes, W.F., & Agwani, N. (1993). Stability of activity across the lifespan. *Activities, Adaptation & Aging, 19*, 19-27.

Stebbins, R.A. (1992). *Amateurs, professionals, and serious leisure.* Montreal: McGill-Queen's University Press.

Sternberg, R. (1990). *Wisdom: Its nature, origin and development.* Cambridge, UK: Cambridge University Press.

Stewart, A.J., & Vandewater, E. (1998). The course of generativity. In D.P. McAdams & E. de St. Aubin (Eds.), *Generativity and adult development: How and why we care for the next generation* (pp. 75-100). Washington, DC: American Psychological Association.

Strain, L., Grabusic, C., Searle, M., & Dunn, N. (2002). Continuing and ceasing activities in later life: A longitudinal study. *Gerontologist*, *42*, 217-223.

Tornstam, L. (2005). *Gerotranscendance*: *A developmental theory of positive aging*. New York: Springer.

Utz, R.L., Carr, D., Nesse, R., & Wortman, C.B. (2002). The effect of widowhood on older adults' social participation: An evaluation of activity, disengagement, and continuity theories. *Gerontologist*, *42*, 522-533.

Vaillant, G. (2002). *Aging well*. New York: Little Brown.

Whitbourne, S.K. (1986). *The me I know: A study of adult identity*. New York: Springer-Verlag.

Whitbourne, S.K. (1996). *The aging individual: Physical and psychological perspectives*. New York: Springer.

Whitbourne, S.K. (2001). *Adult development and aging: Biopsychosocial perspectives*. New York: Wiley.

Whitbourne, S.K., & Collins, K.C. (1998). Identity and physical changes in later adulthood. Theoretical and clinical applications. *Psychotherapy*, *35*, 519-530.

Woerner, M., & Edmondson, R. (2009). Toward a taxonomy of types of wisdom. *Yearbook of the Irish Philosophical Society 2008*, 148-163.

Yarnal, C.M., Chick, G., & Kerstetter, D. (2008). "I did not have time to play growing up . . . So this is my play time. It's the best thing I have ever done for myself": What is play to older women? Leisure Sciences, 30, 235-252.

CHAPTER 4

Studying Leisure in the Context of Aging

Bryan Smale ■ Jennifer Gillies

After reading this chapter, you will be able to

- appreciate the importance of research in understanding the links between leisure and aging,

- understand the importance of epistemological and theoretical considerations in selecting an approach to a research project,

- distinguish between and describe the principal strategies used in quantitative and qualitative research designs, and

- understand the issues associated with each approach to research and how they influence the analysis and interpretation of the information gathered in a study.

uppose you are a public recreation employee working for the local department of parks, recreation, and culture, with primary responsibility for the programs and services provided to the older adults living in your community. You have become more and more aware of the challenges your department might face because the population is aging and the number of older adults in your town is growing. Also, the diversity of your community is increasing as many new residents arrive from a variety of cultures, and these include many older adults, often as part of extended families. Consequently, you are no longer certain that your department is offering programming that is meeting their needs. What are the older adults in your community actually doing in their leisure time? What are their preferences for activities and programs? How do they even *feel* about their leisure time? Is it meaningful to them? You are keen to provide whatever support you can, but what should you do?

These questions cannot be answered by sitting at your desk, guessing at solutions, and hoping for the best. Rather, you need to find the best information available from the people most directly affected by your decisions, organize and analyze the information you gather, and draw conclusions that are based on solid interpretations and sound judgment. There is no better way to do this than by conducting research. When we embark on a research study, we begin by developing a *research design*, which is the framework or overall plan for undertaking a research study. The design describes the people about whom we are interested (i.e., the *sample*), the location where we will conduct our research (i.e., the *study site*), the way in which we intend to gather the information (i.e., the *data*) necessary to answer our questions (i.e., the research *methods*), and the way in which we intend to organize and analyze the information we gather (i.e., *data analysis*). All of these components of the research design lead to the most important outcome of research—the *interpretation* of the results. In other words, what meaning can we make from our research efforts to answer our initial questions?

Epistemological Perspectives Guiding Research

Doing research is really just a matter of asking good questions and coming up with relevant and effective answers. It sounds simple, but *how* we conduct our research depends on making use of strategies and techniques—that is, the methods of research—that are best suited to our questions. However, the methods of research are not disconnected from the broader issues of the way in which researchers examine the social world around them. Even though we do not routinely reflect on our philosophical perspective every time we begin a new study, that perspective has a significant effect on the overall research design. Research is inextricably linked to ideas about how the world operates and how we come to understand it.

Epistemology is how we come to understand the world around us, and two epistemological perspectives (or *worldviews*) have dominated the way in which we currently conduct research in the social sciences. The first perspective comes from *postpositivism*, which is based on traditional assumptions found in the natural sciences, such as objective truths, universal laws or theories that govern actions and beliefs, and knowledge built on evidence and our rational interpretation of it. Postpositivists believe that there is a certain order to the world and research is designed in such a way so as to discover it. Hence, researchers using methods associated with postpositivism typically put forward a theory, gather the necessary data to test it, and then verify the theory or refine it in an effort to better understand the world.

In recent years, postpositivist researchers have relaxed their belief in an absolute truth of knowledge. They now embrace the view that we can never fully understand and describe the behaviors and beliefs of human beings, but we can identify the most important factors that affect people's actions and ideas, and that which remains unknown is idiosyncratic and does not disprove the general theory. For example, a postpositivist researcher might theorize that as people grow older, their physical and psychological well-being decline. To test this proposition, he might gather data from a large group of adults ranging in age from mid- to later life, including data on both physical well-being (perhaps using a test of physical fitness) and psychological well-being (perhaps using a standardized scale). After analyzing all of the data, the researcher may discover that lower levels of both physical and psychological well-being are indeed more often associated with later life. For those people who do not conform to this pattern, the researcher acknowledges that there are many other factors that might help to maintain people's well-being as they age, such as exercise and nutrition, but this acknowledgment does not refute the basic truth that aging leads to lower levels of well-being.

The second perspective is *constructionism*, which arose in part as a response to the tenets of positivism. Constructionism argues that meaning is constructed by people, not discovered as an objective truth. Crotty (1998) describes this perspective well when he says that, in constructionism,

> all knowledge, and therefore all meaningful reality as such, is contingent upon human practices, being constructed in and out of interaction between human beings and their world, and developed and transmitted within an essentially social context. (p. 42)

A key element in constructionism is that knowledge and meaning are socially constructed; in other words, meanings are *subjective*, arrived at through our interactions with others as we strive to make sense of the world. Further, meaning is rooted in our historical and cultural backgrounds because they inform our current understandings.

Research methods associated with constructionism are not confined to any one approach, and the underlying ideas of this perspective have led to diverse modes of inquiry, some of which will be introduced later in this chapter. Nevertheless, most constructionist approaches tend to be characterized by such qualities as the following:

- *Reflection on values*—Who will benefit from the research? Will anyone be discredited? Will any of the participants be exploited in any way?
- *Voices of participants*—Will the voices of the participants be heard and validated by the process, or will they be hidden?
- *Collaborative participation*—Will the participants engage fully in the generation of knowledge along with the researcher? Will the participants also benefit from the research?
- *Multiple perspectives*—Will all perspectives be represented and honored?

By reflecting on these aspects, researchers are better positioned to understand how meaning is constructed and acted upon by the people directly engaged in the circumstances of interest.

The Role of Theory

As the previous discussion suggests, *theory* plays a critical role in research. Theory provides researchers with a framework within which to organize and understand the social phenomena of interest. This framework identifies and defines the concepts central to the researcher's inquiry and describes the relationships among them. Most researchers rely on middle-range theories to inform their work rather than grand theories. Grand theories are quite abstract and provide a framework for organizing ideas. They attempt to provide overall principles and a unifying explanation of, for example, all social life or the totality of human experiences. In the context of human life and health, Parse's (1981, 1987, 1992) theory of human becoming is an example of a grand theory. Middle-range theories, on the other hand, are generally focused on describing how specific phenomena within a given context are related. Some classic middle-range theories focused on aging and leisure (i.e., the context) include activity theory (Havighurst, 1961; Lemon, Bengtson, & Peterson, 1972), disengagement theory (Cumming & Henry, 1961), and continuity theory (Atchley, 1971, 1989, 1999). Each of these theories describes the nature of a person's leisure as she ages and the factors that contribute to changes in leisure patterns and social relationships. A researcher interested in exploring how the leisure lifestyles of adults continue, adapt, or completely change might embrace one of these theories as a guiding framework when developing the study.

The role of theory in research differs depending on the epistemological perspective you embrace. For postpositivist researchers, theory comes first, guiding the research questions to be answered and determining the design of the research project. Many postpositivist researchers set out to test their theories by generating hypotheses based on propositions suggested by a theory to see if the propositions can be supported by the evidence generated in their studies. Researchers who conduct their studies in this fashion are engaged in *deductive inquiry* because their questions are deduced from theory and guide the data collection and analysis.

In contrast, for researchers based in constructionism, theory might provide some initial guidance concerning salient issues to explore, but new theory or refinements to existing theory typically emerge from interpretation of the data gathered during the research process. This is characteristic of *inductive inquiry*, which generates theory rather than tests it. Elements of both deductive and inductive inquiry are typically present to some degree in most studies, but the point in the process at which the researcher places the most emphasis on theory reflects whether he is most likely engaged in deductive inquiry (and embracing a postpositivist perspective) or inductive inquiry (and embracing a constructionist perspective).

Two Broadly Defined Approaches to Research

In the social sciences, approaches to research have typically been described as falling into two general categories: quantitative and qualitative. These two labels for the approaches to research have emerged because of the types of methods used and the character of the data that are gathered. **Quantitative research designs** typically rely on surveys of many people to gather information on issues of interest and then convert that information into numeric format for subsequent analysis and interpretation. This approach is therefore most often associated with a postpositivist epistemology. In contrast, **qualitative research designs** usually involve personal interviews and the participants' words are the data to be analyzed. Hence, qualitative approaches are usually linked to a constructionist epistemology.

The general characteristics of quantitative and qualitative approaches to research are summarized in table 4.1. Though these features are most often associated with one approach, they are not necessarily restricted to that approach; for example, either approach could focus on both depth and breadth.

Quantitative Inquiry

As suggested in table 4.1, a number of features characterize quantitative approaches to inquiry. In this section, we focus on those things with which researchers most often concern themselves when designing a study: how to define and measure the concepts central to their inquiry, who will make up their sample of study participants, how they will gather their data, and finally, how those data will be analyzed.

Concepts and Measurement

The phenomena in which we are interested in knowing more about are the *concepts* or constructs that are the focus of our research. When we develop specific definitions of those concepts, we are engaging in the process of *conceptualization*. Conceptualization involves defining each of our concepts in theoretical terms; in other words, a conceptual definition describes the way in which we have come to understand the essence of the concept. For example, even familiar ideas such as age and aging need to be defined conceptually to clarify how we are thinking about them and how we are distinguishing between them.

When we set out to devise measures of our concepts, we become engaged in the process of *operationalization*, which involves converting our abstract concepts into measureable form. A well-operationalized measure is one that adheres closely to the theoretical definition of the concept—it provides an indicator that reflects the essence of the concept. Ultimately, the process of measurement means assigning numbers to attributes or levels associated with each concept. An important consideration when assigning numbers to the various attributes of a concept is the meaning those numbers possess. Different measures place more or less importance on the actual value of the number assigned to each attribute. This is known as *level of measurement*, and there are four levels, each with numbers assigned that have specific meanings.

The first level of measurement is *nominal*. Nominal-level measures simply distinguish between distinct *categories* or attributes associated with a concept. In nominal-level measures, the assignment of numbers serves only to distinguish between each of the categories. So, to measure a person's gender, we might assign a number 1 to represent the category *male* and a number 2 to represent the category *female* (see table 4.2 on page 72). We could use any discrete numbers because they are simply markers of categories.

The second level of measurement is *ordinal*, which introduces the idea of *rank order* to the measure. The categories are discrete, but now their order is important. For example, if we want to ask older golf players to indicate if they feel their skill level is low, moderate, or high, those three categories have a clear rank order and so the numbers we assign to them should reflect that order (see table 4.2 on page 72).

The third level of measurement is *interval*, and it introduces the property of *equal distance* between each category of a measure. Interval-level measures are most often associated with scales that are used to assess attitudes and perceptions. For example, older adults might be asked to rate the quality of the recreational services offered by the local senior center according to a 5-point scale where 1 = strongly disagree, 2 = disagree, 3 = neutral, 4 = agree, and 5 = strongly agree (see

Characteristics of Quantitative and Qualitative
Approaches to Research

Characteristic	Qualitative	Quantitative
GETTING STARTED		
Intent of the study	Focus on depth	Focus on breadth
Relationship to theory	Inductive—theory developed from data as the research progresses; grounded theory	Deductive—theory is the starting point for research; testing of hypotheses; analyzing results in light of theory
Role of concepts	Typically work with grounded concepts where definitions come from the participants	Concepts defined carefully beforehand; definitions lead to operationalization of variables (i.e., measurement)
Scientific method	Interpretivist paradigm and spiraling process of method not consistent with the scientific method as it is exemplified by traditional experimental design	Commitment to scientific method in order to achieve objectivity; control of variables; rigor in measurement; replication of procedures
GENERAL APPROACHES		
Designs	Case study; ethnography; phenomenology; grounded theory; action research	Experiments; quasi-experiments; survey designs
Techniques	In-depth interviews; participant observation; focus groups; analysis of documents and media sources (latent content analysis)	Secondary data analysis; structured observational methods; questionnaires; analysis of nonverbal forms of data
Process	Flexible; has clear starting point but method evolves as the research progresses	Adheres to original design to maintain reliability and validity of measurements
STRATEGIES AND TECHNIQUES		
Form of data	Uses words	Uses numbers
Setting	Natural setting; no controls imposed	Laboratory or field site where the goal is to control or manipulate the setting; specific setting may not be important
Sampling	Often uses smaller samples; focuses on selective (purposive) sampling or theoretical sampling	Uses much larger samples; focuses on representative samples of specific population using random sampling procedures
Role of researcher	Researcher immersed in the phenomena and is an instrument of qualitative research; researcher's role is to see the world through another's eyes	Researcher maintains distance to retain objectivity and to limit personal bias (separation of object and subject)
MAKING MEANING		
Verification of results	Often bring results back to participants to verify if researcher's interpretations are in fact true for the participants	Results are statistically verified for reliability and validity
Outcomes	Thick descriptions of experiences and perceptions of participants; uses quotations and profiles to support patterns and themes	Explanations or predictions of relationships among phenomena based on descriptive and inferential statistics
Negative cases and outliers	Interested in both commonalities and negative cases or inconsistencies	Focus is on common or generalizable patterns; outliers help inform but are not the focus

■ TABLE 4.2

Levels of Measurement

Level	PROPERTY				MEASUREMENT	
	Discrete categories	Rank order	Equal distance	Absolute zero	Examples	Measure
Nominal	✓				Gender	1 = male 2 = female
Ordinal	✓	✓			Skill level SES[a]	1 = low 2 = moderate 3 = high
Interval	✓	✓	✓		Attitude scales	5- or 7-point agreement scale
Ratio	✓	✓	✓	✓	Time Distance	Minutes Kilometers miles

[a] *Note*: SES is used to indicate levels of socioeconomic status (usually a combination of education, income, and occupational prestige).

table 4.2). In this instance, not only do the categories reflect a rank ordering of agreement, with higher numeric scores indicating greater degrees of agreement, but they also represent equally spaced points along a continuum of agreement. Consequently, the numbers used to represent each category must appear at equal intervals or distances along the continuum, and those equal distances are meaningful; in other words, the relative distance between points 2 and 3 on the 7-point scale is equivalent to the distance between points 6 and 7.

The last and highest level of measurement is *ratio*, and it possesses the highest level of meaning when numbers are assigned to each category. The basic property of a ratio-level measure is that it has an *absolute zero*. Ratio-level measures use familiar *units of measure* such as minutes or hours for time, inches or centimeters for height, miles or kilometers for distance, and raw counts of things or behaviors such as number of people living in a household or number of times per week that someone participates in walking for exercise. Each of these measures has a clear zero value (e.g., someone who watches no television), even if people might not realistically report it (e.g., zero distance to nearest park).

As shown in table 4.2, there is a clear relationship between the levels of measurement, with higher levels carrying all of the properties of the lower levels. In other words, a ratio-level measure not only has the unique property of an absolute zero, but it also possesses the properties of discrete categories, rank order, and equal distances between categories. So, if we have a higher level

of measurement, we also have the potential to treat it as a lower-level measure, but a lower-level measure cannot be raised to a higher level. For example, we could take a measure of the time spent each day watching television measured in minutes and create ordinal-level categories such as "none," "1 to 60 minutes," "61 to 120 minutes," and "over 120 minutes." However, if television viewing were originally measured using these four categories, we would not be able to determine the actual number of minutes spent watching per day.

With nominal- and most ordinal-level measures, the principal challenge is to ensure that the attributes associated with a measure are mutually exclusive and exhaustive. The attributes of a measure are *mutually exclusive* when someone can be assigned to only one category. For example, for a measure of a concept like gender, each person could only be included in one category—either male or female. For an ordinal measure such as categories of age, a measure would not be mutually exclusive if the categories were defined as "under 16 years," "16 to 25 years," "25 to 35 years," and so on, because someone who was 25 years of age could be assigned to two different categories. When a measure is *exhaustive*, all of the relevant categories or attributes have been included in the measure. For example, if a questionnaire asked which neighborhood the respondent lived in but only provided the names of half of the neighborhoods in the city, then the list would not be exhaustive. The names of all of the neighborhoods would have to be included in the list.

The main consideration when using interval- and ratio-level measures is deciding how precise we want our measure to be. This is often a balance between the amount of detail we would like to have as researchers and how reasonable it is to expect the study participants to provide minute details. For example, we might want to know how much television older adults are watching, but asking them to report how many total hours in the past year they spent watching would be an unreasonable request for anyone. Researchers usually consider how much detail is necessary to adequately answer their questions, so a more reasonable request might be to ask, for example, how many hours the person watched television in the previous week or in a typical week.

Validity and Reliability

When we attempt to measure concepts, such as people's behaviors, perceptions, or attitudes, we want to be sure that what we measure is, in fact, measuring what we think it is. This is what we mean when we say a measure is valid. *Validity* refers to the extent to which the measure we use to represent a concept actually measures what it is intended to measure. For example, if we were to measure someone's height in centimeters, few people would question whether that measure was a valid indicator of the concept *height*. However, if we were to argue that the measurement of a person's height was an indicator of intelligence, everyone would accuse us of using an invalid measure of the concept *intelligence*. Consequently, we make every effort to ensure that our measures are as valid as possible. Converting difficult concepts such as attitudes or perceptions into valid measures—a process called *operationalization*—is more challenging, so there are several ways to assess the validity of a measure. Here are three of the more common approaches:

- *Face validity*—Face validity exists if a measure clearly reflects the content of the concept. In the judgment of others, does the measure get at the concept in question? This is an intuitive process of examining the measure and judging that it does indeed capture the essence of the concept.
- *Content validity*—A measure possesses content validity if it provides complete coverage of all aspects of a concept's definition. For example, if we conceptualize the motivation for leisure as comprising social, physical, emotional, spiritual, and aesthetic motives, then the measure of leisure motivation should include indicators of each of these motives.

- *Concurrent validity*—We can assess the concurrent validity of a measure by comparing it with other measures of the same concept that were developed previously. We can argue that our measure is valid if it shows high correspondence with the results of the previously validated measure.

For the most part, the validity of a measure is based on a solid conceptual definition of the concept of interest. The better we understand and clearly define the concept, the more confidence we have in judging the validity of the measures we use to reflect the concept.

An associated and equally important characteristic of a good measure is its *reliability*, or the extent to which a measure captures a concept consistently over time and across various groups of people. If we think of a concept as a target, then the closer the measure hits the center of that target, the more valid it is, and the more consistently our repeated use of the measure hits the same spot, the more reliable it is. For example, in figure 4.1 on page 74, we want our measure to produce results like those shown in target A—it has consistently hit the center. In target B, we have a reliable measure because it consistently gets the same results, but it has missed the target; in other words, it is measuring something else other than the concept in which we are interested. The measure reflected in target C is neither reliable nor valid, which is the result of both poor conceptualization and poor operationalization.

Some researchers feel that validity is more important than reliability because unless a measure accurately captures the intended concept, it has little value. However, if it is valid but somewhat unreliable, we can usually detect the reasons for the lack of reliability (e.g., younger people might feel differently from older adults about what is important in their leisure). Nevertheless, a measure that is both valid and reliable is most desirable and will provide researchers with results in which they can be confident.

Sampling Strategies

If we wanted to know something about the leisure interests of the older adults living in our community, we probably would not have the resources to include everyone in our study. Hence, we set out to select a smaller group of participants—our *sample*—that is representative of all the people that compose the group of interest—our *survey population*. **Sampling** strategies used to select

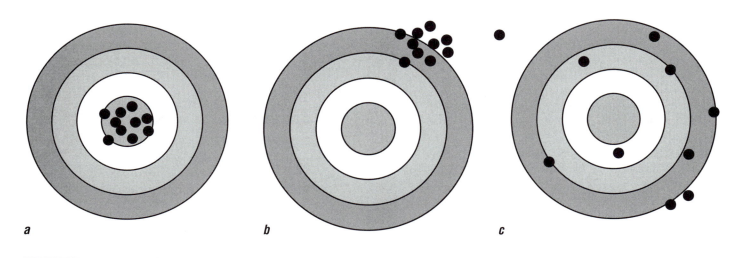

a   b   c

Figure 4.1 Validity and reliability in measuring concepts. Results may be *(a)* valid and reliable, *(b)* reliable but not valid, or *(c)* neither reliable nor valid.

participants for quantitative studies have an essential goal: to ensure that the sample is *representative of* and *generalizable to* the wider population from which it is drawn. In order to meet this goal, researchers can choose from a variety of sampling strategies, each of which is based on *probability sampling*. Strategies based on probability sampling are designed to give every person within the survey population an equal chance of being selected to participate in the study, thereby ensuring a representative sample.

Some of the more frequently used strategies of probability sampling are

- simple random sampling,
- systematic sampling,
- cluster sampling, and
- stratified sampling.

To illustrate how each strategy is used, let's assume we want to draw a representative sample of 100 older adults from the list of 500 members of a local seniors' recreation center. That list of members is referred to as our *sampling frame*, which provides a complete listing of everyone in the survey population from which our sample will be drawn.

In the case of *simple random sampling*, everyone listed in the sampling frame would be assigned a number from 001 to 500, and then using a random numbers table or a computer that randomly generates three-digit numbers, 100 participants would be selected to form the sample. This is similar to pulling names from a

hat and ensures that everyone on the list has an equal probability of being selected.

A somewhat simpler but just as effective strategy would be to use *systematic sampling*. We would take the same list of 500 members of the recreation center and select every fifth person on the list after choosing a random starting point on the list. Every fifth person is the *sampling interval* (i.e., number of people in the sampling frame divided by the desired sample size: 500 / 100 = 5), and it ensures that all of the members listed have an equal chance of being selected; hence, the systematic sample is just as representative as a simple random sample.

Let's assume we do not have a reliable sampling frame and cannot use either of these first two sampling strategies. This could occur if, for example, the membership list is not up to date or if the recreation center only has lists of older adults who register for the programs that are offered. In this case, we could use *cluster sampling* by first compiling a complete list of all of the programs and then creating the sample by randomly selecting enough programs to enlist at least 100 older adults to be part of the sample. Each program represents a *cluster* of older adults, and all of the participants in the program would be invited to be part of the study. As with simple random and systematic sampling, the process of randomly selecting from the complete list of programs ensures that all older adults at the recreation center would have an equal chance of being part of the final sample.

We might choose to use *stratified sampling* if the survey population is relatively small or we want to ensure that certain groups within the population are adequately represented in the final sample. If, for example, one of our research questions concerned differences in the leisure lifestyles of older women and men, we would want to ensure accurate and adequate representation of both sexes, so we would stratify by sex. If the survey population were three-quarters women, then a *proportionate* stratified sample would also be three-quarters women, or 75 people in the final sample of 100. In contrast, if we wanted to ensure we had an equal number of men to compare to the women, we would select a *disproportionate* sample of 50 men and 50 women, overrepresenting the men but ensuring that enough men were included for meaningful comparisons.

Sometimes, however, researchers might have to use a *nonprobability sample*, identifying a group of people that meet the specific criteria but that might not be entirely representative of the larger population. For example, assume a researcher is looking to enlist older adults from across an entire community to complete a questionnaire on their leisure interests. Because a suitable sampling frame of all older adults in the community likely is not available, the researcher might ask members from all of the seniors' recreation centers to participate in her study. This approach is known as *convenience sampling* and is often used when the population of interest is not easily accessible. By using a convenience sample, the researcher will not know how representative the sample is of the entire population of older adults because not all older adults are necessarily members of these centers, and consequently, she cannot generalize her findings to the larger community of older adults. Nevertheless, her hope is that she can still make some inferences from the results of the study as long as she recognizes who has been included and who has not.

One of the challenges in sampling is deciding on the size of the sample. How many people need to participate in our study so we are confident that the sample will be representative and allow us to make inferences about the population? There are formulas for calculating sample size that ensure small margins of error in the inferences we draw about large populations, but as a rule of thumb, we can have confidence in the results from a sample of at least 300 to 350 people drawn from a population of over 25,000. Nevertheless, a simple guideline is to include as many people as your resources permit, that is, to maximize the size of the sample based on financial and human resources as well

as available time. Also, when the population of interest is relatively small (e.g., the 200 members of a seniors' walking club), a researcher could choose to include everyone in the study.

Common Design Strategies

While a researcher is deciding on the key concepts to explore, how to operationalize those concepts into measurable form, and from whom to gather information using those measures, he also is considering which research design is most suited to the types of questions to be answered. Over the years, two strategies have emerged that have dominated the way in which social scientists have conducted their research—the **survey** and the **experiment**. Arguably, many of the other strategies described in the literature, such as observational research, content analysis, and program evaluation studies, are variations on one of these two general approaches. For example, in content analysis, the participants in the study are not people but rather artifacts such as magazine articles, newspaper editorials, brochures, or even images. These artifacts are surveyed by measuring their characteristics using a structured instrument (similar to a questionnaire) to determine which features appear most frequently and whether certain features are associated with other characteristics. Most textbooks on social research methods provide descriptions of these strategies (see, for example, Babbie, 2007; Bryman, Teevan, & Bell, 2009; Neuman & Robson, 2009), and others focus on specific strategies such as content analysis (e.g., Neuendorf, 2002) or program evaluation (e.g., Royse, Thyer, & Padgett, 2010).

Survey Research

Perhaps the defining approach to gathering data in the social sciences, and certainly one of the most frequently used, is the survey. Survey research design traditionally has used a self-administered questionnaire, where participants receive a paper copy of the survey form and respond to a series of questions that provide a prescribed set of response options. More open-ended questions, where respondents provide a longer, written response to a question (e.g., "How would you describe the recreation services for older adults in our community?"), can be used in a questionnaire, but they are less common. Surveys also take the form of face-to-face interviews, telephone interviews, and online questionnaires, but these are really just different ways of administering a survey. Just like a questionnaire, a structured format and fixed responses remain the principal features of a survey design regardless of how it is delivered to potential respondents.

There are several considerations when designing a questionnaire. Foremost is providing a clear and comprehensive introduction to potential participants about the purpose of the study and why their involvement is important. Such an introduction not only clarifies why you are asking people to become involved but also leads to a much higher participation rate when people feel their answers are important and can contribute something meaningful. The main body of the questionnaire should reflect the researcher's thoughtful consideration of its presentation to respondents. Researchers should try to think how respondents would react to the questionnaire and ask these questions:

- Can the respondent see a logical sequence to the questions? Do the first questions directly address some of the key issues raised in the introduction?
- Are the layout and visual presentation appealing and easy to read and follow?
- Are there clear instructions for each of the question formats so a respondent would know exactly how to answer?
- Is the wording of each question clear, unambiguous, and relevant to the research objectives?

With respect to presentation, the researcher must provide clear instructions on how to questions should be answered (e.g., "Please select the *one* response that best describes *how you feel*" versus "Please select *as many* of the responses as you feel *apply to you*"). The wording of questions can be much more complicated than we might imagine. Depending on the sample, the language that is used must be familiar and accessible. Here are some of the more common issues encountered when creating questions:

- **Avoid double-barreled questions.** A question is double-barreled when it asks two or more questions at once. For example, "Do you enjoy taking the bus or a taxi to the recreation center?" cannot be answered by someone who likes taxis but hates the bus. This question needs to be made into two separate questions.
- **Use clear and simple language.** The question, "Do you think there is a paucity of

adequately colossal parks in your neighborhood?", would be better asked as, "Do you think there are enough large parks in your neighborhood?"

- **Avoid questions that require lengthy recall.** The longer the time frame you ask about, the more difficult it is for people to remember their behaviors accurately. For example, if you are asking about participation in certain leisure activities, be sure to select a reasonable time frame. Rather than asking how many times someone visited the local farmer's market in the past year, ask about the past week or past month.
- **Avoid using negatives.** A question such as "To what extent do you agree that the city should not further develop the local swimming pools?" could be confusing, or worse, someone could easily miss seeing the *not* and answer quite differently.
- **Make sure the response options are mutually exclusive.** Ensure that the response options are completely independent; in other words, there is no overlap between them such that a respondent would fall into two categories. For example, when asking respondents to indicate how many times they attended the seniors' recreation center in the past month, do not have overlapping categories like these:

☐ 1 to 3 times last month
☐ 3 to 5 times last month
☐ 5 to 10 times last month

Which of the first two categories should be selected by a respondent who went three times last month? Mutually exclusive categories would be more like these:

☐ 1 to 3 times last month
☐ 4 to 5 times last month
☐ 6 to 10 times last month

- **Make sure the response options are exhaustive.** The response options you provide should cover all of the possible responses without making the list too long. In the example just given, there is not an option for someone who does *not* go to the seniors' recreation center or for someone who went more than 10 times in the last month. So, categories of "never" and "11 or more times last month" need to be added to make the list exhaustive. In its final form, the question might look like this:

How many times in the past month did you go to the seniors' recreation center? Please select the *one* option that best describes your attendance:

- ☐ 0 times (I never attend)
- ☐ 1 to 3 times last month
- ☐ 4 to 5 times last month
- ☐ 6 to 10 times last month
- ☐ 11 or more times last month

Once you have prepared a draft of the questionnaire, you should conduct a *pilot test* before distributing it to the people in your intended sample. A pilot test involves having a small group of people with characteristics similar to those in the sample fill out the questionnaire and then provide feedback on its readability, clarity, and ease of completion. The feedback is especially helpful for determining the suitability of the questionnaire for the specific sample of people who will be surveyed. For example, even though older adults are increasingly active and healthier, your sample might require your questionnaire design to accommodate people with visual limitations of some nature. For example, by simply using a larger font (e.g., 14 point rather than 11 or 12), the questions and response options are easier to read and complete. Some people might also require more time to complete the questionnaire or might even need someone to answer any questions they have about the survey. Based on all of the preceding considerations, an example of a self-administered questionnaire that might be distributed to and completed by the members of a seniors' recreation center is illustrated in figure 4.2 on page 78.

The 2006 study by Payne, Mowen, and Montoro-Rodriguez is a fairly typical example of a survey design involving older adults. Beginning with a conceptual framework based on ideas from successful aging and clear definitions of their key concepts, they set out to determine the extent to which leisure lifestyle explains perceptions of physical and mental health among older adults living with arthritis. They enlisted 464 older adults (over 50 years of age) to complete a self-administered questionnaire about their leisure, health, social interactions with friends, and selected demographic characteristics. The questionnaire used closed-ended questions that were converted by the researchers into numeric form to provide measures of the key concepts. Based on the results, they found that older adults with more diverse leisure repertoires and more frequent interactions with friends reported higher levels of perceived physical and mental health, which helped them overcome the negative aspects of living with arthritis.

Surveys do not necessarily have to be just about people. For example, Dupuis, Smale, and Wiersma (2005) sent questionnaires to long-term care facilities (e.g., nursing and retirement homes) across Canada to discover what types of and how often community recreation programs were provided for residents. In their study, even though the questionnaires were completed by administrators at the facilities, the unit of analysis was the facility, not the administrator. In other words, the results of the study described the facilities, using measures such as the numbers of residents, staff, and volunteers and the types of recreation programs offered and how frequently they were provided.

Experiments

Experiments are often thought of as being the sole domain of scientists working in laboratories, yet experiments can be used anytime we want to discover whether the introduction of some activity or program (i.e., an intervention) leads to a change in a group of people. When an experiment evaluates the effectiveness of medications, medical devices, or treatments, it is referred to as a *clinical trial* and is typically the domain of medical researchers. For leisure researchers, experiments can be designed to evaluate, for example, the effect of introducing a new recreation activity to a group of older adults in an effort to enhance their quality of life.

In a classic experimental design (see figure 4.3 on page 79), study participants are randomly assigned to one of two groups: an experimental group and a control group. Both groups are given a pretest, which usually involves the completion of a questionnaire or interview that gathers baseline information on the researcher's specific area of interest. The experimental group is then exposed to an intervention such as a program or task that is being examined to determine if it is effective in bringing about a change in the participants' behavior or perceptions. The control group does not receive the intervention. Following the completion of the program, participants in both the experimental and control groups complete a posttest that assesses them again on the area of interest. If an intervention is successful, we would expect to see a significant change in the scores from the pretest to the posttest among participants in the experimental group but virtually no change in the control group. Such a result would

Treetown Park and Recreation Department: Maple Recreation Center for Seniors

In this survey, we would like to know more about your preferences for and participation in the recreation activities provided by the center. Based on the information we collect, we hope to provide you with better programs and services at the Maple Recreation Center for Seniors.

Your Participation in Recreation Activities

Following are a number of recreation activities. Please indicate how often you participate in each activity in a typical week. If you do *not* participate in the activity, put in a 0 (zero).

Recreation activities	Frequency of participation
Playing cards	_____ times per week
Walking for exercise	_____ times per week
Bicycling	_____ times per week
Social dancing	_____ times per week
Eating out	_____ times per week
Swimming	_____ times per week
Bowling	_____ times per week
Exercising	_____ times per week
Gardening	_____ times per week
Reading	_____ times per week

Your Reasons for Participating in Recreation Activities

People give many reasons for participating in recreation activities. Following are a few of the more common reasons people have given. For each reason, please indicate the extent to which you agree or disagree that it is true for you by placing a mark [X] in the appropriate box.

Reasons for participating in recreation activities	Strongly disagree	Disagree	Neutral	Agree	Strongly agree
To keep in shape physically					
To use my imagination					
To meet new people					
To gain a sense of belonging					
To discover new things					
To be creative					

Some Things About You

- What is your gender? ☐ Female ☐ Male
- What is your age? _____ years of age
- In which neighborhood of Treetown do you live? _____
- How long have you been a member of the Maple Recreation Center? _____ years and _____ months

Figure 4.2 Self-administered questionnaire for members of a seniors' recreation center.

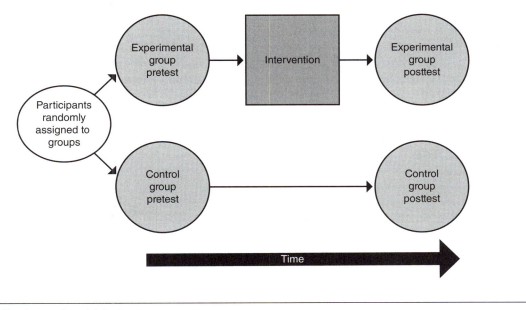

Figure 4.3 Classic experimental design.

tell us that the intervention has had the expected outcome and is an effective means of bringing about change in those who engage in the activity or program; otherwise, we would have seen a comparable change among those who did *not* participate in the activity.

Garcia-Villamisar and Dattilo (2010) used an experimental design to determine whether people who participated in a leisure program reported higher scores on several indicators of quality of life than people who did not participate. They enlisted 37 adults aged 17 to 39 years who had been diagnosed with autism spectrum disorder (ASD) to participate in a year-long leisure education program (the experimental group). These participants were compared with 34 similarly aged adults, also with ASD, who did not participate in the program (the control group). After establishing baseline measures for both groups before the experimental group participated in the program (the pretest), the researchers were able to see if the adults who participated in the program were significantly different from the nonparticipating adults in the control group by comparing baseline scores with scores gathered after the program was completed (the posttest). At the end of the year, they found that the experimental group showed significantly higher scores on four aspects of quality of life as well as lower levels of stress.

In Garcia-Villamisar and Dattilo's (2010) study, the one-year time frame between the pretest and posttest is comparatively long for most experiments. The length of time between the pretest and the posttest depends on the nature of the intervention. For example, a researcher might want to determine if a preretirement financial planning course (i.e., the intervention) helps older adults prepare better for their impending retirements. Such a course might last six to eight weeks, and consequently the time between the pretest and posttest also would be that long.

Some researchers might add two or three posttests to the experiment design, with each one being administered several weeks or even months after the completion of the program. Doing so allows the researchers to determine if the change attributed to the intervention has been sustained over time. Assessing the staying power of an intervention has become increasingly important as researchers have discovered that many programs have immediate positive effects that diminish over time. Clearly, programs that have a sustained effect are regarded as more beneficial to participants.

Designing a classic experiment is not always feasible, especially in a natural environment. It might not be possible, for example, to assign participants randomly to the experimental and control groups or to conduct a pretest. Under certain circumstances, a researcher might be faced with identifying an experimental and a control group based solely on convenience. For example, the experimental group might be self-selecting in that it is formed simply by those individuals who have signed up to take part in a new recreation program offered by a local seniors' recreation center. A researcher might then enlist another group of older adults at the center to form the control group and hope that the two groups are relatively comparable on all characteristics apart from their participation in the new program. In other situations, a researcher might not feel that she can ethically create a control group because it would deny a group of participants the same access to an intervention provided to an experimental group. In each of these situations, when a researcher cannot design a classic experiment, such a variation is referred to as a *quasi-experimental* design—the study would still be an experiment but modified to meet the special circumstances.

Data Analysis Strategies

Most data gathered using quantitative research designs use numeric measures of the characteristics concerning their samples. Numeric data lend themselves to the use of descriptive and inferential statistics for analysis and interpretation, and researchers often plan their data analysis strategies when they design their studies to ensure they gather the type of data needed for statistical analyses. This means that the researcher considers the level of measurement of each indicator being collected and knows which statistics can be used to summarize and describe the sample once all of the data have been collected. For example, for characteristics like gender and neighborhood of residence (see the sample questionnaire in figure 4.2), which are nominal-level measures, a researcher would report the results in frequency tables, reporting the numbers and percentages that fall within each category. For interval-level measures, such as the agreement scale used to assess older adults' reasons for participating in recreation, or ratio-level measures, such as the questions about the number of times per week of participation and the length of time that the person has been a member of the center, a researcher could generate descriptive statistics such as the *mean* (i.e., the arithmetic average) to describe the average response and the *standard deviation* to describe how much the participants vary in their responses.

Further, knowing beforehand the level of measurement of each indicator allows the researcher to plan which *inferential statistics* to use to answer questions such as, "Are men different from women in the reasons they report for participating in recreation activities?" or "Is there a relationship between how long people have been members at the center and how often they participate in all of the recreation activities?" These research questions can be answered with greater confidence by using inferential statistics, which are tests of the probability that the differences between groups or the strength of the relationships between concepts are *significant*, that is, they did not occur by chance but are valid reflections about the population from which the sample was drawn.

Qualitative Inquiry

As reflected earlier in table 4.1, a number of features distinguish qualitative research designs from quantitative approaches. Similar to quantitative approaches, qualitative research involves many design strategies, each of which is based on a different orientation. Complicating the desire to come up with a single definition of qualitative research is its constantly evolving form (Denzin & Lincoln, 2005b). Nevertheless, as noted earlier, most qualitative research designs are based on the idea that to understand the world around us, we must understand and interpret the ways in which people experience their everyday lives and ultimately how they construct meaning, often in social contexts. This means that qualitative researchers embrace the subjective nature of experience and "study things in their natural settings, attempt to make sense of, or interpret, phenomena in terms of the meanings that people bring to them" (Denzin & Lincoln, 2005a, p. 3).

These researchers believe that knowledge is socially constructed by people as they interact with the world, so concepts such as *aging* and *leisure* are not unchanging phenomena similarly experienced by all. Rather, these are constructs that each person interprets differently, and these interpretations can change over time, especially when people interact. For example, how others thought about aging in the past might be different from how they think about aging today. Consequently, the most commonly used methods of qualitative research gather data through interviews with people, analyze those data in the form of verbal texts, interpret them in the context of the interviewees' experiences, and attempt to represent those experiences as faithfully as possible. This is what makes qualitative research interpretive—it typically relies on the researcher to be the principal instrument of research.

Concepts

If meaning is constructed by people, then the relationship between theory and research is somewhat more ambiguous in qualitative research. As noted in table 4.1, theories and concepts are usually the outcomes of qualitative research because researchers examine and interpret the meanings offered by participants. However, theory can also initially inform the research process by providing researchers with a sense of the current understanding of the phenomena and processes in which they are interested. Consequently, qualitative research adheres less rigorously to a step-by-step process characteristic of quantitative research and is in a constant state of revision, reevaluation, and reflection as the research advances.

The concepts with which researchers are interested take two forms in qualitative research. First, unlike in quantitative research where concepts are defined a priori and used to develop measurable indicators, in qualitative research, the concepts initially are regarded as *sensitizing concepts*. Researchers use sensitizing concepts as interpretive devices that typically emerge from existing theories and ideas that researchers consult in preparation for their inquiries, and they provide a general direction for entering the process without being bound to them. Charmaz (2003) describes sensitizing concepts most succinctly:

> Sensitizing concepts offer ways of seeing, organizing, and understanding experience; they are embedded in our disciplinary emphases and perspectival proclivities. Although sensitizing concepts may deepen perception, they provide starting points for building analysis, not ending points for evading it. We may use sensitizing concepts *only* as points of departure from which to study the data. (p. 259)

Second, concepts typically emerge from the data provided by study participants. Following a careful analysis of the data provided by participants, concepts emerge that might confirm the validity of the initial sensitizing concepts, but perhaps more importantly, entirely new concepts emerge that are more reflective of the participants' experiences and the meanings they attach to them. It is the emergence of these new concepts and how they are connected that advances our understanding of the phenomenon under research and leads to new theories. In essence, concepts—and the theories that might be developed from them—are the outcomes of qualitative research rather than the features that guide the approach. This is why qualitative research is frequently described as being inductive and emergent.

Data Sources and Settings

In qualitative research, both the type of data gathered and the settings in which research takes place are different from quantitative research. As noted earlier, the qualitative researcher typically uses data taken from the narrative texts arising from interview transcripts and other published documents; from photographs, videos, or any other images; from audio media such as recordings, speeches, or music; or from observations of behaviors in their natural settings. Regardless of the type of data gathered and analyzed, they are richly descriptive in their portrayal of the phenomenon and of the participants.

Qualitative researchers also seek to understand and interpret phenomena as they exist in their *natural settings*. This means that a researcher goes directly to the participants and the research sites where the phenomenon of interest naturally occurs. When participants are reflecting on their experiences, the data will be richer and imbued with meaning if they are gathered in a way and at the place most associated with those experiences.

For example, as an alternative to the survey design described earlier to look at patterns of behavior among older adults using the seniors' recreation center, a researcher might interview older adults about their experiences at the center in order to understand the meanings that they attach to their participation in certain leisure activities. The interviews would be recorded and transcribed so the researcher has a written account of each interview, and the transcripts serve as data for analysis and interpretation. The researcher also may include observations of the older adults and their interactions while participating in leisure activities at the center in order to better understand their experiences in context. His field notes would then be included as data in the subsequent analysis and interpretation.

Common Strategies of Qualitative Inquiry

Researchers can choose from a variety of strategies of qualitative inquiry depending on the purpose of the study and the specific nature of the research questions. These strategies provide not only a guiding framework for the way in which the study is conducted and the data are to be analyzed but also provide a guiding philosophy on how to explore the experiences and meanings of participants. Among the most commonly employed of these strategies are grounded theory, phenomenology, and ethnography.

Of these, **grounded theory** has been the approach most frequently used by qualitative researchers in leisure studies. Grounded theory is a strategy of inquiry that leads to the development of an overarching theory or understanding that is grounded in the perspectives of participants, which is why it is regarded as a truly inductive approach. However, grounded theory has evolved into a family of methods, with each approach reflecting a slightly different orientation to data collection, analysis, and theory development. Nevertheless, grounded theory can most often be characterized by three essential properties:

- Theoretical sampling (which is discussed in the next section)
- Data analysis using the constant comparative method to derive themes and categories
- Theory development based on the saturation of derived categories

Charmaz (2006) summarizes grounded theory in this way:

> Grounded theory involves taking comparisons from data and reaching up to construct abstractions and then down to tie these abstractions to data. It means learning about the specific and the general—and seeing what is new in them—then exploring their links to larger issues or creating larger unrecognized issues in entirety. An imaginative interpretation sparks new views. (p. 181)

The popularity of grounded theory among researchers is in part due to its comparatively clear procedures, especially the traditional means of analyzing interview data. A clearly presented example of the steps in a grounded theoretical approach and subsequent data analysis is provided by Hardy and Grogan (2009). Using the data gathered during focus groups from 48 adults between 52 and 87 years of age, they developed a theoretical model representing how older adults' participation in physical activity is influenced by a desire to prevent further decline in health as well as the presence of social support.

Phenomenology is typically selected as a strategy of inquiry if the researcher is seeking to understand the essence of a phenomenon by exploring the lived experiences of participants. In other words, a researcher using phenomenology wants to carefully describe the everyday experiences of participants and the meanings they attach to those experiences, thereby moving from simply describing a phenomenon to determining the *nature* of what it is. Hence, phenomenology

seeks to describe and interpret the essential meanings of people's lived experiences with as much richness and depth as possible. In this respect, phenomenology differs from grounded theory in that theory is not a planned outcome of the exploration. Rather, as van Manen (1997) has argued,

> [phenomenology] attempts to gain insightful descriptions of the way we experience the world pre-reflectively, without taxonomizing, classifying, or abstracting it. So phenomenology does not offer us the possibility of effective theory with which we can now explain and/or control the world, but rather it offers us the possibility of plausible insights that bring us in more direct contact with the world. (p. 9)

Benisovich and King (2003), for example, used a phenomenological approach in their examination of 12 older adult Russians who immigrated to the United States during the previous five years and the meanings they attached to health and their experiences with the health care system. The researchers found four themes reflecting the experiences of the Russian immigrants—feelings of stress, distrust, alienation, and helplessness—all of which provided insights into why they did not engage the U.S. health care system.

Ethnography is a qualitative form of inquiry arising from cultural anthropology where researchers seek to uncover and describe the sociocultural interpretations and daily lives of those within a specific culture. In other words, unlike phenomenology, which focuses on individual experiences and meanings, ethnography is concerned with the social or cultural context within which groups of people live and act. The defining feature of ethnography is *fieldwork*, especially fieldwork that uses a naturalistic approach in that researchers immerse themselves in the natural environments in which people live in order to examine and interpret firsthand their behaviors.

Ethnographers use a variety of techniques to enlist participants, frequently relying on their judgment of who might be the best people to represent key roles within the culture, as well as to gather data about the people within the cultural group of interest. For example, an ethnographer might begin by examining the history, language, and norms of the cultural group before initiating observations of and interviews with key members of the group. Indeed, observation is the method of data collection most often associated with ethnographic research. By immersing herself in the everyday lives of people, the ethnographic researcher is better able to understand and contextualize their basic beliefs, hopes, fears, and expectations. Consequently, an ethnographer is sometimes described as the instrument of research because data collection and interpretation relies on his senses, thoughts, and feelings about the culture as various events and behaviors occur and are recorded, typically using a combination of observation and interviews.

A good illustration of an ethnographic study is provided by Paulson (2005), who used a variety of techniques to explore how cultures of fitness evolved among older adult participants in fitness and dance exercise classes. She participated in and observed the exercise classes for an entire year, kept notes on the observations she made about the classes, recorded stories that arose naturally from interacting with participants, and conducted interviews with the participants as well as the class instructors. From all of these sources of data, Paulson was able to construct a rich description of the participants' experiences and how cultures of fitness evolved and influenced their experiences of growing older.

Sampling Strategies

Two main sampling strategies are most often associated with qualitative approaches to research: purposeful sampling and theoretical sampling. *Purposeful sampling* is used by qualitative researchers to identify data sources judged to be the most relevant to the research questions. Data sources are most often people, but they could also be documents, sites, visual materials, or other artifacts—any source of information that best enables a researcher to uncover and understand the topic under study. Unlike random sampling in quantitative studies, there is no expectation that the sample used in a qualitative study is representative of the general population; rather, the sample is judged as soundest and trustworthy if it is closest to the experiences and issues being explored. Purposeful sampling is especially appropriate when a researcher is trying to enlist unique or difficult-to-reach populations. For example, to study the experience of ballroom dancing for older adults, a researcher would purposefully recruit people who were engaged in the activity because they would be in the best position to describe the personal meaning resulting from their participation.

The second type of sampling typically occurs during the research process rather than at its outset. *Theoretical sampling* is used when a qualitative researcher becomes aware of emerging theoretical constructs as the study is progressing and

feels further exploration is required. So, he may seek out additional information by including other people, activities, or events in the sample to facilitate the development of emergent categories and themes. As Morse (2007) succinctly states, "The main principle of theoretical sampling is that the emerging categories, and the researcher's increasing understanding of the developing theory, now direct the sampling" (p. 240). Although theoretical sampling is linked primarily to grounded theoretical approaches, it is increasingly used by qualitative researchers in an effort to reach *theoretical saturation*, that point in the research process when "gathering more data about a theoretical category reveals no new properties nor reveals any further theoretical insights" (Bryant & Charmaz, 2007, p. 611). The goal is not simply to increase the sample size but to enhance the development of emerging themes by going back to the data. For example, a researcher whose participants were primarily women may decide to interview more men because the data were suggesting that gender played a prominent role in the experience being explored.

The sample size selected for a project varies depending on the research question, the experience of the researcher, available resources (i.e., time, financial, and human), and the population with which the researcher is working. For example, a researcher working on a small-scale exploratory project might choose to interview 7 to 10 participants, whereas an experienced researcher working on a large-scale project might interview 20 to 30 participants in order to fully examine the topic from a variety of perspectives. Similarly, if a researcher wanted to explore an issue or experience in greater depth, she might interview fewer participants over longer periods of time and in greater detail.

It may be difficult to gauge ahead of time exactly how many participants will be enough for a project because of the emergent nature of qualitative research. Qualitative researchers typically collect and analyze data simultaneously, and they may realize as they near the end of their expected data collection that they need to recruit more participants (i.e., theoretical sampling). On the other hand, the researchers might *not* collect more data because they feel they have reached theoretical saturation. Saturation occurs when new data being analyzed fit into categories or themes that have already been created or the relationships between them have been well established during the ongoing data analysis process. Once data analysis ceases to yield any new insights, researchers may feel that they have reached saturation on an issue and hence no further sampling is required.

Common Strategies for Collecting Data

The three most common strategies used to gather data in qualitative studies are interviews, focus groups, and observations. Researchers sometimes even combine two or more strategies in the same study depending on the issue being explored. For example, as illustrated by Paulson's (2005) ethnographic study on cultures of fitness, a researcher might interview participants as well as observe them in the environments where the activity of interest takes place.

Interviews

The most frequently used strategy by qualitative researchers to gather data involves *interviews* with participants. Typically done face to face but sometimes over the telephone or even online in real time, interviews provide an opportunity to explore and understand firsthand participants' experiences and perspectives. Here are some key characteristics of an interview in a qualitative study:

- **Interviews are generally less structured.** They are not like questionnaires where participants respond to the same questions presented in the same order. After introducing the topic or issue of interest, there is more emphasis on exploring ideas and the participants' perspectives and allowing the questions to follow the participants' lead.

- **Interviews are participant focused.** Even though the researcher usually introduces the topic of inquiry, the direction and nature of the interview is determined by the participant. Rambling or occasionally going off on tangents is even encouraged because such departures can reveal unanticipated insights about what the participants regard as relevant.

- **New questions can be introduced in an interview.** During an interview, the researcher does not have to confine herself to predetermined questions. When new ideas or issues are introduced by the participants, the researcher has the freedom to introduce new questions to explore those ideas more fully.

- **Interviews are flexible.** As the previous point suggests, an interview does not have to

adhere to a prescribed set of questions, and it can place more or less emphasis on certain questions depending on what the participant feels is relevant.

There are many styles of interviewing. Each style largely depends on the extent to which the researcher takes an active part in the discussion with the participant. Structured interviews typically mean the researcher is more of a listener than an engaged discussant. More active interviews involve the researcher in the conversation with the participant, and both people explore and collaborate in building an understanding of the participant's experience.

Regardless of style, the qualitative researcher prepares for the interview by developing an *interview guide*, which can be a list of specific questions to be asked in sequence during the interview (i.e., a more structured approach), or more often, a list of basic questions on the topics related to the research questions that serve as memory prompts to facilitate the conversation with a participant. The interview guide is just that—a guide to help the researcher steer the interview. It is especially helpful when more than one person is conducting the interviews so that the principal issues are all introduced and in roughly the same order to allow a degree of comparability of differing styles. Along with the basic questions, researchers often include *probes* following each question that encourage participants to delve more deeply and elaborate on their responses. Probes may include questions such as "Can you tell me more about that?" or "What was that like for you?" Also, probes should not be leading; in other words, the researcher should *not* ask, "Do you mean this . . . ?", because it presumes to know what a participant intended and could direct the subsequent conversation in the direction the researcher wants.

Interviewing people might seem easy, but the questions must be probing without leading, the pace and sequencing must be carefully choreographed without being too structured, and most importantly, researchers must listen carefully to the participant and take advantage of new and unexpected topics that might arise. Consequently, researchers new to interviewing should practice their skills in a couple of pilot sessions before engaging the real participants.

Interviews should be recorded to ensure that an accurate record of the conversation is made and to allow the researcher to focus on the participant. The audio recording should then be transcribed immediately following the interview, and these transcripts become the data used for subsequent analyses. When transcribing interviews, an exact record is made, including all of the pauses, the laughing, and even the "umms" and "ahhs," because the researcher is interested in not just *what* participants say but also the *way* in which they say it. For this reason, a researcher may also insert notes in the transcript concerning body language, facial expressions, and emotions to capture emphases not evident in the words themselves. All of this information becomes data for analysis.

Focus Groups

A *focus group* is like an interview except it involves more than one participant. It is, in effect, a group interview. Participants with a connection to the topic of interest are gathered together by the researcher to participate in a group discussion in which the researcher serves as facilitator or moderator rather than interviewer. The purposes of a focus group are to

- give several people an opportunity to explore a specific theme or issue in depth,
- explore how people respond to an issue as members of a group rather than simply as individuals, and
- explore and understand how the meaning of an issue or experience is constructed collaboratively by the group members.

In other words, the data that are gathered in a focus group represent the group culture and shared meaning about an issue rather than a single person's perspective obtained in an interview. By discussing an issue as a group, the conversation often stimulates recall and a variety of perspectives as participants negotiate and construct a collective understanding. Participants probe one another to understand why others have certain perspectives, and through this process, the researcher gains insight into the ways in which meaning is constructed and shared in everyday life.

Focus groups give researchers a collective perspective on research issues.

Unlike interviews, a researcher does not have to decide on the number of participants but rather must decide on the size of the focus group (i.e., how many people to include) and the number of focus groups to organize and facilitate. Depending on the issue to be discussed and the level of participant engagement anticipated, a researcher would usually have 4 to 12 people in each focus group. If the issue is particularly meaningful to participants or is controversial, people are likely to have more to say, so a smaller group is advisable. Smaller groups are also more likely to encourage involvement from all of the participants. The number of focus groups to conduct is primarily a function of two considerations. First, a researcher might continue to organize focus groups until he feels theoretical saturation has been reached. Once that point has been reached, no more groups are needed. Second, a researcher might feel that the perspectives on an issue to be discussed are affected by demographic factors such as gender, class, and race. Consequently, more focus groups with a diverse range of participants are desirable to ensure that multiple perspectives are represented.

As the facilitator of the focus group, a researcher must

- initiate discussion but not dictate its direction,
- be nonintrusive and allow the discussion to evolve based on what the participants feel is relevant while helping to maintain focus,
- provide clarification on issues when asked by the participants, and
- encourage participation from everyone in the group.

The researcher should also monitor the discussion for a *polarization effect*, which can occur when the attitudes or opinions of each participant become more extreme or entrenched as a result of strong feelings on an issue. As with interviews, the researcher makes notes about which participant is speaking, nonverbal responses shown by each person, and dynamics of the interactions among participants to supplement the transcripts created from the audio recording of the discussion.

Observations

Observations are usually conducted in conjunction with other strategies such as interviews, especially in ethnographic studies, and are less often done on their own. Normally, the researcher is a *participant observer* in that she actively engages in the social setting and with members of the group of interest to observe their behaviors and activities and to elicit the meanings associated with those behaviors, the participants' interactions, and importance of the setting where they occur. If done in conjunction with individual interviews, observations can provide context to the perspectives described by the participants.

The researcher records observations and thoughts in *field notes*, which usually focus on the researchers' reflections and initial interpretations of what has been observed but can also include additional information such as photographs, video or audio recordings, documents, and diagrams. Usually, the participants are made aware of the researcher's involvement in their social world, so the researcher taking field notes does not distract them. However, the role of the researcher can vary. In some situations, the researcher may be a complete observer but not an active participant in the event or setting because involvement might be disruptive to the participants. For example, a younger researcher might feel that participating in a 10-week aquacise program designed for older adults would affect the natural interactions among the participants or make them feel uncomfortable, so he might choose to observe from a discrete distance. In contrast, the researcher may become an active participant in the program but choose to conceal his identity as a researcher. Concealment might reveal natural patterns of behavior and interactions that might not occur with a researcher present, but situations might arise that demand confidentiality and hence the researcher cannot report on them. So although the decision to reveal or conceal the researcher's identity to the group is typically linked to the issue at hand, it also raises ethical concerns.

Data Analysis and Presentation

The approach taken to the research study typically determines the type of **data analysis** that a researcher will use. Nevertheless, most strategies of qualitative data analysis involve complete immersion in the data (e.g., frequent reading and rereading of transcripts), an ongoing process of critical reflection in order to understand the experience of participants and to infer overall meaning, and an exploration of the possible relationships among emerging concepts. The starting point for most analysis of qualitative data is *coding*, which involves the assignment of labels (and sometimes notes) to particularly relevant parts of the data source, such as a transcript, that appear to have theoretical significance (i.e., aspects relevant to answering the research questions) or seem to be meaningful within the social worlds of the people being studied. In conjunction with coding the data source, a researcher will often keep a journal to record her thoughts and impressions as they emerge throughout the entire research process. These journal entries—usually called *memos*—help the researcher reflect more deeply on the data and identify emerging categories and themes.

Here are some of the guidelines that researchers follow when preparing for and performing coding, especially when analyzing interview data:

- **Read through the initial transcripts and field notes repeatedly.** Reading all of the transcripts as they become available allows the researcher to begin to see interesting patterns and important aspects of the participants' perspectives and experiences.

- **Begin coding early in data collection.** Coding can begin immediately with the transcribing of the first interview. This helps the researcher develop a feel for the data, and as coding progresses, codes and notes can be revisited and reconsidered as new categories and possible themes emerge.

- **Continually review the codes.** If two or more codes appear to be describing the same phenomenon or experience, consolidate them or reflect on what the difference between them might be. This is where the researcher may begin to see the connections between significant ideas represented by the codes.

- **Consider how the codes and emerging categories might be related to more general theoretical ideas.** Building on possible connections between codes, consider what the core concepts might be and what relationships exist among them. This process assists the researcher in identifying potential themes that capture the essence of the participants' experiences.

Three common problems can occur that researchers must try to avoid when coding qualitative data. First, coding is not the analysis itself; it is simply a way of facilitating the researcher's thinking about the perspectives and meanings captured in participants' words and reducing a huge amount of data into a more manageable number of key ideas. Second, even though coding helps in identifying those key ideas, it can result in a loss of the context in which the ideas were expressed. Pulling fragments out of transcripts might mean that a critical social setting in which an idea arose might be missing from the code and ultimately missing from the researcher's interpretation of its meaning. Third, a researcher might be tempted to create codes that fit his preconceived notions of what the experiences and meanings are like for participants. This can happen if researchers allow theoretical literature to sway their perspectives rather than being sensitive to the meanings expressed by the participants themselves.

Once the researcher has identified meaningful themes from the data, the results of the analyses are typically presented through the use of the participants' actual words (i.e., direct quotations from transcripts) or images (i.e., photographs or drawings made by participants) intertwined with the researcher's interpretations and detailed descriptions. The words and images selected for presentation are those the researcher feels have best captured the nature of the participants' experiences and will resonate most with the reader. The researcher's choices must be as faithful to the participants' perspectives as possible and not reflect the biases (intentional or not) of the researcher. This critical part played by the researcher in representing the experiences of the participants is another unique feature of qualitative research—the researcher is the primary research tool responsible for analyzing and especially interpreting data.

Roles and Responsibilities of the Researcher

Beyond the technical decisions concerning the design and administration of any research study, the researcher has certain roles and responsibilities that she must embrace to ensure that neither the data nor the participants are affected adversely. This means the researcher must be aware of any places where personal bias might enter the process, be constructively critical of all decisions regarding the research process, and ultimately maintain a high level of personal integrity.

Data Collection and Analysis

In qualitative research, the researcher is the primary research instrument responsible for collecting, analyzing, and interpreting the data. Unlike the approaches used by quantitative researchers, who gather data with structured survey instruments and analyze the data using statistical procedures, qualitative researchers are the conduits through which data are gathered, and they are the instruments of analysis. Even though the final interpretation of the data is subject to the biases and values of both qualitative and quantitative researchers, qualitative researchers have more often had to defend the quality and integrity of their research because of its subjective nature. At one time, this subjectivity was considered detrimental to the validity of qualitative research, but increasingly the researcher's experiences, emotions, and intuitions are seen as essential aspects of the research process (Dupuis, 1999). Qualitative researchers' proximity to the participants and their context brings strength, humanity, credibility, and sincerity to their work. For example, it could be an asset for a researcher exploring the impact of dementia on families if she herself has experienced caring for someone with dementia. Even though the researcher would need to consciously reflect on how her personal experiences might influence the research process, she would bring sensitivity, awareness, and a level of understanding to the study that would enhance its legitimacy and credibility.

Since qualitative researchers are integral parts of the data collection and analysis processes, they must exercise *reflexivity*, meaning they must be aware of their personal biography, biases, values, investments, and interests and how all of these factors shape every aspect of the study. Researchers are encouraged to openly reflect on the choices they make throughout the research process, who and what they choose to include or omit, and how any emotions that they experience might influence the direction and outcomes of the study. Reflections on these issues should occur at all phases of the research process, should be captured in a research journal, and should be constantly considered during data analysis and interpretation.

Acting Ethically

Although ethical considerations are just as important in quantitative research approaches, they are more often confronted by qualitative researchers because of the close interaction between the researcher and the participants. Acting ethically in their treatment of and interactions with participants is a fundamental and nonnegotiable responsibility of the researcher. Consequently, all researchers must consider how ethical issues will be addressed even before their studies begin. Researchers must anticipate any potential stress or harm, be it physical, psychological, or emotional, that involvement in their study may cause to participants, and *take every possible step to ensure that participants do not experience harm*. At no time should the needs of the researcher and the study take precedence over the personal welfare of the participant.

As a first step, the researcher needs to provide potential participants with accurate details about the nature of the study, what will be expected of them, and most importantly, any aspects that could lead to potential harm. All of this information is necessary so participants can provide *informed consent* of their involvement. Once engaged in the study, the identity of the participants must be kept completely confidential and never revealed in any reports or other documents concerning the study (e.g., by using pseudonyms rather than real names). Further, when interviews are being conducted with people with illnesses or disabilities, the researcher needs to be sensitive to such things as the length and location of the interview, the language used, and especially the capabilities and limitations of each participant. Being aware of body language and subtle cues in the language used by the participant can alert a researcher to potential stressors being experienced. Upon completion of the study, the researcher has an obligation to follow up with participants, share the knowledge gained, and in some instances discuss how the findings might lead to change on issues of concern to the participants. As noted previously, by exercising reflexivity, a researcher is better able to ensure that the research process adheres to ethical principles and practices.

Doing Research Well

To do research well, every researcher should embrace certain essential values. First, the researcher must have a clear idea of what he wants to know, because that establishes the path to follow. Second, and perhaps more importantly, the researcher must follow some guiding principles. Adherence to these principles can ultimately ensure the quality and integrity of the research.

Choosing a Path

The first and often most difficult step in conducting research well is w*riting clear and concise* *research questions.* The research questions provide an anchor for the researcher, reminding her of the focus of study and keeping the process on track toward meaningful answers. Research questions that are too vague or broad do not provide clear direction and inevitably lead to similarly vague answers. Also, the nature of the questions will imply the approach to be taken. For example, a research question that asks, "Is the frequency of attendance at an exercise program for older adults related to their overall well-being?", suggests a postpositivist approach where data gathered in a survey would indicate whether a significant relationship exists between attendance and well-being. In contrast, a research question that asks, "What is the nature of the experience for older adults participating in an exercise program?", suggests an interest in the individual perspectives and meanings held by older adults about the exercise program, so a more constructionist approach would be appropriate.

As the previous examples indicate, once the research questions have been established, *choose an approach and a strategy that best fit the research questions.* Does the nature of the research questions suggest a postpositivist or a constructionist approach? Is a certain perspective better suited to the nature of the study? In the second example of a research question ("What is the nature of the experience for older adults participating in an exercise program?"), would an ethnographic or a phenomenological approach be better? Once an approach is taken, which specific strategy is better suited to gather the necessary data? Interviews? Observations? Perhaps both? Some researchers are tempted to select several strategies for gathering data, thinking more is better; however, if the data gathered do not directly contribute to answering a research question, then an additional strategy might be a waste of resources.

Guiding Principles for the Researcher

Regardless of the approach taken to a study or the specific strategies used for collecting, analyzing, and interpreting data, there are several principles for doing research well that should guide all of the researcher's decisions.

- Maintain the highest level of honesty and integrity throughout the research process.
- Think critically about every stage in the research process.

- Be reflective about all of the decisions that are made and the implications of each one for the research.
- Treat all of the participants well, be ethical, and follow up after the study is complete.

Returning to your role as a public recreation employee working for the local department of parks, recreation, and culture, how are you going to find out about the behaviors, preferences, and experiences of the older adults living in your community? What specifically do you want to know—that is, what are your research questions? What approach will you use to answer your research questions? What strategies will you use to draw a sample and to gather information?

KEY TERMS

data analysis—The systematic and rigorous examination of a collection of information (i.e., the data, such as all of the responses to a questionnaire or the text in all of the transcripts from personal interviews) to identify patterns, themes, and relationships.

ethnography—A form of qualitative inquiry focused on the description and interpretation of culture and cultural behavior. Ethnography typically involves fieldwork where participant observation, interviews, and field notes are used to gather data.

experiment—A strategy of data collection and analysis associated with the scientific method where an event or intervention is examined for its effect on some outcome. An experimental researcher controls and manipulates the participants, variables, setting, and timing of the process to ensure that any effect on the outcome variable can be attributed to the event or intervention.

grounded theory—A set of procedures for generating substantive theory concerning social phenomena. Grounded theory is normally linked to induction, where theory is derived from the analysis of data using a process called *constant comparison* and theoretical sampling of people or events.

phenomenology—Often considered both a philosophy and a methodology, phenomenology involves the in-depth exploration and detailed description of the subjective meanings and experiences of everyday life.

qualitative methods—Typically associated with an interpretivist or constructionist perspective of research and with strategies of data collection, organization, analysis, and interpretation involving text, images, audio media, or observations.

quantitative methods—Typically associated with an objectivist or postpositivist perspective of research and with strategies of data collection, organization, analysis, and interpretation involving data gathered in or converted to numeric form.

sampling—The process involving the systematic procedures for the selection of research participants. In quantitative approaches, sampling procedures are focused on generating a large group of participants who are representative of the population to allow for the generalization of results. In qualitative approaches, sampling procedures are focused on gathering key informants (i.e., people judged to have particular insights into the phenomenon under study).

survey—A research design using a representative sample of individuals drawn from the population who complete questionnaires or structured interviews to generate data used to make inferences about the population. The principal part of survey design is the development, administration, and collection of a questionnaire (i.e., the specific instrument of data collection) that provides the data, usually handled numerically, for subsequent analysis and interpretation.

LEARNING ACTIVITIES

At the beginning of the chapter, you were asked to imagine that you are a public recreation employee working for the local department of parks, recreation, and culture, and you have the responsibility of developing and planning programs and services for the older adults living in your community. Suppose you are interested in identifying the leisure behaviors, perceptions, and experiences of older adults in your midsized community and how these aspects of their lives might be related to their quality of life. You decide to conduct a study to explore these ideas in greater detail.

We will work with this scenario through each stage of the hypothetical study. You will find it useful in designing your study to consult some of the resources referred to throughout the chapter.

Stage 1: Writing the Purpose and Research Questions

As a first step, you have decided to establish a clear purpose for the study and develop research questions that will bring you closer to understanding the lives of the older adults.

Quantitative Research Approach

a. Write a statement of purpose that will guide your research based on a quantitative research approach.

b. Develop three research questions on specific aspects of the study that need to be examined in order to achieve your purpose.

Qualitative Research Approach

a. Write a statement of purpose that will guide your research based on a qualitative research approach.

b. Develop three research questions on specific aspects of the study that you feel need to be examined in order to achieve your purpose.

Once you have developed your purpose statement and research questions for each research approach, reflect on these questions: (1) How do the purpose statements differ between your qualitative and quantitative research approaches? In what way? (2) How do the research questions differ between your qualitative and quantitative research approaches? In what way?

Stage 2: Designing the Study

Now that you have determined the purpose of your study and developed the research questions, the next step involves selecting an appropriate research design. The approach you select will differ depending on whether you choose to conduct a qualitative or quantitative research design.

Quantitative Research Approach

a. Assuming you are going to distribute a self-administered questionnaire, design a sampling strategy that would generate a representative sample of all adults in the community aged 65 years and older. As you consider your plan, ask yourself the following questions:

– How would you define the survey population?

– Is there a sampling frame you could use from which to select a representative sample?

– How many participants do you hope to include in the final sample?

– What sampling strategy will you use for selecting potential participants?

– In what ways would you try to increase your response rate?

b. Design a two-page questionnaire with a set of close-ended questions for the older adults to complete. Be sure that the questions you create will gather the data you need to answer your research questions.

Qualitative Research Approach

a. Assuming you are going to conduct personal interviews, design a strategy to recruit a sample of participants that will best enable you to conduct your study. As you consider your plan, ask yourself the following questions:

– What criteria might you use to recruit potential participants?

– How many participants do you anticipate including in the final sample? What factors might affect the final number?

– How will you select and recruit potential participants?

b. Design an interview guide with an initial three or four questions and some appropriate probes you might use in your interview that explore the participants' perspectives and experiences associated with your research questions.

Stage 3: Conducting the Study Ethically

You have a clear purpose of study and research questions and you have developed and settled on a research design. Now, you are planning to begin data collection. As part of the entire research process, you want to ensure that you are acting as ethically as possible.

Regardless of whether you are using a quantitative or a qualitative approach, ask yourself the following questions to ensure you are acting ethically throughout the research process:

a. What steps should you take to ensure that the participants are able to provide informed consent?

b. How might you provide the opportunity for meaningful engagement by participants? How would this opportunity differ between the two approaches (e.g., even though the older adults might be completing your questionnaire anonymously, how could they be more engaged)?

c. How will you provide feedback to participants to ensure that they are informed about the progress and outcomes of your study?

d. What steps you will take to protect the confidentiality of your participants?

SUGGESTED READING

The resources suggested here by no means represent a comprehensive list of the references on specific research methods and approaches to analysis. Nevertheless, they are among the most popular sources in the social sciences, especially in leisure research.

Survey Design and Research

A large number of books dedicated to survey research design are available that go into great detail on all aspects of survey development, design, administration, collection, and analysis. Here are some of the more popular sources.

Dillman, D.A. (2000). *Mail and Internet surveys: The tailored design method* (2nd ed.). Toronto: Wiley.

Fink, A. (Ed.). (2003). *The survey kit* (Vol. 1-10). Thousand Oaks, CA: Sage.

Fowler, F.J., Jr. (1993).*Survey research methods* (2nd ed.). Newbury Park, CA: Sage.

Vaske, J.J. (2008). *Survey research and analysis: Applications in parks, recreation, and human dimensions.* State College, PA: Venture.

Experimental and Quasi-Experimental Research Designs

Shadish, W.E., Cook, T.D., & Campbell, D.T. (2002).*Experimental and quasi-experimental designs for generalized causal inference.* Boston: Houghton Mifflin.

Descriptive and Inferential Statistics for Quantitative Data Analysis

Gravetter, F.J., &Wallnau, L.B. (1992). *Statistics for the behavioral sciences* (3rd ed.). St. Paul, MN: West.

Kiess, H.O. (2002). *Statistical concepts for the behavioral sciences* (3rd ed.). Boston: Allyn and Bacon.

Rowntree, D. (2004). *Statistics without tears: A primer for non-mathematicians.* Boston: Allyn and Bacon.

Williams, F., & Monge, P. (2001). *Reasoning with statistics: How to read quantitative research.* Orlando, FL: Harcourt College.

The analysis of quantitative data can be facilitated with the application of the popular statistical software package, SPSS (now called *PASW*). These are helpful guides for the latest versions:

Norušis, M.J. (2009). *SPSS 17.0 guide to data analysis.* Upper Saddle River, NJ: Pearson Education.

Norušis, M.J. (2010). *PASW statistics 18 guide to data analysis.* Upper Saddle River, NJ: Pearson Education.

Grounded Theory

Bryant, A., & Charmaz, K. (Eds.). (2007). *The Sage handbook of grounded theory.* Thousand Oaks, CA: Sage.

Charmaz, K. (2006). *Constructing grounded theory: A practical guide through qualitative analysis.* London: Sage.

Ethnography

Atkinson, P., Coffey, A., Delamont, S., Lofland, J., & Lofland, L. (Eds.). (2001). *Handbook of ethnography.* Thousand Oaks, CA: Sage.

Interviews

Gubrium, J.F., & Holstein, J.A. (Eds.). (2002). *Handbook of interview research: Context and method.* Thousand Oaks, CA: Sage.

Kvale, S., & Brinkmann, S. (2009). *Interviews: Learning the craft of qualitative research interviewing* (2nd ed.). Thousand Oaks, CA: Sage.

Wenger, G.C. (2002). Interviewing older people. In J.F. Gubrium & J.A. Holstein (Eds.), *Handbook of interview research: Context and method* (pp. 259-278). Thousand Oaks, CA: Sage.

Focus Groups

Krueger, R.A. (1988). *Focus groups: A practical guide for applied research.* Newbury Park, CA: Sage.

Krueger, R.A. (1998). *Moderating focus groups.* Thousand Oaks, CA: Sage.

Morgan, D.L. (1998). *The focus group guidebook.* Thousand Oaks, CA: Sage.

Morgan, D.L. (2000). Focus group interviewing. In J. Gubrium & J. Holstein (Eds.), *Handbook of interview research: Context and method* (pp. 141-160). Thousand Oaks, CA: Sage

Analysis and Interpretation of Qualitative Data

Many approaches to the analysis of data gathered in qualitative studies have been developed, most of which are linked to a particular research design. For example, the constant comparative method of data analysis is specific to grounded theory. Some practical guides to strategies of analysis include the following:

Bernard, H.R., & Ryan, G.W. (2010). *Analyzing qualitative data: Systematic approaches.* Thousand Oaks, CA: Sage

Coffey, A.J., & Atkinson, P.A. (1996). *Making sense of qualitative data: Complementary research strategies.* Thousand Oaks, CA: Sage.

Gibbs, G.R. (2008). *Analyzing qualitative data.* Thousand Oaks, CA: Sage.

Reflexivity

Alvesson, M., & Sköldberg, K. (2009). *Reflexive methodology* (2nd ed.). Los Angeles: Sage.

Ethics in Research

Palys, T. (2003). *Research decisions: Quantitative and qualitative perspectives* (3rd ed.). Scarborough, ON: Nelson.

REFERENCES

Atchley, R.C. (1971). Retirement and leisure participation: Continuity or crisis? *Gerontologist, 11,* 13-17.

Atchley, R.C. (1989). A continuity theory of normal aging. *Gerontologist, 29,* 183-190.

Atchley, R.C. (1999). *Continuity and adaptation in aging: Creating positive experiences.* Baltimore: Johns Hopkins University Press.

Babbie, E.R. (2007). *The practice of social research* (11th ed.). Belmont, CA: Thomson Wadsworth.

Benisovich, S., & King, A. (2003). Meaning and knowledge of health among older adult immigrants from Russia: A phenomenological study. *Health Education Research, 18,* 135-144.

Bryant, A., & Charmaz, K. (Eds.). (2007). *The Sage handbook of grounded theory.* Thousand Oaks, CA: Sage.

Bryman, A., Teevan, J.J., & Bell, E. (2009). *Social research methods* (2nd ed.). Don Mills, ON: Oxford University Press.

Charmaz, K. (2003). Grounded theory: Objectivist and constructivist methods. In N.K. Denzin & Y.S. Lincoln (Eds.), *Strategies for qualitative inquiry* (2nd ed., pp. 249-291). Thousand Oaks, CA: Sage.

Charmaz, K. (2006). *Constructing grounded theory: A practical guide through qualitative analysis.* London: Sage.

Crotty, M. (1998). *The foundations of social research: Meaning and perspective in the research process.* London: Sage.

Cumming, E., & Henry, W. (1961). *Growing old.* New York: Basic Books.

Denzin, N.K., & Lincoln, Y.S. (2005a). The discipline and practice of qualitative research. In N.K. Denzin & Y.S. Lincoln (Eds.), *The Sage handbook of qualitative research* (3rd ed., pp. 1-29). Thousand Oaks, CA: Sage.

Denzin, N.K., & Lincoln, Y.S. (Eds.). (2005b). *The Sage handbook of qualitative research* (3rd ed.). Thousand Oaks, CA: Sage.

Dupuis, S.L. (1999). Naked truths: Towards a reflexive methodology in leisure research. *Leisure Sciences, 21,* 43-64.

Dupuis, S.L., Smale, B., & Wiersma, E. (2005). Creating open environments in long-term care settings: An examination of influencing factors. *Therapeutic Recreation Journal, 39,* 277-298.

Garcia-Villamisar, D.A., & Dattilo, J. (2010). Effects of a leisure programme on quality of life and stress of individuals with ASD. *Journal of Intellectual Disability Research, 54,* 611-619.

Hardy, S., & Grogan, S. (2009). Preventing disability through exercise: Investigating older adults' influences and motivations to engage in physical activity. *Journal of Health Psychology, 14,* 1036-1046.

Havighurst, R.J. (1961). Successful aging. *Gerontologist, 1,* 8-13.

Lemon, B.W., Bengtson, V.L., & Peterson, J.A. (1972). An exploration of the activity theory of aging: Activity types and life satisfaction among in-movers to a retirement community. *Journal of Gerontology, 27,* 511-523.

Morse, J.M. (2007). Sampling in grounded theory. In A. Bryant & K. Charmaz (Eds.), *The Sage handbook of grounded theory* (pp. 229-244). Thousand Oaks, CA: Sage.

Neuendorf, K.A. (2002). *The content analysis handbook.* Thousand Oaks, CA: Sage.

Neuman, W.L., & Robson, K. (2009). *Basics of social research: Qualitative and quantitative approaches* (Can. ed.). Toronto: Pearson Education.

Parse, R.R. (1981). *Man-living-health: A theory of nursing.* New York: Wiley.

Parse, R.R. (1987). *Nursing science: Major paradigms, theories, and critiques.* Philadelphia: Saunders.

Parse, R.R. (1992). Human becoming: Parse's theory of nursing. *Nursing Science Quarterly, 5,* 35-42.

Paulson, S. (2005). How various 'cultures of fitness' shape subjective experiences of growing older. *Ageing &Society, 25,* 229-244.

Payne, L.L., Mowen, A.J., & Montoro-Rodriguez, J. (2006). The role of leisure style in maintaining the health of older adults with arthritis. *Journal of Leisure Research, 38,* 20-45.

Royse, D., Thyer, B.A., & Padgett, D.K. (2010). *Program evaluation: An introduction* (5th ed.). Belmont, CA: Wadsworth Cengage Learning.

van Manen, M. (1997). *Researching lived experience: Human science for an action sensitive pedagogy* (2nd ed.). London, ON: Althouse Press.

CHAPTER 5

Leisure Across the Later Life Span

Galit Nimrod ■ Megan C. Janke

After reading this chapter, you will be able to

- recognize how developmental and systems theories can be used to explain changes in leisure across the life course;
- understand how leisure behavior changes across the later life span and what sociodemographic factors influence older adults' leisure involvement;
- discuss how the meaning of leisure may be influenced during later life;
- explain how common later-life transitions, such as retirement and spousal loss, can affect older adults' leisure; and
- identify leisure as a resource in coping with the changes associated with aging.

eisure is not static—not when we are young, not when we are old. Our lives change all the time. We become adults, we acquire education, and many of us get married and have children. Sometimes we change our jobs and careers. We might move to another neighborhood, city, or country. Some of us get divorced and remarry, establishing a new family or changing the dynamics in our existing families. As we age, our children will likely leave home and start their own independent lives, changing our home dynamics once again. As our lives change, we experience changes in our leisure as well.

Leisure across the life span has been studied extensively for several decades. This area of research has both theoretical and practical implications. From a theoretical perspective, the motivation is to understand why and how leisure changes as we age. Each new phase in life brings about new circumstances, new needs and motivations, and sometimes even new constraints. For example, having children may lead to changes in a person's living environment as well as in hours spent working outside the home. It may increase the need and desire for family recreation but may also lead to new limitations in spending time with loved ones such as less energy and a lack of time. Investigating such changes can contribute to our understanding of the role of leisure in adjusting to and **coping** with changes in life. It also enhances our knowledge about the central and peripheral components of leisure and about the role of continuity and change in leisure, which in turn influences theory (for example, continuity theory and innovation theory described in chapter 3). From a practical perspective, such investigations in changes in leisure across the life span may enhance leisure service providers' understanding of their audiences. Enhanced awareness of the needs and constraints experienced during various life phases may eventually lead to better programming and services in the field.

Life-Span Development Models

In the last 50 years, models of individual development across the life course have emerged from various disciplines such as psychology, sociology, economics, and marketing. Two of the most prevalent models are **life-span developmental theory** (Baltes, 1979) and **life-course perspective** (Elder, 1974). Both of these theories suggest that human development is a multidirectional and continual process—that is, that development across the life

span is characterized by gains and losses from birth to death. These theories also indicate that transitions occur throughout the life span, including later life, which may change the trajectory of a person's development. Some influential transitions in later life include the birth of a grandchild and becoming a grandparent, the onset of disease or disability, retirement from the workforce, and the loss of a spouse. All of these experiences have the ability to affect adults' physical, mental, and social well-being as well as their leisure behavior. In addition, important components of our identities may change as a result of these transitions.

Life-span models also address the notion that the context of a person's development is crucial. Contextual factors such as historical events, the timing of events in a person's life, and socioeconomic and cultural factors shape how a person develops and adapts across the life span. These contextual factors allow for a great degree of difference in the development of people while providing some rationale for similarities in the development of people of similar ages, birth cohorts (groups of people born during a particular period, such as the baby boomers), or backgrounds. For example, these models provide a framework for examining differences among older adults who have never married, those who have become widowed, and those who have postdivorce or postwidowhood remarriages. They also allow us to explore cohort differences among adults and to examine the effect of change in this context, such as the influence of computers and the Internet on older adults' development.

Soon after the life-span models were introduced, researchers began to explore aspects of leisure behavior across the life cycle. For example, some studies examined how family and changes in family structure influenced leisure across stages of development (Rapoport & Rapoport, 1975). They noted that leisure is an important factor in creating a meaningful life, but what is meaningful varies according to one's personality and life-cycle stage. Another study (Osgood & Howe, 1984) furthered this movement by exploring psychological aspects of leisure across the life course. This investigation related specifically to white, middle-class, American adults and identified the importance of people's values, motives, and meanings of leisure. These relevant works enhanced our knowledge about leisure behavior across the life course and increased interest in the importance of leisure involvement in various stages of life, such as older adulthood.

The Internet as a Leisure Resource Across the Later Life Span

The percentage of Internet users among people who are 60 years old and over grows rapidly every year. Consequently, the Internet is a significant resource in older adults' leisure in various ways, the first being as an activity in itself. Older adults use many leisure activities offered by the Internet, such as watching the news, playing games, and engaging in virtual hobbies (Opalinski, 2001). Moreover, the Internet is an instrument for learning, planning, and purchasing leisure services. The endless information available on the Internet helps seniors learn about various leisure opportunities, make plans, and even purchase leisure services and products, such as flights, books, or hiking shoes.

Another role of the Internet as a resource is in maintaining social networks with family and friends. It helps remove geographic and transportation limits, and it even assists in bridging the generation gap with children and grandchildren (Burdick, 2001). It can also provide context for forming new friendships, as in the case of seniors' online communities (Nimrod, 2010). Such new relationships may compensate for the loss of friends as a result of retirement, relocation, physical or mental disability, or death.

Since the Internet offers both leisure activity and social interaction, it may help older adults to cope with stress, losses, and negative events, thus contributing to their well-being. Research (e.g., Dickenson & Hill, 2007; Fokkema & Knipscheer, 2007) has demonstrated that Internet use is associated with higher levels of social connectivity, higher levels of perceived social support, decreased feelings of loneliness, lower levels of depression, and generally more positive attitudes toward aging. In addition, involvement in the virtual world is likely to strengthen the self-image and self-confidence of elderly people.

Internet use is an indoor activity that does not require any physical effort; therefore, it is suitable for people who are physically constrained, who lack mobility, or who are afraid to leave home for various reasons. Except for the initial cost of purchasing a computer, an Internet connection is usually inexpensive, so it is quite available in terms of cost, and its potential benefits are many. In the case of the oldest old, it may offer an alternative to the television viewing that occupies most of their leisure time. This alternative may allow not only for passive exposure to content but also more active participation in various online activities that involve social interactions, intellectual challenges, and creative outlets.

Other life-span development models have approached the study of development from the perspective of the environment and the nested systems involved in human development. One such model is Bronfenbrenner's (1979) **ecological systems theory**, which highlights the structures and systems in the environment that shape people's growth and experiences (see chapter 3). As discussed earlier in the text, this model defines four levels of our environment: the microsystem (immediate environment such as a person's work or family), mesosystem (connections between two or more microsystems), exosystem (external environments such as community service providers), and macrosystem (such as culture, customs, or political climate). All of these environments provide a context that can affect and be affected by involvement in leisure across the life span.

The current knowledge on continuity and change in leisure across the life span has been derived from three types of studies:

- **Cross-sectional investigations** examine the general population at a certain point in time, split the sample into age groups, and then compare the leisure patterns of the groups. Cross-sectional studies may provide thorough knowledge about both age differences and cohort differences. As suggested by the previously discussed theories and models, adults' leisure may be affected by the specific circumstances they grew up in, their life history, and their values. Cross-sectional studies cannot quantify the effect of these intergenerational differences, and thus they cannot accurately determine which changes result from aging and which result from differences in cultural, social, or historical events in their lives.

- **Retrospective examinations** explore changes in leisure participation following transitions or important events in life. In these studies, people are interviewed about changes in their leisure after the life transition occurred and are asked to reflect on their past leisure patterns and behaviors. The methods used may be qualitative or quantitative (see chapter 4). Since the changes are examined for each individual, retrospective-based studies do not reflect cohort differences in older adults' leisure. However, retrospective-based studies might be biased because they raise reasonable doubts as to the credibility of adults' reports of their involvement, particularly if respondents are asked to report what happened in their lives many years ago. The described changes in these studies should be regarded then as perceived changes rather than actual ones.

- **Longitudinal research** involves repeating the same measurement with the same population and even with the same group of people (i.e., panel study). Longitudinal studies are beneficial in that they allow us to examine actual change within and between people over time. These studies can avoid the aforementioned cohort effects and memory biases. Yet, findings might be influenced by the changing social, economic, and technological environment and therefore might not reflect the effect of aging alone.

Most studies use only one of these methodologies and thus do not provide a complete picture of adults' leisure behavior in later life. Yet, comprehensive integration of findings from a variety of studies may provide rather consistent and detailed descriptions of change in leisure across the life span in general and in later life in particular.

One problem with the existing body of knowledge regarding leisure across the later life span is that most studies have disregarded certain phases of the life course. The life-span models reinforce that later life is not one homogeneous phase and that many stages or transitions, such as empty nest (children left home), retirement, widowhood, and physical disability, occur during this period. Yet, these stages have rarely been differentiated in leisure research. In many studies, for example, no distinction was made between changes in leisure that occurred due to entering the retirement phase and those related to the onset of physical disability or other transitions. Moreover, some research has not differentiated the retired from those still in the workforce, simply characterizing the older adult population in general. Furthermore, most studies about continuity and change in leisure in later

life have examined only the behavioral aspect of leisure without addressing the consequential psychological effects of such behavior. In addition, previous studies have examined continuity and change without taking into account individual inclinations or type segmentation in leisure. These studies presented the overall leisure patterns of older people in aggregate form (presenting the average) while not exploring or referring to the patterns of behavior that were evident in leisure involvement in later life.

Changes in Leisure Behavior as People Age

Despite some methodological and conceptual weaknesses of previous research, most studies conducted since the early 1960s have provided a detailed picture of leisure in later life. Based on findings from hundreds of studies, it is possible to argue that there are four main changes in leisure behavior as people age.

1. **Decline in participation.** As people age, they tend to decrease their participation in leisure. They reduce the number of activities they take part in as well as the frequency of their participation in continued activities (Katz, Hass, Weitz, Adoni, Gurevitch, et al., 2000; Iso-Ahola, Jackson, & Dunn, 1994; Lefrancois, Leclerc, & Poulin, 1998; van der Meer, 2008).

2. **Shift from active to more passive leisure.** With age, people tend to reduce their involvement in physical activities and move to activities that demand less physical effort. This tendency is intensified by the occurrence of constraining health conditions and aggravations from chronic conditions (Lefrancois et al., 1998; McPherson, 1984). In fact, the decline in adults' involvement in physical leisure activities may likely be more a result of the onset of disease and disability than age (Janke, Davey, & Kleiber, 2006).

3. **Shift from outdoor leisure to indoor activities.** In accordance with the shift to more passive leisure, there is also a shift to indoor activities. Particularly for the oldest old, the outcome is substantial time spent in discretionary activities done alone and at home, with television viewing being most prevalent (Robinson & Godbey, 1997). This may also lead to more activities done with

family members and close friends, since these activities may be considered as more salient to adults during this phase of life.

4. **Decline in search for novelty.** As people age, they are less interested in exploring new leisure pursuits and tend to prefer activities they are accustomed to. Cases have been reported in which peripheral or unsatisfying activities are abandoned and more time given to the most enriching activities (Atchley, 1989; Iso-Ahola et al., 1994). This may also relate to social activities—the **socioemotional selectivity (SES) theory** (Carstensen, 1993) suggests that with age, adults' desire to meet new people and form new relationships decreases, and they are most interested in spending time with close family and friends.

Two classic cross-sectional studies may demonstrate these four main changes. Robinson and Godbey (1997) compared time use of age groups and also examined subgroups within the older population. Comparing people who were 65 and older with people who were 55 to 64 years old demonstrated that the former spent more time watching TV, reading, and volunteering. They participated less than the younger group in studies, physical activities, social gatherings, and cultural events. Dividing the older group further into two segments (65-74 and 75 and older) revealed that the oldest segment spent more time on media and was less involved in physical activities, traveling, and hobbies.

A study by Iso-Ahola and colleagues (1994) examined changes in leisure among age groups across the life span (23 and younger, 24-43, 44-63, and 64 and older). Findings indicated that the number of people adding new activities declined with age, while the number of people who continued activities grew. There were also differences in the type of activities added—older adults were less inclined to add a new physical activity such as team sport or outdoor recreation, and they tended to add more hobbies and home-based recreation.

Although the four changes characterizing leisure in later life describe general trends, they do not apply to all activities and all subgroups. Personal resources such as income and education may buffer the impact of age on leisure activities (Katz et al., 2000) and influence involvement in these activities. There are also significant differences in leisure involvement by gender. Older

women's leisure may be less affected by health decline (Stanley & Freysinger, 1995), and women tend to be more innovative and take up more new activities than do men (Iso-Ahola et al., 1994). Women in later life also tend to be less involved in physical leisure activities compared with men and more involved in social and community activities (Janke et al., 2006), patterns that are generally consistent across the life span. Additionally, the living environment has an effect on adults' leisure; people who live in more urban areas maintain higher levels of involvement in leisure activities compared with people living in rural areas (Lefrancois et al., 1998).

Therefore, even though the general trend is reduced involvement in leisure during later life, we may still find people who have broad activity patterns into their late 80s and 90s (van der Meer, 2008) and who maintain a high level of leisure satisfaction due to continued participation in perhaps more limited, but still valued, activities (Griffin & McKenna, 1998). There are even some adults who try out new leisure activities despite chronic health conditions that limit their abilities to participate in various activities (Nimrod & Hutchinson, 2010).

Changes in Leisure Meanings as People Age

Parallel to the changes in leisure behavior, there seem to be various changes in the meaning of leisure as people age. Many of these changes are associated with the *centrality* of leisure in the lives of older adults. During adulthood people have three main sources of meaning in life: their careers, their families, and their leisure activities. Moreover, leisure is sometimes secondary in importance to work and family at points across the life course. When adults retire from work and their children leave home and start their own families, leisure may become a more central life domain in which they find meaning. Thus, at some points leisure may become one of the most important factors that shape older adults' sense of identity (Frazier, 2002). Yet at other times during older adulthood, such as when dealing with caregiving responsibilities for a spouse, leisure may again need to be put on the back burner to focus on family (Bedini & Guinan, 1996; Bedini & Phoenix, 2004).

As the centrality of leisure in our lives changes, the impact of leisure on well-being may also be affected. The role of leisure activity in later life

iStockphoto / Eduardo Jose Bernardino

For older adults, involvement in activities is strongly associated with well-being.

has been examined in numerous studies (see chapters 7-9). Although its effect on older adults' well-being appears to vary in different contexts and subgroups, most evidence shows a strong positive association between activity involvement and well-being in old age (e.g., Fernandez-Ballesteros, Zamarron, & Ruiz, 2001; Nimrod, 2007a, 2007b). Leisure can become a replacement for work, especially when a person is involved in hobbies, amateur activities, or volunteer activities that can be described as serious leisure (Stebbins, 2006). This type of involvement may lead to many durable psychological benefits such as self-esteem and sense of belonging.

Relatively few studies have explored change and continuity in adults' perceptions of leisure or the meaning that leisure has in the lives of adults. Gibson, Ashton-Shaeffer, Green, and Autry (2003/2004) examined perceptions of leisure among retirement-aged women. Their findings

indicated that women who had valued leisure throughout their lives tended to have positive attitudes toward retirement and perceived leisure as a reward. Conversely, women with low leisure ethic resisted retirement and felt that they were being viewed as old and unproductive (Gibson, Ashton-Shaeffer, Green, & Corbin, 2002). A Study of Leisure During Adulthood (ASOLDA) was a longitudinal study of adults conducted by Carpenter from 1987 to 1996. This study collected information from people every year regarding their perceptions of leisure and the events that occurred in the past 12 months. The results from this study indicate that the meaning of leisure in one's life and perceptions of leisure remain relatively constant across adulthood (Carpenter, 1989). However, the findings also suggest that social roles, responsibilities, and life events are key factors that shape adults' perceptions of leisure (Carpenter & Murray, 2002).

The centrality of leisure in later life is also threatened by the continual increase in the number and level of constraints to leisure that characterize old age. Four types of constraints influence older adults' leisure (Nimrod, 2003):

- Cultural-environmental constraints, such as social isolation, the need to behave according to certain age-related norms, and a lack of companions as a result of friends' and relatives' increasing limitations and mortality
- Health-related constraints, including physiological (e.g., disabilities, chronic illness, or decreased energy) and psychophysiological (e.g., concentration or memory problems)
- Psychological constraints, such as lower motivation, low self-efficacy, and fear
- Technical constraints, such as income, availability of activities, mobility, and time

As a result of these constraints, continuous involvement in leisure activities becomes a challenge.

Research has provided contradictory findings regarding the strength and dominance of various constraints. Yet, it consistently demonstrates that the number and impact of **leisure constraints** increase as people age (McGuire, 1985; McGuire & Norman, 2005). Several studies identified various positive responses to constraints, such as resilience and deepened commitment, attention to other goals, exploration and self-discovery, and changes in attitude toward life and leisure (Kleiber, McGuire, Aybar-Damali, & Norman, 2008; Kleiber

& Nimrod, 2009). However, constraints may also lead to frustration and eventually the reduction and elimination of leisure involvement (Kleiber & Nimrod, 2009; van der Meer, 2008).

Facing more constraints to leisure with age, adults are commonly forced to give up activities they love. As a result, the diversity of activity patterns among people in their eighth or ninth decade of life decreases, and the role of leisure and its importance in their lives may change. At the same time, the salience of other issues such as health, life review, values, and ideals may expand (Frazier, 2002; Prager, 1997). People often become less activity-oriented and more self-reflecting and preoccupied with their personal lives. This shift may be explained by several theories of adult development that emphasize internal growth in later life, such as Vaillant's (2002) model and gerotranscendence theory (see chapter 3).

As people age, leisure seems to be less of a goal and more of a means (Nimrod, 2011). Among their reasons for choosing specific activities, very old adults report a variety of instrumental motives such as keeping healthy and maintaining cognitive abilities (Kolt, 2002). In addition, some leisure activities, such as exercising or social activities, are perceived as preserving one's youth (Dionigi, 2006; Yarnal, 2006), and social activities may provide an opportunity to connect with loved ones. This change in meaning proposes that leisure has a distinctive role in the lives of the oldest old, which may be described as a *resource for resilience* (Nimrod, 2011). Leisure provides cumulative protective factors that help older adults cope with and resist the cumulative risk factors posed by the aging process.

Leisure and Later-Life Transitions

Changes in leisure behavior, as well as in the meaning and significance of leisure, are often catalyzed by **life transitions**. There are many possible life transitions in later life. Some of them, such as retirement, are predictable, and people may plan and prepare for them many years in advance. Others, such as the sudden death of one's spouse, are unexpected. Although these events may be normative for this period in life and adults are aware that they are a possibility, they still may come as a shock and require a long process of acceptance and coping. Even those events that are anticipated may be accompanied by some degree of stress.

Later-life transitions may occur suddenly, and some last only a short time. Others, such as health deterioration, may be gradual and occur over several months or even years. Transitions such as widowhood are typically perceived as negative, while others, such as becoming a grandparent, are positive. Often, transitions such as retirement or widowhood after several years of caregiving may result in mixed emotions from older adults. Moreover, the same transition may be perceived as positive by one person and as negative by another. For example, to some people, moving to a seniors' community may represent an opportunity for more social interactions and leisure activities. For others, however, it represents a loss of independence and a move to the last station in life (see chapters 12 and 13). To further complicate the issue, adults may experience several of these changes simultaneously. These changes and how they are perceived affect people's development and leisure.

Several studies have explored how transitions affect older adults' leisure patterns and engagement in leisure activities, but it is less certain how these transitions affect adults' perceptions of leisure and the meaning of leisure in later life. One recent study using the ASOLDA dataset found that although adults' attitudes about leisure and their perceptions of freedom to engage in leisure appear relatively stable across time, life experiences and events appear to affect how we view leisure in our lives (Janke, Carpenter, Payne, & Stockard, 2011). It seems that when adults experience positive life events, their attitudes about leisure tend to be more positive. In addition, when adults view their lives to be in a period of stability, when no major changes or transitions are occurring, they report a greater perception of freedom to engage in leisure activities. A study by Gibson and colleagues (2002) examined perceptions of leisure among retirement-aged women. Findings indicated an association between perceptions of the life event (i.e., retirement) and leisure attitudes and behavior. Women who resisted retirement or needed to be useful tended to deemphasize the importance of leisure and create second careers for themselves, usually as volunteers, whereas other women felt entitled to leisure and constructed their lives around it.

Whether predicted or unexpected, sudden or gradual, negative or positive, all life transitions require some level of adjustment. They all represent a move to a new life phase and thus involve changes in roles that may be reflected in leisure behaviors and meanings. In addition, leisure appears to be a central factor explaining successful coping with later-life transitions and negative life events (Duggleby, Bateman, & Singer, 2002). Maintaining relationships with family and friends, pursuing spirituality, and staying physically and mentally active and involved have all been related to more effective coping with retirement (Nimrod, 2007a, 2007b; Nimrod, Janke, & Kleiber, 2008), spousal loss (e.g., Janke, Nimrod, & Kleiber, 2008a, 2008b, 2008c), and adapting to disability and major changes in health status (e.g., Duke, Leventhal, Brownlee, & Leventhal, 2002; Silverstein & Parker, 2002).

The scope of this chapter does not allow an elaboration on every possible life transition in later life, but two common transitions are worth closer attention here: retirement and spousal loss. How older adults perceive these experiences can vary widely based on the circumstances leading to these transitions. For example, retirement has a different connotation for adults who choose to leave the workplace than for those who leave due to a change in health status, the onset of caregiving responsibilities, or being forced into taking early retirement. In the same manner, the loss of a spouse may be experienced differently based on several factors such as closeness of the marital relationship, the role of the spouse as a caregiver, gender, age, and availability of a support system. Participation in leisure activities may vary widely as people adapt to these life events, and research suggests that patterns of leisure involvement may be related to older adults' coping and well-being.

Retirement

Retirement is a relatively new concept and did not emerge in the United States until the 1930s. As stated earlier in this chapter, adults are often perceived as looking forward to retirement and planning for this transition, but this is not always the case. Some people have difficulty contemplating

Early Retirement

Sigal Naim*

Early retirement is defined as retiring before the determined mandatory age. In many cases, such retirement is used by organizations as an efficiency mechanism for releasing older employees without firing them. Thus, it is based on a financial agreement with the employer. There are two types of early retirement: willing and unwilling. While some employees choose to retire, others are forced to do so by the employer. This appears to be a key distinction in understanding the experience of early retirement. Forced retirement for any reason may cause a sense of humiliation, loss of control, and trauma (Beck, 1982; Kimmel, Price, & Walker, 1978).

As with mandatory and late retirement, early retirement requires preparation and adjustment. Adjustment can take place in several ways, including starting a new career, taking a part-time job, or volunteering (Stein, 2000). Such behaviors are known as bridge behaviors, providing a gradual transition from the workforce to full retirement (Feldman, 1994; Stein, 2000).

In a qualitative study (Naim, 2009) with Israeli men who chose to retire early (i.e., before the mandatory age of 67 years old), interviewees provided two types of justifications for early retirement: organizational (i.e., changes in the workplace) and personal (i.e., strong wish to retire). The construction of early retirement was usually a combination of the two. None of these men considered themselves as aged, and all of them stressed the importance of mental and financial preparation for retirement. The early retirement was perceived as a turning point affecting the person's identity. Past employment was still a strong component in postretirement identity, but other activities, such as volunteering, caring for a grandchild, or hobbies, took central place. Although these were freely chosen leisure activities, they were usually described as work and were characterized by high levels of involvement and responsibility. The major difference was that in their new leisure-jobs, interviewees felt they were their own bosses and had greater control over the time and pace of the activity.

*Sigal Naim is a PhD candidate in the department of communication studies at Ben-Gurion University of the Negev, Israel.

retirement because their work is such an integral part of their identity. Others wish to retire but are unable to do so because of their financial situations. Research typically proposes two types of retirement—blurred and crisp. A **crisp retirement** fits the traditional view of retirement. In this situation, an older person retires from the workforce and never returns. In a **blurred retirement**, people transfer in and out of the workforce in older adulthood. This may be due to factors such as economic pressures, boredom, a need to feel productive, part-time work as a hobby, and so on. Blurred retirement is becoming much more typical among older adults in the United States. Yet, neither of these types may accurately depict a person's retirement experience. For example, the retirement literature (e.g., Calasanti, 1996) suggests that women never fully retire. Although they leave the paid workforce, they do not give up their work in the home.

Two studies (Nimrod, 2007a; Nimrod, Janke, & Kleiber, 2009) explored how adults' involvement in leisure activities changed as they entered retirement by examining both the types of activities engaged in (scope) and the frequency of involvement in such activities. Based on changes or continuity in the scope and frequency of leisure involvement across this transition, four classifications were created: expanders, concentrators, diffusers, and reducers. Those adults who increased the number of activities they engaged in and had more activities with increased frequency than activities with decreased frequency were classified as **expanders**. **Concentrators** were those who had more maintained activities with increased frequency than maintained activities with decreased frequency but did not change or decrease the number of types of activities they engaged in during

the transition to retirement. Adults who increased the number of activities they were involved in but did not increase (or decreased) the frequency of their involvement in those activities were **diffusers**. **Reducers** were defined as those who did not increase (or decreased) the number of their leisure activities and had the same or more maintained activities with decreased frequency than maintained activities with increased frequency.

Using this typology, studies of recent retirees in Israel (Nimrod, 2007a) and in the United States (Nimrod et al., 2009) found that despite having more free time, the majority of retirees in both countries reduced their involvement in leisure, while expanders made up the second largest group. Concentrators and diffusers constituted only small parts of the samples (see table 5.1). These findings demonstrate that there is great variability in how adults use their time in retirement. It also highlights that although we often believe that retirement is a time of leisure and that older adults will increase their involvement in leisure activities once they leave the workplace, this is not necessarily true for a large percentage of people.

Research suggests that health and well-being during the transition to retirement are relatively stable as long as the transition is voluntary. Theories of successful aging such as the activity theory and innovation theory of successful aging (see chapter 4) suggest that maintaining involvement in productive activities later in life, such as leisure, is important to our health. As such, what is the effect of our patterns of activity during retirement on our well-being? Studies have suggested that patterns and frequency of leisure involvement do not appear to significantly affect Americans' life satisfaction or the presence of depressive

■ TABLE 5.1

Changes in Leisure Activity Involvement After Retirement

Group	Postretirement changes		Country	
	Scope	Frequency	United States (N = 430)	Israel (N = 383)
Reducers	Decreased or unchanged	Decreased or unchanged	51%	43%
Expanders	Increased	Increased	21%	35%
Concentrators	Decreased or unchanged	Increased	16%	11%
Diffusers	Increased	Decreased or unchanged	12%	11%

Data from Nimrod 2007 and Nimrod, Janke & Kleiber 2009

symptoms, but this is not necessarily the case for adults in other countries, such as Israel, where increased participation in some types of activities (e.g., physical activity) does seem to affect satisfaction with life (Nimrod et al., 2008). Overall, it is likely that being able to maintain or increase involvement in activities that hold meaning and purpose for older adults is much more important than just the frequency with which they engage in particular activities. It is also probable that benefits gained from participation, such as strengthening primary relationships, self-expression, and personal development (Kelly, 1987), are more important than the frequency of participation.

Widowhood

The loss of a spouse has been identified as one of the most stressful life events that can occur among adults (Bisconti, Bergeman, & Boker, 2004), and the majority of people who experience this are older women. Recent statistics suggest that in the United States, 52% of women 75 to 84 years of age are widowed, and this number increases to 76% of women over the age of 85 (Federal Interagency Forum on Aging-Related Statistics, 2008). The loss of a spouse is often accompanied by changes in adults' leisure behavior. This life event may constrain leisure participation due to the loss of a leisure partner, a decline in expendable income, or the loss of transportation to and from activities (McGuire, 1985). Yet some types of leisure activities may increase with the loss of a spouse. In particular, the death of a spouse often leads to increased contact and social activities with friends and family (Janke et al., 2008a).

One study noted several trends in adults' leisure behavior as a result of widowhood (Janke et al., 2008c). There was great variability in adults' leisure participation in specific leisure activities after the loss of a spouse. The most common leisure activities of widows were talking and visiting with friends and family, with almost all older adults reporting some involvement in these leisure pursuits. Many widows maintained or increased their involvement in religious activities (64%), gardening (43%), and walking (51%). Several adults indicated that they started a new leisure activity by becoming involved in community groups or organizations during widowhood (17%), while almost 55% maintained their involvement in this type of leisure activity. The activity with the greatest percentage of adults ceasing participation after the death of their spouse was physical activity and exercise (17%);

however, 20% of older adults added this type of activity to their repertoire after this life event, representing the greatest percentage of adders of all the activities examined.

Participation in leisure activities after the loss of a spouse does appear to be related to adults' health and well-being. Reducing participation in many leisure activities, such as participation in clubs, walking, gardening, and sport after the loss of a spouse, has been associated with greater levels of depressive symptoms, and reducing the amount of time spent visiting with family and friends or gardening has been related to slowed recovery from the loss over time (Janke et al., 2008c). These findings are consistent with earlier studies (e.g., Patterson, 1996; Patterson & Carpenter, 1994; Sharp & Mannel, 1996) that have found leisure activity to be an important mechanism for coping with widowhood.

However, these findings cannot determine whether widows' reduction in leisure activities caused them to have more depressive symptoms and a slower recovery or if their inability to cope with the loss of a spouse was the cause of the reduced leisure participation. In fact, one study suggested that it is likely that a person's well-being has more of an effect on reducing participation in leisure activities than a reduction of activities has on well-being (Janke et al., 2008b). Yet, studies comparing older adults who have become widowed with those who are continuously married over time have supported claims that leisure behavior is affected by this transition and that reduced involvement in leisure has a different effect on older widows than older people who are married (Janke et al., 2008a).

One factor that has been addressed in the literature on marital satisfaction and leisure but has yet to be examined during widowhood is the role of separate and joint leisure. Among married couples, joint leisure activities, or those activities done together as a couple, have been significantly related to better relationship quality (Johnson, Zabriskie, & Hill, 2006), while parallel activities (engaged in together but with minimal interaction, such as watching TV) or separate leisure (independent pursuits engaged in without the spouse) have less of an effect on marital satisfaction. It is possible that the context of how widows once engaged in the activity (joint, parallel, or separate) could also influence their patterns of engagement in these activities and the effect of involvement in these activities on their health and coping after the loss of a spouse.

Time Misuse in Later Life

Based on the findings regarding changes in leisure following major transitions and well-being, there seem to be better ways to use leisure as a coping mechanism to face life transitions. Yet, most seniors do exactly the opposite of what is associated with better well-being (i.e., reduce their involvement in leisure activities). Why? Possible explanations have to do with constraints to leisure involvement related to these transitions, a lack of education about the role and importance of leisure during these life events, and inadequate or inaccessible services provided to older adults.

For example, in the transitions we just discussed, it was evident that, at least in the studies highlighted, the majority of retirees reduce their involvement in leisure activities after leaving the workforce or at least do not appear to increase their involvement. This could be attributed to how they define retirement and their attitudes toward work and leisure (Gibson et al., 2002, 2003/2004). Yet our perception is that retirement is a time for leisure, affording the time and energy to engage in meaningful activities. Although this reduced involvement does not appear to have a major impact on the immediate health and well-being of retirees in the United States based on

Older Adults in the Czech Republic

Donald N. Roberson, Jr. *

Older adults in the Czech Republic have lived through a difficult period, yet they are a resilient and very active group. Let's consider some aspects of their modern lives.

At the age of 65, people in the Czech Republic retire and begin to draw a pension (up to 60 percent of their former salary). However, a person can continue to work if all parties agree, or may retire as early as age 57 with fewer benefits. Many of those who are retired are living in their own homes or flats and are without disabilities. They enjoy recreational activities such as gardening, tourism, cycling, and skiing with friends or with organized clubs.

Many cities and towns have clubs for older adults where they can play basketball, volleyball, and football. Some of these have well-known athletes who are now older.

Some local governments offer senior organizations that meet once or twice a week for social and recreation activities. Every community or town has its own official senior or older adult center with activities organized for older adults, from simple coffee time or card games to some organized travel. Most towns also have a special home for older adults, a place where they can live if they have no family near or if they need some special care. However, most older adults live in their own flats until they can no longer care for themselves. At this time, they may move in with family, or their family will secure their care and personal health. Family is important, and the role of the grandparent is very significant in central Europe. Many of the grandparents are active in the raising of their grandchildren, and many of them will even live with the family. This is especially true in rural areas.

Gardening is a popular free-time activity with older adults. Many families in central Europe have small garden areas or even weekend houses with garden areas. Most of the entire family will be involved in this activity, but it is especially important for older adults. Older adults, in retirement, finally have the time to devote to the gardening and the weekend house. Casual and social dancing is another popular recreational activity for older adults. Organized dances can draw groups of 75 to 100 aged from 50 to 85 years or so.

In comparing older adults in the Czech Republic with their peers in Western nations, older adults in the West seem to be involved move in volunteerism. For example, many schools, recreation centers, cultural events, and museums are heavily supported by volunteer activities in the West. Also, they continue to have jobs, especially part-time jobs. Older adults in the West seem to be more active in their communities as well as politics. And in contrast, Western grandparenting seems to be thought of as a time to indulge grandchildren, taking them out for evenings, or even taking them on trips.

*Donald N. Roberson, Jr., teaches in the College of Physical Culture at Palacky University in the Czech Republic.

the studies discussed, this may largely be due to adults' already substantial involvement in leisure activities. However, for people who are forced to retire due to illness, family responsibilities, or cutbacks in the workplace, finding ways to replace time spent in work with leisure activities may be important in terms of providing opportunities for productive involvement and social roles, which have been demonstrated to be salient factors in successful aging (Rowe & Kahn, 1998).

Another reason why adults may not increase their involvement in certain types of leisure activities once they retire is that although there are community programs for older adults, they may not be as widespread as programs offered for youth and adolescents (Henderson, Neff, Sharpe, Greaney, Royce, et al., 2001). In addition, the advertising of these programs may not be as extensive, making it more likely that adults are not aware of these opportunities. Another possible cause of decreased participation after retirement is the cost of activities. Many people who are retired are living on a limited budget, and they may no longer have the finances available to pay for leisure services.

In terms of widowhood, research has suggested that a decline in several types of activities with the loss of a spouse may exacerbate negative health outcomes; reductions in leisure have been associated with more depressive symptoms, more difficulty coping, and greater decline in physical functioning (Janke et al., 2008c). There are several possible explanations for this change in leisure involvement. The loss of a spouse may affect leisure participation by decreasing financial security and income, making it more difficult to find a partner with whom to engage in leisure activities. In addition, the sadness and grief associated with this loss may reduce the motivation to engage in leisure activities. These constraints appear to be specific to older widowed women; continuously married women of the same age and demographic backgrounds do not reduce their participation (Janke et al., 2008a). Again, this relationship may also depend on what leisure patterns were like (i.e., joint, separate, or parallel) prior to the loss. Thus, one solution would be to increase adults' awareness of the importance of leisure to their health and well-being during this difficult transition via leisure education programs offered by joint collaborations between health and leisure service providers in the community. In addition, grief support groups for widows should incorporate leisure activities into their programs rather than focusing solely on discussion and seminars to promote opportunities for positive experiences and development.

Conclusion

The different events and experiences we have over our life course shape who we are as older adults. Thus, the leisure behavior of adults in later life is very diverse. The meaning of activities also varies among older adults, and one activity that provides purpose and a sense of identity to one individual may not be enjoyed by others. While some common changes in adults' leisure do occur with age, such as increases in home-based and passive activities, this does not mean that all older adults reduce their involvement in leisure activities over time. When planning leisure programs and services for the aging population it is important to take all of these factors into consideration given that meaningful leisure activities can promote better health and well-being.

KEY TERMS

blurred retirement—Retirement style in which one transfers in and out of the workforce.

concentrators—People who have more maintained activities with increased frequency than maintained activities with decreased frequency but do not change or actually decrease the number of types of activities they engage in following a life transition.

coping—A process of accepting and adjusting to life transitions and negative life events (Duggleby, Bateman, & Singer, 2002).

crisp retirement—Retirement style in which one leaves the workforce and never returns.

cross-sectional investigations—Studies that explore age-related differences by comparing age groups at a certain point in time.

diffusers—People who increase the number of activities they are involved in but do not increase (or decrease) the frequency of their involvement in these activities following a life transition.

ecological systems theory—Theory that defines four levels of the environment (microsystem, mesosystem, exosystem, macrosystem) that shape our growth and experiences.

expanders—People who increase the number of activities they are engaged in and have more activities with increased frequency than activities with decreased frequency following a life transition.

leisure constraints—Factors limiting participation in desired leisure activities or the ability to benefit from such participation (McGuire, 1985).

life-course perspective—A theoretical framework that focuses on the role of social events and phenomena in shaping one's development, highlighting the importance of the timing, context, process, and meaning of events.

life transition—Significant change in one's life. It can be positive or negative, predicted or unexpected, and in such various domains as family, health, work, and leisure (Kleiber, 1999).

life-span developmental theory—Theory suggesting that human development is lifelong, occurs in multiple domains (e.g., physical, cognitive, social), is multidirectional (e.g., experience gains and losses), and is shaped by one's age, historical context, and life experiences.

longitudinal research—Studies that examine change within and between people over time by repeating the same measurement with the same population (and even with the same group of people).

reducers—People who do not increase or actually decrease the number of their leisure activities and have the same or more maintained activities with decreased frequency than maintained activities with increased frequency following a life transition.

retrospective examinations—Studies that explore age-related changes in people by asking them to reflect on their present circumstances and compare them with their past.

socioemotional selectivity (SES) theory—Theory proposing that in their social relationships, older adults base their goals on emotional aspects, leading them to pursue interactions with familiar people and avoid unfamiliar relationships that may lead in unpredictable and unpleasant directions.

REVIEW AND DISCUSSION QUESTIONS

1. What do we know about changes in leisure preferences and behavior as we age?
2. How may the meaning of leisure be influenced during later life?
3. How can developmental and systems theories be used to explain these changes?
4. How can leisure assist in coping with later-life transitions?
5. What are implications for leisure programming and management?

LEARNING ACTIVITIES

1. Think about how the ecological levels proposed in the ecological systems model (chapter 3 and earlier in this chapter) could explain the four main changes in leisure behavior characterizing later life. Come up with at least two examples for each of the described systems.

2. List five specific barriers or constraints that older adults might face in their leisure (e.g., hearing loss). Describe what effect each constraint might have on their leisure and overall health and development. Suggest ways in which leisure professionals can help adults overcome these constraints.

3. Interview an older relative, neighbor, or friend about a recent life transition. In one page, summarize how this transition affected the interviewee's leisure involvement and meanings of leisure.

4. Interpret the findings regarding one of the life transitions presented in this chapter using the theories described in chapter 3.

5. Search the Internet for an online seniors' community (e.g., Buzz50, 50 Plus, IDF50). Pick one community and review its contents. Identify 10 ways through which the content in the community may contribute to older adults' well-being.

CRITICAL-THINKING ACTIVITIES

Imagine your life at age 80. Write a one- to two-page story describing an ordinary day in your life. As you read over your response, reflect on the following questions:

1. What role does leisure play in your daily routine?
2. What meaning do these activities have in your life?
3. What constraints do you face in your leisure activities?
4. What experiences (past, present, and future) influence your leisure at this phase in your life?

SUGGESTED READING

DiGiulio, R.C. (1989). *Beyond widowhood: From bereavement to emergence and hope.* New York: Free Press.

Kelly, J.R. (1987). *Peoria winter, styles and resources in later life.* Lexington, MA: Lexington Books.

Kleiber, D.A. (1999). *Leisure experience and human development: A dialectical interpretation.* New York: Basic Books.

Robinson, J.P., & Godbey, G. (1997). *Time for life: The surprising way Americans use their time.* State College, PA: Pennsylvania State University Press.

Weiss, R.S. (2005). *The experience of retirement.* Ithaca, NY: Cornell University Press.

REFERENCES

Atchley, R. (1989). The continuity theory of normal aging. *Gerontologist, 29,* 183-190.

Baltes, P.B. (1979). Life-span developmental psychology: Some converging observations on history and theory. In P.B. Baltes & O.G. Brim, Jr. (Eds.), *Life span development and behavior* (pp. 255-279). New York: Academic Press.

Beck, S.H. (1982). Adjustment to and satisfaction with retirement. *Journal of Gerontology, 37*(5), 616-624.

Bedini, L.A., & Guinan, D.M. (1996). "If I could just be selfish . . .": Caregivers' perceptions of their entitlement to leisure. *Leisure Sciences, 18,* 227-239.

Bedini, L.A., & Phoenix, T.L. (2004). Perceptions of leisure by family caregivers: A profile. *Therapeutic Recreation Journal, 38,* 366-382.

Bisconti, T.L., Bergeman, C.S., & Boker, S.M. (2004). Emotional well-being in recently bereaved widows: A dynamical systems approach. *Journals of Gerontology Series B: Psychological Sciences & Social Sciences, 59B*(4), P158-P167.

Bronfenbrenner, U. 1979. The ecology of human development: Experiments by nature and design. Cambridge, MA: Harvard University Press.

Burdick, D. (2001). *Digital divide or tool for understanding and collaboration: Computers and intergenerational relationships.* Paper presented at the 54th Annual Scientific Meeting of the Gerontological Society of Americas, Chicago.

Calasanti, T. (1996). Gender and life satisfaction in retirement: An assessment of the male model. Journal of Gerontology, 51, S18-S29.

Carpenter, G. (1989). Life change during middle adulthood and valuing leisure. *World Leisure & Recreation, 31*(1), 29-31.

Carpenter, G., & Murray, S. (2002). Leisure behaviors and perceptions when midlife death is imminent: A case report. *Journal of Park and Recreation Administration, 20*(4), 12-36.

Carstensen, L.L. (1993). Motivation for social contact across the life span: A theory of socioemotional selectivity. In J.E. Jacobs (Ed.), *Developmental perspectives on motivation: Nebraska Symposium on Motivation* (Vol. 40, pp. 2090-2254). Lincoln, NE: University of Nebraska Press.

Dickenson, A., & Hill, R.L. (2007). Keeping in touch: Talking to older people about computers and communication. *Educational Gerontology, 33*(8), 613-630.

Dionigi, R. (2006). Competitive sport as leisure in later life: Negotiations, discourse, and aging. *Leisure Sciences, 28*(2), 181-196.

Duggleby, W., Bateman, J., & Singer, S. (2002). The aging experience of well elderly women: Initial results. *Nursing & Health Sciences, 4*(3), 10.

Duke, J., Leventhal, H., Brownlee, S., & Leventhal E.A. (2002). Giving up and replacing activities in response to illness. Journals of Gerontology Series B: Psychological Sciences and Social Sciences, 57(3), 367-376.

Elder, G.H. (1974). *Children of the great depression: Social change in life experience.* Chicago: University of Chicago Press.

Federal Interagency Forum on Aging-Related Statistics. (2008). Older Americans 2008: Key indicators of well-being. Washington, DC: U.S. GPO.

Feldman, D.C. (1994). The decision to retire early: A review and conceptualization. *Academy of Management Review, 19*(2), 285-311.

Fernandez-Ballesteros, R., Zamarron, M., & Ruiz, M. (2001). The contribution of socio-demographic and psychosocial factors to life satisfaction. *Ageing and Society, 21*(1), 25-43.

Fokkema, T., & Knipscheer, K. (2007). Escape loneliness by going digital: A quantitative and qualitative evaluation of a Dutch experiment in using ECT to overcome loneliness among older adults. *Aging & Mental Health, 11*(5), 496-504.

Frazier, L.D. (2002). Psychosocial influences on possible selves: A comparison of three cohorts of older adults. *International Journal of Behavioral Development, 26*(4), 308-317.

Gibson, H., Ashton-Shaeffer, C., Green, J., & Autry, C. (2003/2004). Leisure in the lives of retirement-aged women: Conversations about leisure and life. *Leisure/Loisir, 28*(3-4), 203-230.

Gibson, H., Ashton-Shaeffer, C., Green, J., & Corbin, J. (2002). Leisure and retirement: Women's stories. *Loisir et Societe/Society and Leisure, 25,* 257-284.

Griffin, J., & McKenna, K. (1998). Influences on leisure and life satisfaction of elderly people. *Physical & Occupational Therapy in Geriatrics, 15*(4), 1-16.

Henderson, K.A., Neff, L.J., Sharpe, P.A., Greaney, M.L., Royce, S.W., & Ainsworth, B.E. (2001). "It takes a village" to promote physical activity: The potential for public park and recreation departments. *Journal of Park and Recreation Administration, 19*(1), 23-41.

Iso-Ahola, S.E., Jackson, E., & Dunn, E. (1994). Starting, ceasing and replacing leisure activities over the life-span. *Journal of Leisure Research, 26,* 227-249.

Janke, M.C., Carpenter, G., Payne, L.L., & Stockard, J. (2011). The role of life experiences on perceptions of leisure during adulthood: A longitudinal study. *Leisure Sciences, 33,* 52-69.

Janke, M., Davey, A., & Kleiber, D. (2006). Modeling change in older adults' leisure activities. Leisure *Sciences, 28,* 285-303.

Janke, M.C., Nimrod, G., & Kleiber, D.A. (2008a). Leisure activity and depressive symptoms of widowed and married women in later life. *Journal of Leisure Research, 40*(2), 250-266.

Janke, M.C., Nimrod, G., & Kleiber, D.A. (2008b). Reduction in leisure activity and well-being during the transition to widowhood. *Women and Aging, 20*(1-2), 83-98.

Janke, M.C., Nimrod, G., & Kleiber, D.A. (2008c). Leisure patterns and health among recently widowed adults. *Activities, Adaptation & Aging, 32*(1), 19-39.

Johnson, H.A., Zabriskie, R.B., & Hill, B. (2006). The contribution of couple leisure to involvement, leisure time, and leisure satisfaction to marital satisfaction. *Marriage & Family Review, 40*(1), 69-90.

Katz, E., Hass, H., Weitz, S., Adoni, H., Gurevitch, M., Schiff, M., & Goldberg-Anabi, D. (2000). *Tarbut hapnai beIsrael: Tmurot bedfusei hapeilut hatarbutit 1970-1990* [Leisure patterns in Israel: Changes in cultural activity 1970-1990]. Tel Aviv: The Open University.

Kelly, J.R. (1987). *Peoria winter, styles, and resources in later life.* Lexington, MA: Lexington Books.

Kimmel, D.C., Price, K.F., & Walker, J.W. (1978). Retirement choice and retirement satisfaction. *Journal of Gerontology, 33*(4), 575-585.

Kleiber, D.A. (1999). *Leisure experience and human development: A dialectical interpretation.* New York: Basic Books.

Kleiber, D.A., McGuire, F.A., Aybar-Damali, B., & Norman, W. (2008). The paradox of leisure constraints: Having more by doing less. *Journal of Leisure Research, 40*(3), 343-359.

Kleiber, D.A., & Nimrod, G. (2009). „I can't be very sad": Constraint and adaptation in the leisure of a 'learning in retirement' group. *Leisure Studies, 68*(1), 67-83.

Kolt, G.S. (2002). Exercise participation motives in older Asian Indians. *Psychological Studies, 47*(1-3), 139-147.

Lefrancois, R., Leclerc, G., & Poulin, N. (1998). Predictors of activity involvement among older adults. *Activity, Adaptation and Aging, 22*, 15-29.

McGuire, F. (1985). Constraints in later life. In M.G. Wade (Ed.), *Constraints on leisure* (pp. 335-353). Springfield, IL: C.C. Thomas.

McGuire, F., & Norman, W. (2005). The role of constraints in successful aging: Enabling or inhibiting? In E. Jackson (Ed.), *Constraints to leisure* (pp. 89-101). State College, PA: Venture Press.

McPherson, B.D. (1984). Sport participation across the life cycle: A review of the literature and suggestions for further research. *Sociology of Sport Journal, 1*(3), 213-230.

Naim, S. (2009). *The meaning of early retirement.* Master's thesis, Department of Gerontology, University of Haifa, Israel.

Nimrod, G., (2003). Leisure after retirement: Research review and mapping. *Gerontology, 30*(1-2), 29-46.

Nimrod, G. (2007a). Expanding, reducing, concentrating and diffusing: Postretirement leisure behavior and life satisfaction. *Leisure Sciences, 1*, 91-111.

Nimrod, G. (2007b). Retirees' leisure: Activities, benefits, and their contribution to life satisfaction. *Leisure Studies, 26*(1), 65-80.

Nimrod, G. (2010). Seniors' online communities: A quantitative content analysis. *Gerontologist, 50*(3), 382-392.

Nimrod, G. (2011). The impact of leisure activity and innovation on the well-being of the very old. In L.W. Poon & J. Cohen-Mansfield (Eds.), *Understanding the well-being in the oldest-old*, pp. 240-257. New York: Cambridge University Press.

Nimrod, G., & Hutchinson, S. (2010). Innovation among older adults with chronic health conditions. *Journal of Leisure Research, 41*(1), 1-24.

Nimrod, G., Janke, M., & Kleiber, D.A. (2008). Retirement, activity, and subjective well-being in Israel and the Unites States. *World Leisure Journal, 50*(1), 18-32.

Nimrod, G., Janke, M.C., & Kleiber, D.A. (2009). Expanding, reducing, concentrating and diffusing: Activity patterns of recent retirees in the U.S. *Leisure Sciences, 31*(1), 37-52.

Opalinski, L. (2001). Older adults and the digital divide: Assessing results of a web-based survey. *Journal of Technology in Human Services, 18*(3/4), 203-221.

Osgood, N.J., & Howe, C.Z. (1984). Psychological aspects of leisure: A life cycle developmental perspective. *Society and Leisure, 7*, 175-193.

Patterson, I. (1996). Participation in leisure activities by older adults after a stressful life event: The loss of a spouse. *International Journal of Aging and Human Development, 42*, 123-142.

Patterson, I., & Carpenter, G. (1994). Participation in leisure activities after the death of a spouse. *Leisure Sciences, 16*, 105-117.

Prager, E. (1997). Sources of personal meaning in life for a sample of younger and older urban Australian women. *Journal of Women and Aging, 9*(3), 47-65.

Rapoport, R., & Rapoport, R.N. (1975). *Leisure and the family life cycle.* London: Routledge & Kegan.

Robinson, J.P., & Godbey, G. (1997). *Time for life: The surprising way Americans use their time.* State College, PA: Pennsylvania State University Press.

Rowe, J.W., & Kahn, R.L. (1998). *Successful aging.* New York: Pantheon Books.

Sharpe, A., & Mannell, R.C. (1996). Participation in leisure as a coping strategy among bereaved women. In *Proceedings of the Eight Canadian Congress on Leisure Research* (pp. 241-244). Ottawa: University of Ottawa.

Silverstein, M., & Parker, M.G. (2002). Leisure activities and quality of life among the oldest old in Sweden. *Research on Aging, 24*(5), 528-547.

Stanley, D., & Freysinger, V.J. (1995). The impact of age, health, and sex on the frequency of older adults' leisure activity participation: A longitudinal study. *Activities, Adaptation & Aging, 19*(3), 31-42.

Stebbins, R.A. (2006). Serious leisure. In C. Rojek, T. Veal, & S. Shaw (Eds.). *A handbook of leisure studies* (pp. 448-456). New York: Palgrave Macmillan.

Stein, D. (2000). The new meaning of retirement (Report No. EDO-CE-00-217). Columbus, OH: ERIC Clearinghouse on Adult, Career, and Vocational Education.

Vaillant, G. (2002). *Aging well.* New York: Little, Brown.

van der Meer, M.J. (2008). Sociospatial diversity in the leisure activities of older people in the Netherlands. *Journal of Aging Studies, 22*(1), 1-12.

Yarnal, C.M. (2006). The Red Hat Society: Exploring the role of play, liminality, and *communitas* in older women's lives. *Journal of Women & Aging, 18*(3), 51-73.

CHAPTER 6

Leisure and Diversity in Later Life: Ethnicity, Gender, and Sexual Orientation

Steven E. Mock ▪ **Susan M. Shaw**
Erica M. Hummel ▪ **Carissa Bakker**

LEARNING OBJECTIVES

After reading this chapter, you will be able to

- define *ethnicity*, *gender*, and *sexual orientation* as understood by social science researchers;

- identify factors that contribute to marginalization and create constraints to leisure by minority ethnic and racial groups, women, and sexual minorities; and

- develop an awareness of how experiences of marginalized groups can be better understood by investigating common experiences, unique challenges and perspectives, and within-group diversity.

Jamila is a woman in her 60s, born in Pakistan, living in England. Leisure in the form of tourism plays an important role in maintaining her Pakistani cultural identity (Ali & Holden, 2006). In her own words, "I arrived in England in 1962. I was only 24 . . . I know my *desh* [culture/roots] . . . I haven't lost them" (Ali & Holden, 2006, p. 229). For 40 years, Jamila has returned to Pakistan to visit family and friends, and she plans to return permanently one day.

A study of participation by older women in a lawn-bowling club in Australia illustrates another way leisure helps to maintain cultural norms, in this case traditional gender roles (Boyle & McKay, 1995). For example, all food preparation and service at the club is handled by women, with a rare exception on Mother's Day. As described by Lavinia, an 85-year-old club member, "It was a bit of a lark really, and the men thoroughly enjoyed it. They would dress up with aprons and wigs on and we really appreciated it. It was their way of saying thank you," albeit in a way that emphasized the gendered nature of the work (Boyle & McKay, 1995, p. 564).

For Rosita, recreation and leisure experiences at a community center focused on the needs of sexual-minority (nonheterosexual) older adults provided support and helped her to navigate the death of her same-sex partner, a transition without a well-established normative template (Libre de Marulanda, 2008). Rosita describes how she "felt the support of a room full of women who understood what it is like to love another woman" (Libre de Marulanda, 2008, p. 3).

The experiences just described highlight some of the key themes of leisure for older adults in general and marginalized groups in particular. Leisure can play an important role in fostering cultural identity, social ties, physical health, and psychological well-being for all adults in later life. But a closer examination of the experiences of marginalized groups, such as racial and ethnic minorities, women, and sexual minorities, reveals sources of social inequality and exclusion that shape and sometimes limit their opportunities and experiences, including leisure (Baars, 2006).

In this chapter we explore diversity in the leisure experiences of older adults, focusing in particular on race and ethnicity, gender, and sexual orientation. We base this discussion on a critical gerontology approach, which incorporates issues of power and inequality and can enhance understanding of leisure among marginalized groups. We take a threefold approach to this overview of the recreation and leisure experiences of older adults and marginalized groups by recognizing that

1. there are common benefits and challenges involved in the recreation and leisure of all older adults,
2. marginalized status shapes leisure experiences in unique ways, yet
3. within marginalized groups there is also heterogeneity in leisure experiences.

Critical Gerontology

Critical gerontology is a macrotheoretical approach that addresses the social structures that shape life's opportunities and choices. It pays particular attention to structured relations of power and the age structuring of power (Estes, 2004), which constrain older adults' access to economic and material resources. Thus, this critical approach to gerontology examines sources of empowerment and disempowerment, social inequality, and inclusion and exclusion over the life course in terms of positive and negative life chances and cumulative advantages and disadvantages (Dannefer, 2003).

Power relations endure not only through unequal access to resources but also through ideological processes that influence and reflect dominant beliefs about aging. That is, if aging is associated primarily with reduced abilities, lack of independence, and marginalized status, such beliefs affect how older adults are viewed. This, in turn, can lead to inferiorization and the perpetuation of negative stereotypes. In this way, critical gerontology challenges traditional forms of gerontological research that adopt a medical model of solving the problems of aging and managing older adults' lives.

For many critical gerontologists, the notion of *identity* is central, since dominant perspectives of older adulthood can influence individual beliefs and self-images. Living in a world where the young and middle-aged are valued can create self-devaluation for older people. According to Twigg (2004), living in a youth-obsessed culture can lead older adults to see signs of aging as evidence of personal failure. Biggs' (2004) notion of the masquerade and how older adults seek to conceal signs of aging through surgery, clothing, and cosmetics provides a powerful image of this process of devaluation. The masquerade, he argues, sends a message that aging is something to be ashamed of and so needs to be hidden away (see Dionigi and Horton, this volume).

Yet critical gerontology is not simply a critique of the oppressive nature of ageism and age relations. Researchers who adopt this approach actively seek solutions through notions of agency, choice, and resistance. Through individual and collective agency, it is argued, older adults can challenge dominant (and oppressive) perspectives, taking advantage of the choices that are available and negotiating their own identities in more positive and self-affirming ways. Thus critical gerontology also focuses attention on individual fulfillment, solidarity with others, and human dignity (Baars, 2006).

In recent years, critical gerontologists have paid increasing attention to issues of diversity among older adults. No longer can older adults be seen as a homogeneous group that is uniformly oppressed; they are a diverse group of people responding to the challenges they face in a variety of ways. Clearly some adults face more challenges than others, and this is related not only to their individual situation but also to the effect of other axes of power such as class, race, ethnicity, gender, and sexual orientation. Recognition of these multiple dimensions of power has led to the concept of **intersectionality** (e.g., Collins, 1998), which pays attention to the interconnections among racism, sexism, heterosexism, and ageism. This, in turn, suggests the need not only to take diversity into consideration but also the need for information about how intersectionality affects the aging experiences for individuals and groups in a variety of life situations. Throughout this chapter we consider commonalities, unique challenges, and diversity in the experiences of marginalized groups. Consistent with our approach, although much research on intersectionality has explored the possibility that multiple devalued identities compound disadvantage, recent research suggests that intersectionality may be more complex than this additive view. To be specific, the intersection of multiple marginalized statuses may place some people outside the prototype for those marginalized groups, creating *intersectional invisibility* (Purdie-Vaughns & Eibach, 2008).

This chapter builds on the ideas and insights of critical gerontology and intersectionality and applies these ideas to leisure. Although the notion of leisure has been given scant attention by critical gerontologists to date, we believe that an analysis of leisure from this perspective has much to offer.

First, leisure plays a particularly important role in the lives of older adults because of retirement and the loss or reduction of work roles and responsibilities. Leisure is also important for seniors in terms of improved health and psychological well-being as well as coping with negative life events (see Nimrod & Janke, this volume; Stanley & Freysinger, 1995). In addition, leisure is potentially significant for older adults because it represents a sphere of life that is relatively free of constraints and obligations, and it provides increased freedom of choice and opportunities for self-expression. Thus it has been recognized as an important site for action, including resistance against oppressive and constraining ideologies (Shaw, 2001) and the creation and negotiation of identities (Wearing, 1998).

A number of leisure scholars have suggested the need to address diversity in terms of power and privilege (e.g., Fox, 2006; Henderson, 2009; Henderson & Shaw, 2006; Kivel, Johnson, & Scraton, 2009), taking account of discourses on gender, culture, race, and sexual orientation. We examine some of the relevant literature to date, focusing specifically on diversity among older adults. We also suggest a framework for future research that incorporates issues of power and inequity, takes account of commonalities as well as differences between groups, and seeks to counteract negative stereotypes and ideological beliefs associated with ageism, **Eurocentrism**, **androcentrism**, and **heterosexism** (Mock, Taylor, & Savin-Williams, 2006).

Ethnicity and Race

Ethnicity comprises a constellation of language, beliefs, social views, and identities related to country of origin or cultural group, and **race** typically refers to visible physical characteristics (Henderson & Ainsworth, 2003). Categories of ethnicity and race sometimes overlap, and personal identification with ethnic and racial groups may differ from the ways in which these categories are defined. In addition, definitions may change over time. For example, *Irish* and *Jewish* used to be defined as racial categories but are now thought of as ethnic categories (Jacobson, 1998). Patterns of leisure participation are influenced by race and ethnicity in multiple ways. For example, race-based or ethnicity-based discrimination may enhance leisure opportunities for some but restrict opportunities for others (Shinew, Floyd, & Parry, 2004). In addition, cultural norms related to ethnicity may shape individual preferences for certain kinds of leisure (Gvion, 2009; Outley & McKenzie, 2007). Thus, ethnicity and race are sometimes related to leisure experiences through structural forces (e.g., discrimination, leisure constraints) (Philipp, 1995) or individual-level forces of personal preference and personal identification shaped by internalization of cultural norms.

Some research shows common patterns of leisure meanings and outcomes across ethnic and racial groups. For example, in a study comparing leisure participation, health, and well-being of African American and white female retirees in the United States, greater leisure participation (e.g., hobbies, socializing with friends, exercising) was significantly associated with better self-rated health for both racial groups (Riddick & Stewart, 1994). Other research has shown a pattern of declining participation in various forms of leisure associated with worse physical health and psychological well-being across cultural contexts from Sweden (Agahi, Ahacic, & Parker, 2006), to Brazil (Benedetti et al., 2008), to African American and white older adults in the United States (Janke, Davey, & Kleiber, 2006).

Although there are similar associations among health, well-being, and leisure activity participation for older adults across ethnic and racial groups, patterns of decline or lower rates of leisure participation are often more pronounced for ethnic and racial minorities. In a study of older adults, Janke and colleagues (2006) found that above and beyond the effect of age, African American participants had lower levels of participation in leisure activities compared with white participants. In another longitudinal study of older adults' physical leisure activity, Mexican American participants reported less participation compared with white participants. This difference was shown to be due to socioeconomic status, particularly income, rather than to racial group per se (Dergance, Mouton, Lichtenstein, & Hazuda, 2005), although in the same study, structural assimilation conceptualized as having close friendships with members of the majority group and integration into the neighborhood, workplace, and school system was associated with greater leisure participation for older Mexican American adults.

When older adults describe barriers to participation in leisure activities, they often talk about constraints related to health, transportation, or income (Martinez, Tanner, Fried, & Seeman, 2009) rather than any overt discussion of prejudice as a barrier to participation. This suggests that racism

and racial prejudice may sometimes be a hidden rather than an overt form of discrimination. It has been well established that poor health and socioeconomic disadvantage can be the result of historic and present inequalities between racial and ethnic groups (Wilson, 1980). Research comparing leisure participation of minority and majority groups (but not focused on older adults) showed that compared with white participants, African Americans were significantly less comfortable participating in several outdoor activities (e.g., camping, going to beaches, skiing) and going to country clubs and museums (Philipp, 1995). Whether the African American participants saw this as overt racism or not, the author suggests that this situation stems from current or historic patterns of discrimination and being made to feel unwelcome.

Leisure participation itself can help relieve stress related to prejudice (Iwasaki, MacKay, MacTavish, Ristock, & Bartlett, 2006), as found in a study of older African American women who participated in a bid-whist card-playing group (Outley & McKenzie, 2007). For these women, the card group provided not only a forum for enjoyable socializing and relaxation but also sometimes a coping mechanism as an outlet for discussing daily hassles, including discrimination. As one woman described, "I would go into the store and the clerk would wait on others [white ladies] . . . sometimes never waited on you at all. It made you feel like your money was no good even if it was the same color as theirs" (Outley & McKenzie, 2007, p. 32). Thus frustration was alleviated through participation in social leisure.

Leisure can play a unique role in maintaining minority cultural heritage as well, as described in Gvion's (2009) study of Yiddish sing-along nights in Israel. In a study of tourism motivations among a Pakistani diaspora in the United Kingdom, Ali and Holden (2006) examine how the so-called myth of return helps to maintain a Pakistani cultural identity with the idea of regular returns and eventually a final return to Pakistan. Here there is a clear linkage to identity negotiation, with the hope of mobility allowing for the reconstruction of identity associated with country of origin and resistance to an identity associated only with the current country of residence. However, the authors also point out that travel motivations among the second and third generation become more diverse and less tied to Pakistan, indicating a diversity of experience among racial and ethnic groups.

The Myth of Return

During the last century, postcolonial Pakistanis arrived in the United Kingdom intending temporary settlement primarily for economic reasons. Originally, the intent of many immigrants was to return eventually to Pakistan, but families often ended up settling permanently in Britain. First-generation Pakistanis frequently recalled experiences of racism since their settlement, which aroused feelings of *unbelonging* and led to the questioning of their identity and place of belonging. The issue of belonging is a central theme of identity: Where they belong and how they belong were anxieties transferred through mobility between England and Pakistan. There is therefore a subsequent dependency upon return trips to Pakistan to ease the discontents of migration associated with feelings of exclusion and being a *pardesi* (foreigner) in the host society.

Tourism-based mobility performs a crucial role in the survival of the myth of return in the postmigration lives of the Pakistani diaspora. Will the myth of return survive among future (e.g., second and third) generations of Pakistanis born in Britain, whose birth country is different from that of their parents? This depends on family dynamics in the Pakistani community and the extent to which first-generation Pakistanis ingrain the myth (as a tourist motivation) into the imaginations, minds, and movements of their children.

Research by Nazia Ali.

Luton, UK

Punjab Province, Pakistan

Photo courtesy of Nazia Ali.

Although members of marginalized groups may share unique characteristics shaped by both structural and individual-level forces, an important component of understanding diverse perspectives includes an examination of within-group heterogeneity (Henderson, 2009; Mock et al., 2006; Shinew, Floyd, McGuire, & Noe, 1996). As we just discussed, although travel to Pakistan may play an important role in maintaining cultural identity for members of the Pakistani minority in the United Kingdom, there appears to be heterogeneity in the significance of that travel depending on cohort. Similarly, diversity in experiences of other

racial and ethnic groups is influenced by several factors, including level of acculturation to the dominant society and socioeconomic factors such as income and education level (Dergance et al., 2005). For example, a study of older adult Chinese immigrants in Canada found that senior centers were used more often by those who were older, lived alone, had a religious affiliation, and had a lower level of self-rated competency with English (Lai, 2006). Thus, both commonalities and divergences are evident in the literature on race and leisure among older adults and the significance of not only predetermined (i.e., research-defined) categories of race and ethnicity but also personal identities and perspectives.

Gender

The term **gender** does not refer to biological differences between men and women but rather to the constellation of beliefs and practices that give meaning to being male or female. Since these ideas and beliefs are socially constructed, they vary among cultures, societies, and historical periods. Though the biological notion of sex has been used to justify or reify socially constructed gender roles (Bem, 1993; Hare-Mustin & Marecek, 1988; Unger, 1979; Young, 1980), this notion is rejected by feminist researchers who emphasize the need to critique essentialist notions of sex and gender (Henderson & Shaw, 2006). Further, although there are dominant beliefs about gender in any one society, and these beliefs often become taken-for-granted assumptions, they can be challenged, negotiated, and reconstructed over time (Shaw, 2001, 2006).

Dominant beliefs about gender and old age influence ideas about which leisure activities are appropriate or desirable for men and women. Social expectations for gender roles and responsibilities also affect access to resources and opportunities. Research has shown, for example, that women have less leisure time than men, especially women with multiple responsibilities, such as caring for children and other family members (Shaw, 1999). Data on participation rates in various leisure activities also show that both men's and women's leisure is gendered, and that gender-based discrimination and gender ideologies influence and constrain leisure.

There is a considerable body of literature on gender and leisure, mostly research on women's rather than men's leisure and the constraints on women's leisure. Nevertheless, there remains relatively little research on the gendered nature of leisure among older adults, and the research that has been conducted has typically focused somewhat narrowly on gender differences and similarities. We begin with a consideration of common predictors and consequences of leisure participation regardless of gender, moving on to the various ways in which gendered relations of power and gender ideologies contribute to leisure constraints, particularly for women. Finally, we consider within-gender heterogeneity of older adults' recreation and leisure experiences.

Although several studies show that, for both women and men, maintaining an active lifestyle and involvement in recreation and leisure are associated with lower rates of mortality, better physical health, and greater psychological well-being (Armstrong & Morgan, 1998; Lennartsson & Silverstein, 2001; Ruchlin & Lachs, 1999), involvement in recreation and leisure activities tends to decline during older adulthood (Armstrong & Morgan, 1998). In one study in the United Kingdom, the physical activity, leisure experiences, and health of men and women aged 65 and older were followed over an eight-year period (Armstrong & Morgan, 1998). The authors found that for both men and women, those who were active were more likely to survive over the eight-year period, and this effect held even in a comparison of subgroups contrasting 65- to 75-year-olds to those over 75. Similarly, a study of involvement in leisure activities and mortality (Lennartsson & Silverstein, 2001) showed that for both women and men, greater participation in solitary-active activities (e.g., working in the garden, hobbies) reduced risk of mortality.

For both women and men, there is a general pattern of declining involvement in various activities, including leisure, with age (Janke et al., 2006; Kleiber & Genoe, this volume; Lennartsson & Silverstein, 2001; Nimrod & Janke, this volume), but some activities show continuity, such as reading and television watching, and for women in particular, involvement in religious activities and theater and movie attendance (Strain, Grabusic, Searle, & Dunn, 2002). Heuser's (2005) study of the participation of older women in a lawn-bowling club illustrates this decline and adaptation. Specifically, even though physical impairment limited or decreased some women's participation in lawn bowling, they often shifted their involvement to volunteering or fund-raising, activities that helped maintain social involvement.

Dominant beliefs and ideologies of gender, reinforced by structural constraints and social interactions, often lead to gender-typical behavior and censure gender atypicality (Bem, 1993). Generally, males are encouraged to be agentic (active, physical, and independent) and females are encouraged to be communal (passive, dependent, and nurturing) (Baumrind, 1980). Multiple studies on the recreation and leisure of older adults document differences in the kinds of activities men and women engage in. For example, men are more likely than women to be involved in outdoor activities such as fishing, hunting, gardening, and sport (Armstrong & Morgan, 1998; Bennett, 1998; Janke et al., 2006; Lennartsson & Silverstein, 2001;

Mobily, Leslie, Lemke, Wallace, & Kohout, 1986). Women are more likely than men to be involved in home-centered activities and hobbies such as sewing, decorating, baking, and quilting (Armstrong & Morgan, 1998; Mobily et al., 1986; Nilsson, Löfgren, Fisher, & Bernspång, 2006), and women show greater continuity over time than men do in religious-service attendance, theater and movie attendance, and general social activities (Stanley & Freysinger, 1995; Strain et al., 2002).

However, recreation and leisure activities also provide relief from or resistance to traditional gender roles for older women. For example, in the study of the bid-whist group discussed previously (Outley & McKenzie, 2007), some of the women in the study talked about how the camaraderie of the card group provided space for personal time and the chance to let their hair down, so to speak. Similarly, the Red Hat Society is a leisure-based social group for older women with the specific aim of having fun without rules or responsibilities (Yarnal, Chick, & Kerstetter, 2008), and for many women, the group provides stress relief from daily hassles and major life events (e.g., widowhood, adult children's problems) as well as a forum for play and freedom from obligations.

Resistance, though, is rarely complete and often contradictory. In a study of older competitive athletes (60 years of age and older), Dionigi (2006) found coexistence of both challenge and conformity to stereotypical ideas of aging among men and women. Negative stereotypes of old age were challenged through the continuation of highly competitive sporting activities, and women were also resisting dominant views of femininity. At the same time, there was an evident denial of aging, suggesting conformity to the devaluation of older adults.

Although gender beliefs and the reinforcement of gender norms may create a somewhat dichotomized experience for men and women, factors such as age, education, income, and race contribute to variability in the recreation and leisure experiences of older men and women. Earlier in this section we considered age as a common factor shared by men and women that is associated with decline or changes in leisure participation. However, aging also creates within-gender variability for older women and men. Research by Bennett (1998) shows that for both men and women, time spent walking and participating in outdoor recreation is greater at younger ages (65 to 74) compared with older ages (75 and older). However, Bennett found that men's participation in indoor activities is greater for the older group compared with the younger group, perhaps as a substitution for the time given up on outdoor activities, which is more substantial for men than women. Tinsley and colleagues (Tinsley, Colbs, Teaff, & Kaufman, 1987) conducted an analysis of the psychological benefits older adults derived from a variety of leisure activities. They found that leisure activities associated with social interaction, including provision or receipt of support, were more likely to be engaged in by older women with lower socioeconomic status, suggesting that motivations for participation in certain kinds of leisure activities may vary depending on age, income, and education.

On a related note, employment status may have an impact on women's leisure experiences in older adulthood. Pinquart and Schindler (2009) found that women in Germany who had been employed and transitioned to collecting a state pension had a sharper increase in leisure satisfaction than women who had not been employed before the transition to collecting a state pension. The authors propose that women who had been employed before retirement likely had a greater share of household work compared with men, with the end of paid work resulting in more leisure time.

Finally, there is some evidence of racial and ethnic variation in the leisure experiences of older women. In a study of older women in Singapore, over half of whom had never been employed and the majority of whom were married, leisure activities were typically confined to those consistent with a nurturing role, such as cooking, visiting family, and caring for grandchildren (Teo, 1997). In addition, for some married women, the husband's retirement tended to curtail the wife's free time due to expectations that she should cater to his needs. In a study by Eyler et al. (1999) that examined social support for older women's physical activity across diverse racial groups in the United States (black, Hispanic, American Indian or Alaskan native, and white), Hispanic women and white women had higher levels of participation in physically active leisure than women in the other two racial groups. In addition, Hispanic women were more likely to have high scores on social support for physical activities compared with the other three groups, although the authors did not propose an explanation for these differences.

Relatively little of the research on gender and leisure for older adults has incorporated a critical gerontology approach or looked at the intersection of power structures associated with age and gender. Nevertheless, some feminist researchers (e.g., Gibson, Ashton-Schaeffer, Green, & Autry, 2003; Wearing, 1998) have shown that gender and gender relations do influence the leisure behavior and experiences of older adults in a variety of ways. Paying greater attention to structural factors as well as to agency may lead to enhanced understanding of the role that gender plays in older adults' leisure lives, for example whether older women are doubly disadvantaged and whether age facilitates resistance to dominant relations of power.

Sexual Orientation

Sexual orientation is a complex construct typically defined as a constellation of sexual or romantic attraction, sexual behavior, and sexual-orientation identity (Laumann, Gagnon, Michael, & Michaels, 1994; Savin-Williams, 2006). Depending on which characteristic is chosen, the percentage of people who could be defined as sexual minorities varies from around 20% (i.e., ever experienced same-sex attraction) to approximately 1% (i.e., consistently self-identified as gay, lesbian, or bisexual) (Savin-Williams, 2006). There is ample evidence that sexual minorities face pervasive homophobic stigmatization that creates considerable distress for some, resulting in poor mental and physical health outcomes (Meyer, 2003). Homophobic stigmatization is a fundamentally social phenomenon (i.e., rooted in social norms and expressed in attitudes and social interaction) (Herek, 2000). Negative attitudes toward sexual minorities stem partially from the threat that nonheterosexual identity poses to pervasive cultural norms of gender polarization and androcentrism (Bem, 1993). Thus, macro-level homophobic cultural ideology is expressed in policy, social structures, and negative interpersonal interactions (Mock & Cornelius, 2003). Due to the social nature of the prejudice and stigma that sexual minorities face, the social benefits associated with some forms of recreation and leisure may be particularly helpful. For example, Iwasaki and colleagues' (Iwasaki et al., 2006) study of Aboriginal adults, people with disabilities, and gay and lesbian adults in Canada found that recreation and leisure participation was an important source of physical and psychological well-being and enhanced a sense of community and social integration.

However, there are several potential challenges and drawbacks to recreation and leisure involvement for sexual minorities. For example, team sports are often homophobic environments (Ander-son, 2002; Clarke, 1998). Partially in response to this homophobic climate, sporting options exclusive to sexual minorities are becoming increasingly popular (Jones & McCarthy, 2010). Although gay and lesbian bars are important venues for socializing and community building, frequent bar attendance is a risk factor for alcoholism and substance abuse (Bux, 1996; Greenwood et al., 2001; Heffernan, 1998). Thus, some forms of recreation may have barriers to participation for sexual minorities (e.g., team sports), and some leisure options carry potential health risks.

In addition to social-structural factors (e.g., stigmatization and discrimination) that shape the recreation and leisure experiences of sexual minorities, there are individual-level factors that could potentially have an impact on recreation and leisure choices. For example, there is evidence of greater gender nonconformity among gay men and lesbians (Bailey, Kim, & Linsenmeier, 1997). In contrast, amplification of typical gender patterns has been found in the decision making of same-sex couples (Mock & Cornelius, 2007; Mock, Taylor, & Savin-Williams, 2006). Although there is a growing literature on the recreation and leisure experiences of sexual-minority adolescents (Caldwell, Kivel, Smith, & Hayes, 1998; Johnson, 2000; Kivel & Kleiber, 2000) and adults (Casey, 2009; Clarke, 1998; Herrara & Scott, 2005; Johnson & Samdahl, 2005; Pritchard, Morgan, & Sedgely, 2002), little has been written on the experiences of older sexual-minority adults (Jacobson & Samdahl, 1998). Thus, in addition to a review of research on recreation and leisure of older sexual-minority adults, we draw on broader themes from the literature on the experiences of sexual-minority older adults that are likely to influence their recreation and leisure.

Older adults often mention the role of recreation and leisure as an opportunity to socialize and as a forum for providing and receiving social support (Heuser, 2005; Riddick & Stewart, 1994; Tinsley et al., 1987). Similarly, research with sexual-minority older adults has identified social support as a key theme. A study of 80 lesbian women and gay men over the age of 50 in the American Midwest found a high level of involvement in the gay community (Quam & Whitford, 1992). Specifically, approximately 76% of the women and 53% of the men were active in lesbian and gay social groups, and roughly a third of both women and men participated in lesbian and gay religious organizations. In a study of the social embeddedness of older lesbian, gay, and bisexual adults, Fokkema and Kuyper (2009) found that the vast majority had consistent monthly contact with family and friends, over a third were involved in volunteer organizations, and social contact and volunteer work were associated with less perceived loneliness.

Although there is evidence that many, if not most, sexual-minority older adults have meaningful social ties and engage in community activities, discrimination has an impact on their lives. Homophobic stigmatization is a challenge noted in virtually all research on the experiences of sexual-minority older adults. Also, a sexual-minority identity is typically considered a concealable identity. Concealing a stigmatized identity requires vigilance that can lead to preoccupation and anxiety about the potential negative consequences of disclosure (Pachankis, 2007). Thus, most sexual minorities face the dual chal-

lenge of coping with discrimination and managing a concealable stigma. The impact of discrimination takes various forms, from overt social exclusion to fear of potential future discrimination. In a study of leisure experiences of lesbians over age 60 in the United States (Jacobson & Samdahl, 1998), one participant noted acceptance from heterosexual neighbors on a day-to-day basis but exclusion from larger get-togethers: "Never does one get invited to their homes when one is having one of those great big beautiful barbecues for friends or family" (p. 243).

A top concern among sexual-minority older adults is the fear of rejection by service providers or in long-term care settings (Brotman, Ryan, & Cormier, 2003; Orel, 2004). As one study participant put it, "Most people are terrified of going into any of the care facilities, and having to be hidden, losing their lovers, their partners, their friends . . ."

Services and Advocacy for Gay, Lesbian, Bisexual, and Transgender Elders (SAGE)

Services and Advocacy for Gay, Lesbian, and Transgender Elders (SAGE) is the world's oldest and largest nonprofit agency dedicated to serving lesbian, gay, bisexual, and transgender older people. Since its inception, SAGE has pioneered programs and services for the aging LGBT community, provided technical assistance and training to expand opportunities for LGBT older people across the country, and provided a national voice on LGBT aging issues.

A SAGE client named Rosita spoke of its impact on her:

Photo courtesy of Services & Advocacy for GLBT Elders (SAGE).

SAGE gave me a place to go when my partner died. I felt the support of a room full of women who understood what it is like to love another woman and the acknowledgment of the group-leader therapist for the issues that I raised and the feelings that I shared. I met two other lesbian widows who avidly listened to my story afterward and eagerly told me theirs. They role-modeled for me in that very crucial moment and filled me with hope and assurances that there would be life beyond my loss.

Because of SAGE I witnessed a vibrant community of elders hopping on the dance floor on a Sunday afternoon, attending job skill workshops and retirement counseling, putting on summer barbecues and holiday dinners, celebrating birthdays, and bravely experiencing their dwindling health and the passing of relatives, partners, and lifelong friends (Libre de Marulanda, 2008, p. 3).

(Brotman et al., 2003, p. 197). To help counter these concerns, sexual-minority adults often express a preference for at least awareness by practitioners of their unique issues (e.g., historic and ongoing discrimination, provision for same-sex partners) and preferably services, recreation and leisure opportunities, and senior housing specifically for sexual minorities (Orel, 2004).

Sexual minorities are flexible in how they meet their social needs. For example, their friendship networks have been characterized as families of choice, that is, a supportive friendship network of people who are not related (Weeks, Heaphy, & Donovan, 2001; Weston, 1991). Perhaps as evidence of this, they are more likely to have more monthly contact with friends than relatives compared with heterosexual adults (Fokkema & Kuyper, 2009). However, social networks of sexual-minority older adults often differ significantly by gender. Specifically, women have a higher proportion of female friends compared with men, who have a higher proportion of male friends (Grossman, D'Augelli, & Hershberger, 2000). This gender difference is reflected in older sexual-minority adults' preferences for not only services and housing focused on sexual minorities but also male- and female-focused options (Jacobs, Rasmussen, & Hohman, 1999).

This is not to say that sexual-minority older adults have no contact with relatives. In fact, grand-parenting presents unique joys and challenges for sexual-minority adults. In a study of lesbian grandmothers (Orel, 2006), one woman said, "I couldn't love my grandkids any more. They mean everything to me and my son knows that. He's great about bringing them over here to visit me and I'm always included in all the family gatherings"(p. 189). About managing her identity, another woman said, "I'm assuming that if my granddaughter did have difficulty with my lesbianism, my daughter would set her straight—no pun intended"(p. 185). Some grandparents do face barriers, though; as one woman said, "I know [my ex-husband] has said some terrible things about me. He was the one who told my grandkids that I was a lesbian, and ever since my relationship with them hasn't been the same. . . . It's sad. It breaks my heart" (p. 190).

Gender beyond the typical dichotomous categories is another form of diversity in the lives of older sexual-minority adults. Although there is little information documenting the experiences of transgender older adults and even less research on their recreation and leisure experiences, there is evidence that they have unique needs. **Transi-**tion refers to a process during which a person is perceived as changing gender identity from either female to male (FTM) or male to female (MTF). Some transgender people do not transition until midlife or older adulthood (Cook-Daniels, 2006). In addition, not all transgendered people transition to definitely male or female; some prefer different genders in different contexts, and some identify as trans but do not modify their appearance. Compared with other sexual minorities, transgender older adults sometimes face unique and potentially dangerous forms of discrimination, as experienced by an FTM person whose doctor would not treat his ovarian cancer (Cook-Daniels, 2006). The implications of noncongruent bodies (Cook-Daniels, 2006) for the recreation and leisure experiences of older adults remains unexplored by researchers, but such work has the potential to offer valuable insight into how people cope with stigmatization and meet their recreation and leisure needs, and it may suggest ways we can facilitate inclusive recreation and leisure opportunities for a diverse population.

Conclusion

Critical gerontology provides a useful framework for analysis of diversity, leisure, and aging through its emphasis on power relations, stigma, exclusion, constraints, and lack of resources. Critical gerontology also directs attention to human rights, human dignity, and social justice through its focus on agency, identity, resistance, individual action, and construction of the self through leisure. Additionally, intersectionality is a powerful concept, emphasizing the need to explore multiple axes of oppression and constraints and recognizing that people's lives and leisure are influenced by their connection to a variety of dimensions of power.

Yet, despite the resonance of the concept of intersectionality, relatively little discussion exists in the literature about how this concept specifically, and critical gerontology in general, can be applied to the analysis of leisure behavior, experience, and practice among older adults. This leads us to suggest a model that might be useful for future research, encouraging an investigation of common experiences among older adults, the unique perspectives of marginalized groups, and sources of diversity within groups. This three-part approach to research of marginalized groups is a synthesis of research recommendations from the study of race and ethnicity (Kivel et al., 2009), gender (Henderson, 2009), and sexual orientation

(Mock, Sedlovskaya, & Purdie-Vaughns, 2011; Mock et al., 2006; Savin-Williams, 2001).

First, investigating common experiences of older adults would enhance our understanding of aging in general as well as factors that facilitate healthy leisure participation. This would help to counteract negative stereotypes, stigma, exclusion, and other constraints linked to ageism that limit older adults' leisure.

Second, there is a clear need for more research on factors unique to diverse groups of older adults, such as groups identified by race, ethnicity, gender, and sexual orientation. This research is needed to direct attention, currently lacking in the field of leisure and aging, to issues of Eurocentrism, androcentrism, and heterosexism. Clearly there are differences in leisure experiences and opportunities among older adults in terms of the structural constraints they face due to various dimensions of power. But there are also opportunities to resist, challenge, or counteract the disadvantages and demeaning ideological systems of belief both individually and collectively.

Third, there is a need to also counteract the out-group homogeneity bias (Judd & Park, 1988) that threatens the credibility of research looking at shared experiences, meanings, and responses to specific types of inequities, such as racial discrimination. The out-group homogeneity bias can occur if intersectionality and multiples axes of power are ignored. Investigating variation within groups also recognizes agency and allows for individual meanings, interpretations, and responses to leisure-related settings, opportunities, and challenges.

It may not be feasible for all research and practice to incorporate all components of this model simultaneously. Rather, we see this as a heuristic model that can help to guide and facilitate a range of studies on aging, leisure, and diversity and raise awareness among practitioners about similarity, difference, and heterogeneity among mainstream and marginalized groups. Though any one study may focus primarily on one component of the model, awareness of the other components and other issues might help to prevent overinterpretation and overgeneralization of findings.

As a final thought, research on diversity and leisure, as mentioned earlier, has tended to focus on disadvantaged groups (i.e., people of color, women, gays and lesbians). Yet, critical theorists are increasingly talking about the need to understand privilege, such as the advantages associated with being white, being male, and being heterosexual (Calasanti, 2004; see also Kleiber &

Genoe, this volume). Understanding privilege, it is argued, provides insight into power relations and may lead to ways to reduce discrimination and facilitate social justice and equity. The idea of intersectionality lends itself to the recognition of multiple advantages as well as disadvantages. We suggest, therefore, that the model discussed here, through comparisons between and within groups, could also be used to understand the role of privilege in the leisure lives of some segments of the older adult population. This could contribute to the growing body of knowledge on leisure, aging, and diversity, and ultimately the critical gerontology goal of individual freedom, fulfillment, solidarity, and human dignity.

KEY TERMS

androcentrism—An assumption expressed in multiple contexts, implicitly or explicitly, that *male* is the normative or default gender and other genders must be explained or accounted for.

critical gerontology—A macrotheoretical approach that focuses on constraints to older adults' access to economic and material resources and examines sources of empowerment and disempowerment, inequity, and inclusion and exclusion.

ethnicity—A constellation of language, beliefs, and social views and identities related to country of origin or cultural group.

Eurocentrism—An assumption expressed implicitly or explicitly that the European cultural experience is the normative cultural experience, and other cultural perspectives must be explained or can only be understood in relation to a European cultural comparison.

gender—A constellation of beliefs and practices that give rise to an understanding of what it means to be male or female.

heterosexism—An assumption expressed implicitly or explicitly that the default sexual orientation for all people is heterosexual and that other sexual orientations must be explained.

intersectionality—The interconnections and interlocking relationships between multiple marginalized statuses (e.g., racism, sexism, heterosexism, ageism).

race—Socially constructed identities that relate to visible physical characteristics and are often linked to a corresponding ethnic or cultural group.

sexual orientation—A constellation of sexual or romantic attraction, sexual behavior, and sexual-orientation identity.

transition—A process during which a person is perceived as changing gender identity from either female to male (FTM) or male to female (MTF).

REVIEW AND DISCUSSION QUESTIONS

1. Define *race*, *ethnicity*, *gender*, and *sexual orientation* as understood by social science researchers.

2. Define *critical gerontology*.

3. Describe the roles leisure plays in the lives of older adults.

4. What are some of the constraints to leisure participation among older adults? Among marginalized older adults?

5. What are some typical gendered recreation activities among older adults?

6. Describe how a sexual-minority identity (a concealable identity) affects leisure experiences.

7. How do leisure experiences differ among ethnic groups? Identify three ethnic groups and provide one example of a leisure activity specific to each group.

LEARNING ACTIVITIES

1. Visit a local retirement facility and interview the recreation coordinator. What types of activities are offered? If there is no recreation coordinator, interview the staff member responsible for the residents' recreational activities.

2. Visit two or three retirement facilities that target specific ethnic groups. What recreational activities are provided for the residents? Do the activities differ in each retirement home? Explain.

3. Research two or three retirement facilities, each from a different continent. What activities are offered for their residents? Are the activities different? Explain.

4. If you were a recreation coordinator in a retirement facility, describe how you would tailor three different recreation and leisure activities to fit the needs of the marginalized older adults served by the facility.

5. Visit a recreation center in your area and find out what activities it provides for older adults. What activities are specifically designed for older adults? Which activities are general? What activities are specific to marginalized groups? If there are no specific activities for marginalized groups, write a letter to the manager explaining the importance of meeting the needs of various marginalized groups.

6. Design an activities brochure for a recreation center targeting marginalized older adults. Select a marginalized group of your choice. Include the mission statement, activity descriptions, the benefits of the activities for the target group, and pictures. Make it visually appealing.

7. Use a source outside of this textbook to research the Red Hat Society and report your findings. How is the Red Hat Society a form of leisure participation? Visit the local Red Hat Society and conduct an interview. Find out what activities they offer and what the interviewee appreciates about the society. If there is no Red Hat Society within easy access, consider a phone or e-mail interview.

CRITICAL-THINKING ACTIVITIES

1. Defend the need to provide recreation and leisure services to all older adults, especially marginalized older adults.

2. This chapter describes leisure experiences for older adults in various marginalized groups. First, compare the leisure experiences of older adults in the dominant group with those of older adults who are marginalized. Describe how leisure is used by marginalized groups and by nonmarginalized groups. How are they the same? Different? Are their experiences beneficial for them? Why or why not? Second, look at the leisure experiences of older adults in specific marginalized groups (e.g., sexual minorities, gender minorities, racial and ethnic minorities). Describe commonalities and differences in the leisure experiences.

3. This chapter is about marginalized older adults and their leisure experiences. Compare their leisure experiences with those of marginalized youth or young adults in general. What similarities and differences do you discern? How are these leisure experiences beneficial to both youth and older adults? What challenges are common to both? Unique to each? Then look at the specific marginalized groups discussed in this chapter (e.g., sexual minorities, gender minorities, racial and ethnic minorities). Compare the leisure experiences of these specific marginalized groups in terms of age.

4. Has your understanding of leisure experiences among marginalized groups within older adults changed after reading this chapter? If so, in what ways?

SUGGESTED READING

Bem, S.L. (1993). *The lenses of gender.* New Haven, CT: Yale University Press.

Biggs, S., & Daatland, S.O. (2004). Ageing and diversity: A critical introduction. In S.O. Daatland & S. Biggs (Eds.), *Ageing and diversity: Multiple pathways and cultural migrations* (pp. 1-9). Bristol, UK: Policy Press.

Grossman, A.H., D'Augelli, A.R., & Hershberger, S.L. (2000). Social support networks of lesbian, gay, and bisexual adults 60 years of age and older. *Journal of Gerontology: Psychological Sciences, 55B,* P171-P179.

Kivel, B.D., Johnson, C.W., & Scraton, S. (2009). (Re)Theorizing leisure, experience and race. *Journal of Leisure Research, 41,* 473-493.

Martinez, I.L., Kim, K., Tanner, E., Fried, L.P., & Seeman, T. (2009). Ethnic and class variations in promoting social activities among older adults. *Activities, Adaptation, & Aging, 33,* 96-119.

REFERENCES

Agahi, N., Ahacic, K., & Parker, M.G. (2006). Continuity of leisure participation from middle age to old age. *Journal of Gerontology: Social Sciences, 61B,* S340-S346.

Ali, N., & Holden, A. (2006). Post-colonial Pakistani mobilities: The embodiment of the "myth of return" and tourism. *Mobilities, 1,* 217-242.

Anderson, E. (2002). Openly gay athletes: Contesting hegemonic masculinity in a homophobic environment. *Gender & Society, 16,* 860-877.

Armstrong, G.K., & Morgan, K. (1998). Stability and change in levels of habitual physical activity in later life. *Age and Ageing, 27,* 17-23.

Baars, J. (2006). Beyond neomodernism, antimodernism, and postmodernism: Basic categories for contemporary critical gerontology. In J. Baars, D. Dannefer, C. Phillipson, & A. Walker (Eds.), *Aging, globalization and inequality: The new critical gerontology* (pp. 17-42). Amityville, NY: Baywood.

Bailey, J.M., Kim, P.Y., & Linsenmeier, J.A.W. (1997). Butch, femme, or straight acting? Partner preferences of gay men and lesbians. *Journal of Personality and Social Psychology, 73,* 960-973.

Baumrind, D. (1980). New directions in socialization research. *American Psychologist, 35,* 639-652.

Bem, S.L. (1993). *The lenses of gender.* New Haven, CT: Yale University Press.

Benedetti, T.R.B., Goncalves, L.H., Petroski, E., Nassar, S.M., Schwingel, A., & Chodzko-Zajko, W. (2008). Aging in Brazil: Physical activity, socioeconomic conditions, and diseases among older adults in Southern Brazil. *Journal of Applied Gerontology, 27,* 631-640.

Bennett, K.M. (1998). Gender and longitudinal changes in physical activities in later life. *Age and Ageing, 27,* 24-28.

Biggs, S. (2004). Age, gender, narratives and masquerades. *Journal of Aging Studies, 18*(1), 45-58.

Boyle, M., & McKay, J. (1995). "You leave your troubles at the gate": A case study of the exploitation of older women's labor and "leisure" in sport. *Gender and Society, 9,* 556-575.

Brotman, S., Ryan, B., & Cormier, R. (2003). The health and social service needs of gay and lesbian elders and their families in Canada. *Gerontologist, 43,* 192-202.

Bux, D.A. (1996). The epidemiology of problem drinking in gay men and lesbians: A critical review. *Clinical Psychology Review, 16,* 277-298.

Calasanti, T. (2004). New directions in feminist gerontology: An introduction. *Journal of Aging Studies, 18*(1), 1-8.

Caldwell, L.L., Kivel, B.D., Smith, E.A., & Hayes, D. (1998). The leisure context of adolescents who are lesbian, gay male, bisexual and questioning their sexual identities: An exploratory study. *Journal of Leisure Research, 30,* 341-355.

Casey, M. (2009). Tourist gay(ze) or transnational sex: Australian gay men's holiday desires. *Leisure Studies, 28,* 157-172.

Clarke, G. (1998). Queering the pitch and coming out to play: Lesbians in physical education and sport. *Sport, Education and Society, 3,* 145-160.

Collins, P.H. (1998). *Fighting words: Black women and the search for justice.* Minneapolis: University of Minnesota.

Cook-Daniels, L. (2006). Trans aging. In D. Kimmel, T. Rose, & S. David (Eds.), *Lesbian, gay, bisexual, and transgender aging: Research and clinical perspectives* (pp. 20-35). New York: Columbia University Press.

Dannefer, D. (2003). Cumulative advantage/disadvantage and the life course: Cross-fertilizing age and social science theory. *Journal of Gerontology, 58B,* S327-S337.

Dergance, J.M., Mouton, C.P., Lichtenstein, M.J., & Hazuda, H.P. (2005). Potential mediators of ethnic differences in physical activity in older Mexican Americans and European Americans: Results from the San Antonio Longitudinal Study of Aging. *American Geriatrics Society, 53,* 1240-1247.

Dionigi, R. (2006). Competetive sport as leisure in later life: Negotiations, discourse, and aging. *Leisure Sciences, 28,* 181-196.

Estes, C. (2004). Social security privatization and older women: A feminist political economy perspective. *Journal of Aging Studies, 18*(1), 9-26.

Eyler, A.A., Brownson, R.C., Donatelle, R.J., King, A.C., Brown, D., & Sallis, J.F. (1999). Physical activity social support and middle- and older-aged women: Results from a U.S. survey. *Social Science & Medicine, 49,* 781-789.

Fokkema, T., & Kuyper, L. (2009). The relation between social embeddedness and loneliness among older lesbian, gay, and bisexual adults in the Netherlands. *Archives of Sexual Behavior, 38,* 264-275.

Fox, K. (2006). Leisure and indigenous peoples. In E. Jackson (Ed.), *Leisure and the quality of life: Impacts on social, economic and cultural development* (pp. 179-190). Hangzhou, China: World Leisure and Zheijiang University Press.

Gibson, H., Ashton-Schaeffer, C., Green, J., & Autry, C. (2003). Leisure in the lives of retirement-aged women: Conversations about leisure and life. *Leisure/Loisir, 28,* 203-230.

Greenwood, G.L., White, E.W., Page-Shafer, K., Bein, E., Osmond, D.H., Paul, J., & Stall, R.D. (2001). Correlates of heavy substance use among young gay and bisexual men: The San Francisco Young Men's Health Study. *Drug and Alcohol Dependence, 61,* 105-112.

Grossman, A.H., D'Augelli, A.R., & Hershberger, S.L. (2000). Social support networks of lesbian, gay, and bisexual adults 60 years of age and older. *Journal of Gerontology: Psychological Sciences, 55B,* P171-P179.

Gvion, L. (2009). Organised leisure as promoting nostalgia: Israeli senior citizens singing in Yiddish. *Leisure Studies, 28,* 51-65.

Hare-Mustin, R.T., & Maracek, J. (1988). The meaning of difference: Gender theory, postmodernism, and psychology. *American Psychologist, 43,* 455-464.

Heffernan, K. (1998). The nature and predictors of substance use among lesbians. *Addictive Behaviors, 23,* 517-528.

Henderson, K.A. (2009). Just research and physical activity: Diversity is more than an independent variable. *Leisure Sciences, 31,* 100-105.

Henderson, K.A., & Ainsworth, B.E. (2001). Researching leisure and physical activity with women of color: Issues and emerging questions. *Leisure Sciences, 23,* 21-34.

Henderson, K.A., & Shaw, S.M. (2006). Gender and leisure: Challenges and opportunities for feminist research. In C. Rojek, S.M. Shaw, & A.J. Veal (Eds.), *A handbook of leisure studies* (pp. 216-230). Basingstoke, UK: Palgrave Macmillan.

Herek, G.M. (2000). The psychology of sexual prejudice. *Current Directions in Psychological Science, 9,* 19-22.

Herrera, S.L., & Scott, D. (2005). "We gotta get out of this place!": Leisure travel among gay men living in a small city. *Tourism Review International, 8,* 249-262.

Heuser, L. (2005). We're not too old to play sports: The career of women lawn bowlers. *Leisure Studies, 25,* 45-60.

Iwasaki, Y., MacKay, K.J., MacTavish, J., Ristock, J., & Bartlett, J. (2006). Voices from the margins: Stress, active living, and leisure as a contributor to coping with stress. *Leisure Sciences, 28,* 163-180.

Jacobs, R.J., Rasmussen, L.A., & Hohman, M.M. (1999). The social support needs of older lesbians, gay men, and bisexuals. *Journal of Gay and Lesbian Social Services, 9,* 1-30.

Jacobson, M.E. (1998). *Whiteness of a different color: European immigrants and the alchemy of race.* Cambridge, MA: Harvard University Press.

Jacobson, S., & Samdahl, D.M. (1998). Leisure in the lives of old lesbians: Experiences with and responses to discrimination. *Journal of Leisure Research, 30,* 233-255.

Janke, M., Davey, A., & Kleiber, D. (2006). Modeling change in older adults' leisure activities. *Leisure Sciences, 28,* 285-303.

Johnson, C.W. (2000). Living the game of hide and seek: Leisure in the lives of gay and lesbian young adults. *Leisure/Loisir, 24,* 255-278.

Johnson, C., & Samdahl, D. (2005). "The night they took over": Misogyny in a country-western gay bar. *Leisure Sciences, 27,* 331-338.

Jones, L., & McCarthy, M. (2010). Mapping the landscape of gay men's football. *Leisure Studies, 29,* 161-173.

Judd, C.M., & Park, B. (1988). Out-group homogeneity: Judgments of variability at the individual and group levels. *Journal of Personality and Social Psychology, 54,* 778-788.

Kivel, B.D., Johnson, C.W., & Scraton, S. (2009). (Re)Theorizing leisure, experience and race. *Journal of Leisure Research, 41,* 473-493.

Kivel, B.D., & Kleiber, D.A. (2000). Leisure in the identity formation of lesbian/gay youth: Personal, but not social. *Leisure Sciences, 22,* 215-232.

Lai, D.W.L. (2006). Predictors of use of senior centers by elderly Chinese immigrants in Canada. *Journal of Ethnic and Cultural Diversity in Social Work, 15,* 97-121.

Laumann, E., Gagnon, J.H., Michael, R.T., & Michaels, S. (1994). *The social organization of sexuality: Sexual practices in the United States.* Chicago: University of Chicago Press.

Lennartsson, C., & Silverstein, M. (2001). Does engagement with life enhance survival of elderly people in Sweden? The roles of social and leisure activities. *Journal of Gerontology: Social Sciences, 56B,* S335-S342.

Libre de Marulanda, R. (2008). *If it weren't for SAGE.* Poem-prose speech presented at the 30th Anniversary SAGE Gala and Awards Ceremony, New York.

Martinez, I.L., Kim, K., Tanner, E., Fried, L.P., & Seeman, T. (2009). Ethnic and class variations in promoting social activities among older adults. *Activities, Adaptation, & Aging, 33,* 96-119.

Meyer, I.H. (2003). Prejudice, social stress, and mental health in lesbian, gay, and bisexual populations: Conceptual issues and research evidence. *Psychological Bulletin, 129,* 674-697.

Mobily, K.E., Leslie, D.K., Lemke, J.H., Wallace, R.B., & Kohout, F.J. (1986). Leisure patterns and attitudes of the rural elderly. *Journal of Applied Gerontology, 5,* 201-214.

Mock, S.E., & Cornelius, S.W. (2003). The case of same-sex couples. In P.E. Moen (Ed.), *It's about time: Couples' career strains, strategies, and successes* (pp. 275-287). Ithaca, NY: Cornell University Press.

Mock, S.E., & Cornelius, S.W. (2007). Profiles of interdependence: The retirement planning of married, cohabiting, and lesbian couples. *Sex Roles, 56,* 793-800.

Mock, S.E., Sedlovskaya, A., & Purdie-Vaughns, V. (2011). Gay and bisexual men's disclosure of sexual orientation in the workplace: Associations with retirement planning. *Journal of Applied Gerontology, 30,* 123-132.

Mock, S.E., Taylor, C.J., & Savin-Williams, R.C. (2006). Aging together: The retirement plans of same-sex couples. In D. Kimmel, T. Rose, & S. David (Eds.), *Lesbian, gay, bisexual, and transgender aging: Research and clinical perspectives* (pp. 152-174). New York: Columbia University Press.

Nilsson, I., Löfgren, B., Fisher, A., & Bernspång, B. (2006). Focus on leisure repertoire in the oldest old: The Umeå 85+ Study. *Journal of Applied Gerontology, 25,* 391-405.

Orel, N.A. (2004). Gay, lesbian, and bisexual elders. *Journal of Gerontological Social Work, 43,* 57-77.

Orel, N. (2006). Lesbian and bisexual women as grandparents: The centrality of sexual orientation in the grandparent-grandchild relationship. In D. Kimmel, T. Rose, & S. David (Eds.), *Lesbian, gay, bisexual, and transgender aging: Research and clinical perspectives* (pp. 175-194). New York: Columbia University Press.

Outley, C.W., & McKenzie, S. (2007). Older African American women: An examination of the intersections of an adult play group and life satisfaction. *Activities, Adaptation, & Aging, 31,* 19-36.

Pachankis, J.E. (2007). The psychological implications of concealing a stigma: A cognitive-affective-behavioral model. *Psychological Bulletin, 133,* 328-345.

Philipp, S.F. (1995). Race and leisure constraints. *Leisure Sciences, 17,* 109-120.

Pinquart, M., & Schindler, I. (2009). Change of leisure satisfaction in the transition to retirement: A latent-class analysis. *Leisure Sciences, 31,* 311-329.

Pritchard, A., Morgan, N., & Sedgely, D. (2002). In search of lesbian space? The experience of Manchester's gay village. *Leisure Studies, 21,* 105-123.

Purdie-Vaughns, V., & Eibach, R. (2008). Intersectional invisibility: The distinctive advantages and disadvantages of multiple subordinate-group identities. *Sex Roles, 59,* 377-391.

Quam, J.K., & Whitford, G.S. (1992). Adaptation and age-related expectations of older gay and lesbian adults. *Gerontologist, 32,* 367-374.

Riddick, C.C., & Stewart, D.G. (1994). An examination of the life satisfaction and importance of leisure in the lives of older female retirees: A comparison of blacks to whites. *Journal of Leisure Research, 26,* 75-87.

Ruchlin, H.S., & Lachs, M.S. (1999). Prevalence and correlates of exercise among older adults. *Journal of Applied Gerontology, 18,* 341-357.

Savin-Williams, R.C. (2001). A critique of research on sexual-minority youths. *Journal of Adolescence, 24,* 5-13.

Savin-Williams, R.C. (2006). Who's gay? Does it matter? *Current Directions in Psychological Science, 15,* 40-44.

Shaw, S.M. (1999). Gender and leisure. In T.L. Burton & E.L. Jackson (Eds.), *Leisure studies at the millennium* (pp. 271-281). State College, PA: Venture.

Shaw, S.M. (2001). Conceptualizing resistance: Women's leisure as political practice. *Journal of Leisure Research, 26,* 186-201.

Shaw, S.M. (2006). Resistance. In C. Rojek, S.M. Shaw, & A.J. Veal (Eds.), *A handbook of leisure studies* (pp. 533-545). Basingstoke, UK: Palgrave Macmillan.

Shinew, K.J., Floyd, M.F., McGuire, F.A., & Noe, F.P. (1996). Class polarization and leisure activity preferences of African Americans: Intragroup comparisons. *Journal of Leisure Research, 28,* 219-232.

Shinew, K.J., Floyd, M., & Parry, D. (2004). Understanding the relationship between race and leisure activities and constraints: Exploring an alternative framework. *Leisure Sciences, 26,* 181-199.

Stanley, D., & Freysinger, V.J. (1995). The impact of age, health, and sex on the frequency of older adults' leisure activity and participation: A longitudinal study. *Activities, Adaptation, and Aging, 19,* 31-42.

Strain, L.A., Grabusic, C.C., Searle, M.S., & Dunn, N.J. (2002). Continuing and ceasing leisure activities in later life: A longitudinal study. *Gerontologist, 42,* 217-223.

Teo, P. (1997). Older women and leisure in Singapore. *Ageing and Society, 17,* 649-672.

Tinsley, H.E.A., Colbs, S.L., Teaff, J.D., & Kaufman, N. (1987). The relationship of age, gender, health and economic status to the psychological benefits of older persons report from participation in leisure activities. *Leisure Sciences, 9,* 53-65.

Twigg, J. (2004). The body, gender, and age: Feminist insights in social gerontology. *Journal of Aging Studies, 18*(1), 59-73

Unger, R.K. (1979). Toward a redefinition of sex and gender. *American Psychologist, 34,* 1085-1094.

Wearing, B.M. (1998). *Leisure and feminist theory.* London: Sage.

Weeks, J., Heaphy, B., & Donovan, C. (2001). *Same sex intimacies: Families of choice and other life experiments.* London: Routledge.

Weston, K. (1991). *Families we choose: Lesbians, gays, kinship.* New York: Columbia University Press.

Wilson, W.J. (1980). *The declining significance of race: Blacks and changing American institutions.* Chicago: University of Chicago Press.

Yarnal, C.M., Chick, G., & Kerstetter, D.L. (2008). "I did not have time to play growing up . . . so this is my play time. It's the best thing I have ever done for myself": What is play to older women? *Leisure Sciences, 30,* 235-252.

Leisure and Healthy Aging

Part III covers the physical, psychological, social, and spiritual aspects of overall well-being for older adults. It also discusses the role leisure plays in all of these domains.

In chapter 7, Bevan Grant and Mary Ann Kluge analyze the contribution of physical activity to aging well. They adopt a wellness perspective whereby participation in physical activity in later life contributes to overall health. After examining the health benefits of active leisure, Grant and Kluge address potential constraints to active lifestyles and implications for programming for older adults. They suggest that the ultimate goal is the adoption of a leisure lifestyle that includes regular physical activity, and they discuss the growing participation in competitive sport by mid- and later-life adults. They finish their chapter with a view that the future is uncertain. Will health services be inundated with older people suffering from the so-called lifestyle diseases (e.g., type 2 diabetes, heart disease, high blood pressure) due in part to sedentary lives, or will we reap the benefits of increased physical activity among older generations? John Rice contributes the international sidebar with a focus on a New Zealand physical activity program called *never2old*.

In chapter 8, Roger Mannell and Ryan Snelgrove examine psychological well-being. They divide their chapter into two aspects of psychological health. First, psychosocial well-being and the role of leisure in promoting happiness and meaning are discussed. The authors examine theories that help to illuminate the relationship between leisure and happiness and satisfaction as leisure patterns change with increasing age, and they discuss the impact of nonleisure factors such as perceived health. The second aspect of psychological health discussed is cognitive functioning or vitality. This deals with brain health and issues of memory. The authors examine the influence of physical, social, and mental forms of leisure on cognitive functioning. In addition, two scenarios of older adults with different life circumstances and needs are presented, and readers are asked to design programs that meet the needs of these individuals based on the chapter content.

The final chapter in part III examines leisure in relation to social and spiritual well-being. In chapter 9, Paul Heintzman and Erin Patriquin start by providing definitions of social and spiritual well-being before examining the role of leisure in providing context for social and spiritual outcomes. They discuss the therapeutic recreation outcome model as a possible modality to use with older adults in promoting spiritual and social health before going through some of the key research findings in this area. The authors note that although spiritual well-being through leisure has not been examined as extensively as social well-being, there are some key studies that show the importance of spiritual well-being through leisure and how it can also help people with life's challenges such as coping with transitions and stress. A sidebar written by Glen Van Andel provides insights into retirement from a long-time academic who has retired and how he has shaped his life around leisure, family, church, and continued contact with undergraduate students.

CHAPTER 7

Leisure and Physical Well-Being

Bevan C. Grant ■ **Mary Ann Kluge**

After reading this chapter, you will be able to

- describe the benefits of physical leisure for overall health and well-being,
- describe why engaging in physical leisure in later life is about more than just being physical,
- identify constraints to engaging in physical leisure for those aged 65 years and older,
- explain why being physically active as a way of contributing to overall health and well-being is not a high priority for many older adults, and
- identify limitations of relying on the scientific discourse to advance our understanding of aging and physical activity.

Growing old is an inevitable but natural process, and the way it occurs is not fixed. Although not everyone relishes the challenges associated with the later stage of life, many see it as a time for growth and self-fulfillment, an ongoing investment in lifelong development. As Kirkwood (2001) asserts, "We are not programmed to die, but survive and there is much we can do to assist this programming" (p. 49). It is here that physical leisure in its many forms can play a prominent role in helping people in their later years realize the continuing possibilities for a life well lived.

Leisure may once have been viewed as somewhat frivolous, but today there is no dispute that it has a positive impact on wellness and quality of life. It also provides opportunities for reaffirming self and developing a new identity, even in the later years (Atchley & Barusch, 2004; McGuire, Boyd, & Tedrick, 2009). **Physical leisure**, or **active living**, as it is often referred to, and its myriad benefits are seen as a way to offer older people "a transition to a new life, rather than a continuation of the old" (Blaikie, 1999, p. 73). But as Kollard (2007) reminds us, not only is leisure diverse, it takes place in the real world of possibilities and limited resources and responsibilities. As we come to view the advantages of aging as being at least as real as the disadvantages, then what people do with their leisure time becomes highly relevant, particularly given an anticipated increase in life expectancy.

Aging is a universal experience, and no one wants to live a life devoid of good health. Thankfully, in recent years the biomedical view of aging has expanded to embrace a wellness-oriented perspective as a way to reduce the impact of living with a chronic ailment or degenerative disease. This emphasizes the importance of lifestyle and the potential for older people to continue living independent, healthy lives. It is therefore not surprising that greater impetus is given to help people extend not only their life span but also their health span. How this occurs is a complex, multifactorial process that may well be different for each person. Nevertheless, what transpires over time determines one's state of **well-being** and **quality of life**. Although a high level of wellness and life satisfaction is within reach of us all, the way in which this is realized in the later years varies considerably and is not easily predicted. The literature suggests that the way we age is not simply the consequence of a single set of determinants or advances in medicine and technology, but that the environment in which people live and the lifestyle they embrace are also strong predictors of well-being.

Health Maintenance as a Benefit of Physical Leisure

Proclaiming the benefits of physical leisure for older people is not new. Almost 30 years ago, Senator Ray Perrault told attendees of the first Canadian Conference on Fitness in the Third Age, "There is substantial evidence to support the notion that exercise may be an effective way to delay the effects of aging" (Perrault, 1983, p. 3). Since then empirical information has accumulated to present an unequivocal argument that many ailments and illnesses frequently associated with later life (e.g., chronic obstructive lung disease, loss of strength, susceptibility to falls, reduced functional capacity, bone loss, elevated cholesterol levels, arthritis, coronary vascular disease, difficulty with perception, insomnia, reduced cognitive alertness, lessened self-efficacy, social isolation) can be positively influenced by regular physical activity of even mild intensity. This in turn can enhance functionality and quality of life. The message is that people who adopt a sedentary lifestyle are at greater risk of not-so-good health.

Evidence that physical activity benefits health maintenance is so convincing that a few years ago the WHO classified physical *inactivity* as a major health risk. This information is being acted upon in many countries, where physical activity is finding a more prominent place on policy agendas related to the health and well-being of older people. Nevertheless, physical activity in whatever form is not a panacea for a trouble-free existence or a guaranteed solution to avoiding the ailments people are more likely to experience in later life. Rather, being physically active is a lifestyle choice that can make a difference to functionality and well-being. Our leisure results from making choices to do as we want in a way that ensures satisfaction and personal fulfillment. Kirkwood (2001) believes that having "the freedom to make—and continue making—choices is perhaps the greatest single index of well-being" (p. 47).

The relationship between lifestyle and health is complex. Active leisure does positively influence health, but health problems, which are more frequent in old age, can negatively influence

Photo courtesy of Mary Ann Kluge.

Leisure activities should reflect an individual's personal desires and be satisfying and pleasurable.

involvement in such leisure (Godbey, 2008). Older people are in tune with the aging process, and they know it is impossible to be fully liberated from the realities of physical decline associated with age (Kluge, 2002). Some health-related publicity, particularly advertising, suggests, however, that "if you don't work at keeping your [older] body in shape, then it is implied you don't care about it. . . . It has become a duty to resist the onset of signs of decline" (Blaikie, 1999, p. 86). The impact of such messages is not yet fully understood.

Given that some causes of not-so-good health and illness are proximate, it is not useful to blame people for their health problems without contextualizing the many factors that expose them to health risks. After all, older people's lifestyle choices and subsequent behaviors are partially a response to the conditions imposed by their social, political, and environmental circumstances (Bernard, 2000; McElroy, 2002; Stoller & Gibson, 2000). From a life-course perspective,

the current older population was not socialized into participating in regular physical activity, particularly for health, during leisure time. Rest was considered the virtue of old age, and taking it easy was encouraged rather than exerting oneself (Kirk, 1997). Avoiding the supposed risks associated with exercise was inscribed in the dominant pathological discourse that mostly defined later life as a period of decline, frailty, and obsolescence (Vertinsky, 1995). Still today, many people in their later years consider it legitimate to withdraw from physical activity and take a well-earned rest even though we know that exercise takes on greater rather than lesser significance with age (DiPietro, 2007).

Clearly people have some responsibility for their own health, but when taking responsibility for one's health becomes more of a personal project than a pleasurable experience, the likelihood of continued involvement is tenuous. A belief that leisure or downtime must be converted to uptime or body time by engaging in physical activity can be problematic. This is particularly the case for older people who have experienced years of bodily abuses, misuses, disuses, and disease, not to mention limited opportunities and social stigma (Faircloth, 2003). Against such a backdrop, pursuing a physically active lifestyle in order to enhance well-being is not likely to be a high priority. But given the resilience of older people, leisure of the physical kind can help people redefine their identity. After all, "leisure embodies the contention that it is through play, in one form or another, that we find relatively low-risk opportunities" (Hendricks & Cutler, 2003, p. 115).

Modern society has seen the emergence of an age-resisting culture of active leisure with knowledge that health can be achieved through personal effort rather than relying solely on professional ministrations (Gilleard & Higgs, 2000). Times may be changing, but beliefs such as those previously outlined have a lasting effect that is more likely to take decades rather than months or years to change (Bernard, 2000; Roberts, 2006). This does not mean that older people have lost the zest for a physically active lifestyle; rather, participating in some forms of leisure, including physical activity, has never been overly popular with the older population (Crombie, Irvine, Williams, McGinns, Slane, et al., 2004; Grant & Kluge, 2007). This need not be the case, but reversing the trend of inactivity poses a notable challenge for people working in health promotion and recreation.

Constraints to Engaging in Physical Leisure

Changing one's lifestyle in the later years is fraught with numerous challenges, and deciding to engage in a new leisure activity, such as that of the physical kind, is not as easy as it sounds. In recent years a number of researchers (e.g., Booth, Bauman, & Owen, 2002; Crombie et al., 2004; Grant, 2008; Jancey, Clarke, Howat, Maycock, & Lee, 2009; Lees, Clark, Nigg, & Newman, 2005; O'Brien Cousins, 2000; Paulson, 2005; Towers, Flett, & Seebek, 2005) have explored why the majority of older people avoid physical leisure. The reasons cited in these and writings that reflect international findings include the following:

- Lack of time
- Not interested in physical activity
- Concerns about what the older body should and should not do
- Having to justify choice of activity to family and friends
- Lack of support from family, friends, and health professionals
- Ailments and not-so-good health
- Limited physical skills to have success
- Self-consciousness about one's body while exercising
- Fear of injuring oneself
- Inertia
- Feeling too old
- Already healthy enough
- Doubts about the significance of the outcome
- Cost of membership or program fee
- Difficulty of adopting a regular exercise routine
- Physically painful or uncomfortable
- Lack of an exercise companion
- Lack of easy access to open spaces and facilities

Without denying the legitimacy of these reasons, it is difficult to know exactly what they mean at the individual level given that people's day-to-day experiences are strongly influenced by gender, age, educational background, social status, life history, prejudices, expectations, and values of the neighborhood in which they live and grow older. Overall, there is a tendency for people to reduce their leisure activities with age,

and "no type of leisure activity is more likely to be abandoned or avoided by the old as regular physical exercise" (Kelly, 1993, p. 123). This claim of nearly 20 years ago has continued to be affirmed by surveys of physical activity in Western countries. Could the adoption of a sedentary lifestyle be due to the reality of daily life competing with the perception of physical leisure? Or, might there be an unfortunate degree of sensitivity and stigma associated with being old and having a body that does not always function as one wishes? Unfortunately, the twenty-first century is a time where the public appearance of a fit body is a valued currency, and consequently many older people feel their body is both visibly and conceptually out of place (Lupton, 2003; see also Dionigi & Horton in this book).

Implications for Programming

In order to attract adults over the age of 65 to physically active leisure programs and to provide them with safe and meaningful experiences, an understanding of the target population is necessary. This cohort is different in many ways from younger age groups. In general, they have more freedom regarding time, discretionary income, and social roles (Henderson, Bialeschki, Shaw, & Freysinger, 1996). They also have an increased awareness of their mortality and may be experiencing other transitions in life, including some firm ideas about how to live. Given the heterogeneity of this sector of the population, the type of leisure that might attract their interest remains a puzzle and warrants careful consideration (Hendricks & Cutler, 2003).

Some older adults shy away from physical leisure; they are afraid of irritating an ailment or getting hurt (O'Brien Cousins, 2000). Others are seeking meaning in their lives and are looking to either reactivate a part of themselves that has lain dormant for some time or to create a new self. Therefore, it is important when implementing a program to emphasize the process and practice (i.e., the experience) rather than the outcome (e.g., fitness) (Kollard, 2007). Understanding older adults' motives for active living is imperative. Regardless of the reasons for choosing one activity over another, the activities in which one participates must have personal value and meaning in order to be of relevance. It is, after all, the experience rather than the activity per se from which meaning and satisfaction emerge (Kleiber, 1999).

Many strategies, including intervention studies, policy initiatives, community programs, and

Functional Classifications

Older adults comprise a wide span of age groupings: 60+, 70+, 80+, and the oldest old. They also have a wide range of functional ability. In order to understand this range of ability, Spirduso, Francis, and MacRae (2005) formulated a broad description based on five levels of function: physically elite, physically fit, independent, frail, and dependent. The *physically elite* are very active and fit, engaging in intense and frequent episodes of physical activity, sometimes including focused sport-skills training for competition. The *physically fit* are older adults who exercise two to three times per week or even daily. They do so primarily for health benefits, tending not to compete in sporting events or exercise sessions that are as long or as intense as those that the physically elite participate in. *Physically independent* people are healthy enough to take care of activities of daily living (ADLs) on their own and have enough stamina for social activities and travel, but they are not intentionally physically active for health benefits and therefore are not necessarily physically fit. Those who are classified as *physically frail* and *physically dependent* are people who have one or more chronic diseases that compromise their health and challenge them in their daily activities. These people are largely homebound, with differing levels of support needed. Irrespective of the category, all people can benefit from engaging in activities that are developmentally appropriate.

social marketing, have been used to try to increase active living among older people. In spite of good intentions and initiatives based on sound theoretical and conceptual principles, the numerous efforts have "not led to a significant improvement in population-based participation rates or to an increase in exercise adherence" (Rikli, 2005, p. 55). Neither does it seem there will be a sudden uprising where masses of older people become exercise junkies and take to the streets, parks, mountains, gyms, and pools in pursuit of better health through a playful existence. In order to embrace and maintain a physically active lifestyle in a personally rewarding way, the experiences need to be sufficiently meaningful that it is difficult for people to imagine them being absent from their lives (Kretchmar, 2005).

Wanting to adopt an active lifestyle raises questions about how much of a particular type of exercise is enough to achieve which outcome for what age group (Dishman, Washburn, & Heath, 2004). Some recommendations advise 30 minutes of moderate physical activity accumulated throughout the day on most days as sufficient for health benefits. Other recommendations emphasize longer duration and higher intensity. These recommendations need to be positioned against what older adults consider to be the actual purpose for engaging in physical activity during their leisure time. What is supposedly good for you may be supported by empirical evidence, but that evidence is tinged by a difference between the scientific meanings

associated with terms such as **physical activity**, **physical fitness**, and **exercise** and their socially and culturally constructed meanings. Pursuing an active lifestyle derived primarily from expert discourse of the health and exercise industry seems to create a degree of uncertainty and instability among older people (Gilleard & Higgs, 2000).

When developing a program for older adults, it is important to keep in mind that most people do not exercise because the experts hold out some distant and existential advantage such as living longer or living better (Locke, 1996). If one's previous lifestyle has been sedentary and nonphysical leisure pursuits more appealing, then the chances of active living being embraced in the later years will be limited. Many older people believe that for their body to remain functionally effective, staying busy will suffice (Grant, 2008; Katz, 2000). Success in aging requires ongoing adaptation, and unless an activity is enjoyable or worth doing from a personal point of view, rational reasons and facts do little to either entice or sustain participation (Chodzko-Zajko et al., 2005; Kretchmar, 2005; Spirduso et al., 2005). The challenges for program leaders are considerable, and rather than getting older adults caught up in the pursuit of optimal health, adopting the concept of active living might be more appropriate. A myriad of activities that allow participants to reap the associated physical, psychological, social, and spiritual benefits of participating in a way suited to their needs will suffice (Wankel, 1997).

From "Didn't Do" to "Have to Do" to "Get to Do"

Linda Glick

When I got my Medicare card at age 65, I decided I needed to do something different at this time in my life. A younger friend who works with older adults showed me a video with older women competing in Senior Games. On the spur of the moment I decided that I would do that, and my friend became my trainer.

At first I thought the whole shape-up plan was interesting. Then it got a bit hard. But I was determined. For several months I *had to* purposely exercise to train. Sometimes I was tired or sore and didn't want to, but I *had to* because I was signed up for the Senior Games in the 100 meter and the long jump. I had never even been on a track before!

The story becomes long here, but I actually won my events. Winning was amazing, and the larger reward was having a new and healthier me.

I am writing this a couple of years later. Somewhere in that time frame I went from *have to do to get to do*. My body now *wants* to move and be active; part of my leisure time is now about physical activity. I don't even care about that Medicare card anymore.

Photo courtesy of Mary Ann Kluge.

Linda Glick.

Integrating Leisure and Physical Activity

If growing older results in more freedom, then it is reasonable to assume that when one becomes old, life must be replete with greater opportunities for leisure that ultimately affect well-being. Having more discretionary time (i.e., freedom) in later life may provide opportunities for an enriched lifestyle, but too much time can induce a feeling of uselessness and loss of purpose (Csikszentmihalyi, 1997). As Carlsen (1996, p. 188) explained, this can be perplexing for many older people, who ponder:

"How am I going to spend my time?"

"What sorts of things can I do with my time?"

"What motivations, what purposes, what focused activities will give me a 'why' for my time?"

In spite of such dilemmas, we live in an increasingly age-conscious society that affords more and more possibilities for engaging in diverse forms of leisure. To be of benefit, however, leisure requires a certain creativeness, discipline, and personal investment. Physically oriented leisure can provide the self-knowledge to live a full life, but what circumstances and opportunities cue older people to become engaged in an active lifestyle? Something must trigger older adults to take up more active living and ignore the stereotypes of aging (O'Brien Cousins, 2001). The following examples depict two ways in which physical activity and leisure become integrated to enhance quality of life as well as affirm identity.

Active Living Through Sport

Some older adults are intentionally physically active, and the outcomes many desire have functional relevance to their lives (Jones & Rose, 2005).

Some are so focused on maintaining independence, not succumbing to diseases and disability, and preserving or improving their performance capabilities that they devote much of their leisure time to physical activity. Very active older adults indicate that being physically active helps them manage aches and pains, improves their outlook on life, and even "helps keep me from getting old" (Kluge, 2002, p.17). Growth in sport participation in the later years exemplifies this interest in maintaining physical function and independence, something paralleled by an increasing number of organizations promoting masters, seniors, or veterans sporting events. These organizations sponsor sporting events with stated missions such as, "To improve the quality of life for adults aged 50+ by providing athletic competition and social opportunities that promote healthy, active lifestyles." This was accentuated in the publicity for the 2009 World Masters Games held in Sydney where the expression, "ordinary people can have extraordinary experiences" captured the essence of what this form of leisure offered people from over 100 countries competing in 28 sports.

Consider the example of Christel Donley, who has been athletic all of her life. Unlike many women in her cohort (75+ years of age) who were born in the United States and had little opportunity for sport participation, Christel's early roots in Germany provided a strong foundation of skills and confidence in the motor domain. Readers may think that, based on her sport background, remaining physically active in the later years is therefore easy, but Christel was unable to find a place to work out for track and field during the winter months because U.S. athletic facilities supported by tax dollars are often unavailable for adults. She found out about an older women's volleyball team supported by local university faculty and students, and what started out as a utilitarian relationship (accessing indoor workout space) became much more. Before long she became so invested in the group of women she had come to know and the new skills she was learning that she was hooked. Christel's lifelong interest in sport participation is still growing, now as a member of a volleyball team of women aged 65 and older.

Activity as Personal Growth

Life transitions with their multiple meanings and impact on quality of life call for readjustment in social roles and activities (see chapter 5). Life transitions in the later years also provide opportunities for personal growth (Dionigi, 2006; Kluge,

Christel Donley.

Photo courtesy of Chris Stone/Masterstrack.com.

2005). There is, however, a need to be conscious of aging and to move onward and outward rather than inward. This perspective provided a foundation for a workshop called *The Women We're Becoming* (Kluge, 2007). The outdoors added an extra dimension to the workshop focus of personal growth through self-understanding, because "the great outdoors works on the soul as well as the muscles" (Rolston, as cited in Edginton, DeGraaf, Dieser, & Edginton, 2006, p. 27). Women who attended the workshop experienced

- an increased connection with and confidence in their bodies,
- an enhanced ability to identify and articulate their needs, and
- an awareness of the need to reprioritize their lives.

Alina Urbanec grew up in an urban environment. As an adult, Alina would occasionally go for short walks in her neighborhood. Having

Photo courtesy of Mary Ann Kluge.

Alina Urbanec enjoys the outdoors.

few opportunities to be outside or to appreciate nature, Alina was almost squeamish about being outdoors, but she accepted an invitation to attend *The Women We're Becoming.* Experiencing outdoor activities at the workshop opened up a new world for Alina. She discovered a connection with nature she hadn't experienced before and developed feelings of self-control that arose from better understanding and accepting of herself and her needs. One revelation Alina had was, "Now I get it! Hiking is walking in a pretty place!"

Accessing the Meaning of Active Aging

Living in and through an aging body is interwoven with all aspects of day-to-day living. As such, much is to be gained by taking seriously the forms of knowledge that might generate multiple understandings of the aging process and what it is like to have a physically active or inactive body (Phoenix & Grant, 2009). Not surprisingly, there is a belief that our understanding of aging and the way older people live could be enhanced: "If the humanities play a larger role in shaping our common awareness of late life, and if they can balance biomedicine and social science, new

ways of knowing aging may be possible" (Cruikshank, 2003, p. 205). Obtaining quantitative measurements about attributes such as strength, cardiovascular response, mood state, bone density, perceptions of barriers to exercise, and so on advances our understanding about the role of physical activity in later life. This, however, tells only a part of the active aging story, and greater credence needs to be given to the fact that aging cannot be fully understood apart from its subjective experience. "Although it is unlikely that any single physical activity theory will be able to account for all the anomalous data currently emerging, it is clear that many of the current theories used to understand physical activity are inadequate" (Rose, 2008, p. 112).

It is not uncommon for people who engage in a physically active lifestyle to describe their well-being in a positive way. They feel good when physically active, regardless of the level of intensity (Kluge, 2002; Grant, 2008; Whitehead, 2010). This multifaceted feel-good phenomenon that almost everyone experiences, is, paradoxically, "difficult to define operationally" (Spirduso et al., 2005, p. 235). Hence, trying to determine with any degree of precision how and why this phenomenon occurs is difficult. Perhaps we should consider that it might well be that "physical

Never2old Active Aging Program

John Rice

At the beginning of the twenty-first century, two public commentaries stirred the imagination of the sport and recreation staff at Auckland University of Technology (AUT), New Zealand. The first was about the oft-discussed consequences of an increasingly older population, and the second, the adoption of a more sedentary existence with age. A question arising from this gloomy picture was what could be done to encourage more of the 65+ population to adopt a more active lifestyle.

The staff at AUT had not previously considered catering to the older cohort in their community. This was foreign territory. However, that all changed in 2002 when the never2old active aging program (www.never2old.net.nz) was launched. The program continues to flourish and is now offered in 19 centers in the Auckland area serving more than 2,000 adults, with an average age of 73 participating on a weekly basis. At the outset, we so-called experts approached our new venture with great gusto. Somewhat naively, we thought we knew the recipe for improving functional fitness: Just extrapolate from what we did with younger age groups and tone down the intensity while ensuring the activities contributed to overall functionality, strength, cardiorespiratory efficiency, and flexibility.

It soon became evident that we knew little about this age group and many of our ideas reinforced ageist stereotypes. The concept for never2old was okay, but so many elements essential to an ideal program for older people were overlooked. It became glaringly obvious that the scientifically based exercise cocktail being served up was effective but rather bland. Hence, we needed to ensure that the exercise resonated with the needs of the participants. Attending was as much about being with others of a similar age as it was about getting in shape.

Photo courtesy of John Rice.

continued ▶

▶ **Never2old Active Aging Program** (continued)

Since those early hit-and-miss days, much has changed, and the never2old program now provides a multimodal, personalized approach to active aging. This means that the physical may be a prime reason for attending, but it is not the only benefit. Adopting a more holistic approach means we move beyond thinking about the body as a machine to be tuned and give attention to the physical, social, psychological, emotional, and spiritual aspects of life.

More recently some participants expressed an interest in more adventurous activities, so we introduced YAHOO (Young At Heart Outdoor Odysseys) Challenges, a series of outdoor pursuits (e.g., abseiling or rappelling, paddling sea kayaks and outrigger canoes, climbing, orienteering, Nordic walking, and trekking on the beach or in the bush) suited to the older person's capabilities. To our surprise, we found that participants could not get enough of these activities. They also wanted to know more about their aging bodies, so we now offer educational forums that provide information on a range of topics related to health and well-being. The more competitive participants wanted an opportunity to revisit their sporting youth, so a modified sport program is now offered. What's next?

Although the never2old program is far from perfect, it offers a diverse array of opportunities for those over 60 years old. Retention rates are up, membership inquiries are never ending, and participants appear to relish the choice of activities. The bottom line is that we experts have learned that it's not about what *we* can do *to* and *for* older folk; rather, it is about valuing and better understanding the aspirations of our older adults and giving due diligence to these factors when designing a program. In so doing, the experiences in which the participants engage will be meaningful and ensure positive outcomes.

activity influences well-being more through its symbolic than its physiologic impact, which might explain why social participation possesses apparently equal effectiveness in reducing later life morbidity and mortality" (Gilleard & Higgs, 2000, p. 80).

Older adults are individuals with stories that are as mysterious as their bodies and whose biographical aging is as intricate and important as their biological aging, as worthy of study, and as pertinent to their health (Gubrium, 2001). After all, older people are the authentic experts of their lives and have a lifetime of experiences to share. The broad goal of qualitative inquiry is to explore how one constitutes self and to unravel something of the way people make sense of their experiences. This enables an alternative picture to emerge and ensures that the voice of the older person is central in explaining the relationships among aging, physical leisure, and well-being (Grant & Kluge, 2007). Insight into how the various types of physical activities are experienced is useful to help utilize physical leisure as a way to optimize quality of life (Kollard, 2007; Spirduso et al., 2005). However, there is still much to be learned about how best to support older people who wish to remain active or reunite with what was probably a more active lifestyle some years ago.

An Active Future

The changing demographic that favors older adults has led to comparisons between the economic costs of sedentary older adults and those who lead an active lifestyle. It is well documented that older people carry a progressively heavier burden of disease and disability, and this comes at a social and economic cost. No one knows for sure whether an older population will swamp health services or consume an increasingly larger proportion of the health budget, but one thing seems strikingly evident—"the more aging fits the disease model, the more money is spent on it" (Vincent, 2006, p. 687). When such a perspective prevails, it is believed to encourage passivity and consequently the continued high cost of aging (Mullan, 2002). It is therefore not surprising that speculation is rife about future health budgets and the alarm bells are beginning to sound in policy-making circles from Beijing to Washington (Milner & Scoffield, 2009).

Could a more physically active older population curtail some of the concern? According to a recent Canadian study, the answer is a resounding *yes*. The study found that whereas physical inactivity imposes substantial costs on the publicly funded health care system, active people tend to use significantly fewer health care services (Sari, 2009). Given the personal benefits to be gained as well as possible savings in the health budget of a state or country, older people are being encouraged to embrace an active lifestyle. This approach is also advocated by the WHO, who encourages a shift away from intervention to focus more on policy and promotion of action in the community (Chodzko-Zajko & Schwingel, 2009).

There may not be a solution to slowing down the aging process, but older bodies are capable of and relish being activated. Staying relatively fit need not be a struggle, but whether active older people can live up to the ancient Greek adage of dying young at a very old age is still questionable. Following publication of the empirically grounded 2008 Physical Activity Guidelines for Americans (U.S. Department of Health and Human Services [DHHS], 2008), the following position stand was written for the ACSM. It provides a succinct statement about the importance of physical activity.

> Although no amount of physical activity can stop the biological aging process, there is evidence that regular exercise can minimize the physiological effects of an otherwise sedentary lifestyle and increase active life expectancy by limiting the development and progression of chronic diseases and disabling conditions. There is also emerging evidence for significant psychological and cognitive benefits accruing from regular participation. . . . Adults aged 65 years and older gain substantial health benefits from regular physical activity, and these benefits continue to occur throughout their lives. (Chodzko-Zajko, Proctor, Fiatarone, Minson, Nigg, et al., 2009, p. 1510)

Conclusion

Leisure of the physical kind may not be the elixir for well-being, but it can help to decrease morbidity, modify the impact of chronic degenerative diseases, maintain functional capacity, positively influence one's feeling of self-worth, and improve quality of life. It is important to remember, however, that everybody ages differently, and the way the benefits of physical activity accrue varies dramatically. Given that contexts and lifestyle preferences are constantly changing with age, we should accept that there are no rules. Although many older people may seek the magic formula for an active lifestyle, there will never be a one-size-fits-all prescription. Even in later life, leisure is about freedom to be or, perhaps, freedom to become (Roberts, 2006), and how we enact this is an individual choice.

KEY TERMS

active living—A holistic perspective of life that positions physical activity as integral to well-being.

exercise—A subset of physical activity that is planned, structured, and purposeful in the sense that improving an aspect of physical functioning or performance is an objective.

physical activity—Any body movement, be it part of the daily routine or structured activity produced by the skeletal muscles, that results in energy expenditure.

physical fitness—A set of attributes that relates specifically to the ability to perform various physical activities in an efficient manner.

physical leisure—Physical activity that is personally relevant to one's lifestyle; it includes the selection of activities based on personal needs and interests.

quality of life—The physical, psychological, and spiritual aspects of life along with relationships and one's personal aspirations regarding purposeful activity and personal growth.

well-being—The personal feelings people have about their total state of being and quality of life at a given point in time.

REVIEW AND DISCUSSION QUESTIONS

1. How does physical leisure influence life satisfaction and well-being?

2. How might generational differences influence values, attitudes, beliefs, and meanings related to physical leisure?

3. What is your generation's view of physical leisure versus that of your parents, grandparents, or even great-grandparents?

4. What benefits can older people anticipate from physical leisure?

5. Develop an argument for allocating more resources to ensure greater opportunities and support for older people to engage in physical leisure.

LEARNING ACTIVITIES

1. Find a brochure or advertisement that promotes physical leisure for older adults and describe how the words and images are used to reflect the older person.

2. Locate a website that focuses on older adults living active lives and determine the key messages being portrayed.

3. Identify physical leisure opportunities for the older population that are provided by organizations in your area.

4. Interview several older people to find out about their attitudes toward physical leisure.

5. Do an online search to locate what is happening in other countries with regard to the promotion of older adults being more physically active.

6. With a group of classmates, visit a recreation or leisure center and determine how user friendly it is for the older person.

7. Identify a physical leisure program or event designed specifically for older adults. Attend the program or event and observe what occurs. Then write a report highlighting some of the excitements and dilemmas you witnessed.

CRITICAL-THINKING ACTIVITIES

1. Identify a community program or policy from another country that relates to older adults' leisure and physical well-being. Note details about the age group, purpose statements, images and language used to promote active living, program content, costs, facilities, matters pertaining to health, and other key factors. Compare this information with a similar context in your country or community. Using the information from this and other chapters in the book, describe how aging is portrayed with regard to active living, health, and well-being.

2. Choose one leisure or recreation facility in your city and describe some of the challenges for the management team if an additional 250 people aged 65 years and older decided to become members in the next 12 months.

SUGGESTED READING

Chodzko-Zajko, W., Sheppard, L., Senior, J., Park, C., Mockenhaupt, R., & Bazzarre, T. (2005). The national blueprint for promoting physical activity in midlife and older adult population. *Quest, 57,* 2-11.

Grant, B., & Kluge, M. (2007). Exploring 'other body(s)' of knowledge: Getting to the heart of the story about aging and physical activity. *Quest, 59,* 398-414.

Jones, C.J., & Rose, D.J. (Eds.). (2005). *Physical activity instruction of older adults.* Champaign, IL: Human Kinetics.

Spirduso, W., Francis, K., & MacRae, P. (2005). *Physical dimensions of aging* (2nd ed.). Champaign, IL: Human Kinetics.

Taylor, A., & Johnson, M. (2008). *Physiology of exercise and healthy aging.* Champaign, IL: Human Kinetics.

U.S. Department of Health and Human Services (DHHS). (2008). *Physical activity guidelines for Americans.* Rockville, MD: Author.

REFERENCES

Atchley, R., & Barusch, A. (2004). *Social forces and aging: An introduction to social gerontology.* Belmont, CA: Wadsworth/Thomson Learning.

Bernard, M. (2000). *Promoting health in old age.* Buckingham, UK: Open University Press.

Blaikie, A. (1999). *Ageing and popular culture.* Cambridge: Cambridge Press.

Booth, M., Bauman, A., & Owen, N. (2002). Perceived barriers to physical activity among older Australians. *Journal of Aging and Physical Activity, 10,* 271-280.

Carlsen, M. (1996). *Creative aging: A meaning making perspective.* New York: Norton.

Chodzko-Zajko, W., Proctor, D., Fiatarone, M., Minson, C., Nigg, C., Salem, C., & Skinner, J. (2009). Exercise and physical activity for older adults. *Medicine and Science in Sports and Exercise, 41*(7), 1510-1530.

Chodzko-Zajko, W., & Schwingel, A. (2009). Transnational strategies for the promotion of physical activity and active aging: The World Health Organization model of consensus building in international public health. *Quest, 61,* 25-38.

Chodzko-Zajko, W., Sheppard, L., Senior, J., Park, C., Mockenhaupt, R., & Bazzarre, T. (2005). The national blueprint for promoting physical activity in mid-life and older adult population. *Quest, 57,* 2-11.

Crombie, I., Irvine, L., Williams, B., McGinns, A., Slane, P., Alder, E., & McMurdo, E. (2004). Why people do not participate in leisure-time physical activity: A survey of activity levels, beliefs and deterrents. *Age and Aging, 33,* 287-292.

Cruikshank, M. (2003). *Learning to be old: Gender, culture and aging.* Lanham: Rowan and Littlefield.

Csikszentmihalyi, M. (1997). *Finding flow: The psychological engagement of everyday life.* New York: Harper Collins.

Dionigi, R. (2006). Competitive sport as leisure in later life: Negotiations, discourse, and aging. *Leisure Sciences, 28*, 181-196.

DiPietro, L. (2007). Physical activity, fitness and aging. In C. Bouchard, S. Blair, & W. Haskell (Eds.), *Physical activity and health* (pp. 271-286). Champaign, IL: Human Kinetics.

Dishman, R., Washburn, R., & Heath, G. (2004). *Physical activity epidemiology.* Champaign, IL: Human Kinetics.

Edginton, C.R., DeGraaf, D.G., Dieser, R., & Edginton, S.R. (2006). *Leisure and life satisfaction: Foundational perspectives* (4th ed.). New York: McGraw-Hill.

Faircloth, C. (2003). Different bodies and the paradox of aging: Location bodies in images of everyday experience. In C. Faircloth (Ed.), *Ageing bodies: Images and everyday experiences* (pp. 1-26). Lanham, MA: Altra Mira Press.

Gilleard, C., & Higgs, P. (2000). *Cultures of ageing: Self, citizen and body.* London: Prentice Hall.

Godbey, G. (2008). *Leisure in your life: New perspectives.* State College, PA: Venture.

Grant, B. (2008). An insider's view on physical activity in later life. *Journal of Psychology of Sport and Exercise, 9*, 817-829.

Grant, B., & Kluge, M. (2007). Exploring 'other body(s)' of knowledge: Getting to the heart of the story about aging and physical activity. *Quest, 59*, 398-414.

Gubrium, J. (2001). Narrative, experience, and aging. In G. Kenyon, P. Clark, & B. de Vries (Eds.), *Narrative gerontology: Theory, practice and research* (pp. 19-30). New York: Springer.

Henderson, K., Bialeschki, M.D., Shaw, S.M., & Freysinger, V.J. (1996). *Both gaps and gains: Feminist perspectives on women's leisure.* State College, PA: Venture.

Hendricks, J., & Cutler, S. (2003). Leisure in life course perspective. In R. Settersten (Ed.), *Invitation to the life course: Towards new understandings of later life* (pp. 107-134). New York: Baywood.

Jancey, J., Clarke, A., Howat, P., Maycock, B., & Lee, A. (2009). Perceptions of physical activity by older adults: A qualitative study. *Health Promotion Journal, 68*, 196-206.

Jones, C.J., & Rose, D.J. (Eds.). (2005). *Physical activity instruction of older adults.* Champaign, IL: Human Kinetics.

Katz, S. (2000). Busy bodies: Activity, aging, and the management of everyday life. *Journal of Aging Studies, 14*, 135-149.

Kelly, J. (1993). Varieties of activity. In J. Kelly (Ed.), *Activity and aging: Staying involved in later life* (pp. 119-124). Thousand Oaks, CA: Sage.

Kirk, H. (1997). Facing the historical 'rest-in-old-age' paradigm. In G. Huber (Ed.), *Healthy aging: Proceedings of 4th International Congress of Physical Activity, Aging and Sports* (pp. 63-65). Heidelberg: Health Promotion.

Kirkwood, T. (2001). *The end of age: Why everything about ageing is changing.* London: Profile Books.

Kleiber, D. (1999). *Leisure experience and human development: A dialectical interpretation.* New York: Basic Books.

Kluge, M. (2002). Understanding the essence of a physically active lifestyle: A phenomenological study of women 65 and older. *Journal of Aging and Physical Activity, 10*, 4-27.

Kluge, M. (2005). It's never too late to dare: Outdoor adventure programming for the age wave. *Journal of Physical Education, Recreation, and Sport, 76*(5), 39-46.

Kluge, M. (2007). Re-creating through recreating: Using the personal growth through adventure model to transform women's lives. *Journal of Transformative Education, 5*, 177-191.

Kollard, F. (2007). The new leisure world of modern old age: New aging on the bright side of the street. In H. Wahl, C. Tesch-Romer, & A. Hoff (Eds.), *New dynamics in old age: Individual. environmental, and societal perspectives* (pp. 213-237). New York: Baywood.

Kretchmar, R.S. (2005). *Practical philosophy of sport and physical activity* (2nd ed.). Champaign, IL: Human Kinetics.

Lees, F., Clark, P., Nigg, C., & Newman, P. (2005). Barriers to exercise behavior among older adults: A focus group study. *Journal of Aging and Physical Activity, 13*, 23-33.

Locke, L. (1996). Dr. Lewin's little liver patties: A parable about encouraging healthy lifestyles. *Quest, 48*, 422-431.

Lupton, D. (2003). *Medicine as culture: Illness, disease and the body in Western society.* Thousand Oaks, CA: Sage.

McElroy, M. (2002). *Resistance to exercise: A social analysis of inactivity.* Champaign, IL: Human Kinetics.

McGuire, F., Boyd, R., & Tedrick, R. (2009). *Leisure and aging: Ulyssean living in later life* (4th ed.). Champaign, IL: Sagamore.

Milner, B., & Scoffield, H. (2009, July 8). The growing cost of an aging world. *Globe and Mail*, p. 14.

Mullan, P. (2002). *The imaginary time bomb: Why an ageing population is not a social problem.* London: I.B. Tauris & Co. Ltd.

O'Brien Cousins, S. (2000). My heart couldn't take it: Older women's belief about exercise and risks. *Journal of Gerontology: Psychological Sciences, 55B*, 283-294.

O'Brien Cousins, S. (2001). Thinking out loud: What older adults say about triggers for physical activity. *Journal of Aging and Physical Activity, 9*, 347-363.

Paulson, S. (2005). How various 'cultures of fitness' shape subjective experiences of growing older. *Ageing and Society, 25*, 229-244.

Perrault, R. (1983). Opening remarks. *Proceedings of the National Conference on Fitness in the Third Age* (pp. 2-4). Ottawa.

Phoenix, C., & Grant, B. (2009). Expanding the research agenda on the physically active aging body. *Journal of Aging and Physical Activity, 17*, 362-380.

Rikli, R. (2005). Movement and mobility influence on successful aging: Addressing the issue of low physical activity. *Quest, 57,* 46-66.

Roberts, K. (2006). *Leisure in contemporary society* (2nd ed.). Oxfordshire, UK: CABI.

Rose, D. (2008). Aging successfully in the 21st century: Does kinesiology offer the silver bullet? *Quest, 60,* 105-120.

Sari, N. (2009). Physical inactivity and its impact on healthcare utilization. *Health Economics, 18,* 885-901.

Spirduso, W., Francis, K., & MacRae, P. (2005). *Physical dimensions of aging* (2nd ed.). Champaign, IL: Human Kinetics.

Stoller, E., & Gibson, R. (2000). Inequalities in health and mortality: Gender, race and class. In E. Stoller & R. Gibson (Eds.), *Worlds of difference: Inequality in the aging experience* (pp. 269-286). Thousand Oaks, CA: Pine Forge Press.

Towers, A., Flett, R., & Seebeck, R. (2005). Assessing potential barriers to exercise adoption in middle-aged men: Over-stressed, under-controlled, or just too unwell? *International Journal of Men's Health, 4*(1), 13-27.

U.S. Department of Health and Human Services (DHHS). (2008). *Physical activity guidelines for Americans.* Rockville, MD: DHHS.

Vertinsky, P. (1995). Stereotypes of aging women and exercise: A historical perspective. *Journal of Aging and Physical Activity, 3,* 223-237.

Vincent, J. (2006). Ageing contested: Anti-ageing science and the cultural construction of old age. *Sociology, 40,* 681-698.

Wankel, L.M. (1997). The social psychology of physical activity. In J. Curtis & S. Russell (Eds.), *Physical activity in the human experience: Interdisciplinary perspectives* (pp. 93-126). Champaign, IL: Human Kinetics.

Whitehead, M. (2010). *Physical literacy: Throughout the life course.* London: Routledge.

CHAPTER 8

Leisure and the Psychological Well-Being and Health of Older Adults

Roger C. Mannell ■ **Ryan Snelgrove**

After reading this chapter, you will be able to

- explain the difference between the psychosocial and cognitive dimensions of the psychological well-being and health of older adults,
- explain the difference between aging-specific and general theories of leisure and psychosocial well-being,
- explain the ways in which leisure can contribute to the psychosocial well-being of older adults,
- explain the ways in which various types of leisure influence the cognitive health of older adults, and
- apply theory and research on leisure and psychological well-being and health to improving the quality of life of older adults.

anice and Debbie are both 70 years of age, and both retired at age 65 after working for over 25 years as accountants in a large financial firm. They held positions in different departments and do not know each other. Both women were committed to the company and their careers. They have good pensions and, with reasonable planning, they have the financial resources to live comfortably and pursue their interests. Janice has never married and has no children, while Debbie has been divorced for many years and has a son who lives with his family in another city several hundred miles away.

Before retiring, neither Janice nor Debbie had given much thought to retirement and what life would be like once it began. However, both women had enjoyed traveling during vacations and had seen retirement as an opportunity to pursue this passion. The first five years of retirement were quite exciting with the planning of the next trip, being on the go, exploring unfamiliar places, and meeting new people. Both women have been happy with their lives. However, at age 70 the travel bug is losing its grip on both Janice and Debbie. Not only have they experienced a great deal of what they set out to see, but traveling is getting too expensive to make a life of it and security concerns are creating more hassles. It also seems to take more energy than it used to.

Looking toward the next 10 to 20 years of life, the two women have very different outlooks. One is doing well and the other is struggling. Janice is embracing the change with some trepidation but mostly excitement. She feels energized and ready to tackle new projects that will challenge her and allow her to learn new skills. Debbie, on the other hand, is anxious about the future and is already starting to feel depressed. She's worried that she's becoming more prone to forgetting things and doesn't have anything to keep her mind and body active. Retirement has been a vacation up to this point, but she feels that perhaps the vacation is over.

How can we account for these differences in outlooks and the likelihood of the two women establishing new patterns of living that will contribute to their psychological well-being and health as they continue to age? Why didn't these differences affect their enthusiasm and happiness in the first five years of retirement? Could differences in their lifestyles since retirement be playing a role? What are the important psychological needs that retired older adults must meet in order to age successfully and maintain their intellectual

and cognitive health and functioning? How can older adults continue to adapt to the constraints that limit their leisure involvement as they age? Could Debbie benefit from some type of leisure education and counseling? We will ask you to address some of these questions later.

In this chapter we explore the impact of leisure on two aspects of the psychological well-being and health of older adults. The first is **psychosocial well-being**, which refers to people's happiness and how well they cope with the various challenges and changes that occur in their lives as they age. This dimension has received a good deal of attention in the field of leisure studies as well as other fields. Researchers and practitioners are interested in a range of factors that allow some older adults to maintain high levels of psychosocial well-being in spite of the decline in physical health that accompanies aging, particularly in the later stages of life.

Leisure is one of those factors. Of course, it can play an important role in psychosocial well-being for people of any age, and a number of theories about these influences have been developed and studied (Mannell, 2007). These general theories of leisure and psychosocial well-being include the ideas of pleasure-fun, identity formation and affirmation, personal growth, keeping busy, and stress coping. However, the transition to the postretirement years, which is associated with increased free time and an expanded opportunity for meaningful leisure, has led to considerable interest in the ways older people use this time and the implications for their psychosocial well-being (Kleiber, 1999). As we have seen in earlier chapters, this interest has led to the development of aging-specific theories of successful aging (e.g., activity and continuity) that have strong implications for the role of leisure in maintaining psychosocial well-being. As well, recent aging-specific leisure and psychosocial well-being theories (e.g., constraint-adaptation and innovation) have been proposed. These general and aging-specific theories are shown in figure 8.1 and will be discussed later. The general theories share some similarities with the aging-specific theories but also provide important insights into the leisure and psychosocial well-being of older adults that have often been ignored.

Cognitive health is the second dimension of psychological health and well-being dealt with in this chapter. It refers to the effective functioning of memory, attention, inductive reasoning, perceptual and cognitive processing, and social cognition

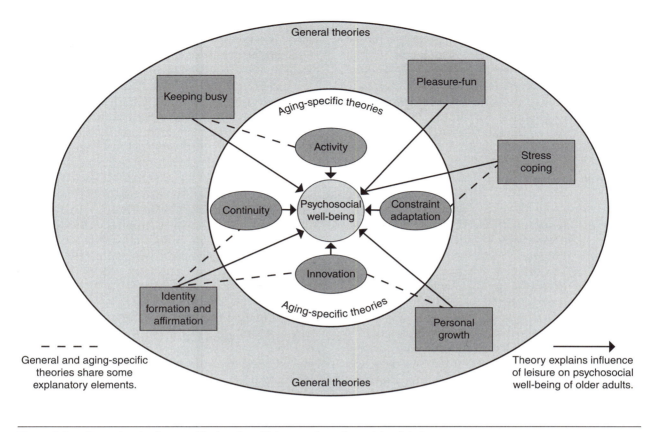

Figure 8.1 General and aging-specific theories of leisure and psychosocial well-being.

as well as use of language, vocabulary, and speech. Until recently it has been given little attention in leisure studies and much of the research comes from other fields. However, there is growing interest in the potential of physical, social, and intellectual leisure pursuits to contribute to cognitive health by enhancing cognitive functioning and reducing declines in cognitive performance due to aging and age-related dementias.

Leisure and Psychosocial Well-Being

In the study of older adults' psychosocial well-being, terms such as *affect, happiness, morale, psychological well-being, quality of life,* and *life satisfaction* are often used (Mannell & Dupuis, 2007). Although these terms refer to different dimensions of psychosocial well-being, they overlap in meaning and are often used interchangeably. **Affect** refers to feelings and moods, and **happiness** is the extent to which positive feelings outweigh negative ones. **Morale** refers to a future-

oriented optimism or pessimism regarding the problems and opportunities associated with aging, and **quality of life** is a broad concept referring to overall well-being. The term **psychological well-being** refers to self-acceptance, personal growth, having purpose in life, effective coping, and feelings of competency. In research on aging and psychosocial well-being, the term **life satisfaction** has most frequently been used by researchers. It has a past orientation and implies an act of judgment, a comparison of what people have versus what they expect in terms of their whole life or a specific part of it.

Nonleisure Factors as a Context for the Influence of Leisure

Not only is leisure one of the factors that has been linked to psychosocial well-being, but its influence occurs in the context of many other determinants (Keyes, 2007). Separating the influence of leisure from the biological changes and other nonleisure influences that occur as a result of getting older is difficult (Mannell & Dupuis, 2007).

For example, some evidence suggests that psychosocial well-being changes systematically over the life course as we age, with lower levels experienced in middle age and higher levels in younger and older adulthood (Blanchflower & Oswald, 2008). However, age itself in the postretirement years is not associated with psychosocial well-being when other factors such as declining health, disability, decreased financial resources, death of a spouse or partner, loss of friends, and decreased leisure activity are taken into account.

Although only a few differences in psychosocial well-being have been found to be directly based on nonleisure factors such as gender, education, and preretirement employment status, these factors are likely to have an indirect influence on psychosocial well-being as well as leisure participation. For example, higher levels of education have an indirect effect on well-being by influencing such things as having retirement plans, better finances, and more leisure interests and opportunities. Even wealth that provides greater opportunities for certain types of leisure, such as travel, does not guarantee well-being. Research suggests that regardless of financial resources, older adults who have focused their leisure and nonleisure retirement goals to maximize the use of their resources appear to experience less financial strain and have higher psychosocial well-being.

As might be expected, the impact of declining physical health on well-being during the later stages of life has been of great interest to researchers, and older adults in poorer health generally have lower psychosocial well-being as well as leisure participation. However, even a good deal of the negative influence of poor health is indirect. Perceptions of health have been found to be better predictors of psychosocial well-being than the actual number or severity of health conditions, and these perceptions are strongly influenced by illnesses that limit or complicate the activities of daily living and interfere with participation in leisure activities. For example, bladder control, visual and hearing impairments, and limitations in mobility negatively affect perceptions of health and well-being more than chronic disorders with established treatments that don't interfere as much with daily activities, including leisure.

Many other factors that play a role in the psychosocial well-being of older adults have been studied. This research often suggests that these factors not only directly influence psychosocial well-being but also leisure participation and are themselves influenced by leisure. For example,

having close friendships and a social network are important for psychosocial well-being. These social relationships are fostered through involvement in leisure and in turn provide opportunities to engage in social leisure. Other factors ranging from psychological characteristics, such as personality traits, to cultural values have also been studied. In the case of personality characteristics, neuroticism and extraversion have been found to be negatively and positively associated with psychosocial well-being, respectively. However, these traits also influence leisure participation in old age (Steca, Alessandri, & Caprara, 2010). Clearly, the complex relationships among nonleisure and leisure determinants and psychosocial well-being need to be kept in mind when the relationship between leisure and psychosocial well-being is considered.

Does Leisure Decline With Age and Threaten Psychosocial Well-Being?

As we will see, participation in leisure activities has been associated with higher levels of psychosocial well-being among older adults, and consequently, researchers and practitioners have been concerned that there appears to be a decline in leisure participation over the life course. Over the years many studies have found that overall leisure activity levels decrease with age. Activities done outside the home and those requiring physical exertion and a high intensity of involvement have shown the highest negative correlations with age. Recent reviews of the evidence suggest that these age-related participation patterns continue to be the case. Janke, Davey, and Kleiber (2006) concluded that leisure participation in the later stages of life is characterized by a decline with increasing age, the substitution of more with less challenging activities, a transition from physical activities to activities that demand less physical effort, and a shift from outdoor to indoor activities. Also, older adults do not typically begin new leisure activities, and if they do increase participation levels, it is more likely to be in activities they were engaged in before retirement. However, in spite of these overall patterns, the authors noted that there are substantial differences among older adults. These differences have implications for psychosocial well-being and need to be taken into account when developing policies and providing leisure services for older adults.

These individual differences in participation have been demonstrated in a number of studies over the past two decades. For example, in a study of people ranging in age from 16 to over 65, Searle, Mactavish, and Brayley (1993) found that about 20% of the people surveyed were *replacers* (during the previous year they had quit an activity they had been participating in for several years and had begun a new activity), 25% were *quitters* (quit an activity and did not begin a new one), 16% were *adders* (did not quit an activity but added an activity), and about 40% were *continuers* (neither added nor quit activities). Nimrod and Kleiber (2007) more recently examined older adults who are adders. They called them **innovators** and proposed that they may have higher psychosocial well-being as a consequence. Nimrod (2008) studied a group of these innovators and found that they did have higher levels of psychosocial well-being. Interestingly, it appeared that the addition of just one new activity was sufficient to enhance well-being.

Janke et al. (2006) examined changes in a variety of leisure activities, including physical activities, among a group of people aged 50 and over. They found most of the decline in leisure with age occurred in physically active leisure. However, as in the studies mentioned previously, they also discovered that participants differed substantially. Clearly, not all older adults are the same, and more research would be useful to help understand these patterns and provide information to help people remain active in their leisure. Of course, the value of staying active in leisure depends on it actually contributing to psychosocial well-being. In the following sections, we review theories and evidence about the ability of leisure to contribute to psychosocial well-being that will help us develop better policies and leisure services for older adults. As we will see, there are many ideas about the ways in which leisure can contribute to the psychosocial well-being of older adults.

Aging-Specific Theories of Leisure and Psychosocial Well-Being

As noted earlier, some ideas about the ways in which leisure contributes to psychosocial well-being have been developed to apply specifically to older adults in the postretirement years. These theories are based on the idea that it is important for older adults to maintain or even increase not only their leisure participation but also their overall activity levels, both leisure and nonleisure. Also, the physical, cognitive, and social changes

that occur as a result of getting older require lifestyle changes and adaptations if psychosocial well-being is to be maintained.

Activity and continuity theories are the oldest theories of successful aging that reflect this idea. In the case of activity theory, older people are happiest and most fulfilled in direct proportion to how much activity they are able to maintain as they age. Older adults must find replacement activities for activities they lose due to retirement, illness, and other difficulties. Continuity theory takes a different approach, suggesting that being active isn't enough. Activities and relationships that have been developed over a long period of time in people's lives are viewed as the most likely to contribute to well-being. They not only allow older adults to maintain a sense of being valued and capable but also continuity with their past. The theory also suggests that continuity without openness to some change may jeopardize older adults' well-being if there is no adaptation to new circumstances (McGuire & Norman, 2005).

Although these ideas have general support and still receive research attention, they are rather vague when it comes to helping us understand the substantial differences among people in the way they use leisure and adapt to the changes associated with aging. This concern recently led Gibson (2006) to suggest that new theories are needed that improve understanding of the ways in which leisure participation can influence well-being and allow the development of more effective interventions. Fortunately, some of these developments are beginning to occur. For example, McGuire and Norman (2005) have applied the general theory of leisure constraint and negotiation (Jackson, 2005) to leisure and aging. Constraint-negotiation theory, which is relevant to people of any age, attempts to explain the ways in which the constraints encountered in daily life can restrict leisure participation and the approaches people use to overcome these constraints to maintain participation and enjoyment. McGuire and Norman extended the theory to older adults, arguing that having to deal with factors that restrict leisure participation can be beneficial even if older adults are not successful in maintaining participation. These benefits may occur as a result of the constraints forcing older adults to adapt and modify their leisure lifestyles to meet their changing capacities and interests in ways that better promote well-being.

Kleiber, McGuire, Aybar-Damali, and Norman (2008) and Kleiber and Nimrod (2009) further developed this constraint-adaptation idea about leisure constraints being beneficial by incorporating ideas from the selective optimization with compensation (SOC) theory (see chapter 3). Recall that SOC theory assumes that older adults face a variety of challenges as they grow older, but they have a range of resources that they can use to make effective adjustments to allow them to feel more in control and happier. For example, Kleiber et al. (2008) suggest a variety of positive responses to leisure constraints that may include a deeper commitment and greater effort to maintaining participation in a constrained activity, a shift in attention to other goals that may be more appropriate at a particular point in a person's life, and the discovery of new capacities.

There is some evidence for these ideas. Kleiber and Nimrod (2009) found that the older adults they studied had responded to age-related leisure

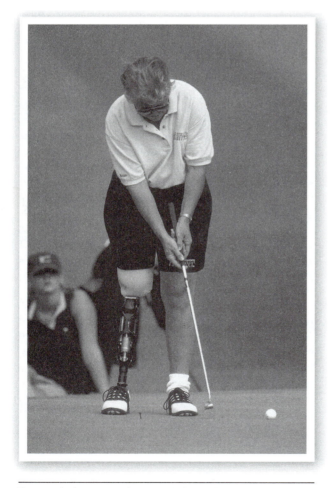

By negotiating constraints to activity, older adults can benefit in ways that go beyond the positive outcomes associated with the activity itself.

constraints by recognizing they couldn't continue to do everything they were doing. They reduced and eliminated activities, and they recognized that a certain activity was important to them and became even more committed or turned a constraint into a project. This latter response is particularly interesting. The researchers give the example of an older adult in their study turning his constraint (a hearing impairment) into a mission to educate others about the challenges during his leisure time. The development of theories such as this leisure constraint-adaptation theory is important. Such ideas will not only help us understand how older adults can remain active in meaningful leisure but also how to provide appropriate support and interventions when needed.

Applying General Theories of Leisure and Psychological Well-Being to Aging

Early in the development of thinking about the influence of leisure on psychosocial well-being regardless of age, the frequency and diversity of leisure activity were often seen as affecting psychosocial well-being—people with higher levels of leisure activity have higher psychosocial well-being. However, as researchers studied this relationship, it was often found to be weak, not applying to all people and differing based on gender, race, and culture. Even when supported, knowing that higher leisure participation contributes to well-being provides little insight for helping people create and adapt their leisure lifestyles to meet changing needs resulting from evolving life circumstances, including aging. In other words, telling people that it is good for them to be more active in their leisure is not very helpful!

Researchers recognized that far more useful would be understanding who might benefit from various types and levels of leisure involvements, when and why some types of leisure are meaningful and contribute to well-being better than others, and how current leisure involvements can be adapted or replaced to allow continued participation and enjoyment when constraints are encountered. Some of the resulting research has been done with older adults, but a great deal has been focused on people of all ages, and there are a number of theories that attempt to explain the influence of leisure on people's psychosocial well-being regardless of age. These general leisure and well-being theories are explicit about the ways and conditions under which leisure can influence psychosocial well-being, and they include ideas that leisure contributes to well-being by keeping people psychologically and behaviorally busy, providing experiences of pleasure and fun that contribute to long-term well-being, developing and confirming identity, promoting personal growth, and serving as a resource for coping with stress (Mannell & Kleiber, 1997). Research on these ideas continues today (Mannell, 2007). We now look at these ideas and the insights they provide for better understanding of how and when leisure can contribute to the psychosocial well-being of older adults.

The theory of *keeping busy* with leisure is one of the most basic explanations of how leisure contributes to psychosocial well-being. In figure 8.1, this link is indicated by the solid arrow between keeping busy in the outer ring of the diagram and the circle in the middle representing psychosocial well-being. The dashed line connecting keeping-busy theory and activity theory on the inner ring indicates that the two theories have some explanatory elements in common—namely, the more activity, the better.

Keeping busy with leisure activities has been thought to provide a way to fill free time with constructive alternatives to negative behavior or thoughts that can jeopardize health and well-being. People are thought to be happiest when they are busy. Having unoccupied free time and leisure is assumed to be risky for some people due to boredom. Interestingly, both juvenile delinquency and apathy in old age are often viewed as a result of having too much free time. In the case of adolescents, if no socially acceptable leisure alternatives are available, boredom can result in risky health behaviors such as smoking, alcohol abuse, vomiting on purpose (bulimia), and attempting suicide (Caldwell & Smith, 1995), and the benefits of structured leisure activity to combat boredom among adolescents have been demonstrated (e.g., Larson, Walker, & Pearce, 2005). In the case of older adults, boredom can result in depression and withdrawal from life (Blazer, 2003). Leisure also is a way of keeping the mind busy, thus diverting people from distressing thoughts that may be triggered by stressful life events such as the death of a spouse. By keeping their minds busy, people may temporarily avoid the stress of these events—in effect, leisure provides a break that can allow more effective coping in the long run (Iwasaki, Mactavish, & MacKay, 2005; Iwasaki & Mannell, 2000).

Another prevalent general theory about leisure and well-being is that psychosocial well-being can result from the experience of *pleasure and fun* in leisure. Leisure can provide relatively brief pleasurable-fun experiences (e.g., joking with friends, playing with your dog, successfully finishing a game of sudoku) that not only enhance the quality of the present moment but cumulatively contribute to long-term psychosocial well-being better than major but less frequent leisure events such as visiting Disney World or attending musical theater. Much of the leisure that people engage in during their daily lives is characterized by fun and pleasure seeking. Leisure pursuits that become meaningful to people are often structured to provide opportunities for fun and pleasure as part of the ongoing experience (Fine, 1989), and more research is showing that such moments do contribute to long-term well-being (Lyubomirsky, King, & Diener, 2005). As can be seen in figure 8.1, the importance of leisure for providing pleasure and fun has not been addressed by aging-specific theories of leisure and psychosocial well-being. This neglect is surprising. Surely pleasure and fun are as important to older adults as to other age groups!

Leisure is also thought to promote psychosocial well-being through *personal growth*. In theories about leisure, personal growth is often referred to as *self-actualization*. However, the concept of personal growth encompasses a wide range of ideas, including developing and maintaining competence, autonomy, mature interpersonal relationships, and a sense of purpose and integrity, and many psychological theories of positive human functioning are based on these ideas. Because it allows freedom of choice, leisure can provide opportunities that foster the development of personal growth, opportunities that often are not as available in other areas of life.

Also, involvement in leisure activities that demand effort, perseverance, and commitment (Stebbins, 2001) and the development of skills to meet new challenges (Csikszentmihalyi, 1997) can lead to personal growth. Kelly and Ross (1989) found that older adults who experienced higher levels of well-being were more involved in freely chosen leisure activities that challenged their knowledge and skills and required an investment of effort. Shary and Iso-Ahola (1989) found that not only did feelings of competency result from enhancing nursing-home residents' choice and control over their lives through leisure participation, but that these feelings of competence were also accompanied by increases in self-esteem. In another study, older adults who engaged in a higher proportion of leisure activities in which their skills and knowledge matched the challenges of the activity had higher psychosocial well-being (Mannell, 1993). Silverstein and Parker (2002) reported that older adults who increased their leisure participation over a 10-year period demonstrated greater personal growth. Interestingly, some of these dimensions of personal growth may help us understand Nimrod and Kleiber's (2007) innovation theory of successful aging (see figure 8.1); that is, adding new activities can provide new challenges that may promote personal growth.

Associated with personal growth is the idea that leisure can provide opportunities for *identity formation and affirmation*. In leisure, people feel free not only to be themselves but also to try out new possibilities and identities. For example, an older adult can try out birding by joining a club or puppy raising and training by volunteering with a service-dog organization. If the activities are enjoyable and competencies are developed, identities as a birder or puppy trainer may be formed and affirmed by ongoing involvement. These leisure identities can express and affirm individual talents and capacities, provide some degree of social recognition, and affirm central values and interests.

People are motivated to engage in leisure behavior that allows them to affirm images they have or would like to have of themselves (Kleiber, 1999). Leisure activities often embody distinct identity images; that is, people in a cultural or social group share beliefs about the characteristics of people who participate in these activities. By participating in activities that embody these identity images, people validate that they are or aspire to be this type of person, and they may be challenged over time to develop new skills and psychological resources so that they can live up to the new identity. Coatsworth et al. (2005) examined identity formation among adolescents in leisure activities with cross-national samples from the United States, Chile, and Italy. Findings indicated that many adolescents reported high levels of identity experiences within leisure activities.

Little research has been reported about the actual psychological process by which participation in leisure activities helps older adults maintain their identities or contributes to the formation of new identities as they age. As indicated in figure 8.1, some of these identity ideas may help explain the positive influence of leisure on psychosocial well-being proposed by the continuity and innovation theories of aging. It's also interesting to note that there is no general theory of leisure and psychosocial well-being that includes the idea of continuity. It might be useful to study the potential value of leisure in providing people of all ages who are going through changes in their lives (e.g., becoming a university student, a parent, or unemployed) with links to their past selves.

Finally, leisure has also been found to influence psychosocial well-being through its ability to facilitate *coping with stress* (Iwasaki & Mannell, 2000; Kleiber, Hutchinson, & Williams, 2002). There are many sources and types of stress that can threaten psychosocial well-being. Older adults struggle with the stress of daily hassles (e.g., financial concerns), role strain (e.g., caregiving), chronic life problems (e.g., long-term disability), life transitions (e.g., retirement), and life crises (e.g., death of a spouse). However, although stress has been linked to decreased psychosocial well-being, some people are able to resist stress or cope better than others. Leisure coping theory suggests that leisure activities and experiences can provide temporary escape, contribute to feelings of control, foster companionship, and enhance moods, all of which appear to be useful for reducing certain types of stress (Iwasaki & Mannell, 2000). Leisure can also contribute to coping with negative life events such as the death of a spouse by promoting self-restoration and post-traumatic growth (Kleiber et al., 2002). Although none of the aging-specific theories explicitly refers to coping with stress, adapting to constraints as suggested by constraint-adaptation theory could be considered a type of coping if we assume that older adults find it stressful when they are constrained in some aspect of their leisure (see figure 8.1).

In summary, there is good evidence that leisure behavior and experience can have a positive influence on the psychosocial well-being of older adults. It is also clear that our knowledge about using leisure to promote well-being among older adults could benefit from incorporating ideas from general leisure and well-being theories. However, in further developing theories and knowledge, it is important to remember that leisure choices and participation are not automatically good, nor do they guarantee psychosocial well-being. Leisure involvement can also have neutral or negative impacts and displace behaviors that contribute to well-being (e.g., television watching can displace socializing with friends or being a leisure innovator). Fortunately, the factors that allow leisure to positively contribute to well-being are the subject of growing research efforts in many Western countries and increasingly in other regions of the world. With respect to older adults, we are not only developing a better understanding of the relationship between leisure and psychosocial well-being but also the processes that influence changes in leisure associated with aging and the ways older adults can maintain, adapt, and innovate in their leisure to experience its psychological benefits.

Leisure and the Cognitive Health of Older Adults

Along with psychosocial well-being, older adults often cite cognitive functioning as a central feature of how they define successful aging (Depp & Jeste, 2010). **Cognitive functioning** refers to attention, episodic and working memory, executive functioning, and processing speed. The ability of the brain to handle information from the environment essential to achieving a particular goal is referred to as *attention*. The most commonly reported cognitive decline experienced by older adults is in *episodic memory*, which represents the ability to recognize, consolidate, and use experiential information. Another form of memory, called *working memory*, temporarily holds auditory, visual, and spatial information that is important for cognitive processes such as recalling instructions and learning a list of words. Processes that describe the planning and execution of goal-directed behaviors

as regulated by the frontal lobes are known as *executive functioning*. Finally, *processing speed* describes mental efficiency or speed of thinking, and it also has an impact on physical action. Evidence suggests that cognitive decline in later life is not inevitable (Perls, Levenson, Regan, & Puca, 2002). So, why do some people experience significant changes in cognitive functioning while others experience little or no change?

Psychological and epidemiological research indicates that engagement in physical, social, and mental leisure activities can influence cognition. The impacts of activities in these three domains are not exclusive, and many leisure activities can be classified in two or more of these domains. Although it is difficult to separate leisure activities into the three domains, doing so may be useful for developing effective intervention strategies and fully understanding the connections between leisure and cognitive functioning (Richards, Hardy, & Wadsworth, 2003).

The cognitive benefits of older adults' engagement in active physical, social, and mental leisure are greater than those derived during young adulthood and midlife (Wilson et al., 2005), and older adults can also benefit from newly adopted leisure behaviors (Bielak, in press; Colcombe & Kramer, 2003). Improving cognitive functioning is important because it is linked to overall psychosocial well-being and provides protection against the onset of dementia and Alzheimer's (Crowe, Andel, Pedersen, Johansson, & Gatz, 2003).

Mr. Game Boy Versus the Renaissance Man

John and Al are lifelong friends, and it's been a long life thus far. They are both 85 years old, have outlived their spouses, and live in a seniors' home that provides meals, housekeeping, and occasional nursing support when needed. Although they now live in their hometown, they and their families lived in different communities at various times during their lives as they moved around with their jobs. However, they have always shared interests in the outdoors, sport, and volunteer work in the community.

Both John and Al have chronic health problems that restrict their activities to some extent, but they both still have reasonably good hearing and sight and are able to walk with the aid of a cane. However, Al has become concerned about his friend John. John seems to have become obsessed with playing video games, doing electronic mind exercises, and completing crossword puzzles to the exclusion of other leisure activities. Al thinks John is foolish to give up so many of his social and physical leisure involvements to focus on mental activities. However, both John's and Al's parents and many of their friends experienced cognitive decline or dementias in their later years, and John believes that he is immunizing himself with these activities.

Is Al justified in his worry about John becoming too specialized in his leisure? Could Al's leisure lifestyle, which involves being as physically active as his limitations allow and continuing to engage in social activities, be effective in protecting against cognitive decline?

Although research has not led to conclusive explanations of the relationship between engagement in various leisure activities and cognition in older adults, the concepts of brain reserve and cognitive reserve have received widespread attention (Stern, 2002). **Brain reserve** can be thought of as brain size, neural density, or the number of connected synapses. It refers to brain capacity, and a larger capacity increases the time before a critical threshold of damage is reached. **Cognitive reserve** presumes that unused cognitive capacity exists regardless of brain reserve and can be stimulated through increased activity. Cognitive reserve helps explain why some older adults who possess the pathology associated with Alzheimer's do not show disease characteristics (Stern, 2002). That is, they have activated a cognitive reserve that helps cope with the pathology by providing new cognitive function that makes up for the lost functioning. The popular phrase "Use it or lose it" is most consistent with the idea of cognitive reserve because brain reserve is more fixed.

Physically Active Leisure

Numerous studies have demonstrated a positive relationship between physically active leisure and cognitive health for older adults (Fratiglioni, Paillard-Borg, & Winblad, 2004; see also chapters 2 and 7. Specifically, frequent engagement in activities such as walking, sport, and exercise is associated with maintained and improved cognitive functioning in older adults. For example, a longitudinal study that followed a group of older American women over a 25-year period found that those who engaged in regular, moderately intense physical activity had higher cognitive functioning than those who engaged in little to no physical activity (Weuve et al., 2004). Also, higher levels of physical activity were associated with less cognitive deterioration over time. Similar results have been found for American men and in other countries such as Canada and the Netherlands (Fratiglioni et al., 2004; Laurin, Vereault, Lindsay, MacPherson, & Rockwood, 2001).

It is believed that a physically active lifestyle can expand brain capacity (brain reserve) and stimulate cognitive reserve directly through a number of vascular and neurological processes and indirectly through a number of health benefits, such as insulin regulation, decreased stress and disease prevention, and increased psychosocial well-being, all of which are associated with positive cognitive functioning (Bielak, in press; Weuve et al., 2004). These findings are consistent

with the association found between health status and cognitive functioning, particularly given that people who are more physically active in their leisure also tend to have a healthier approach to eating and overall better health.

Socially Active Leisure

Engagement in a socially active leisure lifestyle means that people have developed a network of friends and family they see regularly, or they participate in socially oriented leisure activities such as volunteering, dining out, attending church functions, and playing games. A large population-based study of older adults found that people who had a greater number of social networks or a higher rate of participation in socially based leisure activities had lower levels of cognitive decline (Barnes, Mendes de Leon, Wilson, Bienias, & Evans, 2004). The influence that involvement in social networks and activities had on cognitive functioning was found even after taking into account participants' baseline cognitive function, level of mental and physical activity, health status, and certain sociodemographic characteristics. Similarly, other studies have shown that social ties and engagement in social activities not only enhance cognitive function but may in some cases delay the onset of Alzheimer's and dementia (e.g., Scarmeas, Levy, Tang, Manly, & Stern, 2001; Seeman, Lusignolo, Albert, & Berkman, 2001).

Although researchers are less certain about the links between social activities and cognition than they are about links with physical activity (Barnes et al., 2004), two popular theories have been proposed. One idea is that socially active lifestyles stimulate cognitive reserve and specific cognitive functions since older adults have to navigate social cues and rules, organize social engagements, negotiate with challenging people, and deal with disagreements (Bielak, in press). The second idea is that involvement in social networks and activities may indirectly protect cognitive functions by providing emotional support and enhancing psychosocial well-being, which are associated with stress reduction, lowered cortisol levels, and reduced risk of cardiovascular disease and diabetes.

Mentally Active Leisure

The idea that regular participation in activities that are mentally engaging (e.g., reading, doing crossword puzzles, learning a language) provides cognitive benefits seems intuitive, and it has been fueled by the widespread appeal of commercial products, including video games, aimed at improving cognition. Although some evidence suggests that engaging in mental leisure activities is associated with higher cognitive reserve (Scarmeas & Stern, 2003), it is important to consider that in population-based epidemiological studies, it is difficult to isolate mental activities from physical and social activities. Thus, without evaluating the effectiveness of mental activities in isolation, results may be confounded and inconclusive. Evaluations of intervention strategies that involve engaging in mental activities have been employed as a way of partially isolating the efficacy of these activities.

The ACTIVE research group (Willis et al., 2006) conducted the first large-scale study to demonstrate the beneficial effects of cognitive training for older adults without dementia. Using both self-report and performance-based outcome measures, it was shown that cognitive benefits lasted up to five years from the onset of the intervention. Further, this study showed that the intervention strategies aimed at improving cognitive function had a positive, albeit limited, effect on cognitive function in daily life. The limited effect of cognitive training on everyday cognitive tasks is a common critique of intervention strategies that aim to improve cognition in older adults. Such strategies typically result in an improvement in the specific task in which the person engaged but limited improvement in related cognitive tasks. For example, researchers have questioned the cognitive relevance of mental activities such as crossword puzzles for improving anything beyond the ability to complete crossword puzzles (Bielak, in press). However, that is not to say that these mental activities are not beneficial through other means, such as stress reduction or an improvement in psychosocial well-being.

Results supporting the relationship between mental leisure activities and cognition have also been questioned in terms of establishing causality. That is, does engaging in mentally active leisure lead to improved cognitive abilities, or are people with higher cognitive functioning more likely to seek out intellectually stimulating activities (Crowe et al., 2003)? Research has found support for both explanations (e.g., Schooler & Mulatu, 2001), suggesting a mutual influence. The effects of education and participation in mental activities certainly may not be independent or additive. Researchers have found that mental activities may benefit low-educated people more

than highly educated people (Christensen et al., 1996), perhaps because there is more potential for improvement among the former.

In summary, although a considerable amount of research has been reported in recent years, there is a need to further clarify the relationships proposed to exist between various types of leisure and cognition. There are also many unknowns. For instance, the intensity of involvement required to achieve cognitive benefits is unclear. Bielak (in press) comments that "it is unknown to what extent activity duration and intensity matter, making this clearly another potential research focus." Also worth further exploration is the potentially beneficial effect of engaging in leisure activities that are physical, social, and mental. Karp et al. (2006) found that older adults who participated in activities that were high in at least two of these three components had the lowest risk of dementia. Crowe et al. (2003) found similar effects when older adults had leisure lifestyles that included participation in multiple types of activities. However, the benefits of engaging in multiple types of leisure activities should be considered alongside the intensity with which the activities are undertaken. In other words, participating in fewer activities at a higher intensity may be as cognitively beneficial as participating in multiple forms of activities at low or moderate levels.

Conclusion

Current theory and research do not provide a detailed blueprint for enhancing the psychosocial or cognitive psychological well-being and health of older adults through leisure. However, the picture is becoming clearer. It is encouraging that many older adults are active in their leisure and are likely receiving many of the psychological benefits discussed without thinking too much about it. It also seems to be the case that the same physical, social, and mental leisure activities can contribute to both psychosocial and cognitive well-being and health.

However, research suggests that there is tremendous diversity in the leisure lifestyles and developmental paths that people follow over the life course. People who are married or single, parents or childless, partners in heterosexual or same-sex relationships, and members of one ethnic and cultural background or another follow different routes and face different issues as they age and strive for psychological well-being and health. Patterns of leisure participation parallel this diversity. In 1992, Zuzanek and Smale analyzed the time use and lifestyles of 25- to 44-year-old people during a typical week. Even in this restricted age range, they were able to classify the participants into five major life-cycle groups, and they found that the groups substantially differed in their weekly leisure participation rates and patterns. These groups are now approaching retirement and becoming older adults. They have likely brought with them distinct leisure patterns of participation and needs as well as skills in adapting to the changes associated with aging. Consequently, they will require different leisure opportunities and services to meet their needs and maintain psychological well-being and health.

It is also clear that strategies aimed at improving the psychological well-being and health of older adults through changes in leisure lifestyle should not focus solely on level of participation. In particular, the research on the relationship between leisure and psychosocial well-being suggests that the quality and meaning of people's leisure activities is as important as how much they do. Also, as we noted earlier, what people do with their leisure is not automatically a force for well-being and good health. The choices older adults make can be completely benign in their influence on health, and in some cases they even can be destructive, as with activities involving substance misuse and other forms of risky behavior.

Analyses of U.S. and Canadian data suggest that participating in normally beneficial leisure activities, including exercise, can even have negative consequences. For example, if people who are experiencing heavy demands from areas of their lives such as work and family try to pack too much activity into their leisure, stress levels may actually be exacerbated rather than buffered. Having a physically active lifestyle was found to be more strongly related to physical and mental health among older retired adults who may have fewer demands on their time compared with people in other life-cycle groups (Zuzanek & Mannell, 1998). Such differences likely exist among groups of older adults as well. In advocating leisure participation and developing leisure interventions to enhance psychological well-being and health, older adults' life circumstances must be taken into account.

In recent years, there has been more research on the impact of various interventions designed to improve the psychosocial well-being and quality of life of older adults. Programs for health promotion targeted at older adults have been developed and tested, and some research has been reported for leisure interventions, yet much more is needed. The ideas and research reviewed in this chapter suggest that there are and will be many good ideas emerging in the leisure studies field on which to base interventions, and these will need to be evaluated if progress is to be made.

KEY TERMS

affect—Feelings and moods.

brain reserve—Brain size, neural density, or the number of connected synapses; brain capacity.

cognitive functioning—Attention, episodic and working memory, executive functioning, and processing speed.

cognitive health—The effective functioning of memory, attention, inductive reasoning, perceptual and cognitive processing, and social cognition as well as use of language, vocabulary, and speech.

cognitive reserve—The unused cognitive capacity that exists regardless of brain reserve and can be stimulated through increased activity.

happiness—The extent to which positive feelings outweigh negative ones.

innovators—Older adults who add new, never-before-participated-in activities to their leisure repertoires when they are older and retired.

life satisfaction—A past orientation and an act of judgment in comparing what people have versus what they expect in terms of their whole life or some specific part of it. People who feel their life experiences have matched or exceeded their expectations have higher life satisfaction.

morale—A future-oriented optimism or pessimism regarding the problems and opportunities associated with aging.

psychological well-being—Self-acceptance, personal growth, having purpose in life, effective coping, and feeling competent.

psychosocial well-being—People's happiness and how well they cope with the various challenges and changes that occur in their lives as they age.

quality of life—A broad concept referring to overall well-being.

REVIEW AND DISCUSSION QUESTIONS

1. Name and describe the two types of psychological health and well-being.

2. What terms have been used by researchers to describe the psychosocial well-being of older adults?

3. Why are researchers and practitioners concerned that leisure participation appears to decline with age?

4. What are the primary reasons given by traditional theories of aging (e.g., activity and continuity theories) for the importance of leisure for psychosocial well-being?

5. How does the constraint-adaptation theory of aging help us better understand the way in which older adults can benefit from leisure?

6. What are the limitations of activity and continuity theories for explaining the ways in which leisure can influence psychosocial well-being?

7. Describe five psychological leisure and well-being theories that can provide insights into the ways in which leisure can influence well-being.

8. In general, how do leisure activities prevent cognitive decline and contribute to cognitive health?

9. Which types of leisure activities (physical, social, or mental) contribute the most to cognitive health?

10. In what way might psychosocial well-being and cognitive health be linked?

LEARNING ACTIVITIES

1. Based on the definitions of *happiness* and *life satisfaction* provided in the chapter, develop two questions for each of these concepts of psychosocial well-being that you could use to assess the happiness and life satisfaction of a friend.

2. Analyze your own leisure lifestyle during the past year and classify yourself according to Searle, Mactavish, and Brayley's (1993) typology. Are you a replacer, quitter, adder, or continuer? Do you expect this pattern to continue or change over the next five years? Has it changed during the past five years? Why?

3. Personal growth theories of leisure and well-being suggest that providing opportunities for older adults to experience self-determination and competence is critical to psychosocial well-being. Do you think this theory applies

to frail older adults who are confined to bed or wheelchairs? If so, develop a recreation intervention that does more than keep them busy and promotes personal growth.

4. Describe and name a new mental recreational activity or resource that could be used to promote cognitive health.

5. Can video games and game systems be designed to simultaneously promote physical, social, and mental activity? Are you familiar with any such systems or games? How could such games be made attractive to older adults?

CRITICAL-THINKING ACTIVITIES

1. Let's return to the opening story of Janice and Debbie, who spent the first five years of retirement doing a great deal of traveling but who now have different outlooks on the future.
   - Identify how their leisure lifestyles before retiring might account for the differences in their present outlooks.
   - Explain why these differences may not have affected their enthusiasm and happiness in the first five years of their retirement.
   - What are the important psychological needs that these two retired women must satisfy to age successfully and be happy?
   - If Debbie were a family friend and wanted to chat with you about her feelings and concerns, what would you counsel?
   - What is the likelihood of the two women establishing new patterns of living that will contribute to their psychosocial well-being as they continue to age?

2. In the story of the two friends living in a seniors' residence, Al was concerned about John becoming preoccupied with mental leisure activities.
   - If you were a recreation therapist working in the residence, would you be concerned about John's leisure behavior? Is Al justified in his worry about John becoming too specialized in his leisure?
   - Describe the evidence for and against the idea that leisure activities requiring mental activity can prevent cognitive decline.

– Could Al's leisure lifestyle, which involves being as physically active as his limitations allow and continuing to engage in social activities, be effective in protecting against cognitive decline?

– Develop a leisure plan for John that includes recommendations to help meet what he feels are his primary needs yet also provide for a more balanced leisure lifestyle.

SUGGESTED READING

Csikszentmihalyi, M. (1997). *Finding flow*. New York: Basic Books.

Fine, G.A. (1989). Mobilizing fun: Provisioning resources in leisure worlds. *Sociology of Sport Journal, 6*, 319-334.

Karp, A., Paillard-Borg, S., Wang, H.X., Silverstein, M., Winblad, B., et al. (2006). Mental, physical and social components in leisure activities equally contribute to decrease dementia risk. *Dementia and Geriatric Cognitive Disorders, 21*, 65-73.

Kleiber, D.A. (1999). *Leisure experience and human development*. New York: Basic Books.

Klieber, D.A., & Nimrod, G. (2009). 'I can't be very sad': Constraint and adaptation in the leisure of a 'learning in retirement' group. *Leisure Studies, 28*, 67-83.

Mannell, R.C., & Dupuis, S.L. (2007). Life satisfaction. In J.E. Birren (Ed.), *Encyclopedia of gerontology* (Vol. 2, 2nd ed., pp. 73-79). Oxford, UK: Elsevier, Academic Press.

Schooler, C. & Mulatu, M.S. (2001). The reciprocal effects of leisure time activities and intellectual functioning in older people: A longitudinal analysis. *Psychology & Aging, 16*, 466-482.

Snyder, C.R., & Lopez, S.J. (2007). *Positive psychology: The scientific and practical explorations of human strengths*. Thousand Oaks, CA: Sage.

REFERENCES

Barnes, L.L., Mendes de Leon, C.F., Wilson, R.S., Bienias, J.L., & Evans, D.A. (2004). Social resources and cognitive decline in a population of older African Americans and whites. *Neurology, 63*, 2322-2326.

Bielak, A.A.M. (in press). How can we not 'lose it' if we still don't understand how to 'use it'? Unanswered questions about the influence of activity participation on cognitive performance in older age—a mini-review. *Gerontology*.

Blanchflower, D.G., & Oswald, A.J. (2008). Is well-being U-shaped over the life cycle? *Social Science & Medicine, 66*, 1733-1749.

Blazer, D. (2003). Depression in late life: Review and commentary. *Journal of Gerontology: Medical Sciences, 58A*, 249-265.

Caldwell, L.L., & Smith, E.A. (1995). Health behaviors of leisure alienated youth. *Society and Leisure, 18*, 143-156.

Christensen, H., Korten, A., Jorm, A.F., Henderson, A.S., Scott, R., & Mackinnon, A.J. (1996). Activity levels and cognitive functioning in an elderly community sample. *Age and Ageing, 25*, 72-80.

Coatsworth, J.D., Sharp, E.H., Palen, L., Darling, N., Cumsille, P., & Marta, E. (2005). Exploring adolescent self-defining leisure activities and identity experiences across three countries. *International Journal of Behavioral Development, 29*, 361-370.

Colcombe, S.J., & Kramer, A.F. (2003). Fitness effects on the cognitive function of older adults: A meta-analytic study. *Psychological Science, 14*, 125-130.

Crowe, M., Andel, R., Pedersen, N.L., Johansson, B., & Gatz, M. (2003). Does participation in leisure activities lead to reduced risk of Alzheimer's disease? A prospective study of Swedish twins. *Journal of Gerontology: Psychological Sciences, 58*, 249-255.

Csikszentmihalyi, M. (1997). *Finding flow*. New York: Basic Books.

Depp, C.A., & Jeste, D.V. (2010). Phenotypes of successful aging: Historical overview. In C.A. Depp & D.V. Jeste (Eds.), *Successful cognitive and emotional aging* (pp. 1-14). Washington, DC: American Psychiatric.

Fine, G.A. (1989). Mobilizing fun: Provisioning resources in leisure worlds. *Sociology of Sport Journal, 6*, 319-334.

Fratiglioni, L., Paillard-Borg, S., & Winblad, B. (2004). An active and socially integrated lifestyle in late life might protect against dementia. *Lancet Neurology, 3*(6), 343-353.

Gibson, H.J. (2006). Leisure and later life: Past, present and future. *Leisure Studies, 25*, 397-401.

Iwasaki, Y., & Mannell, R.C. (2000). Hierarchical dimensions of leisure stress coping. *Leisure Sciences, 22*, 163-181.

Iwasaki, Y., Mactavish, J.M., & MacKay, K. (2005). Building on strengths and resilience: Leisure as a stress survival strategy. *British Journal of Guidance and Counselling, 33*, 81-100.

Jackson, E.L. (Ed.) (2005). *Constraints to leisure*. State College, PA: Venture.

Janke, M., Davey, A., & Kleiber, D. (2006). Modeling change in older adults' leisure activities. *Leisure Sciences, 28*, 285-303.

Karp, A., Paillard-Borg, S., Wang, H.X., Silverstein, M., Winblad, B., et al. (2006). Mental, physical and social components in leisure activities equally contribute to decrease dementia risk. *Dementia and Geriatric Cognitive Disorders, 21*, 65-73.

Kelly, J.R., & Ross, J.E. (1989). Later-life leisure: Beginning a new agenda. *Leisure Sciences, 11*, 47-59.

Keyes, C.L.M. (2007). Psychological well-being. In J.E. Birren (Ed.), *Encyclopedia of gerontology* (Vol. 2, 2nd ed., pp. 399-406). Oxford, UK: Elsevier, Academic Press.

Kleiber, D.A. (1999). *Leisure experience and human development*. New York: Basic Books.

Kleiber, D.A., Hutchinson, S.L., & Williams, R. (2002). Leisure as a resource in transcending negative life events: Self-protection, self-restoration, and personal transformation. *Leisure Sciences, 24*, 219-235.

Kleiber, D.A., McGuire, F.A., Aybar-Damali, B., & Norman, W. (2008). Having more by doing less: The paradox of leisure constraints in later life. *Journal of Leisure Research, 40*, 343-359.

Klieber, D.A., & Nimrod, G. (2009). 'I can't be very sad': Constraint and adaptation in the leisure of a 'learning in retirement' group. *Leisure Studies, 28*, 67-83.

Larson, R., Walker, K., & Pearce, N. (2005). A comparison of youth-driven and adult-driven youth programs: Balancing inputs from youth and adults. *Journal of Community Psychology, 33*, 57-74.

Laurin, D., Verreault, R., Lindsay, J., MacPherson, K., & Rockwood, K. (2001). Physical activity and risk of cognitive impairment and dementia in elderly persons. *Archives of Neurology, 58*, 498-504.

Lyubomirsky, S., King, L., & Diener, E. (2005). The benefits of frequent positive affect: Does happiness lead to success? *Psychological Bulletin, 131*, 803-855.

Mannell, R.C. (1993). High investment activity and life satisfaction among older adults: Committed, serious leisure and flow activities. In J.R. Kelly (Ed.), *Activity and aging* (pp. 125-145). Newbury Park, CA: Sage.

Mannell, R.C. (2007). Health, well-being and leisure. *World Leisure Journal, 49*, 114-128.

Mannell, R.C., & Dupuis, S.L. (2007). Life satisfaction. In J.E. Birren (Ed.), *Encyclopedia of gerontology* (Vol. 2, 2nd ed., pp. 73-79). Oxford, UK: Elsevier, Academic Press.

Mannell, R.C., & Kleiber, D.A. (1997). *A social psychology of leisure.* State College, PA: Venture Press.

McGuire, F.A., & Norman, W. (2005). The role of constraints in successful aging: Enabling or inhibiting? In E.L. Jackson (Ed.), *Constraints to leisure* (pp. 89-102). State College, PA: Venture Press.

Nimrod, G. (2008). In support of innovation theory: Innovation in activity patterns and life satisfaction among recently retired individuals. *Aging and Society, 28*, 831-846.

Nimrod, G., & Kleiber, D.A. (2007). Reconsidering change and continuity in later life: Toward an innovation theory of successful aging. *International Journal of Aging and Human Development, 65*, 1-22.

Perls, T., Levenson, R., Regan, M., & Puca, A. (2002). What does it take to live to 100? *Mechanisms of Ageing and Development, 123*, 231-242.

Richards, M., Hardy, R., & Wadsworth, M.E.J. (2003) Does active leisure protect cognition? Evidence from a national birth cohort. *Social Science & Medicine, 56*, 785-792.

Scarmeas, N., Levy, G., Tang, M.X., Manly, J., & Stern, Y. (2001). Influence of leisure activity on the incidence of Alzheimer's disease. *Neurology, 57*, 2236-2242.

Scarmeas, N., & Stern, Y. (2003). Cognitive reserve and lifestyle. *Journal of Clinical and Experimental Neuropsychology, 25*, 625-633.

Schooler, C., & Mulatu, M.S. (2001). The reciprocal effects of leisure time activities and intellectual functioning in older people: A longitudinal analysis. *Psychology & Aging, 16*, 466-482.

Searle, M.S., Mactavish, J., & Brayley, R.E. (1993). Integrating ceasing participation with other aspects of leisure behavior: A replication and extension. *Journal of Leisure Research, 25*, 389-404.

Seeman, T. E., Lusignolo, T. M., Albert, M., & Berkman, L. (2001). Social relationships, social support, and patterns of cognitive aging in healthy, high-functioning older adults: MacArthur studies of successful aging. *Health Psychology, 20*, 243-255.

Shary, J.M., & Iso-Ahola, S.E. (1989). Effects of a control-relevant intervention on nursing home residents' perceived competence and self-esteem. *Therapeutic Recreation Journal, 23*, 7-16.

Silverstein, M., & Parker, M.G. (2002). Leisure activities and quality of life among the oldest old in Sweden. *Research on Aging, 24*, 528-547.

Stebbins, R.A. (2001). *New directions in the theory and research of serious leisure.* New York: Edwin Mellen Press.

Steca, P., Alessandri, G., & Caprara, G.V. (2010). The utility of a well-known personality typology in studying successful aging: Resilients, undercontrollers, and overcontrollers in old age. *Personality and Individual Differences, 48*, 442-446.

Stern, Y. (2002). What is cognitive reserve? Theory and research application of the reserve concept. *Journal of the International Neuropsychological Society, 8*, 448-460.

Weuve, J., Kang, J.H., Manson, J.E., Breteler, M.M.B., Ware, J.H., & Grodstein, F. (2004). Physical activity, including walking, and cognitive function in older women. *Journal of the American Medical Association, 292*, 1454-1461.

Willis, S.L., Tennstedt, S.L., Marsiske, M., Ball, K., Elias, J., et al. (2006). Long-term effects of cognitive training on everyday functional outcomes in older adults. *Journal of the American Medical Association, 296*, 2805-2814.

Wilson, R.S., Barnes, L.L., Krueger, K.R., Hoganson, G., Bienias, J.L., & Bennett, D.A. (2005). Early and late life cognitive activity and cognitive systems in old age. *Journal of International Neuropsychological Society, 11*, 400-407.

Zuzanek, J., & Mannell, R.C. (1998). Life-cycle squeeze, time pressure, daily stress, and leisure participation: A Canadian perspective. *Society and Leisure, 21*, 513-544.

Zuzanek, J., & Smale, B.J.A. (1992). Life-cycle variations in across-the-week allocation of time to selected daily activities. *Loisiret Societe/Society and Leisure, 15*, 559-586.

CHAPTER 9

Leisure and Social and Spiritual Well-Being

Paul Heintzman ■ **Erin Patriquin**

LEARNING OBJECTIVES

After reading this chapter, you will be able to

- define *social well-being, spiritual well-being*, and *integrative wellness*;
- understand the relationships among aging, leisure, and social well-being;
- understand the relationships among aging, leisure, and spiritual well-being; and
- understand the interconnections between social well-being and spiritual well-being in the leisure of older adults.

The two previous chapters have examined leisure and aging well in terms of two dimensions of well-being: physical well-being and psychological well-being. In this chapter we continue to focus on leisure and aging well as we explore the social and spiritual dimensions of well-being in the lives of older people. We begin with definitions of the key concepts, followed by sections on aging, leisure, and social well-being; and aging, leisure, and spiritual well-being. We conclude with a presentation of the leisure-spiritual coping model that illustrates the interconnections between social and spiritual well-being in the lives of older people when experiencing stress. As a learning activity, before reading this chapter please write down your definitions of *social well-being*, *spiritual well-being*, and *integrative wellness*. We will return to your definitions in the review and discussion questions at the end of the chapter.

Defining Key Concepts

In this section we present definitions of social well-being, spiritual well-being, and integrative wellness. These concepts are foundational to the rest of the chapter.

Social Well-Being

Social well-being has been defined in a variety of ways, although most definitions focus on the nature and size of social interactions and social networks (Larson, 1996). For example, Adams, Bezner, and Steinhardt (1997) stated that "social wellness refers to the perception of having support available from family or friends in times of need and the perception of being a valued support provider" (p. 212). Keyes (1998) proposed that social well-being, defined as "the appraisal of one's circumstances and functioning in society" (p. 122), includes five dimensions: social integration, social acceptance, social contribution, social actualization, and social coherence. Dupuis (2008, pp. 98-99) has concisely defined these dimensions as follows:

- **Social integration**—Feeling that one has something in common with others and a sense of belonging to one's community and society.
- **Social acceptance**—The capacity for trusting others, believing others are capable of kindness and industriousness, holding a favorable view of human nature, and feeling comfortable with others.

- **Social contribution**—Having a strong sense of social value; believing that one is a vital member of society and contributes in valuable ways to the world.
- **Social actualization**—Understanding that society is continually evolving, being hopeful about its condition and future, and recognizing its potential.
- **Social coherence**—Having a concern about the world and a strong desire to make sense of the world.

When planning and implementing recreation programs that have social well-being objectives, recreation practitioners need to take into consideration these five dimensions of social well-being. Dupuis (2008) has noted that components of social well-being may vary from culture to culture and across the life span, thereby creating difficulties in both the conceptualization of social well-being and the use of this concept by recreation professionals.

Spiritual Well-Being

Based on an extensive review of literature, Hawks (1994, p. 4) identified internal characteristics of people who are spiritually healthy and also ways in which spiritually healthy people express themselves in their external interactions. Internal characteristics include

- a sense of life purpose and ultimate meaning;
- oneness with nature and beauty and a sense of connectedness with others;
- deep concern for and commitment to something greater than self;
- a sense of wholeness in life;
- strong spiritual beliefs, principles, ethics, and values; and
- love, joy, peace, hope, and fulfillment.

External characteristics include

- interactions with other people that are characterized by trust, honesty, integrity, altruism, compassion, and service; and
- regular communion or a personal relationship with a higher power or larger reality that transcends an observable physical reality.

Based on these characteristics, Hawks (1994) developed the following comprehensive definition of **spiritual health**:

A high level of faith, hope, and commitment in relation to a well-defined worldview or belief system that provides a sense of meaning and purpose to existence in general, and that offers an ethical path to personal fulfillment which includes connectedness with self, others, and a higher power or larger reality. (p. 6)

As you can see, social well-being and spiritual well-being overlap with each other. For example, the *connectedness with others* element of spiritual well-being is similar to the *social integration* dimension of social well-being, while *interactions with others characterized by altruism, compassion, and service* in the description of spiritual well-being is similar to the *social contribution* dimension of social well-being.

McDonald and Schreyer (1991) make a helpful distinction between the **content** and **process of spirituality**. Although the content and process are intertwined and one cannot occur without the other, content is the particular object of spirituality while process refers to the spiritual activities and functions that a person engages in. Even though the content of spiritual expressions (e.g., a belief system, content of a prayer) may differ from one spiritual expression to another, the spiritual processes (e.g., prayer, meditation) might be similar across many spiritual expressions. Given the diversity of faith and spiritual traditions in North America and in other regions of the world, recreation practitioners who are planning and implementing recreation programs that have spiritual objectives may want to focus more on spiritual processes than spiritual content.

Integrative Well-Being: Interconnections Between Social and Spiritual Well-Being

Wellness "is the integration of social, mental, emotional, spiritual and physical health at any level of health or illness" (Greenberg, 1985, p. 404). As a wellness dimension, spirituality has been conceptualized from two perspectives: elementalistic and integrative. As an elementalistic dimension, spiritual wellness is a distinct dimension, while as an integrative dimension it is an overarching concept found within each of the other dimensions of wellness. From the **elementalistic view**, spiritual wellness is one part of the whole. It interrelates, interacts, and must remain in balance with each of the other dimensions if optimal wellness is to be maintained. From the **integrative wellness** view, optimal wellness is also dependent on spiritual wellness occurring within each of the interrelated and interactive dimensions of

wellness. If spiritual wellness is an integrative component and not just an elementalistic component of wellness, then it needs to be an important consideration for recreation practitioners who are interested in enhancing the health of the people they work with.

Several dimensions of social well-being (e.g., social integration, social acceptance, social contribution) and many characteristics of spiritual well-being (e.g., life purpose and meaning; compassion and service; spiritual beliefs, principles, ethics, and values; a personal relationship with a higher power) are interwoven in the following reflection on retirement by an older adult. This reflection also illustrates the integrative nature of wellness (sidebar, p. 162).

When working with older adults, the therapeutic recreation outcome model (Van Andel, 1998; see also Carter, Van Andel, & Robb, 2003) is one model that incorporates both social and spiritual well-being (see figure 9.1 on page 163). In this model, therapeutic recreation strives to sustain or enhance the health status, quality of life, and functional capacities of people with specific characteristics (e.g., older adults) through the use of recreation or experiential activities and processes specifically developed for them. **Health status** refers to an integration of the five independent yet interacting health dimensions—physical, mental, spiritual, emotional, and social—that describe a person's level of health and well-being. **Quality of life** is a subjective measure of spiritual and psychological well-being characterized by feelings of self-determination, joy, contentment, and satisfaction. **Functional capacities** refer to a person's ability to function socially, spiritually, psychologically or emotionally, physically, and mentally or cognitively. Thus, this model reflects a holistic understanding of health where there is an integration of body, mind, and spirit.

Research suggests that people who attain integration among life's domains can experience a high level of well-being despite their circumstances. For example, an older person with a terminal illness who exhibits poor physical health may experience a high degree of wellness characterized by mental alertness, appropriate emotional expression, maintenance of meaning and purpose in life, and good relationships with others. Thus, this model and its holistic understanding of health is helpful for recreation practitioners when working with older people who may have limited function in one domain of health but who can experience an overall high level of well-being.

Thoughts on Retirement

Glen Van Andel

As friends and family learned of my intention to retire, they often asked, "What do you plan to do in retirement?" It was a question I shrugged off with a quick list of items, such as do a little traveling, work on projects for my kids, volunteer for some disaster-relief organizations, and enjoy some of my hobbies.

But more recently, as I've begun to experience this new phase of my life, I've realized there is more to this question than I had initially considered. When I took this question seriously, it drove me to ask other philosophical and spiritual questions, such as "Who am I?" and "Why am I here?" These are basic questions I've been asking for most of my life, especially at those transitional times when I began to consider a career, changed jobs, or faced challenges in the routine of life.

My parents were my early role models as they actively engaged in a number of local, state, and national civic and religious organizations. Caring for and serving others were primary values that permeated the small western Washington farming community in which I was raised. Although work was a dominant theme in my youth, I also recall rich times of family holidays and special outings to nearby lakes, hiking in the mountains, and fishing on Puget Sound. Celebrating life while we lived it, every moment brought much laughter and joy to our home. Life had a purpose. We were placed on this earth to serve and enjoy God and others.

My adult life continued to be shaped by these early experiences. My career began with part-time and later full-time work as a recreation therapist in a behavioral health setting where I learned to love adolescents who had experienced more pain and suffering in their short lives than I had ever known. Entering into their chaotic world to lead them to a place of hope and healing was challenging but also deeply rewarding.

Later, my gifts for teaching and leadership were used in a 30-year career as a college professor. It was a joy to engage undergraduate students in the stimulating world of ideas and challenge them to develop and use their gifts in meaningful careers of service to others. But the time came when I knew I had lost some of the passion and energy for this demanding career. It was time for a change.

So now what? What's next? Who am I? Why am I here?

As it turns out, I find myself doing many of the things I've done in the past that have enriched my life with meaning and purpose. My days are filled with a wide variety of activities such as weekly visits with several undergraduate students who have chosen me as a mentor, volunteering at my church and in a prison ministry, traveling with friends and family to those select places on our bucket list, developing deeper relationships with my grandchildren through regular contact often centered around ice cream, and using my interest in woodworking to design and build projects for my grown children and their families.

So, in retirement I'm rediscovering who I am and why I am here. Life is still about the importance of developing and maintaining meaningful relationships and using my God-given gifts to serve others. I'm reminded of a sign on an old Alaskan highway that read, "Choose your ruts carefully; you may be in them the next 200 miles." Retirement is intimately connected to values, beliefs, and attitudes developed in earlier stages of life. I am now even more grateful for the ruts I chose to follow.

Aging, Leisure, and Social Well-Being

A growing body of literature exists on the relationship between leisure and social well-being in later life, although almost all of it is focused on the social integration dimension of social well-being, which is not surprising since most definitions of social well-being focus on social integration. In this section we examine the social integration, social acceptance, and social contribution dimensions of social well-being as they relate to aging and leisure.

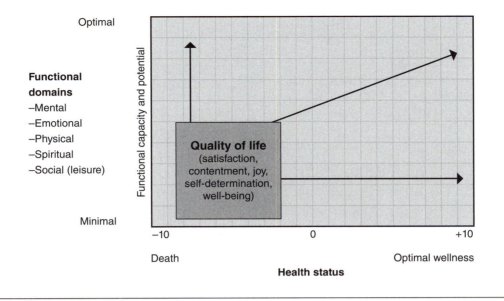

Figure 9.1 Therapeutic recreation outcome model.

Reprinted, by permission, from G. Van Andel, 1998, "TR service delivery and TR outcome models," *Therapeutic Recreation Journal* 32(3): 180-193.

Aging, Leisure, and Social Integration

Adams (1993) suggested that leisure activities provide contexts where older people can meet and make friends and that these activities are important venues for the affective, behavioral, and cognitive processes of friendship development and maintenance. During leisure people can show how they feel about each other through actions such as displaying affection and sharing resources and information. Thus, leisure provides a space for emotional responses such as loyalty, indifference, and empathy to others as well as an opportunity for reflection and evaluation of oneself and others. McCormick (1994) has suggested that for older people in rural areas, where traditional opportunities for social interaction through farming-based social structures, village stores, churches, and school events have declined, provision of leisure services might provide continued opportunities for social interaction and social well-being.

In a study of the relationship between leisure participation and perceived wellness among older people (aged 55-75) in Taiwan, Tsai and Wu (2005) found a significant positive relationship between leisure participation and perceived social wellness. Although few studies have used the concept of social well-being as in Tsai and Wu's study, a number of researchers have documented how leisure can be a means for older people to contribute to their community, reduce loneliness

and social isolation, create a sense of community belonging, and facilitate community social interaction (Dupuis, 2008). For example, in a study of older women who were quilters, Piercy and Cheek (2004) discovered that the quilters used their activity to enhance connections with their grandchildren and contribute to the well-being of the wider community, in addition to developing strong friendships within their quilting groups.

Most of the research on leisure and social well-being has focused on physical leisure activities. In a study of 6,596 American adults over 60 years of age, Bertera (2003) found that social network contacts (visits with neighbors, family gatherings, telephone calls) may be positively influenced by participation in physical activities such as biking, walking, and gardening. In a qualitative study of mall walkers over the age of 60, Duncan, Travis, and McAuley (1995) discovered that, according to the participants, mall walking was an effective way to increase social interaction, social companionship, and a sense of belonging that otherwise would have decreased due to retirement and other factors associated with aging. Another study of older adults who participated in one of two physical activity groups for a 12-month period found that social support from the activity group was associated with reduced loneliness (McAuley et al., 2000). Likewise, Whitaker's (2005) study of older Italian bicyclists discovered that bicycling, whether to make visits around town, do errands, or go on rides with a cycling club, brought older people into contact with others and led to the benefits of friendships, social ties, and social connectedness. The social dimension of bicycling was one of the most important outcomes of the activity mentioned by the study participants. Whitaker (2005) described this social dimension of cycling as follows:

> Many cyclists have been riding with the same friends for years. While these men also enjoy riding alone, they say that it is fun to be in company and to be able to have a conversation during the ride. The more sociable riders are active in their cycling associations, going to weekly meetings, weekend rides, get-togethers for cyclists and their families, and annual cycling trips to other regions or countries. As Michele puts it, he values the "associative life" surrounding his cycling group. (p. 26)

Dionigi's (2002) study of the meaning of competitive sport competition for masters athletes (aged 55 to 94 years) found that a sense of community developed from being with like-minded friends. Comments about "feeling like a big family," "belonging to a team," and "camaraderie" suggest that the social support, social interaction, and friendship resulting from sport involvement were motivation for continued participation.

Some studies have found that leisure engagement compensates for a decrease in social contacts and the size of one's social network as one grows older. In a representative survey of 324 older Swedes living in a community, Silverstein and Parker (2002) discovered that participants increased their leisure activities as an adaptive strategy to offset social deficits associated with aging. This adaptive strategy was especially prevalent among older people who had relatively little contact with their family or who had become widowed. Silverstein and Parker explained that leisure activities may enhance "social integration by linking active individuals to friends and acquaintances in a structured context" (p. 545). Likewise, in a study of female members of a senior center that offered a wide range of activities and volunteer opportunities, Hurd (1999) observed that many of these older women were widows who depended on the center as a social network that took the place of their deceased husbands and the associated social networks based on marriage. A qualitative study of Senior Odyssey, a program to encourage intellectual and social engagement among older adults, suggested that the participants valued the chance to sustain and develop their social networks through the program (Parisi,

Greene, Morrow, & Stine-Morrow, 2007). As one participant stated, "I need this interaction with people . . . because I'm not reaching out as much as I used to . . . to other people . . . I think older people tend to become isolated . . . but this was a chance to interact with other people" (p. 38).

Of particular relevance to this chapter, Dupuis (2008) has noted that religious and spiritual organizations may provide a significant space for networking and social interaction among older people. In a study of religious activities and attitudes of older adults, Koenig, Moberg, and Kvale (1988) found that a majority of respondents stated that of their five closest friends, at least four were members of their religious congregation. The researchers concluded that these congregations were a significant source of social support. These results support previous findings by Stephens, Blau, Oser, and Miller (1978) that increased frequency of attendance at religious services by older people is correlated with higher levels of informal social support.

The extensive research on the relationship between leisure and social integration reviewed in the preceding paragraphs suggests the importance of providing opportunities for older people to meet and to develop friendships with each other. Recreation professionals may also want to refer older people to other organizations (e.g., religious organizations) that provide opportunities for networking and social interaction.

Aging, Leisure, and Social Acceptance

Although there is extensive research on leisure and social integration, there is a paucity of research on the other four dimensions of social well-being. In regard to the social acceptance dimension of social well-being, participation in a program of recreational activities by Arab and Jewish elders in Israel improved the participants' attitudes toward each other (Leitner & Scher, 2000; Leitner, Scher, & Shuval, 1999), which suggests that attempts by recreation practitioners to involve older adults from diverse backgrounds into the same recreation program may lead to social acceptance.

Aging, Leisure, and Social Contribution

The social contribution dimension of social well-being includes the belief that a person is a vital member of society (Keyes, 1998). However, older people are often devalued and viewed as inferior to the young (Dionigi, 2002). Thus, recreation practitioners need to understand that leisure may provide the opportunity to resist ageist social stereotypes and to negotiate and create aging images that are more positive (Dupuis, 2008; cf. Hurd, 1999; Whitaker, 2005). For example, Wearing (1995) documented how leisure that emphasizes what one can do and the importance of choice may be an avenue to resist underuse of mental and physical capabilities in old age. Similarly, Dionigi (2002) found that competitive sport offers a leisure context for older athletes to resist negative stereotypes associated with aging.

Another aspect of the social contribution dimension of social well-being is "a strong sense of social value" and a belief that one "contributes in valuable ways to the world" (Dupuis, 2008, p. 98). In their study about building social capital through leisure in older adulthood, Maynard and Kleiber (2005) suggested that leisure activities may be used by older people not only for social integration but also for community involvement and civic engagement. To facilitate this process, Maynard and Kleiber recommended that interaction and sociability be enhanced through the following types of initiatives by recreation practitioners:

- The integration of neighborhood public leisure centers with public libraries

- The integration of neighborhood public leisure centers with senior centers
- A greater focus on intergenerational programming, especially programming that includes the integration of older adults with youth
- The provision of space for discussing public issues

Aging, Leisure, and Spiritual Well-Being

Compared with the literature on leisure and social well-being in later life, there are fewer studies on leisure and spiritual well-being for this age group. Thus, this section includes some studies that have examined leisure and spiritual well-being for all age groups. First, the relationships between leisure and spiritual well-being are examined, and then leisure-spiritual processes are discussed.

Relationship Between Leisure and Spiritual Well-Being

Ragheb (1993) surveyed 219 people to investigate whether leisure participation and level of leisure satisfaction were related to five components of

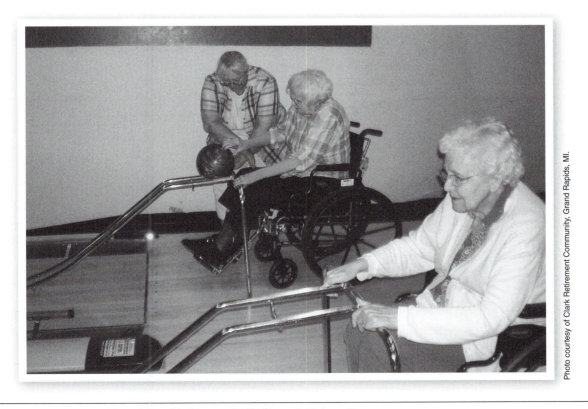

Photo courtesy of Clark Retirement Community, Grand Rapids, MI.

Leisure activities provide older adults with the opportunity for social integration.

perceived wellness. Frequency of leisure participation and level of leisure satisfaction were found to be positively associated with overall perceived wellness, including spiritual wellness. Reading had the highest correlation with perceived wellness and all of its components. Higher levels of satisfaction with leisure related to relaxation, beauty, and the environment were dominant in their contributions to perceived wellness, including spiritual wellness. A limitation of this study was the measurement of spiritual well-being with just one or two questionnaire items, making it difficult to capture the complexity of spiritual well-being and assess the validity of its measurement.

Heintzman and Mannell (1999) conducted a more comprehensive study of leisure and spiritual well-being that investigated the associations between four dimensions of leisure (activity, motivation, setting, and time) and spiritual well-being. Significant positive associations were found between spiritual well-being and overall participation in leisure activities as well as engagement in the specific categories of personal development activities, cultural activities, outdoor activities, and hobbies. There was no significant association between spiritual well-being and the leisure categories of mass media, social activities, sport activities, and travel and tourism. The findings concerning the positive association between spiritual well-being and both cultural activities and outdoor activities are consistent with Ragheb's (1993) suggestion that participation in these types of activities may be conducive to spiritual well-being.

In Heintzman and Mannell's (1999) study, higher levels of leisure motivation were associated with spiritual well-being, as was leisure engaged in for intellectual and stimulus-avoidance motives. The association between spiritual well-being and stimulus-avoidance motivations (e.g., to avoid social contacts, to seek solitude and calm settings, to seek rest, and to unwind; Beard & Ragheb, 1983), is consistent with Ragheb's (1993) finding of the important contribution of the relaxation component of leisure satisfaction to spiritual wellness, suggesting that relaxing leisure experiences with low levels of stimuli may be conducive to spiritual well-being.

Heintzman and Mannell (1999) also found that those who pursued leisure in quiet urban recreation areas and their own homes reported higher levels of spiritual health. There was no significant association between time use and spiritual well-being. Further analyses showed

that participation in personal development activities (e.g., reading for spiritual growth, meditation, tai chi, yoga, attendance at retreats) was the best predictor of spiritual well-being, followed by stimulus-avoidance motivations and frequency of engaging in leisure in one's own home. A mass-media leisure style (low leisure motivation and low leisure participation except for high participation in mass-media activities) was clearly associated with low spiritual well-being. Both those who might be characterized as having a *personal development* leisure style (high level of participation in personal development activities) and those with an *overall active* leisure style (high level of participation in all leisure categories) had higher levels of spiritual well-being. This contrast between a mass-media leisure style and a personal development leisure style is consistent with Nimrod's (2007) study on retirees' leisure where older adults with a high level of radio and television use tended to not participate in religious activities.

Heintzman and Mannell's (1999) findings concerning the importance of personal development activities, stimulus-avoidance motivations, and leisure in one's own home to spiritual well-being suggest that the role of recreation professionals in enhancing spiritual well-being might be one more of leisure referral and education than of leisure activity provision or facility design and management. Stimulus-avoidance motivations also suggest the importance of providing green spaces, parkland, and quiet urban areas where people can get away from the busyness of everyday life.

If we turn to the few studies on the association between leisure and spiritual well-being in older adults, Tsai and Wu (2005) discovered a significant association between leisure participation and perceived spiritual wellness among older people (aged 55-75) in Taiwan. Similarly, in a study of campers at Ontario Provincial Parks, Heintzman (1998) found that the degree to which introspection and spirituality added to satisfaction with the park experience increased with age, with introspection and spirituality adding the most to satisfaction for those over 70 years (Heintzman, 1998).

For the purposes of this chapter, the data set on leisure and spiritual well-being (Heintzman, 1999) that was used in Heintzman and Mannell's (1999) previously described study was reanalyzed to investigate the associations between leisure and spiritual well-being for older adults in comparison with the general population. The data set was divided into two groups, those under 50 years and those 50 years and over. Those in the older age group had significantly higher scores on two measures of spiritual well-being: a behavioral scale of spiritual well-being that measured spiritual behaviors (e.g., spiritual reading, meditation, prayer) and a subjective scale of spiritual well-being (e.g., relationship with higher power, meaning and purpose in life). These findings are consistent with Canadian studies of spirituality where the importance of spirituality increases with age (Bibby, 2002).

When an analysis was done of the older group on its own, only the personal development category of leisure activities had a significant correlation with both behavioral and subjective spiritual well-being. Thus, leisure activities such as reading, meditation, and tai chi were associated with higher levels of spiritual well-being. There were no significant relationships between spiritual well-being and either time use or leisure motivations, but there were significant positive relationships between behavioral spiritual well-being and frequency of participation in the leisure settings of primitive wilderness areas and one's own home. As with the findings from the general population, the importance of personal development activities and leisure in one's home suggests that the role of the recreation professional in enhancing spiritual well-being among older people may be one more of leisure referral and education than of activity provision.

Leisure-Spiritual Processes

Some studies have gone beyond determining if leisure is associated with spiritual well-being to investigating **leisure-spiritual processes**—that is, leisure processes or strategies that offer spiritual benefits. In a qualitative study of 40 retirement-home residents, Roelofs (1999) discovered that *edifying* was one of six strategies participants used to author or actively create leisure experiences. This strategy involved nourishing one's soul and obtaining inner spiritual satisfaction, which was described as a feeling of peace and comfort. One's soul was nourished through reading religious literature and scriptures and listening to or viewing religious programs on the radio, television, and audiotapes. Participants mentioned that nourishing their souls contributed to them being spiritually strong, being a witness for their God, knowing what God wanted them to be, and affirming their sense of belonging to God. Roelofs suggested that this edifying strategy is consistent with the item that states, "I do leisure activities that restore my spirituality" (Beard & Ragheb, 1980, p. 27) in the Leisure Satisfaction Scale, which is "a measure of the extent to which individuals perceive that certain personal needs are met or satisfied through leisure activities" (Beard & Ragheb, p. 22).

Photo courtesy of Clark Retirement Community, Grand Rapids, MI.

This Christmas celebration at Clark Retirement Community is an example of a social and spiritual event.

Professional Profile

Allison Van Orman

Allison Van Orman is the recreation therapy coordinator at Clark Retirement Community, a Methodist facility in Grand Rapids, Michigan. Her background includes a degree in recreation with an emphasis on recreation therapy, CTRS (certified therapeutic recreation specialist) certification, and 10 years of work experience in therapeutic recreation. Currently Allison works in rehab and long-term care, including a secured dementia unit. Her duties involve assessing new residents and patients. This assessment includes sensitively asking questions on religious preference and background as well as providing information on religious services.

Chapel services with a Methodist orientation are provided twice a week, and Catholic mass is held once a month. If patients are Jewish, Allison offers to contact a rabbi for them. The chapel services are broadcast on the facility's TV channel if a resident does not feel like going to the chapel. A 15-minute service with hymns and a short reflection is held on Wednesday afternoons for residents who cannot sit through the longer chapel service due to attention span or physical reasons. The Bible is available on CD and tape for residents to listen to.

In addition to the traditional activity programming of a garden club, a trivia club, outings, socials, music, entertainment, exercise classes, and arts and crafts, there are also spiritual groups. Spirituality may also be integrated into other programs; for example, at times the questions for the trivia club may focus on spirituality. A computer system called *It's Never Too Late* (www.in2l.com), which can be used individually or in groups, has a spiritual element to it. For example, it has a slide show accompanied by hymns, which often relaxes the residents and gives them a sense of peace.

The goal is to assist the residents in whatever way possible, and if that includes praying with them, taking them to chapel, or reading the Bible to them, the staff will do it. Some residents do not have an interest in pursuing spirituality, and that is fine as well. However, for many residents, faith and involvement in their religious community is a big part of their lives, and thus the staff attempt to create avenues for them to maintain their spiritual health. Allison believes that nourishing the residents' souls brings them a sense of peace. Whether it's hearing an old familiar hymn or reading a familiar passage in the Bible, it brings normalcy to their lives.

Heintzman (2009) has identified and summarized the research that supports eight possible leisure-spiritual processes or factors, and in this section we briefly explain each of these processes. *Leisure as time and space* refers to the fact that leisure provides the time for spiritual development and the space necessary to create an environment for spiritual well-being. *Balance in life*, which may have daily, weekly, monthly, and yearly dimensions and stands in contrast to busyness in life, is conducive to spiritual well-being. Settings that have a sense of *personal history* (places associated with childhood or earlier periods of life) or *human history* (old buildings and ancient cultures) tend to be conducive to spiritual well-being.

Although leisure may provide time and space to cultivate spiritual well-being, time does not necessarily guarantee it. A key factor is an *attitude of openness* that people bring to their leisure

activities; it may be characterized by phrases such as *keeping awareness open, seeing with new eyes, gratitude, gratefulness, focus, a different way of seeing things, intentionality, discernment,* and *being awake to seeing*. Probably the most documented factor that contributes to spiritual well-being is that of *natural leisure settings*. However, *being in a different environment* from the setting of one's everyday life may be as important as the natural environment itself. *Solitude*, characterized by silence, quiet, and time alone, is another factor important to spiritual well-being. *Connections with others*, developed through sharing, teamwork, friendship, and emotional support, is a key dimension of social well-being and an important characteristic of leisure experiences that contribute to spirituality.

Although these eight factors have been identified, spiritual well-being is often produced through a combination of these factors. Several empirical studies support each of these factors (Heintzman, 2009), and studies specifically involving older adults support particular processes, including leisure as time and space (Iwasaki & Butcher, 2004; Son & Hutchison, 2009), nature (Bremborg, 2008; Fredrickson & Anderson, 1999; Infantino, 2004-2005; Milligan, Gatrell, & Bingley, 2004), being away (Fredrickson & Anderson; Ouellette, Heintzman, & Carette, 2005), solitude (Bremborg, 2008), and connections with others (Fredrickson & Anderson; Infantino, 2004-2005). It is important for recreation practitioners to take these processes into consideration when planning and implementing programs that include spiritual objectives. We will examine the findings of these studies in more detail later in the chapter when we discuss the leisure-spiritual coping model.

Building upon a qualitative study (Heintzman, 2000) that examined the relationships between leisure and spiritual well-being, Heintzman and Mannell (2001) developed a scale to examine leisure-spiritual processes. This 36-item Spiritual Processes Scale reflects 12 possible processes or ways in which leisure might influence spiritual well-being. In the reanalysis of Heintzman's (1999) data set for this chapter, people aged 50 and over had significantly higher scores than the younger group on the leisure-spiritual processes scale, which means that the older group was more likely to use leisure to facilitate spiritual well-being. Of the 12 leisure-spiritual processes, there were significant positive relationships between behavioral spiritual well-being for the older group and the following processes: time and space (leisure provides time and space for spiritual development), sacralization (leisure sensitizes one to the spiritual), being away (being in a different setting in one's leisure), and compatibility (engaging in an activity that is congruent with one's personality). Therefore, the older group used these leisure-spiritual processes to enhance their spiritual well-being.

The older group also had significantly higher scores than the younger group on three leisure-spiritual processes: attitude, busyness, and sense of place. This means that for the older group, having an attitude of openness and receptivity in their leisure and also being in a special place during their leisure were more likely to facilitate spiritual well-being, while being busy and frantic in their leisure was more likely to detract from their spiritual well-being. Implications for recreation practitioners include providing activities that facilitate the development and maintenance of an open and receptive attitude, providing opportunities to visit special places, and avoiding rushed or busy leisure activities.

Analysis of the leisure-spiritual processes scale by Heintzman and Mannell (2001) revealed three major factors: the process of **sacralization** (leisure sensitizes one to the spiritual), place processes (e.g., nature, sense of place, being away), and **repression** processes (leisure represses a person's spiritual tendency) (see figure 9.2). This quantitative study as well as a qualitative study (Heintzman, 2000) suggest that leisure can both enhance and detract from spiritual well-being. Thus, recreation practitioners should not assume that leisure activities and programs are always spiritually beneficial for participants.

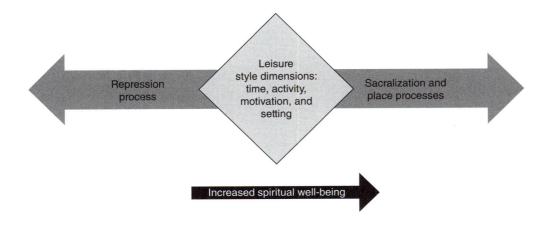

Figure 9.2 Model of leisure and spiritual well-being.

Reprinted by permission from P. Heintzman, 1999, *Leisure and spiritual well-being: A social scientific exploration*. Unpublished PhD thesis. (Ontario, Canada: University of Waterloo), 245.

> ## A Theoretical Model of Leisure and Spiritual Happiness for Older People
>
> Ouellette (2007, 2011) developed a theoretical model of spiritual happiness that applies Benedictine spirituality to the leisure of older people. He suggests that Benedictine spirituality facilitates contemplation that leads to union with God and spiritual happiness. Benedictine spirituality is characterized by community prayer, holy reading of scripture, silence, stability, detachment, moderation, listening, and humility. Ouellette notes that these elements of Benedictine spirituality, also found in other spiritual traditions, facilitate union with God through a contemplative attitude. Older people are predisposed to the practice of contemplation because of their ability to become detached, reminisce, cultivate wisdom, and accept the happy and unhappy events of their lives. The model suggests that in some cases leisure may facilitate contemplation, union with God, and spiritual happiness. If a contemplative attitude permeates leisure, whether as activity, time, or state of mind, then it is more likely that union with God and authentic spiritual happiness will be experienced.

Leisure-Spiritual Coping Model

Heintzman (2008) synthesized theory and research findings on leisure, stress, and spiritual coping into a conceptual model of leisure-spiritual coping (see figure 9.3). **Spiritual coping** refers to the ways that people receive help from spiritual resources (e.g., God or higher power, spiritual practices, faith community) during times of life stress, whereas **leisure-spiritual coping** is spiritual coping that takes place within the context of one's leisure. The model takes into account spiritual appraisals, person factors (e.g., religious orientation), leisure-spiritual coping behaviors (e.g., sacralization, grounding, contemplative leisure, time and space, being away), leisure-spiritual coping resources (e.g., connections with nature, others, and transcendent other), and meaning making (e.g., life purpose, transformation, growth). Since one of the components of this model is the leisure-spiritual coping resource of connections with others, the model is a relevant one to use in synthesizing research related to the interconnection between social and spiritual well-being in the leisure of older adults. Though this model is based on research involving people of all ages, in this section we only include research that involved older adults.

Leisure-Spiritual Coping Behavior

Spiritual coping behavior is a common response to stress and has significant relationships with a great diversity of adjustment factors (Gall et al., 2005). These behaviors may be classified as

- organized religious behaviors,
- private spiritual or religious practices, and
- nontraditional spiritual practices.

All three categories of behaviors may be considered leisure activities or occur during leisure time. Of particular relevance to leisure scholars and practitioners is the third category, nontraditional spiritual coping practices, which may include leisure activities with a spiritual dimension. These leisure-spiritual coping behaviors include sacralization and grounding, contemplative leisure, leisure as space and time, and being away.

- **Sacralization and grounding.** *Sacralization* refers to a process where a person is sensitized to the spiritual. Leisure activities such as meditation and relaxation may assist in sacralization. In stressful situations, leisure activities such as jogging, walking, or gardening may be **grounding** for people, diverting their attention away from the stress.
- **Contemplative leisure.** Historically, leisure has been considered to be not only an activity but also an attitude. Pieper's (1963) well-known conceptualization of leisure as "a mental and spiritual attitude . . . a condition of the soul . . . a receptive attitude of mind, a contemplative attitude" (pp. 40-41) reflects a **contemplative leisure** that can be traced back to Thomas Aquinas (1225-1274 CE) and Augustine (354-440 CE). Contemplative leisure has been viewed as one of the steps of the spiritual journey that empowers an individual

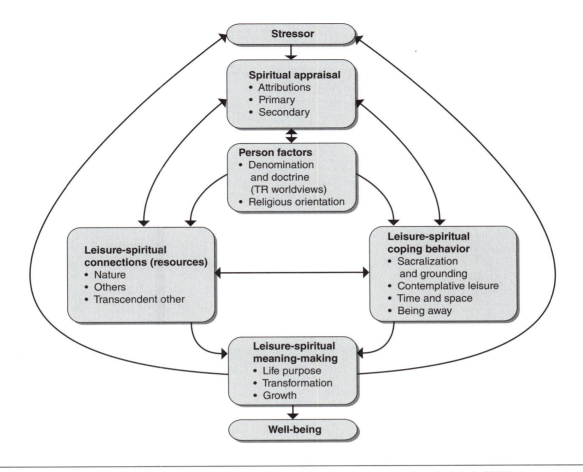

Figure 9.3 Leisure-spiritual coping model. (Adapted from the spiritual framework of coping, Gall et al., 2005).

Reprinted, by permission, from P. Heintzman, 2008, "Leisure-spiritual coping: A model for therapeutic recreation and leisure services," *Therapeutic Recreation Journal* 42(1): 59.

through transcendent life-giving powers to cope with the stresses of the everyday world (Ward, 1999). In support of this view, empirical research has shown that for older women with HIV and AIDS, spiritual transcendence has been facilitated by the quiet of contemplative leisure (Gosselink & Myllykangas, 2007).

▪ **Leisure as time and space.** As mentioned earlier, some people may deliberately use the **time and space of leisure** to spiritually renew themselves. Leisure might be an area of life where a person may develop traditional private and organizational spiritual resources that help cope with stress in life. Some middle-aged and older people suffering from arthritis found that leading an active life spiritually, including spiritual contemplation and prayer, was an effective means to cope with stress (Iwasaki & Butcher, 2004). In a study of 19 American Indian elders aged 56 to 86, which examined the free-time activities

that were mentioned in the context of health beliefs and behaviors, the elders stressed the importance of spirituality for good health (Son & Hutchison, 2009). Free-time activities identified with spirituality included prayer, church attendance, and spiritual activities of a personal nature. Bremborg's (2008) study of mid- and later-life Swedish pilgrims found that a silent walk that provided for individual spiritual experiences was rated the most positive experience of the pilgrimage by almost all participants.

▪ **Being away.** Building on the notion of leisure as time and space, leisure provides the opportunity to get away from the everyday world, consistent with the **being away** feature of restorative environments theory (Kaplan, 1995). This feature of the theory suggests that a different setting from one's everyday environment is conducive to restorative experiences. For example, Ouellette et al. (2005) discovered that monasteries may function as spiritually restorative environments for men over 55 years old who visit them as a leisure activity. Likewise, Fredrickson and Anderson's (1999) study of women's wilderness experiences found that all of the women, most of whom were over the age of 45, had experienced a major life change (deterioration of personal health, major career change, death of a loved one), and therefore the trip provided an opportunity to leave the stresses of everyday life while experiencing spiritual rejuvenation in the wilderness environment.

Leisure-Spiritual Connections

Leisure-spiritual connections are spiritual resources that, along with spiritual appraisals and leisure-spiritual coping behaviors, act as mediating factors in the stress-coping process. These leisure-spiritual connections take the form of connections with nature, others, and the transcendent other.

- **Nature.** Spirituality is frequently associated with a connection to nature (Gall et al., 2005; Heintzman, 2010). Gardening as a leisure activity for older people has been found to sustain spiritual development and renewal as a therapeutic activity that draws upon the healing power of nature (Infantino, 2004-2005; Milligan et al., 2004). For example, in a phenomenological study of five women aged 65 to 75 years who considered themselves lifetime leisure gardeners, Infantino (2004-2005) found that the gardening experience as an evolving lifelong process was a connection to nature that sustained spiritual development. Similarly, Fredrickson and Anderson (1999) discovered that direct contact with the biophysical characteristics of nature in bona fide wilderness played an important role in spiritual inspiration and led to a more contemplative and self-reflective trip experience. A longing for nature was the most common motivation in the study of mid- and later-life Swedish pilgrims (Bremborg, 2008).
- **Others.** Social support and care from others during leisure activities may also contribute to leisure-spiritual coping. Infantino's (2004-2005) study of older female gardeners found that not only was gardening a connection to nature, but it was a connection to friends and family, which helped sustain the women in their spiritual development. Thus, Infantino's

results confirm Adams' (1993) suggestion that leisure activities provide contexts in which older people can develop and maintain friendships.

Beginning with the premise that gardening is a leisure activity that also harnesses the healing power of nature for emotional, physical, and spiritual renewal, Milligan et al. (2003) used ethnographic methods to examine how communal gardening might contribute to the health and well-being of 19 participants between the ages of 65 and 79 over a nine-month period. They observed that older people gained aesthetic pleasure, satisfaction, and a sense of achievement from their gardening. Furthermore, communal gardening "creates inclusionary spaces in which older people benefit from gardening activity in a mutually supportive environment that combats social isolation and contributes to the development of their social networks" (p. 1781). The researchers maintain that communal gardening enhances the emotional well-being and quality of life of older people, and therefore it is a practical way to develop a therapeutic landscape that draws upon the healing power of nature to bring about physical, emotional, and spiritual renewal.

In Fredrickson and Anderson's (1999) study of a wilderness experience where the women had all recently encountered a major life change, a significant theme that contributed to spiritual meaning was group trust and emotional safety. Continual verbal encouragement and ongoing emotional support from other group members, which led to personal bonding and emotional safety, were mentioned as significant contributions to the more meaningful elements and spiritually inspirational aspects of the trip.

- **Transcendent other.** Research suggests that a connection with the transcendent or God has a significant role in coping with stress, particularly if God is viewed as available, protective, comforting, loving, and nurturing (Gall et al., 2005). Gosselink and Myllykangas' (2007) study of older women living with HIV and AIDS found that leisure provided spiritual transcendence that strengthened over time as their disease progressed. Likewise, Fredrickson and Anderson (1999) found that most women were moved to new spiritual heights or transcendence as an outcome of the vastness of the wilderness and their total immersion in it.

Leisure-Spiritual Meaning-Making

Research has documented that spirituality and religion perform a significant role in discovering meaning in a stressful situation (Gall et al., 2005). An illustration of **leisure-spiritual meaning-making** through leisure-spiritual coping is provided by Gosselink and Myllykangas (2007) in their study of the leisure experiences of older American women living with HIV and AIDS. The women in the study were disenfranchised and encountered economic, social, and structural constraints. Following their diagnosis, the meaning of leisure was transformed for all the women in the study. As their disease progressed, the women experienced spiritual transcendence and developed a spiritual view of leisure, which became a metaphor for meaning in life. For some, church took on a new meaning in terms of prayer, connecting with self and a higher power, and acceptance of their disease. For others, spirituality meant a stronger spiritual connection with self, nature, and others. At the same time, leisure advanced the women's well-being through therapeutic benefits, such as resilience in transcending systematic barriers they faced as a result of being female, over 50, and HIV positive. As the disease progressed, the women's transcendence matured and their resolve to overcome obstacles increased. The newfound spirituality of all the women "continued to grow and provide meaning such that they viewed nature, animals, friends, family and advocacy as leisure vehicles through which they could express their spirituality" (Gosselink & Myllykangas, 2007, p. 16).

When applying this model to recreation practice with older adults, recreation professionals are unlikely to be directly involved in the meaning-making of older adults. However, recreation practitioners can facilitate meaning-making by providing opportunities and activities associated with various components of the model: sacralization, grounding, contemplative leisure, leisure as space and time, being away in a different environment, and developing connections with nature, others, and a transcendent other.

Conclusion

In this chapter we reviewed numerous studies that have documented how leisure can assist in the maintenance and strengthening of older people's social well-being, particularly the dimension of social integration. There is also some evidence, although not as much as for social well-being, that leisure can enhance older people's spiritual well-being. Given that some of the characteristics of social well-being overlap with spiritual well-being and that health is integrative or holistic, it is not surprising that social and spiritual well-being are interconnected in the leisure-spiritual coping model. Connections with others—that is, the social integration dimension of social well-being—is a spiritual resource in this model that helps older people cope with the challenges of aging.

The empirical literature reviewed in this chapter suggests a number of implications for recreation practitioners working with older people:

- Take into consideration all dimensions of social well-being (social integration, social acceptance, social contribution, social actualization, and social coherence).
- Recognize that the conceptualization of social well-being may vary across cultures and across the life span.
- In contexts where there are diverse spiritual traditions, focus on spiritual process rather than spiritual content.
- Realize that spiritual wellness is an integrative rather than elementalistic component of wellness.
- Due to its holistic understanding of health, which integrates both social and spiritual health, the therapeutic recreation outcome model is appropriate to use with older people.
- To develop social integration, provide opportunities for older people to meet and develop friendships with others.
- To develop social acceptance, provide opportunities for diverse people to participate in the same recreation activities and programs.
- Recreation activities and programs may be used to resist ageist social stereotypes and to create more positive images of aging.
- To promote social contributions, integrate neighborhood public leisure centers with senior centers and focus on intergenerational programming, including older adults with youth.
- Because personal development activities and leisure in one's own home are important for the spiritual well-being of older adults, offer leisure referral and education services.
- To enhance the spiritual well-being of older adults, facilitate the development of an open and receptive attitude, provide opportunities

to visit special places, and avoid busy and rushed leisure activities.

- Do not assume that leisure always leads to beneficial spiritual outcomes; it may also repress the spiritual tendency.
- Implement the leisure-spiritual coping model and encourage meaning-making by providing opportunities for activities associated with various components of the model: sacralization, grounding, contemplative leisure, leisure as space and time, being away in a different environment, and development of connections with nature, others, and a transcendent other.

KEY TERMS

being away—A different setting from one's everyday environment is conducive to restorative experiences.

contemplative leisure—A mental and spiritual attitude as well as a condition of the soul characterized by receptivity (Pieper, 1963).

content of spirituality—The particular object of spirituality.

elementalistic view—The idea that spiritual wellness interrelates, interacts, and must remain in balance with the other wellness dimensions if optimal wellness is to be maintained.

functional capacities—A person's ability to function socially, spiritually, psychologically or emotionally, physically, and mentally or cognitively.

grounding—The ability of leisure activities to divert a person's attention away from stress.

health status—An integration of the five independent yet interacting health dimensions (physical, mental, spiritual, emotional, and social) that describe a person's level of health and well-being.

integrative wellness—The view that optimal wellness is dependent upon spiritual wellness occurring within the interrelated and interactive dimensions of wellness.

leisure-spiritual connections—Connections with nature, others, and the transcendent other which are spiritual resources that act as mediating factors in the stress-coping process.

leisure-spiritual coping—Spiritual coping that takes place within the context of leisure.

leisure-spiritual meaning-making—The use of spirituality and religion in leisure to discover meaning in a stressful situation.

leisure-spiritual processes—Leisure processes or strategies that offer spiritual benefits.

process of spirituality—The spiritual activities and functions that a person engages in.

quality of life—A subjective measure of spiritual and psychological well-being characterized by feelings of self-determination, joy, contentment, and satisfaction.

repression—Using leisure in a way that represses a person's spiritual tendency.

sacralization—Using leisure to sensitize oneself to the spiritual.

social acceptance—The capacity for trusting others, believing others are capable of kindness and industriousness, holding a favorable view of human nature, and feeling comfortable with others.

social actualization—Understanding that society is continually evolving, being hopeful about its condition and future, and recognizing its potential.

social coherence—Having a concern about the world and a strong desire to make sense of the world.

social contribution—A strong sense of social value; believing that one is a vital member of society and contributes in valuable ways to the world.

social integration—Feeling that one has something in common with others and feeling a sense of belonging to one's community and society.

social well-being—"The appraisal of one's circumstances and functioning in society" (Keyes, 1998, p. 122). It includes five dimensions: social integration, social acceptance, social contribution, social actualization, and social coherence.

spiritual coping—The ways that people receive help from spiritual resources.

spiritual health—A high level of faith, hope, and commitment in relation to a well-defined worldview or belief system that provides a sense of meaning to existence in general and that offers an ethical path to personal fulfillment, which includes connectedness with self, others, and a higher power or larger reality (Hawks, 1994).

time and space of leisure—Leisure provides the time for spiritual development and the space necessary to create an environment for spiritual well-being.

wellness—The "integration of social, mental, emotional, spiritual and physical health at any level of health or illness" (Greenberg, 1985, p. 404).

REVIEW AND DISCUSSION QUESTIONS

1. Review the definitions of *social well-being*, *spiritual well-being*, and *integrative well-being* that you wrote before reading the chapter. Now that you have read the chapter, has your understanding of these concepts changed? If so, how and why?

2. What are the five dimensions of social well-being?

3. What are the eight characteristics of spiritual well-being?

4. What is the difference between the content and process of spirituality?

5. What is the difference between elementalistic and integrative wellness?

6. What are the contributions of leisure to social health?

7. What are the leisure-spiritual processes identified in the chapter?

8. Explain the leisure-spiritual coping model.

LEARNING ACTIVITIES

1. Think of an older person you know, such as a grandparent or an elderly neighbor. Based on what you know of this person, how would you assess her or his social well-being in terms of the five dimensions of social well-being outlined in the chapter?

2. The discussion of spiritual well-being identified six internal and two external characteristics of spiritual well-being. For each characteristic, think of one older person who exemplifies that characteristic. If you cannot think of older people who reflect these characteristics, then choose people of any age. Explain how each person exhibits the specific characteristic.

3. The chapter provides examples of spiritual content (e.g., a belief system, content of a prayer) and spiritual processes (e.g., prayer, meditation). Can you think of other examples of spiritual content and spiritual processes?

4. Draw a diagram of elementalistic wellness and a second diagram of integrative wellness to illustrate the difference between the two. Each of the diagrams should include the social, mental, emotional, spiritual, and physical health dimensions. If wellness is integrative and not elementalistic, how will this affect your work as a recreation practitioner?

5. Maynard and Kleiber (2005) suggested four ways to build social capital through leisure in older adulthood. Can you think of additional ways to build social capital through leisure for older adults?

6. Ouellette's theoretical model of leisure and spiritual happiness suggests that older people are predisposed to the practice of contem-

plation due to a number of factors, and this contemplation can lead to authentic spiritual happiness. Consider the older people you know. Are they predisposed to the practice of contemplation compared with younger people? Explain.

7. Heintzman (2009) identified eight leisure-spiritual processes. How might your knowledge of these eight processes influence the development of a recreation program that has an objective of enhancing spiritual well-being?

8. Make a list of the ways you think leisure may repress spiritual well-being in older adults.

9. Describe a scenario in which you could use the leisure-spiritual coping model as a leisure services practitioner.

CRITICAL-THINKING ACTIVITIES

1. Do you think Hawks' (1994) characteristics and definition of spiritual health are applicable across cultures to people of a variety of religious and spiritual traditions?

2. After providing Hawks' (1994) definition of spiritual health, we discussed how social well-being and spiritual well-being overlap with each other. How are these two dimensions of well-being different? What are the distinctive characteristics of social versus spiritual well-being?

3. Explain how the therapeutic recreation outcome model incorporates both social and spiritual well-being.

4. In the studies cited on the positive relationship between aging and enhanced spiritual well-being, why do you think that (a) the degree to which introspection and spirituality added to satisfaction with park experiences increased with age (Heintzman, 1998), and (b) the older age group (50 and over) had significantly higher spiritual well-being scores than the younger age group (under 50) (Heintzman, 1999)?

5. Explain how the leisure-spiritual coping model integrates both social and spiritual well-being.

6. To what extent should recreation professionals be involved in providing leisure activities and programs with a spiritual dimension? Would it be better for recreation practitioners to refer older people to spiritual and religious organizations?

SUGGESTED READING

Adams, R.G. (1993). Activity as structure and process: Friendships of older adults. In J.R. Kelly (Ed.), *Activity and aging* (pp. 73-85). Newbury Park, CA: Sage.

Heintzman, P. (2009). The spiritual benefits of leisure. *Leisure/Loisir, 33*(1), 419-445.

Heintzman, P., & Coleman, K. (2010). Leisure and spiritual health. In L. Payne, B. Ainsworth, & G. Godbey (Eds.), *Leisure, health and wellness: Making the connections* (pp. 71-82). State College, PA: Venture.

REFERENCES

Adams, R.G. (1993). Activity as structure and process: Friendships of older adults. In J.R. Kelly (Ed.), *Activity and aging* (pp. 73-85). Newbury Park, CA: Sage.

Adams, T., Bezner, J., & Steinhardt, M. (1997). The conceptualization and measurement of perceived wellness: Integrating balance across and within dimensions. *American Journal of Health Promotion, 11*(3), 208-218.

Beard, J.G., & Ragheb, M.G. (1980). Measuring leisure satisfaction. *Journal of Leisure Research, 12*, 20-33.

Beard, J.G., & Ragheb, M.G. (1983). Measuring leisure motivation. *Journal of Leisure Research, 15*, 219-228.

Bertera, E.M. (2003). Physical activity and social network contacts in community dwelling older adults. *Activities, Adaptation and Aging, 27*(3/4), 113-127.

Bibby, R.W. (2002). *Restless gods: The renaissance of religion in Canada.* Toronto, ON: Stoddard Publishing Co.

Bremborg, A.D. (2008). Spirituality in silence and nature: Motivations, experiences and impressions among Swedish pilgrims. *Journal of Empirical Theology, 21*, 149-165.

Carter, M.C., Van Andel, G.E., & Robb, G.M. (2003). *Therapeutic recreation: A practical approach* (3rd ed.). Prospect Heights, IL: Waveland Press.

Dionigi, R.A. (2002). Resistance and empowerment through leisure: The meaning of competitive sport participation to older adults. *Loisir et société/Society and leisure, 25*(2), 303-328.

Duncan, H.H., Travis, S.S., & McAuley, W.J. (1995). An emergent theoretical model of interventions encouraging physical activity (mall walking) among older adults. *Journal of Applied Gerontology, 25*(2), 303-328.

Dupuis, S.L. (2008). Leisure and ageing well. *World Leisure Journal, 50*(2), 91-107.

Fredrickson, L.M., & Anderson, D.H. (1999). A qualitative exploration of the wilderness experience as a source of spiritual inspiration. *Journal of Environmental Psychology, 19*, 21-39.

Gall, T.L., Charbonneau, C., Clarke, N.H., Grant, K., Joseph, A., & Shouldice, L. (2005). Understanding the nature and role of spirituality in relation to coping and health: A conceptual framework. *Canadian Psychology/Psychologie canadienne, 46*(2), 88-104.

Gosselink, C.A., & Myllykangas, S.A. (2007). The leisure experiences of older U.S. women living with HIV/AIDS. *Health Care for Women International, 28*, 3-20.

Greenberg, J.S. (1985). Health and wellness: A conceptual difference. *Journal of School Health, 55*(10), 403-406.

Hawks, S. (1994). Spiritual health: Definition and theory. *Wellness Perspectives, 10*(4), 3-13.

Heintzman, P. (1998). The role of introspection/spiritual in the park experience of campers at Ontario Provincial Parks. In *Culture, environment, and society: Book of abstracts from the Seventh International Symposium on Society and Resource Management* (pp. 169-170). Columbia, MS: University of Missouri-Columbia.

Heintzman, P. (1999). Leisure and spiritual well-being: A social scientific exploration. Unpublished PhD thesis, University of Waterloo, Ontario.

Heintzman, P. (2000). Leisure and spiritual well-being relationships: A qualitative study. *Society and Leisure, 23*(1), 41-69.

Heintzman, P. (2008). Leisure-spiritual coping: A model for therapeutic recreation and leisure services. *Therapeutic Recreation Journal, 42*(1), 56-73.

Heintzman, P. (2009). The spiritual benefits of leisure. *Leisure/Loisir, 33*(1), 419-445.

Heintzman, P. (2010). Nature-based recreation and spirituality: A complex relationship. *Leisure Sciences, 32*(1), 72-89.

Heintzman, P., & Mannell, R. (1999). Leisure style and spiritual well-being. In W. Stewart & D. Samdahl (Eds.), *Abstracts from the 1999 Symposium on Leisure Research* (p. 68). National Congress for Recreation and Parks, Nashville, TN, October 20-24, 1999.

Heintzman, P., & Mannell, R. (2001). Leisure-spiritual health processes: A social scientific study. In M. Havitz & M. Floyd (Eds.), *Abstracts from the 2001 Symposium on Leisure Research* (p. 85). Auburn, VA: National Recreation and Park Association.

Hurd, L.C. (1999). "We're not old!" Older women's negotiation of aging and oldness. *Journal of Aging Studies, 13*(4), 419-439.

Infantino, M. (2004-2005). Gardening: A strategy for health promotion in older women. *Journal of the New York State Nurses Association, 35*(2), 10-17.

Iwasaki, Y., & Butcher, J. (2004). Common stress-coping methods shared by older women and men with arthritis. *International Journal of Psychosocial Rehabilitation, 8*, 179-208.

Kaplan, S. (1995). The restorative benefits of nature: Toward an integrative framework. *Journal of Environmental Psychology, 15*, 169-182.

Keyes, C.L.M. (1998). Social well-being. *Social Psychology Quarterly, 61*(2), 121-140.

Koenig, H.G., Moberg, D.O., & Kvale, J.N. (1988). Religious activities and attitudes of older adults in a geriatric assessment clinic. *Journal of the American Geriatrics Society, 36*, 362-374.

Larson, J.S. (1996). The World Health Organization's definition of health: Social versus spiritual health. *Social Indicators Research, 38*, 181-192.

Leitner, M.J., & Scher, G. (2000). A follow-up study to peacemaking through recreation: The positive effects of intergenerational recreation programs on the attitudes of Israeli Arabs and Jews. *World Leisure and Recreation*, *42*(1), 33-37.

Leitner, M.J., Scher, G., & Shuval, K. (1999). Peace-making through recreation: The positive effects of intergenerational activities on the attitudes of Israeli Arabs and Jews toward each other. *World Leisure and Recreation*, *41*(2), 25-29.

Maynard, S.S., & Kleiber, D.A. (2005). Using leisure services to build social capital in later life: Classical traditions, contemporary realities, and emerging possibilities. *Journal of Leisure Research*, *37*(4), 475-493.

McAuley, E., Blissmer, B., Marquez, D., Jerome, G.J., Kramer, A.F., & Katula, J. (2000). Social relations, physical activity and well-being in older adults. *Preventive Medicine*, *31*, 608-617.

McCormick, B. (1994). "People aren't together too much anymore": Social interaction among rural elderly. *Journal of Park and Recreation Administration*, *12*(4), 47-63.

McDonald, B.L., & R. Schreyer. (1991). Spiritual benefits of leisure participation and leisure settings. In B.L. Driver, P.J. Brown, & G.L. Peterson, *Benefits of leisure* (pp. 179-194). State College, PA: Venture.

Milligan, C., Gatrell, A., & Bingley, A. (2004). Cultivating health: Therapeutic landscapes and older people in northern England. *Social Science & Medicine*, *58*(9), 1781-1793.

Nimrod, G. (2007). Retirees' leisure: Activities, benefits, and their contribution to life satisfaction. *Leisure Studies*, *26*(1), 65-80.

Ouellette, P. (2007). Regards bénédictins sur le bonheur, le vieillissement et le loisir. Unpublished PhD thesis, l'Université de Sherbrooke avec la l'Université Laval, Quebec.

Ouellette, P., Heintzman, P., & Carette, R. (2005). Les motivations et les effets d'une retraite faite par des personnes âgées dans un monastère bénédictin. In T. Delamere, C. Randall, & D. Robinson (Eds.), *The two solitudes: Isolation or impact? Book of abstracts from the Eleventh Canadian Congress on Leisure Research* (pp. 448-452). Nanaimo, BC: Department of Recreation and Tourism Management, Malaspina University-College.

Ouellette, P., Snyder, P., & Carette, R. (2011). L'application de la spiritualité bénédictine au loisir des personnes âgées : un modèle théorique du bonheur spirituel. *Studies in Religion / Sciences Religieuses, 40*(1) 21–44.

Parisi, J.M., Greene, J.C., Morrow, D.G., & Stine-Morrow, E.A.L. (2007). The Senior Odyssey: Participant experiences of a program of social and intellectual engagement. *Activities, Adaptation & Aging*, *31*(3), 31-49.

Pieper, J. (1963). *Leisure: The basis of culture.* New York: New American Library.

Piercy, K.W., & Cheek, C. (2004). Tending and befriending: The intertwined relationships of quilters. *Journal of Women and Aging*, *16*(1/2), 17-33.

Ragheb, M.G. (1993). Leisure and perceived wellness: A field investigation. *Leisure Sciences*, *15*, 13-24.

Roelofs, L.H. (1999). The meaning of leisure. *Journal of Gerontological Nursing*, *25*(10), 32-39.

Silverstein, M., & Parker, M.G. (2002). Leisure activities and quality of life among the oldest old in Sweden. *Research on Aging*, *24*, 528-547.

Son, J.S., & Hutchison, S.L. (2009). Conceptualizing leisure self-care in an exploratory study of American Indian elders' health beliefs and behaviours. *Leisure/Loisir*, *33*(2), 479-509.

Stephens, R.C., Blau, Z.S., Oser, G.T., & Miller, M.D. (1978). Aging, social support systems, and social policy. *Journal of Gerontological Social Work*, *1*(1), 33-45.

Tsai, C-Y., & Wu, M-T. (2005). Relationship between leisure participation and perceived wellness among older persons in Taiwan. *Journal of ICHPER*, *41*(3), 44-50.

Ward, V.E. (1999). Leisure: Spiritual well-being and personal power. *Spiritual life*, *45*, 231-236.

Wearing, B. (1995.) Leisure and resistance in an ageing society. *Leisure Studies*, *14*, 263-279.

Whitaker, E.D. (2005). The bicycle makes the eyes smile: Exercise, aging, and psychophysical well-being in older Italian cyclists. *Medical Anthropology*, *24*, 1-43.

Van Andel, G.E. (1998). TR service delivery and TR outcome models. *Therapeutic Recreation Journal*, *32*(3), 180-193.

Community, Aging, and Leisure

Part IV examines various aspects of community and aging. In particular, this section addresses older people who are still independent and are able to travel the world if they so choose.

In chapter 10, Richard Gitelson and Julie Freelove-Charton describe three types of communities for older adults: active adult communities, continuing-care communities, and naturally occurring communities. The authors examine the leisure services available in these communities, the idea of walkable communities as concerns grow about incorporating sufficient physical activity in the lifestyles of older adults, and the role of senior centers in communities. The authors also discuss the history of active adult communities, or what are commonly called retirement communities, that are pervasive in the warmer U.S. states such as Arizona and Florida. These communities are centered on recreation and leisure and are age restricted. The authors conclude their chapter by discussing the various employment opportunities available for people wishing to work with older adults in various community services.

In chapter 11, Ian Patterson and Shane Pegg continue the focus on independent older adults and examine participation in travel and tourism among older adults. They examine who is likely to travel, their motivations and experiences, and potential constraints. Bus travel and RVing are two popular modalities, and travel lifestyles such as snowbirds and grey nomads are discussed. The authors finish their chapter by looking at two popular types of travel among older adults today—adventure and educational tourism.

CHAPTER 10

The Role of Community in Encouraging Healthy Aging Among Older Adults

Richard Gitelson ■ **Julie Freelove-Charton**

After reading this chapter, you will be able to

- describe the various communities in which older adults live,
- discuss the role that communities can play in encouraging and supporting healthy aging for older adults,
- give examples of how communities are meeting the challenge of providing environments that encourage healthy aging,
- describe a specific type of community for older adults (i.e., active adult communities that are designed specifically for healthy aging),
- describe the crucial role that senior centers play in supporting healthy aging among older adults, and
- identify job opportunities related to the topics discussed in this chapter.

In the previous chapters, you have learned about the importance of healthy aging and the many components that make up a healthy lifestyle; for example, we should exercise, maintain close friendships, eat a nutritionally balanced diet, engage in stimulating activities, and continue to learn throughout our lives. There are three components (Rowe & Kahn, 1997) we must keep in mind if we want to age healthily:

■ We must continue to be engaged with life.

■ We must maintain our physical and cognitive function.

■ We must minimize the risk of disease and disability.

The community in which we live plays a major role in whether we are able to maintain a healthy lifestyle and age successfully. Each community provides a unique environment in which aging occurs. The extent to which a community supports healthy aging depends on many factors, such as population, natural environment, transportation systems, financial conditions, health and exercise facilities, amenities, housing, safety, climate, policies, and attitudes toward older adults and healthy living.

Communities can be social groupings of people who live within a specific locality and share a government structure, such as the city or town you lived in growing up (see chapter 13 for more discussion on communities). The school you are now attending meets the criteria for this definition of community. Communities are also groups of individuals who share common characteristics or interests and who perceive themselves as distinct from the larger community in which they live; for example, sororities and fraternities, religious organizations, and social clubs are types of communities. A community is influenced by the policies of the government, neighborhood, and family.

Based on this definition, each of us will live in and be associated with a variety of communities during our lives. This chapter focuses on how the environment created by these various communities affects the aging process. Consider the community in which you now live (e.g., the school you are attending and the community in which the school is located). Are there gyms, exercise facilities, and recreation centers? Does your community encourage biking, skateboarding, walking, or other transportation alternatives? Are there food co-ops, public gardens, and other entities that encourage healthy eating? Are there libraries, cultural venues, and public parks that provide opportunities for learning, relaxing, enjoying the outdoors, or socializing with others? Are there clubs you can easily join in order to pursue your hobbies and interests? And if these things exist, are they easily accessible, offered at convenient times, and affordable?

If you attend a university or college, you were probably able to answer *yes* to most, if not all, of those questions. Nearly all campuses provide state-of-the-art exercise and gym facilities. If you live on a school campus, you probably have access to tennis, basketball, and racket courts. There are tracks to run on and fields dedicated to playing sports such as softball, rugby, and ultimate Frisbee. There are varsity teams as well as intramurals that offer competitive and fun leagues in a wide variety of sports. There are undoubtedly many kinds of clubs and social organizations to accommodate just about any interest or hobby you might have. When you are hungry, you will probably have the options of vegan, vegetarian, and organic choices. There are certainly plenty of learning opportunities to challenge you intellectually. And, you have a health facility to go to if you are sick and resources if you are struggling emotionally or psychologically.

Unfortunately, after you graduate, you will most likely leave the campus setting that provides all these readily available resources. You will probably find yourself living in a community where resources for engaging in a healthy lifestyle will become less available, or at the very least, less accessible and affordable. Your gym or exercise facility will not be quite as accessible as it was on your campus. You may find it harder to connect with friends because they are no longer living nearby.

The type of community you live in may not be as important in the ability to live a healthy lifestyle when you are younger, but as you age, community resources begin to matter. In this chapter you will discover how communities promote behaviors that lead to healthy aging by providing resources, facilities, and opportunities specifically for older adults. Older adults are defined in this chapter as people who are 55 years of age and older. In 2007, this segment included about 71 million people in the United States, which represented 23% of the U.S. population. About 30% of people aged 55 and older live in some kind of age-restricted community, such as an active adult community, continuing-care retirement community, or naturally occurring retirement community. The other

70% live in communities that are not segregated by age (National Association of Home Builders & MetLife Mature Market Institute, 2009).

The emphasis in this chapter is on **older adult programming** (i.e., programs, activities, and other opportunities that are specifically targeted at people who are 55 and older). This does not mean that these adults cannot and do not take part in opportunities without an age restriction or that people do not leave their community to go elsewhere for opportunities that are not available locally. But research has indicated that the community we live in and the neighborhood where we reside play a crucial role in shaping our behavior and determining the likelihood that we will maintain a healthy lifestyle (Masotti, Fick, Johnson-Massotti, & MacLeod, 2006; Petrossi, 2005).

Impact of Choice and Environment on Health

Ample evidence indicates that our behavior is important in determining how healthily we age. Petrossi (2005) found that a key to healthy aging is person-driven behavior in roles and activities that promote healthy living, and Depp and Jeste (2006) concluded that nearly 70% of physical decline is related to modifiable behaviors. In a review of the existing literature, Handy (2004) concluded that a supportive built environment was not sufficient in itself to influence physical behavior and that one's motivation to be healthy was based on the motivation to engage in healthy behaviors (Bagley & Mokhtarian, 2002; Giles-Corti & Donovan, 2002). Although personal behavior is obviously important, the behaviors we choose do not exist in a vacuum. For instance, it is easier to find ski opportunities in Colorado than it is to find them in Florida. The quality of the air you breathe differs dramatically depending on whether you live next to the oil refineries in New Jersey or on a New Jersey farm. The weather may be more conducive to walking in Phoenix than it is in Boulder, but Boulder is designed to encourage walking while Phoenix is not.

So, although a community cannot change behavior, it can encourage people to pursue healthy behaviors, which will reduce health costs and allow people to live independently

Martin Rickett/Press Association Images

Communities can be designed in ways that encourage healthy behaviors.

longer (Freelove, 2008). Individual behavior is obviously important, but there is evidence that the built environment can also have an impact on healthy behaviors (U.S. Department of Health and Human Services [DHHS], 1996). The payoff for creating an environment that encourages healthy living can be enormous. According to Frank and Schmid (2004), a study in Atlanta found that for each kilometer walked per day, there was a 5% reduction in the likelihood of the person becoming obese. And research has found that environmental factors (e.g., uneven walking surfaces, the absence of sidewalks, having destinations to walk to, safety) are important determinants that make a community or neighborhood walkable (Baranowski, Perry, & Parcel, 2002; Gallagher, 2010; Wang, 2009). In short, what a community does to encourage healthy behaviors, especially in underrepresented populations such as those with lower education and income levels and people with disabilities, does matter (Centers for Disease Control and Prevention [CDC], 2003).

Active Adult Communities

Want to live in a college setting but without the assignments and pressure related to term papers and exams? Where you could join the organizations you wanted, work out at the full-function recreation center, swim at the pool, and even take classes that interested you but without the pressure of tests and grades? Where you would be around people who shared your interests and where there were clubs based on these interests? This section describes such a place—an **active adult community.** What's the catch? You have to meet a certain age requirement, which often is 50 or 55 but can be as low as 45. Although the age requirements vary, most of these communities require at least one person living in the household to be a certain age or older. In 2007, about 3% of people living in households with at least one member aged 55 years or older lived in this type of community (National Association of Home Builders & MetLife Mature Market Institute, 2009).

The development of **age-restricted communities,** the forerunner of active adult communities, can be traced back to the 1950s, when a developer named Del Webb created Youngtown, a new town near Phoenix, Arizona. Very little was specifically active about this first community, which offered low-cost housing and no extra amenities and was restricted to people at least 55 or older. However, by 1960, Webb decided to extend this concept to a more affluent group of older adults who were at least 50 years old (Sun City Visitors Center, 2010).

Del Webb's second planned community, Sun City, was located beside Youngtown. The concept was to offer affordable housing in a community that also provided all the amenities that people could hope for in their retirement years, including golf courses, community centers, cultural events, shopping, multiple sporting venues, swimming pools, walking and biking trails, and clubs aimed at every possible interest. The mild winters of southern Arizona were an important selling point since the initial market for this retirement community was older adults residing in the Midwest and Northeast of the United States. The concept of an active adult community was an immediate hit, with nearly 100,000 people visiting the community on opening day and over 200 homes sold during the opening weekend (Sun City Visitors Center, 2010). Within two months, Sun City became the fastest growing town in Arizona (Rubiano & Chan, 2010).

In Southern California, the planned retirement community of Leisure World, another prototype of the active adult community, was also underway. Although the plan to build the community began in 1960, as did Sun City, the first unit in Leisure World was not sold until 1962. Roy Cortese, the builder of Leisure World, used research data from the gerontology program at the University of Southern California to design the community (Rubiano & Chan, 2010). Although Leisure World was much smaller in concept than Sun City, the formula was the same—the project included affordable housing, recreation, and social activities. One major difference was the inclusion of medical and health facilities in Leisure World, which would come later to Sun City (Baker, 2009). The success of both Leisure World and Sun City confirmed the market for older adults wanting to live in a warm climate in an age-restricted environment that provided for all their possible leisure needs. Active adult communities are found in every state, but they are most popular in Arizona, North Carolina, Florida, Texas, and California.

These types of communities are becoming more common around the world. During the first half of 2010, visitors came to Sun City from Germany, Britain, Italy, Denmark, China, and South Korea to study this type of community. Why the interest? An urban planner from the Netherlands, who has visited Sun City several times, indicated that he liked the recreation activities and hobby clubs. According to the planner, "What we want to do, as in Sun City, is have more vitality, more activity, more than what we are used to in our country. Our country is aging heavily. And seniors want to be respected as persons who can be a part of society, can be worthwhile in society" (Rubiano & Chan, 2010).

Although these early prototypes of planned communities were designed to sell houses, they ultimately encouraged healthy aging as well. Exercise and physical activity have been documented as a key to healthy aging (Patterson, Govindasamy, Vidmar, Cunningham, & Koval, 2004; Petrossi, 2005), and active adult communities have state-of-the-art facilities for activity geared toward their residents. For example, most include special flooring for aerobics and dance, fully outfitted exercise equipment rooms, and classes from aerobics to tai chi and yoga. Before signing up to use

the wellness center in Sun City Grand, people are given a complete physical by Sun Health, Inc., a foundation located in Maricopa County, Arizona, that promotes healthy living, research, and health care. They then work with a trainer to design an exercise program based on their physical condition. Some of the exercise equipment even records the progress of those working out.

We do not exercise in a vacuum, and we are encouraged to exercise when we see others exercising who look like us. Research supports the notion that seeing others similar to ourselves engage in exercise makes it more likely we will engage in similar behavior (King et al., 2000). In an active adult community, instead of 80-year-olds working out at the gym with a group one-fourth their age, they are working out with others similar in age. And what about the 80-year-old who has

Meet Paul Girch, Successful Ager

Paul Girch is an 81-year-old who knows that a key to healthy aging is being active. Paul's message is, "Make exercise a part of your life, at any age." In his youth, Paul was always physically active. He was a distance runner and a varsity football and basketball player. Today, he continues his exercise regime by going to the gym three evenings a week, where for one hour you will find him lifting free weights, using weight machines, and jogging on the treadmill. "Strength training is an important part of my weekly routine," Paul says, who maintains perfect posture and gait. And on any given morning, you'll find Paul on the golf course where he walks 18 holes with his buddies at least three times per week. He shoots an 81 on most days, which is both his goal and his age; for most golfers, shooting 90 makes for a good day.

Paul's environment supports his healthy aging. In 1994, he and his wife Patricia moved to Laguna Woods Village in Orange County, California. Previously known as Leisure World, this 55+ age-restricted community supports their active lifestyle. It is located on 2,100 acres (850 hectares) of rolling hillsides just minutes from the beach. The weather is nearly perfect year-round. As natives of Nebraska, the couple appreciates the mild climate. The community is home to 18,000 older adults with an average age of 67. It offers seven clubhouses, a 27-hole golf course, five swimming pools, a computer center, a performing arts center, and an equestrian center. There are more than 300 clubs and organizations to choose from. According to Paul, "There are so many activities available in the community, it is an incentive to get out and be active."

Paul Girch.

Photo courtesy of Julie Freelove-Charton.

never worked out who moves into an active adult community? Is it too late to begin? As we have seen thus far in this book, the research indicates it is never too late to start reaping the positive health benefits associated with exercise (Gregg et al., 2003).

Walking is the number one exercise for older adults for many reasons; it is easy, inexpensive, and can be done by people with varying levels of fitness (Henderson & Ainsworth, 2000; Lockett, Willis, & Edwards, 2005; Singh, 1996). In general, active adult communities encourage walking and biking. The Villages in Florida (www.thevillages.com) is typical in its efforts to encourage walking and biking by connecting all parts of the community with well-designed trails, sidewalks, and paths that lead to interesting destinations and things to do.

In addition to exercise facilities, exercise classes, and walking and biking trails, these communities provide golf courses, tennis courts, lawn bowling, bocce ball, archery, volleyball, pickleball courts, racquetball courts, and other opportunities to continue to play sports or learn new ones. Pickleball, named after the inventor's dog, is played on a court about a third of the size of a regular tennis court. It is one of the fastest growing sports among older adults, although it is fun for any age, and it provides a great workout.

Nearly all research paints a picture of people disengaging from physical activity as they age (CDC, 2003; DHHS, 1996); however, a study of Sun City residents indicated that this does not have to be the case (Gitelson & Ho, 2008). The study compared **baby boomers** (born between 1946 and 1964) and non boomers (born before 1946) and asked if they currently participated in sport. The findings indicated that nearly half of all boomers and non boomers participated in at least one sport. Nearly 8 out of 10 participated in physical activity each day, and 90% used a recreation center on a regular basis. Nearly a quarter of boomers and one-fifth of non boomers performed strength training each day. Sounds like an active group, especially when you consider that nearly 60% of all older Americans were not meeting the U.S. Surgeon General's minimum recommendations for physical activity in 2005 (DHHS, 2000).

Planned communities also encourage healthy aging by facilitating engagement with others and in various activities. Clubs, which proliferate in active adult communities, provide opportunities to meet this need. Most clubs are organized around special interests, such as arts, card or board games,

or hobbies. In nearly all cases, volunteers are in charge. For example, there are more than 120 clubs in Sun City West. There are 6 dance clubs ranging from country and western to ballroom dancing, 15 sport clubs, and over 30 clubs devoted to various arts, hobbies, and crafts. Interested in woodworking, quilting, lapidary, or pottery? You will find state-of-the-art facilities and willing teachers if you want to learn new skills or engage in a new hobby. There is a club for people with arthritis wishing to exercise, an investment club, a model-railroad club, language clubs, reading clubs, and a theater group. And if you cannot find a club to meet your interests, you can organize it yourself. The nice thing about these clubs is the willingness of members to teach new members how to do the activity. The clubs provide a ready-made network to engage socially with others while having fun. Research has indicated that clubs are a good means of increasing social networking, which is important for health (Waldron, Gitelson, Kelly, & Regalado, 2005).

Finally, active aging communities encourage what has become known as *lifelong learning*. The community of Sun City Grand has even added a building dedicated to learning opportunities. Through a partnership with Arizona State University, a wide variety of classes are offered. Though university faculty teach a few of these courses, community residents teach the majority. Learning new activities and challenging oneself intellectually has been linked to lower risk of developing Alzheimer's disease (Miller, 2009). The success of this learning center has been duplicated in other active adult communities such as The Villages in Florida, where it is featured on the home page of its website.

The concept of relocating to an active adult community in our later years provides an alternative to living in place, the idea that we will remain in our homes long after our children have grown and we have retired. It also provides an alternative to the idea of mixed communities in terms of age. It is not for everyone, however; each year, 5% to 10% of residents living in age-restricted communities move back to their former hometowns to be near friends and family (Gitelson & Ho, 2008).

Resources in Communities Without Age Restrictions

By 2030, the U.S. Census Bureau predicts that people aged 65 years and older will represent

20% of the U.S. population. Presently, approximately 70% live in communities that are not age-restricted (National Association of Home Builders & MetLife Mature Market Institute, 2009). So, how do these communities compare to the active adult communities, and how do they support and promote a healthy lifestyle for older adults? This section deals with this question and discusses community features that are targeted specifically toward older adults. The amount and quality of these targeted resources vary widely among communities based on their resources and attitudes toward aging. Finally, keep in mind that older adults are not limited to what is described here; they can take part in any opportunities available to the general population if they are physically and financially able to do so.

Senior Centers

Most cities offer a counterpart to the recreation centers offered in active adult communities. These centers are usually called **senior centers**, although *adult center*, *multigenerational center*, and other terms are becoming more popular for these facilities. According to the National Council

on Aging (2010b), there are now 11,000 to 15,000 centers specifically targeting older Americans. For consistency, these facilities will be called *senior centers* in the rest of this section.

Although there were senior centers before 1965, the **Older Americans Act** (OAA) of 1965 was the main impetus behind the explosive growth in new centers. The OAA designated these centers as community focal points to serve the needs of older adults (National Council on Aging, 2010b).

Local senior centers play a vital role in supporting the quality of life of older Americans. Once thought of as just a place to receive a free meal, many of today's senior centers offer services and programs that support the health and well-being of the entire community. They also provide career opportunities for professionals in the field of aging, recreation, and leisure.

The origin of today's senior centers can be traced back to 1943 with the opening of the William Hodson Community Center in Bronx, New York. This community center was established by social workers in partnership with city officials who recognized the need for a place to provide services to older community members suffering

John Birdsall/Press Association Images

Senior centers create opportunities for successful aging.

from loneliness, isolation, and limited resources. By 1947, membership at the Hodson center had grown to 350 older adults, with a daily attendance of 150 seniors. The successful establishment of this center is considered a seminal event among gerontologists, and its opening marked the beginning of the senior-center movement. Within a decade, similar senior centers had opened in Philadelphia and San Francisco. By the late 1950s, more than 200 senior centers had been established throughout the United States (Krout, 1989).

During the 1960s, the senior-center movement continued to flourish due to the passage of the OAA in 1965. This act was the first federal initiative aimed at providing financial support for senior centers and other services for older Americans. Later amendments to the act added grants for constructing new senior centers, conducting research on community planning, and expanding services. By the late 1970s, senior centers had evolved to offer recreational opportunities, host health-promotion classes and social clubs, provide basic medical care (e.g., blood pressure clinics, dental care), and a daily meal for older residents (Krout, 1989).

It is estimated that nearly three out of four senior-center users visit one to three times a week and stay for an average of three hours (National Council on Aging, 2010b). According to the National Institute of Senior Centers (National Council on Aging, 2010a), senior centers "create opportunities for successful aging in our communities."

Most senior centers maintain a nonprofit status and receive financial support through a variety of mechanisms. For example, the Encinitas Community and Senior Center in California is owned and operated by the City of Encinitas, and it is largely supported by taxpayer money. The center's employees work for the city. In contrast, the Mid-Columbia Senior Center in Oregon is a private nonprofit corporation and receives no taxpayer support. Private donations, fund-raising events, memorials, room rentals, and memberships fund this center.

In addition to operational and funding differences, there is great diversity among senior centers, including the range of services and programs, available resources and amenities, and staffing and volunteer opportunities. Due to the lack of other service providers specifically aimed at older adults, many senior centers have become a community focal point, and they focus on delivering cost-effective, innovative services

to community members of all ages. Services commonly provided by senior centers include meal and nutrition programs; information and assistance; health, fitness, and wellness programs; recreational opportunities; transportation services; arts programs; volunteer opportunities; educational programs; employment assistance programs; intergenerational programs; social and civic engagement opportunities; public benefits counseling; and other special services (National Council on Aging, 2010b).

Senior centers continue to evolve to support the fitness and recreational needs of today's community members. Newly built centers, such as the Chilson Senior Center in Colorado, include fitness rooms featuring state-of-the-art exercise equipment, indoor swimming pools, steam rooms, and group exercise studios for yoga, tai chi, balance and stability training, and line dancing. Some facilities now staff certified personal trainers to assist older adults with their exercise programs and offer on-site massage therapy to promote continued health. Club activities and community events have also expanded to include walking, kayaking, and surfing groups.

In some cases, the senior center is part of a larger community center serving all age groups and conditions. For example, the Red Mountain Multigenerational Center in Mesa, Arizona, houses a day-care facility, the Red Mountain Active Adult Center, and Sirrine Adult Day Health Services. The adult day care provides respite for caregivers caring for an older adult at home.

In 1978, there were only 300 **adult day-care centers** providing programming, services, and social activities for older adults who needed specialized assistance and continual supervision due to dementia, Alzheimer's disease, or developmental disabilities. Today, there are about 4,000 centers in the United States. The centers have been instrumental in allowing people to stay in their homes longer and not be institutionalized. The centers provide social activities, personal care, therapeutic activities including exercise and mental stimulation, and recreation activities (National Adult Day Services Association, 2010).

A study of older adults attending 17 senior centers in Arizona and South Carolina (Gitelson, Ho, Fitzpatrick, Case, & McCabe, 2008) documented the benefits of senior centers. The study focused on a subset of people attending senior centers—those taking part in the lunch program. This program provides a hot, nutritious meal at a nominal price that can be waived. These partici-

Adult Programming in Europe

In 1972, a successful summer school for retired people was begun in Toulouse, France. The organizers called it the **University of the Third Age (U3A)**, and the idea spread rapidly throughout France and in other countries. One of these countries was Britain, where organizers felt that the original model, built around a partnership with a local university, was too restrictive. The British version of the U3A expanded the concept of learning beyond the walls of universities and into the community. The number of U3As has increased from 8 in 1983 to over 200 in 2009, serving over 200,000 people (Third Age Trust, 2010).

One U3A was formed in West Lancashire, Britain, where the biggest demographic group in the city includes those who are 60 years of age and older. The initiative, created in 1980, was a cooperative venture between government and community leaders based on the recognition that providing opportunities for active aging would have positive outcomes (as discussed throughout this book). The goal was to provide activities that would help older adults age healthily by including at least one of the following elements in each activity: mental stimulation, social engagement, physical activity, and creative expression (McMinn, 2009).

Although there were agencies in West Lancashire that provided opportunities for people with high dependency needs, there was a gap of opportunities for older adults looking for an active lifestyle. The U3A was created to meet this need, and within five years, there were more than 5,000 members in the eight groups that formed in the area. One of these groups, the Augton U3A, offers over 80 programs, including physical, educational, and cultural activities. The group is organized as a voluntary charitable organization run by its members. One example of a program offered by the Augton U3A is MindGym, which is run by retired clinical psychologists and occupational therapists in order to help members understand what they can do to improve their mental well-being. Members can take part in classes (e.g., computer advice, creative writing, film appreciation, Italian, Shakespeare, church history), engage in physical exercise (e.g., walking, Pilates, tenpin bowling, badminton, swimming, line dancing, horseback riding), play games (e.g., Scrabble, bridge, snooker), or pursue a hobby or craft (e.g., needlework, painting, photography, philanthropy, bird watching, mah-jongg). There are also occasional tours and opportunities to take part in plays (McMinn, 2009). These organizations exemplify the ability of community members to create their own opportunities for healthy aging. Members share their expertise and knowledge with others and encourage learning, exercise, and social interaction.

pants are usually less well off than those who do not take part in the lunch program. For example, nearly half of those surveyed reported household incomes of less than $12,000, and 60% were either high school graduates or had not graduated from high school.

According to the study, approximately 6 out of 10 people in the study indicated that the centers were important sources of information on nutrition and health, while 40% to 50% found the centers to be important information providers on social service, legal, transportation, and volunteering opportunities. Nearly 80% indicated that the center was an important source of opportunities to make friends and maintain those friendships, have fun, and get a nutritious meal. About three-fourths of those surveyed reported that the center provided them with a place to go, giving them an opportunity to feel part of a group and improving their quality of life. Nearly 60% felt the centers had improved their physical health or allowed them to learn new ideas. Considering the limited financial resources of the lunch group, it is not likely that these older adults would have been able to find these benefits elsewhere in their communities.

Various social and economic factors influence the operations of today's senior centers. For example, through marketing research, many have found that the name *senior center* is associated with a social stigma as a place where old people go, which is a deterrent for many community residents. To make people feel more welcome and to attract younger baby boomers, many senior centers are searching for a hipper name. Additionally, to improve their public image, many centers have joined Facebook and other social networking sites, enabling them to post photographs of activities and events. Senior centers are also facing changes in demographics and language barriers, which require culturally sensitive programming and bilingual staff. For example, many baby boomers are still working, so to be more accommodating, some centers are altering their traditional hours of operation to include evenings and weekends.

Fitness and Exercise Programs

An excellent example of a community-based program that promotes healthy aging through exercise can be found in Madison, Wisconsin. The Goodman-Rotary 50+ Fitness program, which began in 1994, offers a wide variety of programs, including exercise programs such as walking, yoga, tai chi, dance, strength training, and kayaking. The program began as a partnership between local philanthropists and the Rotary Club. The program currently serves more than 5,000 older adults in 224 classes and has had more than 25,000 participants since its creation.

Healthways, a for-profit organization for disease management, created a program in 1992 called **Silver Sneakers** to encourage healthy aging among older adults. The company contracts with local fitness clubs and health insurers to encourage exercise among older adults. Adults who are in qualifying health programs or Medicare plans are offered low-cost memberships in participating fitness clubs, such as 24-Hour Fitness, Bally Total Fitness, YMCAs, and Curves. The program provides exercise classes and personalized training in how to use equipment and set up an exercise regimen. Classes are designed to increase muscular strength, endurance, range of motion, flexibility, balance, agility, and coordination. A *New York Times* article (Abelson, 2008) reported that Healthways stock took a hit in 2008 when it lost one of its big subscribers, Blue Cross and Blue Shield of Minnesota, who decided to create its own disease management program, and when a Medicare study on the impact of a Healthways program had disappointing results, indicating that the disease management program was not cost effective.

Two final examples illustrate how communities are working to create an environment that is conducive to healthy aging. Hartocollis (2010) describes New York City's effort to encourage more walking among older adults. The city wants to be proactive since it is estimated that it will have 1.3 million adults aged 65 and over by 2030, which will represent the same percentage of the population as children do. The city, which held focus groups, found that older adults wanted safer street crossings, places that provide water to drink and restroom facilities, better street drainage, and more places to go. Based on research that shows it takes longer for older adults to cross the street, the city is changing street lights to provide longer crossing times at 400 intersections. The city is also creating two pilot projects that will create private and public partnerships aimed at encouraging more businesses to become age friendly by offering restrooms and drinking fountains, menus with larger type, and happy hours for seniors. The city also plans to add more benches along sidewalks.

The final example is an effort in Seattle that is aimed at promoting exercise among older adults in multicultural areas (Cheadle, Egger, LoGerfo, Schwartz, & Harris, 2010). The goal is to connect community organizations to create physical activity programs for seniors. The effort involves creating coalitions among these organizations to make the necessary environmental and policy changes to create awareness and support for older adults who want to exercise. The initial efforts have resulted in the creation of 16 ongoing exercise and walking groups involving more than 200 older adults in previously underserved areas of Seattle.

Sport Programs

Participating in sport is a fun way to gain the benefits of exercise. (Chapter 8 provides an excellent review of benefits of sport for people who are older.) In addition, sport provides an opportunity to be competitive, to test abilities, to learn new skills, to socialize with others in both team and individual sports, and to maintain a healthy lifestyle. As you learned in chapter 2 in the discussion about the myths related to aging, there is a false assumption that we either do not want to play sports as we get older or we cannot play the sports we played when we were younger. This may be true for tackle football or rugby, but it is not true for most sports. Without access to facilities, however, it is hard to continue to play the sports you played when you were younger. The excuse has always been that there is no demand for this kind of programming, but baby boomers are proving this to be wrong.

Based on this myth that older adults do not play sports, promoting and encouraging physical activity for seniors through sport has not been a high priority for most cities. Most communities, such as Austin, Texas, and Huntsville, Alabama, have only offered adult softball programs aimed at men. One exception is a program in Albuquerque, New

Communities can encourage health by providing opportunities to participate in fitness activities.

Mexico, called the Silver Gloves. Their mission is to have fun and offer softball opportunities for women who are at least 50 years old. The program encourages women who have never played to come out and learn the game (www.senior-sports.org/Silver_Gloves_-_Home.html).

An example of using sport for promoting healthy behaviors can be found in Phoenix. The goal of the Arizona Senior Olympics, a program begun in 1981, is to encourage physical activity among older adults in the community. Participants are encouraged to train year-round and learn new sports through workshops provided by the city, but the program has always been more about encouraging healthy lifestyles through its year-round series of workshops.

Sport is an area where there is a huge difference in the level of opportunities provided in active adult communities and non-age-restricted communities. For example, there are three softball leagues for various skill levels and 30 softball teams in Sun City Grand, an age-restricted community with a population of approximately 14,000 people who are aged 50 and older. There are also women's travel teams in each of the Sun City communities in Arizona. In Sun City West, a

city with a total population of 50,000 older adults, there are tennis leagues, golf leagues, bocce ball leagues, bowling leagues, lawn-bowling leagues, and other sport leagues for its residents. In nearby Glendale, a city with a population of 250,000 and approximately 50,000 adults over 50, there is one spring softball league for men and no other sport opportunities for either men or women.

Community Engagement

Many opportunities for civic and social engagement are provided by nonprofits or privately organized groups that supplement what is offered by local government. For example, in Charlotte, North Carolina, there are a number of clubs that people have created on their own. One is called the *Senior Scholars*, and its mission is to promote intellectual, cultural, and spiritual growth, all important components of healthy aging. The group, which was formed in 1973, holds its meetings in a Baptist church. Meetings are free and held weekly except in July, August, and the last three weeks in December. The aim of the organization is to provide opportunities for fellowship and to broaden members' understanding of subjects of interest to

Employment Opportunities

As the sheer number of older adults increases, directors and managers of senior centers will need a larger number of highly trained staff to assist their patrons. Although the number of professionals required and the type of job varies, the CPRS identified nine positions considered ideal for operating senior centers (see table 10.1). The reported salaries for these positions range from US$25,000 to US$85,000. Many of these positions require a bachelor degree in recreation and leisure, exercise science, gerontology, nutrition, or a related field. Knowledge of community services and evidence-based health programming with an emphasis on health and well-being is often preferred.

■ TABLE 10.1

Employment Opportunities at Senior Centers by Position Title and Primary Function

Title	Function
Senior-center director or manager	Manages all operations of the facility.
Program and recreation coordinator	Responsible for supervising support staff.
Social services coordinator	Supervises additional support staff.
Nutrition coordinator	Supervises volunteers and congregate meals and delivery.
Office manager or administrator	Supervises all staff working for the center.
Volunteer coordinator	Coordinates volunteers who are in charge of various programs, classes, activities, and clubs.
Facility maintenance supervisor	In charge of facility maintenance ranging from classrooms to swimming pools.
Transportation coordinator	In charge of providing transportation to activities, programs, medical appointments, shopping, cultural activities, and so on.
Facility rental coordinator	In charge of rental facilities ranging from meeting rooms to theaters to large attraction venues.

Data from California Parks and Recreation Society http://aging.cprs.org/StrategicPlanningForSeniorServices2001.pdf.

the group. As mentioned in previous chapters, challenging oneself intellectually and learning new things is a key component of healthy aging.

Another aspect of healthy aging is the continued sense of being a valued member of the community. Many cities offer programs that provide opportunities for volunteering, which has several benefits for those who participate, including a feeling of self-worth and meaning (Van Willigen, 2000). This is certainly the case in active adult communities, such as Sun City, which calls itself the *City of Volunteers*, but there are also many programs that specifically provide volunteer opportunities for older adults in non-

age-segregated communities. An example is the Retired and Senior Volunteer Program (RSVP), a program created in 1986 by The Senior Hub, a nonprofit located in Denver. The program matches volunteers with organizations such as food banks, hospitals, schools, assisted-living facilities, religious organizations, senior centers, and other nonprofit organizations.

Senior centers have clearly evolved since their inception in 1943. They are focal points in their communities, employing highly trained professionals, delivering evidence-based programs and services, and maintaining an essential role in supporting the health of older Americans.

Conclusion

Active adult communities and other age-restricted communities provide a wide array of opportunities that encourage healthy aging among older adults; these communities assume that we will remain active in the later stages of our lives. However, the vast majority of older adults, who live in non-age-restricted communities, must rely on a smaller number of opportunities that are aimed specifically at them. Fortunately, these opportunities, such as senior centers, have increased rapidly in the United States since the 1960s, when federal legislation began to recognize and promote the need to provide more resources for an aging population. The key is to recognize that it is in our best interests to build environments and communities that promote healthy lifestyles for older adults.

KEY TERMS

active adult communities—Communities that require at least one person in the household to be a certain age or older, such as 55. Marketing campaigns for these communities emphasize their amenities that encourage healthy aging.

adult day-care centers—Centers that provide programming, services, and social activities for older adults who need specialized assistance and continual supervision due to dementia, Alzheimer's disease, or developmental disabilities.

age-restricted communities—Any community that requires at least one person in the household to be a certain age or older, such as 55.

baby boomers—Adults born in the United States between 1946 and 1964.

communities—Social groupings of people who live within a specific locality and share a government structure, such as the city or town where you grew up.

older adult programming—Programming aimed specifically at people who are 55 years old or older.

Older Americans Act of 1965—The first U.S. federal initiative aimed at providing financial support for senior centers and other services provided to older Americans.

senior center—A community focal point where older adults come together for services and activities that reflect their experience and skills, respond to their diverse needs and interests, enhance their dignity, support their independence, and increase their involvement in the center and the community.

Silver Sneakers—A program developed by a for-profit company to provide programs at health clubs to promote healthy aging behavior among older adults.

University of the Third Age (U3A)—Program begun in France in 1972 to open up learning opportunities within universities for older adults. Later, the program was expanded to include community-based learning opportunities for older adults.

REVIEW AND DISCUSSION QUESTIONS

1. What are the various types of communities in which older adults live?
2. What are some examples of how a community can encourage healthy aging among older adults?
3. How are communities changing their environments to encourage healthy aging?
4. What are active adult communities, and how do they encourage healthy aging?
5. What role do senior centers play in supporting healthy aging among older adults?
6. Given the controversy about the name *senior centers*, what would you call these centers? Explain why you think your name would be more attractive to baby boomers.
7. What are the job opportunities in this field?

LEARNING ACTIVITIES

1. Volunteer at a senior center. Interview participants about the role the center plays in their lives. Describe the various programs, resources, and opportunities that are provided and how they relate to what you have learned about healthy aging. Indicate why you do or do not see yourself going to a senior center when you are older.
2. Using the following questions, critique the community in which you live in terms of its contributions to healthy aging among older adults. What grade would you give your community based on your answers? Defend your assessment and make recommendations that would improve this grade.
   - How are various parts of the community connected? How extensive are the bike paths and walking trails that encourage physical activity? Check out Boulder, Colorado; Davis, California; and Portland, Oregon for three of the best connected cities in the United States.

– Are there modes of public transportation (e.g., buses, subways) that are safe, convenient, and affordable alternatives for those who have physical or financial constraints that keep them from operating private vehicles? Are there alternative transportation means for those who have mobility restrictions and cannot use the biking or hiking trails or public transportation? In larger communities, this may be represented by a service such as Dial-A-Ride. Some cities offer free bus service for older adults, including Eugene, Oregon, and Ann Arbor, Michigan.

– Are there neighborhood, city, and regional parks, lakes, trails, and other outdoor opportunities within the community? Many cities are known for their parks, such as Golden Gate Park in San Francisco or Central Park in New York City. However, even a smaller town like Chico, California, has a park with over 6 miles (9.6 km) of walking and bike paths.

– Does the community sponsor safe-driving programs for older adults? For example, AARP offers these programs in many American cities.

– Are there centers in the community that focus on older adults? Do they provide the types of services and programming discussed earlier in this chapter that aim to meet the physical, psychological, social, emotional, nutritional, and spiritual needs of older adults? Are they accessible (i.e., within 3-5 mi [5-8 km] of everyone in the community)? Are there alternative ways for people to get to the centers without driving their own vehicle? What are the facilities like? What are their operating hours?

– Are there resources that encourage lifelong learning in the community? Many universities offer educational opportunities for older adults who are not seeking a degree. Duke University has an extensive program that offers classes in the community as well as opening up classes on campus to older adults who are not interested in pursuing a degree. The University of North Carolina at Asheville has a multimillion-dollar facility dedicated to providing learning opportunities for older adults.

– Does the community provide safe, affordable housing specifically for older adults?

– What are the medical facilities like? Are there doctors trained in geriatrics?

– What leisure activities are specifically designed for older adults by community entities, including the commercial sector and religious organizations? Are businesses in the community age friendly?

– Is there a local agency on aging (e.g., Area Agency on Aging in the United States), and if so, what does it provide? Are other social services offered for older adults that provide information on nutrition, exercise, legal matters, employment opportunities, alternative living arrangements, help with paying bills, and medical issues?

3. Look up a facility on the Internet that provides an alternative continuum of care for older adults. Would you consider living in this type of community when you are older? Why or why not?

4. To what extent do finances, gender, age, and ethnicity influence the availability of opportunities and resources for healthy aging?

5. If possible, visit an active adult community or retirement community. If you can't visit an active adult community, find one on the Internet (for example, The Villages in Florida or one of the Sun City communities). Using the questions listed in question 2, critique how well the community supports healthy aging. Based on what you find, discuss why or why you would not want to live in this community if you qualified.

CRITICAL-THINKING ACTIVITIES

1. Is healthy living confined to certain hours of the day? For those who rely on senior centers for congregate meals, exercise programs, social interaction, information on needed services, and learning opportunities, what are the implications of limiting access to certain hours (e.g., 8:30 a.m. to 4:30 p.m. on weekdays with no access on weekends, at night, and on holidays)?

2. What should the role of the community be in providing opportunities for healthy aging among older adults? Should the community concentrate on certain segments of the older adult population, such as those with limited resources? How can the community promote healthy aging for all age populations?

3. Justify the spending of tax dollars on community resources aimed at healthy aging among older adults.

4. Why should a society promote healthy aging among older adults?

5. What can we do during the education process to lay the foundation for people to maintain healthy lifestyles throughout their lives?

6. Physical education programs in schools have introduced kids to activities that should be pursued to maintain a healthy lifestyle. Should a community allocate specific times for older adults to use existing sport fields even if it means less programming for school-aged children? Why or why not? What are the implications if communities do not provide these types of activities?

SUGGESTED READING

Butler, R.N. (2010). *Longevity prescription: The 8 keys to a long, healthy life*. New York: Avery.

Committee on Physical Activity Health Transportation and Land Use. (2005). *Does the built environment influence physical activity? Examining the evidence*. Washington, DC: Transportation Research Board and the Institute of Medicine of the National Academes. www.trb.org.

Enguidanos, S.M. (Ed.). (2005.) *Evidence-based interventions for community-dwelling older adults*. New York: Haworth Press.

Gitelson, R., Ho, C.-H., Fitzpatrick, T., Case, A., & McCabe, J. (2008). The impact of senior centers on participants in congregate meal programs. *Journal of Park and Recreation Administration, 26*(3), 136-151.

REFERENCES

Abelson, R. (2008, April 7). For one company, role in Medicare experiment has hurt stock. *New York Times*. Retrieved from www.nytimes.com/2008/04/07/business/07medside.html.

Bagley, M.N., & Mokhtarian, P.L. (2002). The impact of residential neighborhood type on travel behavior: A structural equations modeling approach. *Annals of Regional Science, 36*(2), 279-297.

Baker, T. (2009). The history of Leisure World, 1963-1975. *Historian, 3*(4).

Baranowski, T., Perry, C.L., & Parcel, G.S. (2002). How individuals, environments, and health behavior interact: Social cognitive theory. In K. Glanz, B.K. Rimer, & F.M. Lewis (Eds.), *Health behavior and health education: Theory, research and practice* (3rd ed.). San Francisco: Jossey-Bass.

Centers for Disease Control and Prevention (CDC). (2003). Prevalence of physical activity, including lifestyle activities among adults—United States, 2000-2001. *Morbidity and Mortality Weekly Report, 52*(32), 764-769.

Cheadle, A., Egger, R., LoGerfo, J., Schwartz, S., & Harris, J. (2010). Promoting sustainable community change in support of older adult physical activity: Evaluation findings from the Southeast Seattle Senior Physical Activity Network (SESPAN). *Journal of Urban Health, 87*(1), 67-75.

Depp, C.A., & Jeste, D.V. (2006). Definitions and predictors of successful aging: A comprehensive review of larger quantitative studies. *American Journal of Geriatric Pyschiatry, 14*(1), 6-20.

Frank, L.D., & Schmid, T.L. (2004). Obesity relationships with community design, physical activity and time spent in cars. *American Journal of Preventive Medicine, 27*, 87-96.

Freelove, J. (2008). *The influence of aging-expectations and neighborhood environment on healthy aging behaviors in older adults*. Unpublished PhD dissertation, University of South Carolina, Columbia, SC.

Gallagher, N.A. (2010). *The influence of neighborhood environment, mobility limitations, and pyschosocial factors on neighborhood walking in older adults*. Unpublished PhD dissertation, University of Michigan, Ann Arbor, MI.

Giles-Corti, B., & Donovan, R.J. (2002). Socioeconomic status differences in recreational physical activity levels and real and perceived access to a supportive physical environment. *Preventive Medicine, 35*, 601-611.

Gitelson, R., & Ho, C.-H. (2008). *A comparison of boomers and nonboomers living in Sun City West*. Sun City, AZ: Arizona State University.

Gitelson, R., Ho, C.-H., Fitzpatrick, T., Case, A., & McCabe, J. (2008). The impact of senior centers on participants in congregate meal programs. *Journal of Park and Recreation Administration, 26*(3), 136-151.

Gregg, E.W., Cauley, J.A., Stone, K., Thompson, T.J., Bauer, D.C., & Cummings, S.R. (2003). Relationship of changes in physical activity and mortality among older women. *Journal of the American Medical Association, 289*, 2379-2386.

Handy, S. (2004). *Critical assessment of the literature on the relationships among transportation, land use, and physical activity* (E. Science, Trans.). Department of Environmental Science and Policy, University of California, Davis. Prepared for the Committee on Physical Activity, Health, Transportation, and Land Use.

Hartocollis, A. (2010). Fast-paced New York, promising safety and comfort to elderly. *New York Times*. Retrieved from www.nytimes.com/2010/07/19/nyregion/19aging.html?_r=1&ref=anemona_hartocollis.

Henderson, K.A., & Ainsworth, B.E. (2000). Enablers and constraints to walking for older African and American Indian women: The cultural activity participation study. *Research Quarterly for Exercise and Sport, 71*(4), 313-321.

Krout, J. (1989). *Senior centers in America*. New York: Greenman Press.

Lockett, D., Willis, A., & Edwards, N. (2005). Through seniors' eyes: An exploratory qualitative study to identify environmental barriers to and facilitators of walking. *Canadian Journal of Nursing Research, 37*(3), 48-65.

Masotti, P., Fick, R., Johnson-Massotti, A., & MacLeod, S. (2006). Healthy naturally occurring retirement communities: A low-cost approach to facilitating healthy aging. *Community Matters in Healthy Aging, 96*(7), 1164-1170.

McMinn, A. (2009). Active retirement for healthier ageing. *Perspectives in Public Health, 129*, 158-159.

Miller, C.M. (2009). *The role of adult education participation in successful aging*. Unpublished PhD dissertation, University of Idaho, Moscow, ID.

National Adult Day Services Association. (2010). About Adult Day Services. Retrieved from www.nadsa.org.

National Association of Home Builders & MetLife Mature Market Institute. (2009). *Housing for the 55+ market: Trends and insights on boomers and beyond*. Retrieved from www.metlife.com/assets/cao/mmi/publications/studies/mmi-report-housing-55+-market.pdf.

National Council on Aging. (2010a). National Institute of Senior Centers. from www.ncoa.org/strengthening-community-organizations/senior-centers/nisc/.

National Council on Aging. (2010b). Senior centers fact sheet. Retrieved from www.ncoa.org/press-room/fact-sheets/.

Patterson, D.H., Govindasamy, D., Vidmar, M., Cunningham, D.A., & Koval, J.J. (2004). Longitudinal study of determinants of dependence in an elderly population. *Journal of the American Geriatrics Society, 52*, 1632-1638.

Petrossi, K.H. (2005). *Expanding the science of successful aging: Older adults living in continuing care retirement communities (CCRCs)*. Unpublished PhD dissertation, University of South Florida, Tampa, FL.

Rubiano, S.A., & Chan, C. (2010). Sun City model imitated all over U.S., world. *Arizona Republic*. Retrieved from www.azcentral.com/community/surprise/articles/2010/07/03/20100703sun-city-arizona-model-for-world.html.

Singh, M.A.F. (1996). Physical activity and functional independence in aging. *Research Quarterly for Exercise and Sport, 67*(3), S70.

Sun City Visitors Center. (2010). Sun City: 40 years of success. Retrieved from www.suncityaz.org/History/SC40years.htm.

Third Age Trust. (2010). The U3A story. Retrieved from www.u3a.org.uk/about-u3a/history-of-u3a.html.

U.S. Department of Health and Human Services (DHHS). (1996). *Physical activity and health: A report of the Surgeon General*. Atlanta: DHHS, CDC.

U.S. Department of Health and Human Services (DHHS). (2000). *Healthy People 2010: Understanding and improving health*. Washington, DC: Author.

Van Willigen, M. (2000). Differential benefits of volunteering across the life course. *Journals of Gerontology: Social Sciences, 55B*, S308-S318.

Waldron, V., Gitelson, R., Kelly, D., & Regalado, J. (2005). Losing and building supportive relationships in later life: A four-year study of migrants to a planned retirement community. *Journal of Housing for the Elderly, 19*(2), 5-25.

Wang, Z. (2009). *Nearby outdoor environmental support of older adults' yard activities, neighborhood walking and independent living in the community*. Unpublished PhD dissertation, Texas A&M University, State College, TX.

CHAPTER 11

Tourism and Aging

Ian Patterson ■ **Shane Pegg**

After reading this chapter, you will be able to

- describe the importance of travel and tourism to an emerging market of older adults,
- understand how sociodemographic variables (i.e., gender, income, and education) influence the travel behavior of older adults,
- discuss the main motives that encourage or discourage older adults from traveling and whether they differ from those of other cohorts,
- discuss the most popular modes of transport used by older adults for leisure travel,
- understand the emerging interest of baby boomers in adventure tourism with a focus on their participation in physically challenging soft adventure activities, and
- explore the growing trend of combining travel and learning for older adults.

On a global scale, business operators are becoming increasingly aware of the significant impact that older adults are having on the tourism industry (Paxson, 2009). This growing segment of the population is already starting to exert its significant economic clout by demanding a diverse range of services not previously considered to be mainstream offerings for older adults (Dennis, 2005; Reece, 2004). For example, Walker (2009) noted that 74% of the 50-year-old-plus travel market in Australia reported that they had been on a holiday in the previous year, compared with only 68% of those in generation Y (aged 18-29 years), the cohort that is most often associated with travel and vacation spending.

Tourism researchers and practitioners alike readily appreciate that as a direct consequence of global aging patterns, senior travelers will increasingly account for a larger share of vacation spending globally (Littrell, Paige, & Song, 2004; Sangpikul, 2008; Wang, Chen, & Chou, 2007). For example, in 1999, over 593 million international travelers were aged 60 years and over, accounting for approximately a third of the total amount spent on holidays in that year. By 2050, this figure is projected to exceed 2 billion trips per annum (World Tourism Organization [WTO], 2001). For these reasons, the senior market is becoming more attractive to travel businesses and is often promoted in Europe, especially in response to the fluctuations in seasonal demand of tourists (Fernandez-Morales & Mayorga-Toledano, 2008). That is, older travelers are likely to be less constrained by work and family responsibilities and are able to take vacations outside of the peak travel seasons usually associated with school vacations.

This significant shift will also have a notable impact on the types of vacations and destinations chosen (Patterson & Pegg, 2009). For example, it is likely that the volume of beach trips will fall markedly in the future and educational or cultural tourism will increase since older people generally prefer to take holidays where they learn something new and embark on various historical and cultural experiences (WTO, 2001). This notion is supported by Yarnal (2004), who studied group cruise experiences and found that although familiarity was an important facet of the travel experience for many people over 50 years of age, comfort and security were also provided as a platform for exploration and novelty.

These projections imply that becoming older does not necessarily restrict the desire to travel, and older travelers as a growing but somewhat discrete market segment are increasingly attracting the attention of tourism researchers and marketers. Robertson (2001), for example, felt that tourism researchers needed to more clearly differentiate the impact that the travel experience has on older people in comparison to younger tourists. Robertson posed the following question: "Is travel [for older people] more than materialistic shopping trips, mass tour buses that isolate travelers from locations they desire to see, or self-indulgent trips that take advantage of Third World Countries?" (p. 100).

Despite this somewhat cynical viewpoint, there is little doubt that older people are increasingly placing travel as a higher priority in their retirement years in comparison to previous generations. Part of the reasoning for this shift relates to the fact that today's older travelers are healthier, wealthier, better educated, and more independent than younger people, and they also have an abundance of leisure time and a lessening of social and family obligations (Higgs & Quirk, 2007; Tate, Mein, Freeman, & Maguire, 2006). In Australia, the great majority of people aged 65 years and over regard themselves as fit, well, and independent (Australian Institute of Health & Welfare, 2008). In the United States, the AARP (Davies, 2005) commissioned a study that focused on the older adult travel market. They concluded that over 20 years ago, less than 5% of baby boomers traveled to Europe (4%); Mexico, Central America, or South America (4%); or the Caribbean (4%). Today, nearly double the percentage of boomers are traveling to these international destinations, with 14% traveling to Mexico, Central America, or South America; 10% to the Caribbean; and 7% to Europe. A majority of boomers considered themselves to be adventurous (55%), and nearly 8 out of 10 (77%) considered their travel experiences to be more adventurous than those of their parents.

According to Huang and Tsai (2003, p. 561), "seniors will soon be one of the largest prospective market segments for the hospitality and travel industries," and they will significantly contribute to the leisure sector. This is attributed to the fact that they possess a relatively large share of discretionary money that they want to spend on travel; people over the age of 55 years account for 80% of all vacation dollars spent in the United States (Javalgi, Thomas, & Rao, 1992). This trend was supported more recently by Fortosis (2009), who noted that older North Americans control more than US$7 trillion of wealth, own approximately 77% of the financial assets in the United States, and have no intention of staying home but rather prefer to travel the globe, seeking adventure and experiencing the world. Boomers spend a significant amount of money on leisure travel. Although approximately one-quarter (26%) spent less than $500 on leisure trips, 47% spent between $500 and $3,000. Another 26% spent between $3,000 and $10,000, and 3% spent $10,000 or more (Davies, 2005). Furthermore, there is every indication that seniors prefer to take longer trips and stay away from home for a longer time (Eby & Molnar, 1999; Shoemaker, 2000), and they have a greater concern for personal safety and security while traveling (Jang & Wu, 2006) in comparison to other age segments of the population.

Sociodemographics of Travel

Previous research has concluded that aging is a multidimensional phenomenon and that people age biologically, psychologically, socially, and spiritually at different rates (Keller, Leventhal,

& Larson 1989; Moschis, 1996). Therefore, we need to be careful that we do not lump all people together as *older* or *mature* simply because they are over an arbitrary age such as 55, 60, or 65 years. To do otherwise shows a lack of understanding about what each age cohort is really like, especially in regard to older people's individual needs, interests, and lifestyles (Patterson, 2006). Each cohort group of older adults has lived through a specific time in history that adds to their distinct characteristics, needs, and interests. At the same time, there is individual variability in a person's physiological changes, health status, psychological well-being, socioeconomic circumstances, social and family situation, and ethnic or minority status.

Despite this, some research has indicated that travelers over 50 years old generally spend more time planning their trips and outlay significantly more money than those who are under 50 years old (Penalta & Uysal, 1992). Furthermore, those over 50 years old are more likely to respond to

Red Hat Society and Group Travel

The **Red Hat Society (RHS)** is a leisure- and travel-related social organization that was founded in 1998 by Sue Ellen Cooper for women aged 50 years and older. As of July 2009, there were over 70,000 registered members and almost 24,000 chapters in the United States and 25 other countries. The Red Hat Society is the largest women's social group in the world, and its primary purpose is to encourage social interaction among women that results in fun, friendship, freedom, and fulfillment. The goal is for members to bond as they travel through life together. The society is not a sorority or a voluntary service club, and it does not conduct initiations or fund-raising projects. Red Hatters tend to accessorize by, "wearing full regalia which includes, at a minimum, gaudy red hats and garish blue outfits. It more generally involves frilly bathrobes, fuzzy slippers, 'diamond'encrusted tiaras, elaborate creations with glitzy jewellery, garish hat pins, elaborate feather boas, vivid mesh stockings, and bright red and purple handbags" (Hutchinson, Yarnel, et al. 2008, p. 984). When justifying the formation of this group, Cooper (2004) stated that it provides an antidote to the serious loss of self-esteem that many aging women face as they deal with children leaving home, caring for elderly parents, widowhood, health crises, and altered body image.

The benefits of a group travel experience for older women who are members of the Red Hat Society were explored by Liechy, Ribeiro, and Yarnal (2009). Using self-directed photography, 30 members of the Red Hat Society volunteered to take photographs during one day of their vacation. Later, they expanded on their photographic selections through personal narratives to "show what was 'Red Hattish' about the day" (p. 20). The findings suggested that the group tour provided a multidimensional context for the women to have fun, be self-expressive, and develop social relationships. Participants articulated that Red Hattishness fostered positive emotions that in turn led to expressions of well-being, clearly demonstrating that traveling with other women in a supportive, playful context played a vital role in the enjoyment and benefits derived from the tour. The overall sentiment of the women was that the group tour provided feelings of belonging, freedom, playfulness, and lighthearted fun.

promotions, advertisements, and travel packages that are largely ignored by those younger than 50 years old. As a result, travel businesses have become more aware that the senior market is an important segment and have started to shift their advertising dollars to target the 50-years-and-over segment.

Older women in particular are regular travelers. In 1988, Hawes found that as women grow older, they increasingly preferred to travel overseas, especially those in the 55- to 59-year-old age group, who were more likely to be highly educated and earning higher incomes than younger women. In many cases, older women saw travel as a transitory activity between paid work and retirement; it provided a psychological barrier from work and home life. When traveling, older women preferred shorter trips, were generally more aware of safety issues, and required more opportunities to socialize and interact with other people. Shorter rather than longer trips were seen to be cohort related because of the greater availability of cheaper air travel compared to previous decades (Statts & Pierfelice, 2003). Older women also displayed stronger preferences for local, cultural, and heritage activities and festivals than men. However, in many cases, women were not as confident about traveling alone as men were. They also were more likely to be widowed or divorced and as a result did not have a partner to travel with (Lehto, O'Leary, & Lee, 2001).

Amount of discretionary income has also been found to be an important factor in permitting greater numbers of older people to travel. For example, in the United States in 1995, economic data indicated that the buying power of older adults generally exceeded what they spent during middle age because most of their major investments in their home and family were now completed and their children were no longer dependent on them (Chon & Singh, 1995). In Australia, baby boomers were found to have assets worth an estimated AUS$1 trillion, with 85% indicating that they planned to travel annually either within Australia or overseas. A number also reported that they intended to make as many as 10 domestic trips per annum (Queensland Tourism, 2008).

The financial health of a large percentage of older people has made them an expanding market for luxury goods and services (Penalta & Uysal, 1992). As a result, resorts and hotels are designing programs and activities that specifically target older people. Although group travel and package tours still remain popular choices for many seniors, there is a growing market for more individualized, quality-driven travel options and related products and services. Education has also become a significant factor in determining older people's propensity to travel, especially to overseas destinations. Baby boomers are much more highly educated than their older counterparts; well over half of all American baby boomers have earned at least a high school diploma, and approximately one in four have completed four years of college education (McNeil, 2001).

However, despite these trends, academics need to be careful about overestimating the number of older people who will travel in the future. Because divorce is more common in today's society than in the past, single-parent families and second marriages are likely to diminish family wealth and restrict leisure travel for older adults with younger children (Ryan, 1995). In addition, caregiving of loved ones is a further restriction on older people's travel plans when they must provide long-term care for family members who have chronic health conditions (Bedini & Gladwell, 2006; Gladwell & Bedini, 2004). Even though the number of older people who are traveling may be overestimated, it is still important that older travelers have the opportunity to experience the unique meanings that traveling can provide so as to explain the importance of tourism in their lives and to the world in general.

Meanings of Tourism

Conversations are one way of investigating the meaning of tourism and the role that travel plays in people's lives (Ryan, 1995). Robertson (2001) examined the meaning of the travel experience for older travelers to determine whether their experiences were personally transformative. Four major themes emerged from the data he collected:

- **A new perspective on what they had at home.** Their experiences were examined in a range of countries with various types of architecture, food, money, language, and people. These experiences resulted in a new dimension of knowledge as well as a greater appreciation of life in their home country.
- **A changed sense of self.** One respondent stated that she felt liberated and more self-confident, while another stated that he felt strengthened as a result of visiting holy sites.

- **Disrupted assumptions were caused by these new experiences.** Many of the travelers' initial assumptions had changed because of the travel experience. For example, one respondent stated that he no longer assumed that the world was an unfriendly or hostile place.
- **A deeper understanding of the problems associated with a particular country.** Travel provided a deeper knowledge about the country that was visited. For example, one couple expressed that they had a deeper sense of the economic problems associated with a particular country by staying with a host family during their visit. Of special significance was the tour guides' role; their attitudes were seen as important, especially if they incorporated personal reflections during the tour, were unhurried, and allowed time for discussion and questions. This resulted in learning that had special significance, resulting in a transformative experience for the individual tourist.

Qualitative research was further conducted by Gibson (2002), who interviewed six men and five women between 65 and 90 years of age, asking them specific questions about their leisure travel patterns and the meanings that travel held for them. She concluded that for most of the participants, leisure had played a meaningful role in their lives since retirement. Many stated that they were motivated by a desire to learn more about other cultures and people. One of the respondents, Will, who was in his early 80s, explained that the educational value of travel was very important to him and his wife: "We were both firmly interested in people . . . and history. In fact, that's one of the reasons for going to this Spanish, Portuguese thing [Elderhostel trip, now known as Road Scholar] . . . we hope in every place to have contact with and conversations with the local people" (p. 17).

These studies have shown the value of qualitative research methodologies, which have been largely ignored by tourism researchers in the past. There is a need to further extend and apply the experiences of older people to the study of leisure and tourism (see chapter 4 for more information on methods). This is because qualitative interviews enable the researcher to provide new meanings and understandings about the trip experience from a perspective other than that of quantitative research. For instance, Robertson's (2001) study showed that older travelers faced various disorienting dilemmas (e.g., language, money, travel directions), and although these were not crisis situations, they often resulted in the loss of self-confidence and learning when the challenges were not solved. Most travelers further identified that learning was the main focus of their trip, and learning about the various destinations transformed their lives in subtle yet important ways. This suggests that older tourists may have a variety of motivations for their travel behavior.

Motivations to Travel

What motivates people to travel has fascinated tourism researchers for the last two decades. Tourism motivations include escaping personal and interpersonal environments and seeking out personal and interpersonal intrinsic rewards. Thus, to Iso-Ahola (1983), tourist behavior is the "interplay of forces—avoidance of routine or stressful environments and seeking recreation places for certain psychological rewards" (p. 55). Terms such as *push factors* and *pull factors* have been used by researchers to describe what influences people's choice of a particular destination and to help understand tourist choices. Dann (1977, 1981) described the two stages in the travel decision-making process as push and pull factors:

- **Push factors** are the internal sociopsychological motivators that predispose or push a person to travel. In other words, they are the motives that establish the desire for taking a vacation.
- **Pull factors**, on the other hand, are external motives that pull a person toward a particular destination once the decision to travel has been made. Dann (1981) further suggested that anomie and ego enhancement are underlying reasons for travel.

Dann's ideas about push and pull motivations were extended by Crompton (1979), who identified the motives that influenced pleasure vacationers in their selection of specific destinations. Nine motives were empirically identified and classified into two main categories. The first category included seven motives that he called *sociopsychological* or *push factors*. They included the following: escape from a perceived mundane environment, exploration and evaluation of self, relaxation, prestige, regression, enhancement of kinship relationships, and facilitation of social interaction. The second category, which Crompton called *cultural motives* or *pull factors*, included the last two motives: novelty and education. These two motives have helped researchers to better understand why someone chooses a particular destination.

Older people in particular experience such push factors as the urge to escape from the demands of home and would like to be more active in their leisure activities (Norman, Daniels, McGuire, & Norman, 2001). Older travelers have also shown a strong preference for visiting relatives and friends, socializing with other people, visiting cultural and heritage attractions, and learning more about various cultures (Lehto, Jang, Achaua, & O'Leary, 2008). The most important pull factors are good transportation, high standards of hygiene and cleanliness, and personal safety (You & O'Leary, 1999). Further research has also indicated that older North Americans with higher education, income level, and life satisfaction scores tend to spend most of their discretionary income on recreation and leisure, and they prefer destinations that are the farthest distance from Canada and the United States (Zimmer, Brayley, & Searle, 1995).

Segmentation by psychographic variables (such as VALS typing, which stands for values, attitudes, and lifestyle segmentation), a well-known consumer segmentation tool that has been previously used in studies of older people, has been found to be closely related to lifestyle, making it easier to predict travel search behavior and to develop more precise marketing and promotional strategies. Shoemaker's classic studies (1989, 2000) have shown that it is possible to differentiate among segments of older travelers that have been mainly based on psychographic variables, and these segments tend to remain fairly stable over time. Shoemaker found three main groups of older travelers:

- **The retirees** (19.3%) preferred to return to the same destinations each year rather than visiting a new one.
- **Escape and learn** (41.8%) liked to visit new places and experience new things, visit historical sites, and enjoyed spiritual and intellectual enrichment.
- **Active storytellers** (34.8%) liked to escape routine and to meet and socialize with new people, to do physical activities and to attend festivals.

Shoemaker (2000) noted that in the length of time between his two studies, there was a trend away from package tours. Many older people now prefer to be more independent and organize their own trips since they favor more active vacations that may also involve intellectual learning and visits to a range of historical sites.

Further research has found that active older travelers with higher incomes tend to stay away from home for longer amounts of time (Patterson, 2006). These travelers are more attractive to marketers in the tourism industry because they like to buy or rent luxury properties so as to escape the cold weather, and they prefer to be more active in healthy leisure activities. Relaxation activities and escaping home life seem to be more attractive for the younger older people who are still working in paid employment. Finally, studies have shown that there is a great deal of heterogeneity within the older-adult travel market and that older adults travel for a multitude of reasons, including to experience new places, to learn, to visit family and friends, to meet new people, to participate in active and adventurous leisure activities, to rest and relax, and for nostalgic reasons.

Constraints to Travel

A number of barriers, or **constraints**, have been listed as the main reasons preventing older people from traveling. Among the most common constraints for older adults are a decline in their income in retirement (Hong, Kim, & Lee, 1999) and a deterioration in their health (Bedini & Gladwell, 2006; Fleischer & Pizam, 2002). These findings suggest that the tourism industry needs to concentrate its marketing efforts on the age range of 60 to 70 years old, when health is generally good and income levels are at their peak. Lack of time is not an important issue once the older person has retired. More recently, safety and a sense of security from terrorism attacks have become important considerations for older people (Lindquist & Bjork, 2000). Most studies have also found that it is important to have access to good health care facilities at the destinations that are visited. The main constraints have been summarized by Huang and Tsai (2003), and they fall into two main categories:

- Personal problems such as cost, lack of time, health, age, and family responsibilities
- Tourism providers' responsibilities such as cost considerations and poor provision of information

Photograph courtesy of Tourism Queensland.

Older people who are still working might be more motivated to travel for relaxation and escape.

Governments have a responsibility to ensure safe travel within their jurisdictions. Governments generally post warnings for travellers of potential dangers on their website. This includes external factors such as security concerns and environmental barriers. Environmental factors such as fire, earthquakes, crime, violence, and unhealthy food and water are among the major concerns that restrict older people's travel to many Asian and Middle Eastern countries. In such turbulent times, older tourists generally favor countries that are seen to be safe and that can provide access to high-level health care facilities. Travel is mainly conditioned by people's health needs, which can often deteriorate at a more advanced age and may restrict their ability to travel.

Modes of Travel

The automobile is the preferred mode of pleasure travel for older people in Western societies (Javalgi et al., 1992; Eby & Molnar, 1999). In the United States, there has been an increase in car use, number of trips, and proportion of driver's-license holders among older people. Those without access to a car, mainly older women, experience the most problems with getting around (Rosenbloom, 2001). Airline travel runs a distant second to the car, with only 28% of older adults using plane travel, followed by travel in rented vehicles (8%), motor homes (2%), and bus and train services (1%). Wei and Ruys (1998) found similar results for Australia, with the two preferred modes of travel being personal vehicles (57.3%) and airplanes (37.4%) for people who were aged 60 years and over. The higher percentage of older people who fly has been attributed to the large distances between major cities in Australia compared with the United States. Furthermore, older adults are four times more likely than younger age groups to travel by bus in the United States, with 6% of adults aged 65 years or older preferring to take a vacation on a tour bus during the past year (Dortch, 1995).

The popularity of the automobile decreases as age increases past 65 years (Javalgi et al., 1992), which has been attributed to the general decline in health as people age, resulting in a lack of stamina for driving for long distances. An examination of the types of destinations associated with various modes of travel found that older adults who still use their car tend to visit their children and relatives and to attend entertainment and functions related to their work (Teaff & Turpin, 1996). Travel time was found to be less important for older drivers, who are not as concerned about stops and delays along the travel route compared with younger families. Older travelers are also generally more willing to take side trips, because most have retired and as a result can take their time. Because of this, many older people stay away from home for extended periods of time (up to five weeks), and they mainly travel in the off-season when it is cooler and cheaper accommodation rates are available (Eby & Molnar, 2001).

Although bus travel is not the most popular mode of transportation for taking pleasure trips, it does increase in importance as a person ages. Javalgi and colleagues (1992) attributed this increase in bus travel to the increased use of package tours by older adults since package tours generally incorporate both bus and plane travel. A number of reasons have been given for the increased use of public transport, such as the desire to let someone else do the driving because of eyesight problems, frailty forcing older people

to substitute public transport for private cars, and the high cost of fuel.

Another popular form of travel for older people is by camper or motor home, also known as a **recreational vehicle**, or RV. Campgrounds or RV parks attract large numbers of RVs, resulting in high levels of social interaction and friendship with other travelers. In a study of national park usage in Queensland, Ballantyne, Pegg, and Scott (2008) found that the provision of opportunities to engage with park staff and other travelers was a critical dimension for the overall visitor experience.

Temporary Communities

Many RVers stay in the same location for several weeks and develop a sense of community with their fellow travelers. The social patterns of temporary communities established by mobile travelers in the United States were first investigated by Jobes (1984). He found that temporary communities were often communities of people with special interests, that is, people who consciously came together because of their shared interests, values, and preferred behaviors. Travelers were

Care-A-Vanners

An example of a temporary community of RV users with a special interest is the **Care-A-Vanners**, which is a volunteer section of Habitat for Humanity. Participants travel around North America and build homes for the poor (Gurwitt, 2003). Founded in 1988, today's RV Care-A-Vanners have annually built more than 175 Habitat houses in the United States and Canada. There are as many as 6,000 Care-A-Vanner members, and the builds generally last around two weeks. Usually there are 6 to 10 RVs, so there may be up to 20 Care-A-Vanners helping out.

One volunteer, Paul Tanzer, had volunteered with Habitat for Humanity for 15 years. His knowledge, experience, and leadership made him an invaluable asset to the organization. Paul became involved with the organization shortly after retiring in 1995. He brought with him not only his construction knowledge but also experiences from other Habitat affiliates around the United States. His experience with the earliest phases of home building—foundations and framing—made him invaluable on several builds. "I became the foundation guru," Paul stated. So what kept bringing Paul back to Habitat despite his already busy schedule? "The people," Paul said. "I like these people that I meet. I look forward to meeting all these guys. I don't know how common it is, but there's a group of guys who are really loyal and can get together, have lunch, sit around and talk. We're very compatible. I like the building aspect and get a lot of satisfaction from it, but it's the meeting of the people and getting to talk to them and renewing relationships that brings me back." He further stated, "I like to build stuff. Some people like to push paper, some people like to pry open your mouth and be a dentist, but I like to build—and contribute to the welfare of people in need while I'm at it." (*North Willamette Valley Habitat for Humanity News*, 2010) free to choose when and where they would go and with whom, although to the outsider it may seem quite structured and predictable. The locations changed periodically, but the interaction networks tended to remain relatively stable. Much of the travelers' free time was spent playing cards, sharing meals, and conversing, and people who were injured or ill were taken in and supported by the group until they recovered. Mobile travelers referred to themselves as *gypsies*, *vagabonds*, or *nomads* and developed their own language that included technical jargon associated with their rigs. This sense of freedom was also reflected in the travelers' lifestyle, in that they were experiencing a successful retirement and were economically secure so as to comfortably live a life of leisure.

Older Mobile Travelers

In North America, the term **snowbird** has been commonly used to describe older people who travel from the Northeast and Midwest of the United States and Canada to warmer localities such as California, Arizona, Florida, and Mexico, where they spend a large portion of the winter months enjoying the warmer climate. The Canadian Snowbird Association estimated that in 2007, 70% of Canadian travelers who spent more than one month in the Sun Belt chose Florida as their destination, with the number of visitors to the state totaling over 450,000 older people (Statistics Canada, 2009).

A significant portion of the snowbird community is made up of RVers. Such vehicles are especially popular with the younger and more affluent snowbirds in the United States and Canada. Many of the modern RVs have been described as homes on wheels, with the larger and more expensive ones offering an extensive range of features; for example, the Winnebago Menindee includes an electronically controlled awning, a large outdoor LCD television (one of three onboard), an automatic satellite dish, solar panels, an inbuilt generator, electric entry steps, a tow bar, a BBQ fitting, internal and external showers, and the luxury of being able to slide out some of the external storage bins (www.sydneyrvcentre.com.au/latest-news.html).

Research on Snowbirds

As discussed, a snowbird is a Northerner who moves to a warmer climate in the winter. Mings and McHugh (1995) investigated the snowbird lifestyle in Arizona during the winter months. They interviewed 12 couples from three large Phoenix-area RV resorts. All couples agreed to continue to meet regularly with the researchers

Boondocking

Boondocking has recently become a popular activity for people who own RVs. It is simply RV camping in an area with limited or no facilities. With the growing popularity of boondocking, the U.S. Bureau of Land Management (BLM) has begun to establish areas for longer stays, particularly in Arizona. The permit fee is around $140, which allows you to stay for up to six months. There are temporary towns, such as Slab City in California, complete with bookstores, grocery stores, and other businesses run by RVers. When summer returns, these communities disappear, and they reappear the following winter. The largest gathering of RV boondockers was reported to be in Quartzite, Arizona; up to 200,000 people spent at least part of the year there. Quartzite is near the California border only 20 miles (32 km) from the Colorado River and is famous for gem shows and swap meets (Gillman, 2010).

Several stores in the United States, such as Walmart, also encourage RVs to park overnight in their parking lots. A spokesman for Walmart stated,

Generally we limit it to one night. We do it as a convenience for people who come in late at night, shop with us, and then leave in the morning. Generally RVers are good folks and good customers. Many follow routes where Walmarts are handy because we have prescription drug stores, optical departments, and other items crucial to them. They are very courteous and often check in at the courtesy desk to let us know they are parked in the back of the lot. (Blais, 2002, p. 6) in the future so as to review changes to their lives over the previous year. The authors found that outdoor activities were most popular with snowbirds, especially desert sightseeing, walking, golfing, and swimming—all activities that were virtually impossible during the winter in their home states. The most distinctive aspect of the RV lifestyle was the large amount of time and attention given to a wide variety of leisure activities. Another aspect was the importance of social interaction among RVers. Most were outgoing, group-oriented people with a strong preference for leisure activities that allowed them to socialize. Card playing, dancing, bus tours, potluck dinners, and shuffleboard were stated as the most popular leisure activities. Another common characteristic of the RV lifestyle was the high level of geographic mobility, including a preference for local sightseeing and overnight excursions. For some people, their base resort in Arizona was used as a home base for short trips to nearby attractions such as casinos in Nevada, beaches in California, and the border towns of Mexico.

Most winter residents indicated that they were very involved in leisure activities for most of their waking hours. The resorts themselves organized events such as pancake breakfasts, talent nights, dance and art classes, tennis, golf, and pool. When the snowbirds returned home, their range of leisure activities was much more limited and the pace of participation slowed down considerably. At home all their friends and neighbors were not retired, whereas in Phoenix, most people were full-time pleasure seekers. As a result, when they were away, snowbirds generally welcomed a lifestyle that included periods of high activity where they enjoyed easy access to leisure facilities and programming as well as the ready availability of leisure partners in the RV resort. On return to their home city, there was a period of relative calm and a slower-paced lifestyle with a reduction in the number of leisure activities.

Grey Nomads

Grey nomads is a term used to describe older adults who travel around Australia. They are "people aged over 50 years, who adopt an extended period of travel (at least three months) independently within their own country" (Onyx & Leonard, 2005, p. 61). Most grey nomads have retired from paid work and now have time at their disposal to travel around Australia at their own pace. Mings (1997) interviewed 306 couples in 41 caravan parks between Mossman and South Mission Beach in Queensland, concluding that there were major differences between the lifestyles of snowbirds and grey nomads.

For instance, Mings concluded that there was appreciably less social interaction in Queensland caravan parks in comparison to RV resort parks, with 76% of grey nomads stating that they did not know anyone else in the park. There were also fewer group-oriented leisure activities, such as dances, classes, dinners, and sporting tournaments, compared with American RV resorts. Grey nomads stayed an average of 35 days in Queensland caravan parks compared with 4.4 months in RV resorts in Phoenix. The return rate for grey nomads was 2.2 visits versus 5.9 visits by snowbirds to Phoenix. This was because Australian grey nomads preferred to travel longer distances at a more leisurely pace, sometimes between 300 and 500 kilometers per day, rather than staying for a long time in one RV park. Grey nomads also preferred to sightsee along the way and were not in a rush to get to their particular destination. Indeed, grey nomads tended to be on the road for a considerable amount of time, with a mean of 128 days (4 months), and were generally more mobile than most North American snowbird travelers.

Onyx and Leonard (2005) further researched grey nomads to ascertain their main motivations for traveling around Australia. They found that one of the main motivations was to establish new social networks of acquaintances and friends. The majority of respondents indicated that although they traveled with their spouse, they felt that meeting other people was also important. In addition, communication by word of mouth with other travelers was seen as important to ascertain the best places to visit and to stay. A 52-year-old woman explained this by stating, "Once you camp somewhere and you get to know your neighbour and you really talk to them. We've kept in contact with a few of them . . . from all walks of life" (p. 65).

Adventure Tourism

Muller and Cleaver (2000) defined **adventure tourism** as "physically bracing, adrenalin-driven, somewhat risky, with moments of exhilaration punctuated by many opportunities to assess and reassess what has been done or accomplished" (p. 156). An essential component of adventure tourism is travel to unusual, exotic, and remote wilderness destinations (Kane & Tucker, 2004; Millington, Locke, & Locke, 2001). Activity, experience, environment, motivation, risk, and competence were identified as primary dimensions that often characterize the traveler's perception of adventure travel (Sung, Morrison, & O'Leary, 1997). Examples of adventure activities are white-water rafting, horseback riding, hiking, skiing, scuba diving, mountain biking, backpacking, and camping.

Swarbrooke, Beard, Leckie, and Pomfret (2003) concluded that adventure is not defined according to the specific activities that are undertaken but more by the state of mind and approach of the participant. However, there is no doubt that adventure denotes action, which is not a passive experience and is generally found to be engaging and absorbing. Adventure also involves effort and commitment, and mental and physical preparation or training is often necessary. Studies have suggested that older travelers are finding adventure tourism more appealing and are becoming more adventurous than previous cohorts, wanting to travel to experience something they find personally satisfying.

The adventure experience varies along a number of dimensions, including type of travel, group membership, and amount and spectrum of risk (Cleaver & Muller, 2002; Ewart & Jamieson, 2003; Muller & Cleaver, 2000). Thus, participants can engage in the adventure activity according to several dimensions, such as location (a remote wilderness trip traveling alone versus a trip to Cancun on a cruise ship), which suggests that there are a variety of levels and types of risk and danger that need to be seriously considered (Bentley & Page, 2001).

Baby boomers in particular often crave adventurous and authentic learning experiences and prefer to be part of the decision-making process. Some older adults are now demanding trips that "involve physical challenge, if not actual danger, travel that involves an inner journey, intellectual challenge, as well as exploration of new places and cultures" (Lipscombe, 1995, p. 44). This finding is supported by Fortosis (2009), who contended that many baby boomers desire a stimulating cultural and social experience that entails lots of interaction and adventure.

The research indicates that baby boomers prefer soft adventure experiences under controlled conditions that are less physically demanding and the use of trained guides who are employed to provide an educational component (Muller & Cleaver, 2000). Travel companies should be aware of these preferences as well as of the importance of catering to their customers' health needs, providing activities that are less physically demanding, slower-paced tours, greater choice in regard to food menus, and plenty of social activities so as to enable the group to mix and get to know each other (Massow, 2000). Gender differences have been noted, with older males preferring more physically demanding activities, such as white-water rafting, rock climbing, and caving, and older females preferring less physically demanding but more educational activities, such as bird watching, horseback riding, and bush walking (Muller & O'Cass, 2001).

Adventure tourism is one of the fastest growing segments of the tourism market. It has become so popular that approximately 100 million adults have chosen vacations that are classified as soft adventure (Miller, 1997). In the past, the tourism industry has focused on young, wealthy, and able-bodied adventure tourists; however, this is slowly changing as marketers become increasingly more aware of the active and adventurous baby boomers (Lehto et al., 2008; Muller & O'Cass, 2001; Patterson, 2002). It has been acknowledged that people over 50 are more adventurous than their parents, and they are often driven to discover new destinations and to try out new and exciting leisure activities (Sellick, 2004).

Strategic Management (2007) suggests that seniors are flocking to adventure travel, with interest so high it is now regarded as one of the hottest niches in the travel business. This has been attributed to the fact that baby boomers often become bored with merely being mass tourists and passively sightseeing, indicating strong preferences for more exciting, challenging, and authentic experiences at travel destinations (Boksberger & Laesser, 2009). This new generation of retirees is "hungry to get off the beaten path" and is driven in part by "more and more retirees with time, money, and a yen for the exotic" (Symonds, 1998, p. 102).

BrandX Pictures

Adventure tourism is often appealing to younger, wealthier retirees.

Many older adults want to escape the stress and boredom of their everyday routine, spend their vacation time on pleasure-filled trips with a range of exciting and new physically challenging activities, and meet people and build new friendships (Camden & McColl-Kennedy, 1990; Kluge, 2005). Gene Wellman, a 71-year-old retired environmental consultant from Klamath Falls, Oregon, typifies this type of traveler: "Wellman has no desire to be herded onto sightseeing buses. So he and his wife Genevieve joined a small group trip to French Polynesia and Peru" (Symonds, 1998, p. 102).

Although there is general acceptance that the baby boomer travel market is a heterogeneous group of submarkets, there is an awareness that adventure tourism is likely to grow more quickly than other segments of the market over the coming years (Kane & Tucker, 2004). Independent adventure travel is becoming more popular than group tours, with the emphasis being on interacting with local residents and gaining in-depth knowledge of an area. Multiactivity trips are also becoming more popular, combining outdoor activities such as trekking, rafting, and diving with an added cultural component.

Based on an examination of the current research literature, future marketing campaigns must place greater emphasis on authentic statements by older people describing their experiences, such as feelings associated with a sense of adventure, escapism, and the challenge of actual involvement. Terms such as *enjoyment*, *flow*, and *meeting new friends* should be emphasized so as to encourage feelings associated with a sense of freedom, fun, and escape from a mundane lifestyle (Coke & Perkins, 1998; Patterson, 2002). These feelings can also be experienced through educational tourism, as discussed in the following section; many older travelers prefer a cultural or heritage experience, mixing with the locals and learning about their culture and traditions.

Educational Tourism

Educational tourists are people who take part in study tours, or who attend workshops to learn new skills or improve existing ones while on vacation (Gibson, 1998). **Educational tourism** involves travel as part of the learning experience and caters to the preference to experience the subject matter in its natural context and original location. Educational tourism has become most popular with older people who have recently retired, particularly college-educated women (Gibson, 1994; Patterson & Pegg, 2009).

To many older travelers, educational travel is intrinsically motivating, and these types of travelers are generally more interested in enriching their lives with experiences rather than being entertained. Pennington-Gray and Lane (2001) state, "This suggests that the preference for learning while traveling is a large component of the older generation's travel preferences" (p. 89). Women in particular are often looking for the opportunity to explore further avenues for self-expression, creativity, and growth in their lives. According to Gibson (1994), men (20%) were less interested in educational tourism than women (25%), because many were still dealing with postretirement transitions and the negative feelings associated with feelings of uselessness and loss of identity. Gibson concluded that older men who were attracted to educational tourism tended to be in their 60s, college educated, and relatively affluent. A further study found that older adults preferred to visit historical places and buildings, museums, cultural events and festivals, and casinos. The main motivations to travel were intellectual curiosity and obtaining greater knowledge about other cultures and historical events (Achkoyan & Mallon, 1997).

Elderhostel (now known as Road Scholar) was the first educational travel program in the United States that was specifically designed for people aged 55 years and older. The program has grown from 220 participants in 1975 to over 4 million in 2008 (Elderhostel, 2008). Nearly 8,000 educational tours have now been run in all 50 states and in more than 90 countries. Generally, the program involves participants living in campus accommodations and eating in campus dining rooms, although they do not have to do homework, take exams, or compete for grades (Miller, 1997). International programs last two to three weeks, including field trips as well as social activities. Participants indicated that they were more motivated to travel because of the *seeking* and *intellectual stimulation* motives rather than the *escape* motive, which was not found to be a strong motivator for the leisure or tourism behavior of older adults undertaking Elderhostel trips (Thomas & Butts, 1998).

The location of the educational trip was also a key factor in its appeal for potential partici-

pants. Once the particular trip destination was selected, participants were keen to explore the natural environment and surroundings in addition to being actively engaged in their learning. For domestic participants, the course topic was the main motivating factor. Future programs have been planned to include a variety of educational institutions, such as museums, outdoor centers, and parks. New courses, where participants are exposed to a number of disciplines, are likely to be introduced in the future to trace a particular historical period through experiential learning opportunities (Goggin, 1999).

Conclusion

Lehto and colleagues (2008) contended that with so many baby boomers about to retire, the critical question now facing the tourism and travel industry is whether or not it fully understands the needs and wants of this aging cohort. This is a critical issue; as Green (2010) stated, baby boomers who were born between 1946 and 1964 will shatter forever the stereotypes and traditional assumptions about people who are in their 60s and 70s. In particular, baby boomers are seeking out services and products that speak to deeper values, and they demand real-life experiences that facilitate learning and broadening of the mind (Green, 2010; Patterson & Pegg, 2009).

As a result, older travelers not only represent a growing market segment but also an increasing challenge for the tourism industry as they demand a range of educational experiences that are often focused on historical and cultural settings. This notion is supported by Goodman (2007), who contends that travel operators need to look for ways to motivate older adults who have been there, done that, so to speak, and this might be achieved by creating tourist opportunities that tap into their renewed interest in history and nostalgia and that are also perceived as being new or adventurous but still relatively safe. Most new seniors are experiencing a reduction in their social and family obligations, which has opened the door to engagement in travel activities and opportunities that in the past may have been considered atypical for this generation (Lehto et al., 2008).

Nimrod and Rotem (2010) concluded that when planning tourism services for older adults, the tourism market must demonstrate greater flexibility with respect to consumer interests and be guided by a benefits continuum that ranges from relaxation to excitement. Glover and Prideaux

(2009) acknowledged this fact when they suggested that destinations that focus on older travelers need to adapt their offerings to better align with more sophisticated travelers who know the type of product and level of service that they should be receiving.

KEY TERMS

adventure tourism—A type of tourism that includes exciting experiences that are often physically demanding. It may involve exploration or travel to remote, exotic, and possibly hostile areas.

boondocking—RV camping in an area with limited or no facilities that often encourages the establishment of temporary communities.

Care-A-Vanners—A volunteer program run by Habitat for Humanity, which is a nonprofit organization that seeks to eradicate substandard housing by building simple, decent houses for low-income earners in the United States.

constraints—Limitations that stop people from traveling. Research has shown that socioeconomic variables such as age, income, and life stage are the main constraints to travel.

educational tourism—Travel as part of the learning experience, which may involve taking part in study tours or attending workshops to learn new skills or improve existing ones while on vacation.

grey nomads—Older adults who independently travel around Australia over an extended period of time. They are often retired and have time at their disposal to travel at their own pace.

pull factors—External motives that pull a person toward a particular destination once the decision to travel has been made.

push factors—Internal sociopsychological motivators that predispose or push a person to travel. In other words, they are the motives that establish the desire for taking a vacation.

recreational vehicle (RV)—A motorized vehicle such as a camper or motor home that is used for traveling and recreational activities.

Red Hat Society (RHS)—A leisure- and travel-related social organization for women aged 50 years and older.

snowbirds—Older people who are mobile and travel in their RVs from the northern states of the United States and Canada during the winter months to localities in the United States and Mexico where they enjoy the warmer climate.

REVIEW AND DISCUSSION QUESTIONS

1. Why are older travelers becoming a primary target for the tourism industry? Discuss this question in relation to the following:
   - Retirement and more free time
   - Increased wealth and greater prosperity
   - Health and fitness needs

2. "Many older people want to feel young again or at least to relive some of the more pleasant experiences that characterized their youth." Discuss this statement in regard to the interest in adventure tourism among the baby boomer generation.

3. Should chronological age be used as the main measure in tourism research on market segmentation? If not, what other psychographic measures might be used?

LEARNING ACTIVITIES

1. Interview three older people: one aged between 60 and 69 years, another between 70 and 79 years, and the third one between 80 and 89 years. Ask them about their travel behavior during the past 12 months. If they have traveled during this time, examine differences based on the
   - age and gender of the person,
   - type of travel (international versus domestic),
   - time of year,
   - type of tourism (e.g., adventure, educational),
   - benefits and constraints,
   - health issues, and
   - safety concerns.

2. Organize a small focus group of older people to discuss the following questions:
   - How do you generally obtain information about taking a vacation?
   - How do you feel about using computers and the Internet to gain information on your vacation information search?
   - Once you have selected a specific vacation, would you use a credit card over the Internet to pay for it?

CRITICAL-THINKING ACTIVITIES

1. Do you think that older people increase their tourist behavior when they retire, or does it depend on their previous lifestyle, their current style of living, and their health?

2. Research suggests that there are some major similarities and differences between snowbirds and grey nomads and their travel behavior. Divide a page in half and jot down several similarities and differences between the two groups. Is culture a factor that encourages differences between them?

3. For many North Americans, retirement marks the chance to take a long-awaited trip. Based on what you have read about travel motivations and meanings, in what ways can tourism contribute to a satisfying retirement? Discuss some of the common issues that travel companies need to consider when catering to the older traveler, such as the following:

   – Needs, interests, motivations, and constraints of older travelers

   – Specific marketing messages directed toward older adults

   – Vacation products directed toward the senior market

SUGGESTED READING

AARP Services, Inc. (2007). The sky's the limit: Travel trends among the baby boomer generation and beyond. *Focalyst.* Retrieved from http://assets.aarp.org/rgcenter/general/travel_trends_1.pdf.

Centers for Disease Control and Prevention (CDC). (2007). The state of aging and health in America report. Retrieved from http://apps.nccd.cdc.gov/SAHA/Default/Default.aspx.

Ianniello, J. (2006). *Baby boomers: A lucrative market for the Pacific Asia region.* Presentation at the 55th PATA Annual Conference, Pattaya, Thailand, April 23-27, 2006. Retrieved from www.roymorgan.com/resources/papers/babyboomers/.

National Tour Association. (2002). Current assessment report for the baby boomer market. Retrieved from www.agingsociety.org/agingsociety/links/car_boomer.pdf.

Patterson, I.R. (2006). *Growing older: Tourism and leisure behaviour of older adults.* Oxfordshire, UK: CABI.

Plunkett Research. (2009). Travel and tourism market research. Aging baby boomers will cause significant changes in the leisure sector, including sports and activity-based travel. Retrieved from www.plunkettresearch.com/industry%20news/plunkett%20research%20indentifies%20sports%20trends%2006-25-09.

REFERENCES

Achkoyan, M., & Mallon, P. (1997). American retired people: A promising market. *Marketing Touristique et Tranches d'age, 54,* 40-44.

American Association of Retired Persons (AARP) & Roper Organization. (1992). *Mature America in the 1990s.* New York: Maturity Magazine Group.

Australian Institute of Health & Welfare. (2008). *Australia's health 2008.* Canberra: Author.

Ballantyne, R., Pegg, S., & Scott, N. (2008). *Queensland national parks visitor satisfaction report.* Brisbane: School of Tourism, University of Queensland.

Bedini, L., & Gladwell, N. (2006). Barriers to leisure travel of family caregivers. *Topics in Geriatric Rehabilitation, 22,* 322-333.

Bentley, T.A., & Page, S.J. (2001). Scoping the extent of adventure tourism accidents. *Annals of Tourism Research, 28,* 705-726.

Blais, P. (2002). On the road again: They're big; they're slow; they're often the vehicle of choice for tourists. *Planning, 68,* 6-11.

Boksberger, P., & Laesser, C., (2009). Segmentation of the senior travel market by means of travel motivations. *Journal of Vacation Marketing, 15,* 311-322.

Botterill, T.D., & Crompton, J.L. (1996). Two case studies exploring the nature of the tourist experience. *Journal of Leisure Research, 28,* 57-83.

Camden, D., & McColl-Kennedy, J. (1991). Travel patterns of the over 50s: Practical implications. In *Papers on the over 50's in the 90': Factors for successful marketing of products and services.* Amsterdam: Esomar.

Chisholm, P. (1989). Postponed pleasures: The over-fifties are spending freely on fun, and now the marketplace is beginning to take notice. *Maclean's, 102*(January 9), 24-25.

Chon, K., & Singh, A. (1995). Marketing resorts to 2000: Review of trends in the USA. *Tourism Management, 16,* 463-469.

Cleaver, M., & Muller, T. (2002). The socially aware baby boomer: Gaining a lifestyle-based understanding of the new wave of ecotourists. *Journal of Sustainable Tourism, 10*(3), 173-190.

Coke, P., & Perkins, H.C. (1998). Cracking the canyon with the awesome foursome: Representations of adventure tours in New Zealand. *Society and Space, 16,* 185-218.

Cooper, S.E. (2004). *The Red Hat Society: Fun and friendship after fifty.* New York: Warner.

Crompton, J.L. (1979). Motivations for pleasure vacation. *Annals of Tourism Research, 6,* 408-424.

Dann, G.M. (1977). Anomie, ego-enhancement and tourism. *Annals of Tourism Research, 4,* 184-194.

Dann, G.M. (1981). Tourist motivation: An appraisal. *Annals of Tourism Research, 6*, 408-424.

Davies, C. (2005). *Travel and adventure report—a snapshot of boomers' travel and adventure experiences.* Washington, DC: AARP.

Dortch, S. (1995). Vacation vehicles. *American Demographics, 17*, 4-5.

Dennis, H. (2005). Evolution of the link between business and aging. *Generations, 28*(4), 8-14.

Eby, D.W., & Molnar, L.J. (1999). *Guidelines for developing information systems for the driving tourist.* Ann Arbor, MI: University of Michigan Intelligent Transportation System Research Center for Excellence.

Eby, D.W., & Molnar, L.J. (2001). Age-related decision factors in destination choice for United States driving tourists. *Journal of Hospitality and Leisure Marketing, 9*, 97-111.

Elderhostel. (2008). *Elderhostel annual report.* Retrieved from www.roadscholar.org/support/annual_report_nodonors_apr09.pdf.

Ewart, A., & Jamieson, L. (2003). Current status and future directions in the adventure tourism industry. In J. Wilks & S. Page (Eds.), *Managing tourist health and safety in the new millennium* (pp. 67-83). Boston: Pergamon.

Fernandez-Morales, A., & Mayorga-Toledano, M.C. (2008). Seasonal concentration of hotel demand in Costa Del Sol: A composition by nationalities. *Tourism Management, 29*, 940-949.

Fleischer, A., & Pizam, A. (2002). Tourism constraints among Israeli seniors. *Annals of Tourism Research, 29*, 106-123.

Fortosis, D. (2009). *The upcoming baby boomer travel boom.* Retrieved from http://searchwarp.com/swa548233-the-upcoming-baby-boomer-travel-boom.htm.

Gibson, H. (1994). *Some predictors of tourist role performance for men and women over the adult life course.* Unpublished doctoral dissertation, University of Connecticut, Storrs, CT.

Gibson, H. (1998). The educational tourist. *Journal of Physical Education, Recreation & Dance, 69*(4), 6-9.

Gibson, H. (2002). Busy travelers: Leisure-travel patterns and meanings in later life. *World Leisure, 44*, 11-20.

Gillman, S. (2010). RV boondocking. Retrieved from http://ezinearticles.com/?RV-Boondocking&id=59959.

Gladwell, N.J., & Bedini, L.A. (2004). In search of lost leisure: The impact of caregiving on leisure travel. *Tourism Management, 25*, 685-693.

Glover, P., & Prideaux, B. (2009). Implications of ageing for the development of tourism products and destinations. *Journal of Vacation Marketing, 15*, 25-37.

Goggin, J.M. (1999). Elderhostel meets the silent revolution. *Tourism Recreation Research, 24*, 86-89.

Goodman, P. (2007). Adventure, entertainment & fantasy take over. Retrieved from www13.mawebcenters.com/gtm2/Industries.ivnu.

Green, B. (2010). Marketing and advertising to baby boomers. Retrieved from www.bgassociates.com/marketing_to_boomers.htm.

Gurwitt, R. (2003). Have tools will travel: Meet the Care-A-Vanners. *Mother Jones, 28*, 28-32.

Hawes, D.K. (1988). Travel-related lifestyle profiles of older women. *Journal of Travel Research, 26*(Fall), 22-32.

Higgs, P., & Quirk, F. (2007). Grey nomads in Australia: Are they a good model for successful aging and health? *Annuals of the New York Academy of Sciences, 1114*, 251.

Hong, G.-S., Kim, S., & Lee, J. (1999). Travel expenditure patterns of elderly households in the U.S. *Tourism Recreation Research, 41*, 43-52.

Huang, L., & Tsai, H.T. (2003). The study of senior traveler behaviour in Taiwan. *Tourism Management, 24*, 561-574.

Hutchinson, S. L., Yarnal, C. M., Staffordson, J., & Kerstetter, D. L. (2008). Beyond fun and friendship: the Red Hat Society as a coping resourse for older women. *Ageing and Society, 28*, 979-999.

Iso-Ahola, S. (1983). Towards a social psychology of tourism. *Leisure Studies, 2*, 45-56.

Jang, S.C., & Wu, C.M. (2006). Seniors' travel motivation and the influential factors: An examination of Taiwanese seniors. *Tourism Management, 27*, 306-316.

Javalgi, R.G., Thomas, E.G., & Rao, S.R. (1992). Consumer behavior in the U.S. travel marketplace: An analysis of senior and non-senior travelers. *Journal of Travel Research, 31*, 14-19.

Jobes, P.C. (1984). Old-timers and new mobile lifestyles. *Annals of Tourism Research, 11*, 181-198.

Kane, M., & Tucker, H. (2004). Adventure tourism: The freedom to play with reality. *Tourist Studies, 4*, 217-234.

Keller, M.L., Leventhal, E.A., & Larson, B. (1989). Aging: The lived experience. *International Journal of Aging and Human Development, 29*, 67-82.

Kluge, M. (2005). It's never too late to dare: Outdoor adventure programming for the age wave. *JOPERD, 76*(5), 39-46.

Lehto, X. Y., Jang, S-C., Achana, F. T., & O'Leary, J. F. (2006). Exploring tourism experience sought: a cohort comparison of baby boomers and the silent generation. *Journal of Vacation Marketing, 14*, 237-252.

Lehto, X.Y., O'Leary, J.T., & Lee, G. (2001). Mature international travelers: An examination of gender and benefits. *Journal of Hospitality and Leisure Marketing, 9*, 53-72.

Liechy, T., Ribeiro, N., & Yarnal, C. (2009). "I traveled alone but never felt alone": An exploration of the benefits of an older women's group tour experience. *Tourism Review International, 13*, 17-29.

Linquist, L-J., & Bjork, P. (2000). Perceived safety as an important quality dimension among senior tourists. *Tourism Economics, 6*, 151-158.

Lipscombe, N. (1995). Appropriate adventure: Participation for the aged. *Australian Parks and Leisure, 31*, 41-45.

Littrell, M., Paige, R., & Song, K. (2004). Senior travelers: Tourism activities and shopping behaviours. *Journal of Vacation Marketing, 10*, 348-362.

Massow, R. (2000). Senior sojourns. *Travel Agent, 299*(12), 1-2.

McNeil, R.D. (2001). Bob Dylan and the baby boom generation: The times they are a changin'—again. *Activities, Adaptation and Aging, 25*, 45-58.

Miller, B. (1997). The quest for lifelong learning. *American Demographics, 19*, 20-22.

Millington, K., Locke, T., & Locke, A. (2001). Occasional studies: Adventure travel. *Travel and Tourist Analyst, 4*, 65-97.

Mings, R.C., & McHugh, K.E. (1995). Wintering in the American Sun Belt: Linking place and behaviour. *Journal of Tourism Studies, 6*, 56-62.

Mings, R.C. (1997). Tracking "snowbirds" in Australia: Winter sun seekers in far north Queensland. *Australian Geographical Studies, 35*, 168-182.

Moschis, G.P. (1996). *Marketing to older consumers.* Westport, CT: Quorum Books.

Muller, T.E., & Cleaver, M. (2000). Targeting the CANZUS baby boomer explorer and adventurer segments. *Journal of Vacation Marketing, 6*, 154-169.

Muller, T., & O'Cass, A. (2001). Targeting the young at heart: Seeing senior vacationers the way they see themselves. *Journal of Vacation Marketing, 7*, 285-301.

Nimrod, G., & Rotem, A. (2010). Between relaxation and excitement: Activities and benefits gained in retiree's tourism. *International Journal of Tourism Research, 12*, 65-78.

Norman, W.C., Daniels, M.J., McGuire, F., & Norman, C.A. (2001). Whither the mature market: An empirical examination of the travel motivations of neo-mature and veteran mature markets. *Journal of Hospitality and Leisure Marketing, 8*, 113-130.

North Willamette Valley Habitat for Humanity News. (2010). *23*(2), 6. www.nwvhabitat.org/uploads/Fall_2010.pdf.

Onyx, J., & Leonard, R. (2005). Australian grey nomads and American snowbirds: Similarities and differences. *Journal of Tourism Studies, 16*, 61-68.

Patterson, I. (2002). Baby boomers and adventure tourism: The importance of marketing the leisure experience. *World Leisure Journal, 44*(2), 4-10.

Patterson, I. (2006). *Growing older: Tourism and leisure behaviour of older adults.* Oxfordshire, UK: CABI.

Patterson, I., & Pegg, S. (2009). Marketing the leisure experience to baby boomers and older tourists. *Journal of Hospitality Marketing & Management, 18*(2), 254-272.

Paxson, M. (2009). Boomer boom for hospitality: Opportunities and challengers. *Journal of Hospitality Marketing & Management, 18*(1), 89-98.

Penalta, L.A., & Uysal, M. (1992). Aging and the future travel market. *Parks and Recreation, 27*, 96-99.

Pennington-Gray, L., & Lane, C.W. (2001). Profiling the silent generation. *Journal of Hospitality & Leisure Marketing, 9*, 73-95.

Reece, W. (2004). Are senior travelers different? *Journal of Travel Research, 43*(1), 11-18.

Robertson, D.N. (2001). The impact of travel on older adults: An exploratory investigation. *Tourism, 49*, 99-108.

Rosenbloom, S. (2001). Sustainability and automobility among the elderly: An international assessment. *Transportation, 28*, 375-408.

Ryan, C. (1995). Learning about tourists from conversation: The over 55s in Majorca. *Tourism Management, 16*, 207-215.

Sangpikul, A. (2008). Travel motivations of Japanese senior travelers to Thailand. *International Journal of Tourism Research, 10*, 81-94.

Sellick, M. (2004). Discovery, connection, nostalgia. *Journal of Travel and Tourism Marketing, 17*, 55-71.

Shoemaker, S. (1989). Segmentation of the senior pleasure travel market. *Journal of Travel Research, 20*, 14-21.

Shoemaker, S. (2000). Segmenting the mature market: 10 years later. *Journal of Travel Research, 39*, 11-26.

Statistics Canada. (2009). *Types of Canadian travelers: Snowbirds.* Retrieved from www.canadainternational.gc.ca/miami/commerce_can/economic-economique_2008/tourism-tourisme/types-categories.aspx?lang=eng#n1.

Statts, S., & Pierfelice, L. (2003). Travel: A long-range goal of retired women. *Journal of Psychology, 137*, 483-494.

Strategic Management. (2007). *Travelers embrace growing tourism trend.* Retrieved from www.thematuremarket.com/SeniorStrategic/travelers_growing_tourism_trend-8753-5.html.

Sung, H.Y., Morrison, A.M., & O'Leary, J.T. (1997). Definition of adventure travel: Conceptual framework for empirical application from the provider's perspective. *Asia-Pacific Journal of Tourism Research, 1*, 47-67.

Swarbrooke, J., Beard, C., Leckie, S., & Pomfret, G. (2003). *Adventure tourism: The new frontier.* Oxford, England: Butterworth Heinemann.

Symonds, W.C. (1998, July 20). Far from the tour bus crowd: Track gorillas in Uganda, explore a rainforest, or pedal across France. *Business Week, 3587*, 102.

Tate, J., Mein, J., Freeman, H., & Maguire, G. (2006). Grey nomads: Health and health preparation of older travelers in remote Australia. *Australian Family Physician, 35*(1/2), 70-72.

Teaff, J.D., & Turpin, T. (1996). Travel and the elderly. *Parks & Recreation, 31*(6), 16-19.

Thomas, D., & Butts, F. (1998). Assessing leisure motivators and satisfaction of international Elderhostel participants. *Journal of Travel and Tourism Marketing, 7*, 31-38.

Tourism Queensland. (2008). Accessible tourism target markets: The ageing population in Australia. Retrieved from www.tq.com.au/fms/tq_corporate/special_interests/accessible/TQU7218%20Accessible%20Target%20Markets%20Trends%20&%20Insights_V2.pdf.

Walker, K. (2009). Aussie research shows importance of boomer travelers. Retrieved from www.thematuremarket.com/SeniorStrategic/boomer_travelers-10822-5.html.

Wang, K., Chen, J., & Chou, S. (2007). Senior tourists' purchasing decisions in group package tour. *Anatolia*, *18*(1), 139-154.

Wei, S., & Ruys, H. (1998). *Industry and senior perception survey*. Brisbane: Department of Families, Youth and Community Care.

World Tourism Organization (WTO). (2001). *Tourism 2020 vision: Global forecasts and profiles of market segments*. Madrid: Author.

Yarnal, C.M. (2004). Missing the boat? A playfully serious look at a group cruise tour experience. *Leisure Sciences*, *26*, 349-372.

You, X., & O'Leary, J.T. (1999). Destination behaviour of older UK travelers. *Tourism Recreation Research*, *24*, 23-34.

Zimmer, Z., Brayley, R.E., & Searle, M. (1995). Whether to go and where to go: Identification of important influences on senior's decisions to travel. *Journal of Travel Research*, *33*, 3-10.

Leisure in Long-Term Care

In part V, the transition into long-term care communities is addressed. In addition, the experiences of older adults in these communities are discussed.

In chapter 12, Sherry Dupuis, Colleen Whyte, and Jennifer Carson provide an overview of long-term care settings and discuss models, philosophies, and cultures associated with the various types of long-term care. Starting with the total institution underpinned by a biomedical approach, they suggest that leisure in such settings is largely viewed as therapy. The authors introduce several alternative approaches to long-term care, including person-centered, relationship-centered, and partnership-centered approaches, and they show how the role of leisure is shaped according to these philosophical approaches. Two therapeutic recreations specialists, Karen Megson-Dowling and Christy Parsons, write about their professional experiences working in long-term care. The chapter concludes with an extensive discussion on quality of life for older adults in long-term care settings and how leisure can enhance overall well-being.

Chapter 13, the last chapter in part V, examines the transition from independent community living to various types of long-term care. Elaine Wiersma and Stephanie Chesser review definitions of community before examining the transition process and the needs that motivate the change from independent living to long-term care settings. The authors describe the adjustment process and the characteristics of leisure in these settings. They point to the importance of maintaining social relationships in long-term settings and how leisure can facilitate this need. They also discuss the role of staff in these settings and how they can also promote social well-being of older adults. Benjamin Mireku contributes an international sidebar about caring for seniors in Africa.

CHAPTER 12

Leisure in Long-Term Care Settings

Sherry L. Dupuis ■ Colleen Whyte ■ Jennifer Carson

LEARNING OBJECTIVES

After reading this chapter, you will be able to

- explain what long-term care is and factors that influence the move to a long-term care setting,

- understand the culture of long-term care settings and the impact of the culture on residents and the provision of recreation and leisure within those settings,

- list alternative approaches to care and discuss the implications of these approaches for recreation and leisure,

- explain the meaning of *quality of life* as defined by residents and the role of leisure in enhancing quality of life in long-term care, and

- understand how to incorporate reflective practice into the provision of meaningful activities in long-term care.

Grace is an 82-year-old mother of 4 and grandmother of 11 who recently moved into a long-term care home (LTCH) after a fall in her own home resulted in a fractured hip and concussion. Living independently in her apartment since her husband died nine years ago, Grace was admitted to a local hospital for 12 weeks to recuperate. While at the hospital, Grace was assessed for placement and transitioned into an LTCH 30 minutes away from her home. Although Grace was initially overwhelmed by the commotion of institutional living and her heartbreak at leaving her two cats with a friend, in the past six weeks she has started to get to know her new neighbor across the hall and to enjoy the afternoon recreation programs. However, she wonders why her friends from the apartment building never come to visit. The routine of rising at 7 a.m. also frustrates Grace, since she considers herself a night owl and had always started her day after 10 a.m. In an attempt to make Grace feel more at home and reduce the boredom she has been complaining about, her two daughters have brought in some small furniture from her apartment as well as her quilting and knitting supplies, a small television, and countless photo albums and picture frames, but due to space restrictions, they are unable to bring her most cherished table set built by her husband.

When you think of long-term care, what comes to mind? How does the concept of long-term care differ from the concept of long-term care *settings*? What does Grace's story tell you about the experience of long-term care?

Long-term care is not a straightforward concept to define. It can refer specifically to residential facilities, such as nursing homes or homes for the aged, that provide care for people who are no longer able to fully care for themselves (Hollander, 2002). Alternatively, long-term care may describe a continuum of care, including services received at home such as home care and meal and day programs, hospital-based care, retirement homes, small group homes, supportive housing and assisted-living facilities, and nursing homes (Banerjee, 2009; Hollander, 2002). As described by the U.S. Senate Special Committee on Aging (2000), "Long-term care encompasses a wide array of medical, social, personal, and supportive and specialized housing services needed by individuals who have lost some capacity for self-care because of a chronic illness or disabling condition" (p. 154). In this chapter, we focus on those living environments designed for older adults who are no longer able to live independently in their own homes and who require 24-hour care and supervision within a secure setting over a prolonged period of time.

The proportion of older adults living in long-term care settings varies depending on where you are in the world. For example, the percentage of older adults living in LTCHs in Canada has been declining over the past several decades (Statistics Canada, 2007) but still remains higher in comparison to some other countries. In 2001, approximately 7% of all older Canadians lived in some type of health care facility (e.g., nursing home, hospital setting). This compares with 4.3% of people over the age of 65 who live in long-term care in the United States and 3.3% in countries within the European Union (Marin, Leichsenring, Rodrigues, & Huber, 2009).

The majority of Canadian residents living in LTCHs are 85 years or older (Statistics Canada, 2007). A profile of residents in long-term care also highlights its gendered nature. Although there is a similar proportion of men and women between the ages of 65 and 74 years, after 74 years of age, there are more women residing in long-term care, and by 85 years of age, women account for two-thirds of residents, "prompting many to note that long-term care is not just a health issue, but a woman's issue" (Banerjee, 2009, p. 34). Being female is not a risk factor in and of itself for long-term care; rather, other factors associated with being an older woman, such as higher life expectancy, lack of a spouse, and fewer income sources, contribute to greater numbers of women living in long-term care (Trottier, Martel, Houle, Berthelot, & Légaré, 2000).

Look back at Grace's story—what are some of the factors that might have contributed to her move to long-term care? There are a number of reasons why a person might move to long-term care. In most cases, older adults make the transition when their care needs are no longer able to be met in the community. This occurs when a person has a complex, chronic health condition (e.g., musculoskeletal disorder, stroke); an illness causing dementia (e.g., Alzheimer's disease); other mental health issues (e.g., depression); or a combination of health issues that cause significant functional limitations (Tomiak, Berthelot, & Mustard, 2000). Therefore, older adults living in long-term care settings tend to have limited mobility and independent ambulatory functioning and limitations in performing activities of daily living (ADLs) such as toileting, bathing, and eating. In addition, older adults are far more likely to be admitted to long-term care if they do not have a primary caregiver, such as a spouse or adult child, who is able to provide day-to-day care or if their caregiver is experiencing high stress due to the caregiving role and is no longer able to provide care. Higher levels of past service utilization, a recent hospital stay, and residency in a retirement or supervised housing facility are also associated with greater risk of moving to long-term care (Pitters, 2002).

Predominant Culture Within Long-Term Care Settings

Erving Goffman (1961) likened homes established for the care of older adults to **total institutions** (see also Wiersma and Chesser in this text). This concept refers to places where all aspects of daily life are conducted within one place, such as the LTCH, with limited or no access to the world outside its walls. Total institutions are characterized by "the attempt to handle all of the needs of whole blocks of people (e.g., patients, inmates, [older adults]) by a clearly separated supervisory staff operating within a tightly structured bureaucratic organization" (Teague & MacNeil, 1992, p. 221). Care within these environments is routinized and regimented, allowing little flexibility in how care is provided. It is assumed that the needs of residents living within a long-term care setting can be met solely within the confines of the facility and that this is the most cost- and time-efficient way to provide care to large groups of people.

Similar to the notion of total institutions, long-term care facilities have also been described as **closed environments** (Teague & MacNeil, 1992). Closed environments limit residents' opportunities for choice and control in their lives as well as their involvement in decision making about care, resulting in the disintegration of ties to the community and the connection to one's past life. An example of this might be George's situation. George participated in a day program in the community for a number of years. This provided his wife, Helen, with some much-needed respite and

provided George with an opportunity to meet new friends and learn new activities. George's wife, however, had a sudden health crisis of her own, and without other options, George was moved to an LTCH. Although George had loved his trips to the day program each week, once he moved to long-term care, policies did not allow George to participate in the community day program. His recreational needs were now only to be met by the LTCH. Think about your own recreational needs. Would they be met completely within an LTCH? Unfortunately, although new approaches and policies to long-term care have been emerging, research suggests that a total-institution or closed-environment approach is still evident in long-term care settings around the world (Dupuis, Smale, & Wiersma, 2005).

As LTCHs developed in North America, they drew on the acute **biomedical model of care** that was being used in hospitals at the time. Guidelines and regulations for long-term care reinforced this approach (Eliopoulos, 2010). The biomedical model constructs aging as a medical problem (Estes & Binney, 1989). Old age is seen as a process of decremental physical decline and is placed under the domain of biomedical practice. The focus is on meeting physical needs and the clinical treatment of symptoms and signs of disease. The health care professional is seen as the expert, the primary custodian of the necessary information to provide adequate care. Staff members are encouraged to be emotionally neutral and use standardized, objective measures in their assessment of patient outcomes. Thus, the patient is viewed as a passive recipient of care, and compliance with treatment is expected (Wade & Halligan, 2004).

Both the total-institution and closed-environment approach and biomedical philosophy have significant implications not only for residents in long-term care settings but also for the provision of recreation and leisure within those settings. Many studies have demonstrated that "older adults living in long-term care settings participate in fewer activities, spend larger amounts of time doing nothing, . . . have less social contact than their counterparts living in the community," and have few opportunities to participate in community (Dupuis et al., 2005, p. 278). As a consequence, feelings of isolation, loneliness, helplessness, boredom, decreased self-esteem, and depression are often reported by residents. It is not surprising, then, that a person's sense of self and self-worth can be threatened and changed within total institutions (Antonelli, Rubini, & Rassone, 2000; Hormuth, 1990).

Karen Megson-Dowling*

The decision to pursue a career working with the elderly came fairly naturally to me. Initially I viewed a career in therapeutic recreation (TR) and gerontology as a means of securing employment for years to come, given the aging baby boomer population. However, early in my career I realized this was more than just a job; it was an enriching experience from which I continue to learn every day. The richness in the relationships that I developed with the residents soon became a passion I craved to excel at. Every day provides a new and exciting opportunity to enhance the quality of life of our elderly population. The wisdom and experience that our elderly population are so willing to share is inspiring, and their desire to continually try to learn different things is motivating.

Karen Megson-Dowling.

I have spent the last 15 years working on a level 2 cognitive-support unit, so a typical day is never typical—which is one of the best things about my day, because I never know what to expect. There are, however, some common TR goals and themes that I try to provide each day, including physical, social, and emotional programs.

- Physical programs, such as gardening, walking group, sensory stimulation, and armchair exercise, are usually held between 10 a.m. and 12:30 p.m. since this is the best time for energy. The goals of these programs are strength, endurance, coordination, fine and gross motor skills, mobility, and ambulation.

- Social programs, such as pet therapy, music groups, baking, and community outings, are usually held between 2 and 3 p.m., following the usual cycle of socializing after a meal. The goals of these programs are to develop social skills, self-esteem, and a sense of community.

- Emotional programs, such as one-on-one interactions, horticultural therapy, sensory stimulation, reading, and experiencing the Snoezelen room (a multisensory environment), are usually held between 3 and 4 p.m. as fatigue settles in and it becomes a more emotional time of the day. The goal of these programs is an opportunity for release and self-expression.

In addition to structured programs, I try to provide opportunities for spontaneity. My office is located directly beside the dining room, which provides both myself and the residents the opportunity to drop in for a visit at any time. This is often when the residents feel most comfortable sharing their thoughts and feelings; some of the best conversations have taken place in this informal setting. I think one of the most rewarding parts of my job is the feeling of safety and security that I am able to provide to the residents. The residents might not remember my name or know what my job entails, but they do know that I do not wear a uniform, am not threatening, and always have the time to listen.

I think the most important thing to remember is that residents value the time they spend with you regardless of the activity. Residents enjoy socializing, contributing to the group, and being involved in meaningful activities. Being with the resident involves humor, a unique approach to each resident, and communication that is reciprocal.

*Karen Megson-Dowling works as a recreation therapist at the Sunnybrook Health Sciences Centre in North York, Ontario.

Recreation and leisure from this approach to long-term care are most typically viewed as therapy, valued primarily as a clinical intervention used to reach some greater end (Sylvester, 1985). Recreation is understood as a viable treatment in managing challenging, aggressive, disruptive, or disturbing behaviors (e.g., Buettner & Fitzsimmons, 2003) and used as a rehabilitation tool to restore functional abilities (e.g., Brill et al., 1998). Recreation assessments tend to focus on measuring functional levels in order to identify areas of need for treatment and rehabilitation (e.g., Boothman & Savell, 2004). With a focus on biomedical aspects of care, emotional, social, spiritual, and environmental aspects of wellness receive minimal consideration (Eliopoulos, 2010), and little attention is given to continued abilities and how residents themselves think about recreation and leisure in their lives.

Let's return to Grace. What would recreation and leisure look like for Grace in a long-term care facility dominated by a total-institution and biomedical approach? What are some of the limitations of such an approach to recreation and leisure in LTCHs?

Alternative Approaches to Care in Long-Term Care Settings

Mounting criticisms of the biomedical approach to care have resulted in calls for a reexamination of the culture within long-term care (Kane, 2001; Pioneer Network, 2010; Rahman & Schnelle, 2008; Thomas, 1996). Since the early 1990s, there has been a shift in the philosophy of long-term care from more traditional, top-down approaches focused on simply providing care to more humanistic, resident-centered care philosophies that foster thriving and living (Clark, 2002; Nolan, Davies, Brown, Keady, & Nolan, 2004). This shift in philosophy emphasizes the building of relationships among residents, family members, and staff, with a more respect-oriented focus and decision making being initiated at the ground level (Ragsdale & McDougall, Jr., 2008). Critical of the biomedical emphasis on technical tasks of physical care without regard for affective or communicative aspects (Thomas, 1996), advocates for **culture change** seek to restore the interactional nature of living and working within long-term care.

Proponents of culture change support principles such as

- resident-led decision making in which residents have choices with regard to their care and are encouraged to make their own decisions about personal issues;
- the recognition of the whole person and a fuller appreciation of the holistic needs required for quality of life;
- the creation of a homelike atmosphere;
- close relationships among staff and residents;
- staff empowerment that moves decision making as close to the residents as possible, if not with the resident themselves; and
- a collaborative decision-making process in which frontline staff and residents are included in the planning of menus, activities, and daily routines (Hooyman & Kiyak, 2008; Koren, 2010).

Under the umbrella of culture change, alternative approaches have emerged from person-centered, relationship-centered, and authentic partnership approaches that all have important implications for the recreation and leisure profession. These approaches have had significant influences on the quality of living for people residing in LTCHs and their family members and staff. In a literature review of client-, family-, patient-, person-, and relationship-centered care, Hughes, Bamford, and May (2008) concluded that these initiatives all shared a number of core elements, including

- respect for individuality and values,
- individual meaning,
- promotion of the therapeutic alliance,
- recognition of social context and relationships,
- an inclusive model of health and well-being,
- legitimation of expert lay knowledge,
- shared responsibility,
- open communication,
- autonomy, and
- valuing of the professional as person.

The authors write that these elements "work as they do because of the interconnecting and interrelating nature of the fibres running through them" (p. 460). The following section outlines all three broad philosophical approaches to care and their application to recreation and leisure.

Person-Centered Care

The **person-centered** approach is rooted in the humanistic philosophical traditions of Carl Rogers (1961) and his description of the *helping relationship* (McCormack, 2004). According to Rogers (1956), if one person can provide a genuine relationship, the other person will "discover within [him- or herself] the capacity to use that relationship for growth, and change and personal development will occur" (p. 10). Within the context of long-term care, this approach has been advanced through the influential work of Tom Kitwood and his peers at the Bradford Dementia Group. In his seminal book on person-centered care within the dementia context, *Dementia reconsidered: The person comes first*, Kitwood (1997) outlined the importance of respectful, trusting, and understanding relationships to the maintenance of personhood. The key feature of this care philosophy is that it places the person, not disease or illness, at the center of all care decisions. Choices are offered to residents and all decisions are in keeping with the person's wishes, desires, and aspirations. Person-centered care focuses on the continued strengths and capabilities of people, considering what they are still able to do rather than what they are no longer able to do (Dupuis, 2010). Person-centered care recognizes that no matter what physical or cognitive challenges people face, everyone has a future and is still able to experience good quality of life and well-being. The four major elements of Kitwood's person-centered approach that are relevant to long-term care include the following (Brooker, 2007, p. 216):

1. **Valuing all people living in long-term care and those who care for them.** Person-centered care is about valuing all people.

2. **Treating people as individuals.** Residents are considered as individual men and women with all their unique strengths and vulnerabilities.

3. **Looking at the world from the perspective of the resident.** The person's subjective experience is seen as reality.

4. **Nurturing a positive social environment in which the resident can experience relative well-being.** People are given the opportunity for social and loving relationships with those around them.

Applying a person-centered philosophy to the practice of recreation and leisure shifts our focus from the traditional highly structured, large-group diversional activities and instead encourages resident involvement in a variety of activities based on individual interest and abilities (McNown Johnson & Rhodes, 2007). It means providing residents and family members with opportunities for meaningful engagement (Train, Nurock, Manela, Kitchen, & Livingston, 2005). Within such an approach, residents are perceived as individuals, and daily activities and care routines are provided in a more flexible way. All care staff are supported in working together to provide a program of meaningful activities and experiences tailored to residents' preferences and needs. Rather than the traditional professional roles of telling, advising, managing, and controlling, staff look for ways to become better listeners, explorers, participators, and clarifiers in their relationships with residents (Pedlar, Hornibrook, & Haasen, 2001). From this perspective, it is vital for staff to recognize and value the life history, personality, and routines that are important to the resident as well as the resident's current preferences, values, interests, and perception of needs.

Person-centered care practices are not without their critics. Some have shown how person-centered care is challenging in practice, especially when practitioners do not take the time to listen to what residents are saying. For example, de Medeiros (2009) examined care plans, interviewed family members and staff about their views of individual residents, and then compared all of these perspectives with those of the residents. She found that the residents' views of themselves and what was important to them did not coincide with staff or family views. For instance, for one of the residents, Rose, the care plan listed reminiscing and bingo as those things most important to her. The family and activity staff felt that visiting family was the most important to her, while the care staff indicated that breakfast and having a bowel movement were the most important. On the other hand, Rose, a former teacher, indicated that teaching and helping young people was important to her. Thus, finding effective ways to capture and understand resident perspectives becomes critical, and when we get it wrong, it can greatly limit opportunities for engagement with what is truly important to the person.

Nolan and his colleagues (Nolan, Ryan, Enderby, & Reid, 2002) critiqued person-centered care for other reasons. They argued that person-centered care fails to "fully capture the interdependencies and reciprocities that underpin caring relationships" (p. 203) and does not recognize the "mutual appreciation of each other's knowledge, recognition of its equal worth, and its sharing in a symbolic way to enhance and facilitate joint understanding" (p. 204). In other words, person-centered care focuses primarily on the resident without recognizing the interactional nature of caring relationships. Thus, a call for a wider and more inclusive approach to care was issued that not only focuses on the person but also engages family members and staff—relationship-centered care.

Relationship-Centered Care

The term **relationship-centered care** was first used by Tresolini and the Pew-Fetzer Task Force (1994) in a report outlining health care conditions within the United States. Describing health care as "an individual, disease-oriented, subspecialty-focused model that has led to a focus on cure at all costs, resulting in care that is fragmented, episodic, and often unsatisfying for both patients and practitioners" (p.16), the authors promoted a paradigm shift with the enhancement of relationships among practitioners and the people with whom they worked as a vehicle for caring, healing, and community. This approach recognizes that quality care depends on strong relationships among all those involved, including the resident, family members, and staff, and it respects and values the perceptions of all involved in the care context. As such, ideas of relationship-centered care are now coming to the forefront of health services.

Within the context of long-term care, relationship-centered approaches are seen as a natural progression from person-centered care. Relationship-centered care adopts a broader perspective and takes into account the social nature of being. Whereas person-centered care focuses on individuals and their needs, relationship-centered care values interdependence and focuses on relationship building. In valuing interdependence, "a reciprocal relationship develops in which both parties grow as a result" (Nolan et al., 2004, p. 47). Proponents of relationship-centered care argue that we can only fully understand people's life experience by situating them within a "rich matrix of relationships and socio-cultural beliefs, an appreciation of which is essential to any attempt to understand the experience of growing older, or to provide meaningful care or services to older adults" (Clark, 2002, p. 300).

At the heart of relationship-centered care practices is the **senses framework** (Nolan, Lundh, Grant, & Keady, 2003; Nolan et al., 2004; Ryan, Nolan, Reid, & Enderby, 2008). The senses framework comprises six senses that are thought to act as a prerequisite for the development of good relationships within the context of care and service delivery. The term *sense* was selected to reflect the subjective and perceptual nature of the important determinants of care for older people, their families, and staff (Nolan, Davies, & Grant, 2002). The senses framework "promotes a way of understanding the factors necessary to creating positive relationships, and highlights some

Eden Alternative

According to William Thomas, a Harvard-educated geriatrician and founder of the Eden Alternative, traditional long-term care practices emphasizing disease and illness perpetuate the three plagues of loneliness, helplessness, and boredom that are at the foundation of resident suffering within long-term care (Thomas, 1996). In *Life worth living: How someone you love can still enjoy life in a nursing home—The Eden Alternative in action*, Thomas (1996) outlines his misgivings with the overemphasis on treatment at the expense of the care environment: "Today, the resident's life is analyzed in great detail, dissected and recombined into a treatment plan that defines every hour of every day of his or her life" (p. 19). The Eden Alternative, the most recognized model of culture change (Ragsdale & McDougall, Jr., 2008), follows three key principles of care. First, it is essential to recognize and promote each person's capacity for personal growth. Second, practitioners must focus on the needs and capacities of the residents rather than on the needs and requirements of the institution. Third, long-term nurturing care is emphasized (Thomas, 1994). Seeking to overcome the institutional nature of long-term care, homes that follow the Eden Alternative seek to normalize the physical environment with the addition of pets, plants, and children (McNown Johnson, & Rhodes, 2007).

of the structures and interactions that maintain such relationships" (Ryan et al., 2008, p. 86). The premise of relationship-centered care is that quality care can only be delivered when *all* the groups involved (i.e., older adults, family members, and staff) experience the following (Nolan et al., 2004, p. 49):

- A sense of security—to feel safe within relationships
- A sense of continuity—to experience links and consistency over time
- A sense of belonging—to feel part of things
- A sense of purpose—to have a personally meaningful goal or goals
- A sense of achievement—to make progress toward a desired goal or goals
- A sense of significance—to feel that you matter

Often criticized for being diversional, traditional nursing-home activities such as bingo, arts and crafts, and current events offer opportunities for busyness and short-lived pleasures (Buettner & Martin, 1995; Voelkl, Battisto, Carson, & McGuire, 2004). In order to foster the development of relationships through the provision of meaningful activities, "an organizational shift must occur, encouraging all staff, from housekeeping to administration, to bring their own interests and talents to work so that they can be used to develop meaningful relationships and enhance quality of life" (Voelkl et al., p. 26). The focus moves from outcome to process, with the central aim of developing and nurturing strong relationships.

Leisure and recreation within this approach are valued as safe spaces where enjoyment of being with others and enlivening relationships are experienced (Sullivan, Pedlar, & Miller, 2002). Related to the senses framework, a sense of security, belonging, continuity, purpose, achievement, and significance and what these mean for residents and family members are considered in the initial assessment. This care approach would then involve open negotiation with both residents and family members as to the type of services they would appreciate (Ryan et al., 2008). Ultimately, staff members would use this intimate knowledge of residents and families to provide leisure activities and experiences that would maintain the most valued aspects of life. Relationship-centered care further emphasizes staff needs, placing responsibility on administration to support the health and wellness of staff, and the time needed to develop and maintain strong relationships with residents and others in the care context.

Although a relationship-centered approach has moved care beyond the individual and offers an understanding of the characteristics of strong relationships, it provides little guidance on how these relationships are developed or maintained over time (Adams, 2005). In addition, all relationships have inherent power dynamics and hierarchies that can marginalize those perceived to be the weakest in the relationship—the residents. What was needed was "a more reflective and critical way of looking at how power is exercised through relationships" so that everyone is equally valued in relationships (Adams, 2005, p. 6).

Partnership Approaches to Care

Building on relationship-centered approaches, some researchers have argued for a move toward partnerships among the resident, family mem-

Family Model of Care

According to Voelkl and colleagues (2004), life-enriching environments that promote familial bonds among residents, family members, and staff are a result of a collaborative culture, a homelike setting, and support for meaningful activities. First, a collaborative organizational culture that provides opportunities for residents, family members, and staff to be involved and ensures that all members of the community feel cared for and nurtured is thought to increase the sense of belonging experienced within the community. Second, a homelike setting that provides ample opportunity for engagement in meaningful relationships and activities (e.g., a dedicated living room for socializing) fosters a sense of equal ownership among all members. Third, opportunities for meaningful activities that incorporate the mutual interests of residents, staff, and family members are believed to be essential not only for maintaining residents' meaningful social roles and activities but also for promoting relationships among residents, staff, and family members.

bers, and professional carers within long-term care (Adams & Clarke, 1999; Dupuis, Gillies, Mantle, Loiselle, & Sadler, 2008; Dupuis et al., in press). This interpretation of the **partnership approach** allows us to move "beyond consensus and collaboration to a mutual appreciation of each other's knowledge" (Adams & Clarke, 1999, p. 5). Authentic partnerships recognize and value the perspectives of all and actively incorporate all voices in decision making (Adams & Clarke, 1999). In working directly with people with dementia, their family members, and professionals on a number of partnership initiatives, Dupuis and colleagues (Dupuis et al., 2008, in press) identified a number of principles and enabling factors necessary to promote authentic partnerships and support residents in the decision-making process. Authentic partnerships are characterized by

- a genuine regard for self and others,
- synergistic relationships where the collective wisdom of the group is seen as richer than the knowledge and skills of any one person, and
- a focus on the process that allows for supportive modifications and creative responses to issues developed from new learning that happens throughout the process.

Authentic partnerships are sustained over time by connecting and committing to others, creating a safe space where all can feel a sense of physical and emotional comfort, valuing diverse perspectives, establishing and maintaining open communication, and conducting critical reflection and dialogue on a regular basis.

A recent example can help illustrate how a partnership approach plays out in practice. The development of a new recreation resource guide brought together people with dementia, family members, professionals (including recreation practitioners), and researchers to work collaboratively to better understand the meanings attached to leisure for people with dementia in various settings and how to support people with dementia in maintaining meaningful activities (Dupuis, Whyte, Carson, Sadler, & Meschino, 2010). In working together and valuing all perspectives in decision making, they came to understand the importance of leisure as experience (rather than activity) for people with dementia and that a new approach to assessment and evaluation was needed in order to ensure meaningful experiences for people with dementia. Rather than developing an assessment tool *for* people with dementia, researchers, professionals, and family members are partnering directly *with* people with dementia to develop an assessment tool and evaluation approach that is most relevant to them as well as to identify strategies to better support people with dementia in continuing to thrive and live a quality life. These strategies incorporate the perspectives and opinions of all key stakeholders involved in the long-term care context, including those of people with dementia.

Figure 12.1 summarizes the key ideas of the three alternative care philosophies. Why is it important to understand the various philosophical approaches to long-term care settings? All philosophical traditions have underlying assumptions,

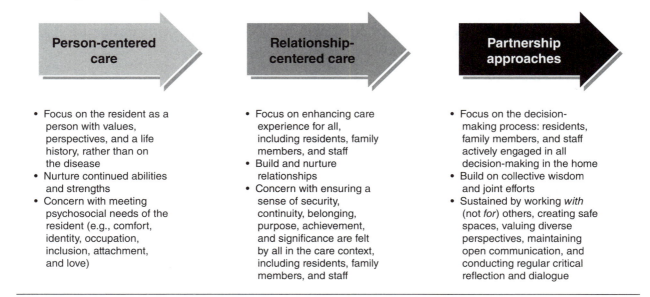

Figure 12.1 Key ideas of three alternative care philosophies.

and these assumptions play a large role in guiding practice. They influence recreation practitioners by supporting or not supporting what is possible in long-term care and by shaping the approach to recreation and leisure in these settings.

Quality of Life Through Leisure in Long-Term Care Settings

Let's move now to a discussion on issues relevant to quality of life in long-term care settings. Is it possible for residents in long-term care to receive excellent health care and yet experience a poor quality of life? This question asks us to consider the difference between quality of care and quality of life, a distinction central to nursing-home reforms and culture change. Although the quality of care provided within long-term care undoubtedly contributes to residents' quality of life, they are not one and the same. One of the most significant acknowledgments of this distinction was set forth in the Omnibus Budget Reconciliation Act of 1987 (OBRA), landmark legislation in the United States that ushered in a series of initiatives designed to improve both quality of care and quality of life in long-term care. Among these initiatives is the mandate that all LTCHs provide "activities designed to meet the interests and the physical, mental, and psychosocial well-being of each resident" (OBRA, 1987, section 1395i-3).

In Canada, legislation on long-term care requires that facilities ensure (a) the provision of supplies and appropriate equipment for the recreational and leisure programs without charge to the residents; (b) the development, implementation, and communication of a schedule of recreation and activity programs that are offered during days, evenings, and weekends; (c) a range of indoor and outdoor recreation, leisure, outings, and social activities that are of a frequency and type to benefit all residents of the home; (d) opportunities for resident and family input into the development and scheduling of recreation programs and activities; and (e) support to help residents participate in activities that may be of interest to them if they are not able to do so independently (Ontario Ministry of Health and Long-Term Care, 2010). These initiatives recognize that quality of life means more than just quality care and that opportunities for leisure and meaningful activity are important to quality of life.

Quality of Life in Long-Term Care

Following OBRA (1987), subsequent reforms and culture change initiatives throughout North America and beyond (e.g., Pioneer Network, 2010; Thomas, 1996) have urged long-term care providers to focus on living, providing excellent health care without making it the central focus. Thus, many contend that quality of life should be the highest priority in long-term care (Edelman, Fulton, Kuhn, & Chang, 2005; Ettema, Dröes, de Lange, Mellenbergh, & Ribbe, 2005; Kane, 2001, 2003; Schölzel-Dorenbos et al., 2007; Whitehouse & Rabins, 1992). But what, specifically, is quality of life? How is it measured and by whom? The assessment of quality of life in long-term care is not a simple endeavor. Perhaps the late M. Powell Lawton (1997) said it best when he explained, "It only takes a short dip into the sea of writing about quality of life to discern that its appeal derives in a major way from its ability to mean anything to anybody—it is only an illusion that consensus exists" (p. 47). **Quality of life** means different things at different times to different people. Take a moment to reflect on the following questions about your quality of life: How do you define it? What does it mean to you? What is the quality of your life? What are the important domains of living that bring meaning, well-being, and contentment to your life? How would you prioritize those domains? Whose judgment can determine your quality of life?

Not only does the global concept of quality of life lack a generally accepted definition, but the life-altering impact of living in long-term care certainly affects aspects of daily life and relationships, thus altering definitions further (Kane et al., 2005). There are more than 1,000 scales available to measure quality of life (Thorgrimson et al., 2003), several of which are specific to long-term care. Conceptualized and informed by a variety of sources, each identifies and prioritizes various domains of what constitutes quality of life. For example, Kane (2001, 2003) developed quality-of-life measures for long-term care along the following 11 domains: security, comfort, meaningful activity, relationships, enjoyment of food, dignity, autonomy, privacy, individuality, spiritual well-being, and functional competence. In comparison, the Quality of Life–Alzheimer's Disease (QOL-AD) scale (Logsdon, Gibbons, McCurry, & Teri, 1999), which was revised for long-term care (Edelman et al., 2005), evaluates quality of life with these

15 items: physical health, energy, mood, memory, living situation, family, friends, ability to do things for fun, ability to take care of self, ability to make choices, relationships with people who work here, ability to keep busy, ability to live with others, self overall, and life overall. How similar are these domains to the domains you identified as being important to you?

When we compare measures, we see similarities and differences. Add to this the tendency for different respondents (e.g., residents, family members, and long-term care staff) to provide different answers and we can surmise that the quality of one's life depends on who you ask. For example, both Kane's measures (Kane et al., 2005) and the QOL-AD (Sloane et al., 2005) demonstrated low levels of agreement when administered to both residents and proxy respondents. Kane et al. conclude "that neither family members nor staff can confidently be expected to report the QOL [quality of life] of NF [nursing facility] residents the same way as the residents do themselves" (2005, p. S322). Parse (1996) reiterates this:

Professional Profile

Christy Parsons*

In my role as recreation and community partnerships consultant, I provide support and leadership to our directors of recreation and their recreation teams. I currently have the opportunity to work with 10 LTCHs and provide support in areas such as program innovation, community interface, education, human resources, administration responsibilities, revenue generation, new facility start-up, and special events. A large part of my role includes acting as an advocate to apply innovative principles to the research, design, implementation, and evaluation of recreation programs and services. I also provide support to the recreation teams as they investigate and integrate best practices in innovative programming in recreation and leisure services for older adults within long-term care.

Christy Parsons.

I am passionate about working with older adults and I learn so much from our residents on a daily basis. Our recreation teams strive to provide meaningful and exciting leisure opportunities for our residents to enhance the quality of their lives. What I truly love about my role is building relationships with residents, staff, family members, and volunteers to collaborate in creating a home for our residents where the possibilities are endless. I believe this is an exciting time in long-term care since we have shifted our focus to providing resident-centered care at its best. It is an honor to serve our residents and the exceptional recreation teams that place a high value on life purpose and satisfaction for each resident.

*Christy Parsons works as a recreation and community partnerships consultant at Schlegel Seniors Villages in Kitchener, Ontario.

Photo courtesy of Murray Alzheimer Research and Education Program.

Who can determine the quality of a person's life? . . . Only the person's own description discloses his or her quality of life. Only the person—there—living the life can describe its quality. . . . This is true of all persons—even those who have been designated by medical diagnoses as having some "cognitive impairment." (p. 126)

In other words, in evaluating quality of life in long-term care, it is the resident's assessment, including residents living with memory loss, that is most important and accurate.

Quantifiable approaches to measuring quality of life may "ignore the symbolic nature and meaning of life to the individual" (Bond & Corner, 2001, p. 101). In their article titled, "Giving Voice to Expressions of Quality of Life for Persons Living With Dementia Through Story, Music, and Art," Jonas-Simpson and Mitchell (2005) offer the following description, a perfect illustration of the symbolic nature and meaning of quality of life:

One participant with severe impairment created a painting of a cabin on the Arabian sea and sand where he described his quality of life as the past and present all at once. In describing the grey and blue brush strokes he said, "veil in the sky . . . peace, peace, and quiet . . . soldiers sleeping . . . waves on the ocean." This quiet contentment is felt when viewing his painting. (p. 56)

Increasingly, quality-of-life assessments are including the perspectives of residents living in long-term care, but often their subjective accounts are limited to self-reports on predetermined response items within domains that may or may not be personally relevant (Dröes et al., 2006; van der Roest et al., 2007). If an evaluation of quality of life fails to include the perceptions of the person whose quality of life is being investigated, or if it fails to assess the most meaningful domains, then that evaluation will not truly reflect the situation. When residents living with dementia in a Canadian LTCH were asked what quality of life means for them, they mentioned feeling content, the importance of relationships, choosing an attitude for living onward, feeling worthy, living with loss, wishes for freedom amid the frustrations with restrictions, struggles with thinking and communicating, and persisting life patterns (Jonas-Simpson & Mitchell, 2005).When Droes et al. (2006) conducted interviews with residents of a psychogeriatric nursing home in the Netherlands, they identified several quality-of-life domains: affect, self-esteem and self-image, attachment, social contact, enjoyment of activities, physical and mental health, financial situation, security

and privacy, self-determination and freedom, being useful and giving meaning to life, and spirituality. Nonetheless, in both examples, we see the key role that leisure can play in enhancing quality of life in long-term care.

Leisure and Quality of Life in Long-Term Settings

Similar to the subjective and multidimensional nature of quality of life, the concept of leisure within long-term care is a complex yet vital matter. Leisure has been identified as the greatest contributor to the life satisfaction and quality of life of older adults (Lloyd & Auld, 2002; Marshall & Hutchinson, 2001; Voelkl, Galecki, & Fries, 1996) and essential to aging well (Dupuis, 2008). Recreation and leisure opportunities have a unique role to play in the maintenance and enhancement of quality of life in long-term care settings, providing a sense of meaning, purpose, pleasure, and accomplishment as well as opportunities to socialize, assist others, and enhance self-esteem (Jenkins, Pienta, & Horgas, 2002; Marshall & Hutchinson, 2001). Participation in leisure and recreation continues when experiences are meaningful to the individual (Ragheb, 1996). Therefore, an important role of people working in long-term care is to assist in providing meaningful opportunities for leisure.

But what is leisure? Similar to our discussion regarding quality of life, leisure, too, means different things at different times to different people. As Lee, Dattilo, and Howard (1994) explain, "Leisure is not a unitary concept, but is often composed of many characteristics. . . . The experience of leisure is transitory and complex and people's interpretation of leisure experiences change over time" (p. 202). Leisure can be characterized as time, recreation or activity, state of mind, places and spaces, or cultural context (Henderson, 2008). If we focus on examining what residents did in the past as a way of identifying leisure interests, will we be able to understand what leisure means for residents today?

Leisure within long-term care is most often characterized as activity—meaningful activity, therapeutic activity, recreational activity, and so on. The focus here is on the types of activities provided. Others have examined the meaning of leisure for people living with dementia in both the community and long-term care and have found that many describe leisure not as an activity but as an experience (Dupuis et al., 2010). People with dementia most valued experiences that provided opportunities to be oneself, make a difference, have fun, seek freedom, be with others, find balance, and grow and develop (Dupuis et al., 2010). Leisure can provide meaningful opportunities for continued engagement in life. It provides a space where we can be all that we can be, where we can feel valued and a sense of belonging, where we can work toward our aspirations and goals, and, as described by Renwick and Brown (1996), continue being, belonging, and becoming (Dupuis, 2006).

What happens to the leisure experience when activities are delivered or prescribed on a structured basis? Long-term care provides a context for much debate within the field of therapeutic recreation, as well as other allied health sciences, as professionals attempt to reconcile two streams of arguably opposing thought. One stream embodies the humanistic, person- and relationship-centered, partnership values of the culture change movement with its emphasis on living, empowerment, collaboration, and choice. The other stream forwards a message of biomedical efficiency, that is, given the societal recognition of the increased demand for health care services and the growing scarcity of health care resources, such as long-term care workers, it is argued that effective health care must also be efficient. In efforts to improve consistency and potentially reduce costs, many long-term care disciplines have prepared evidence-based practice guidelines aimed at reducing the variability of how best to assess and treat selected clinical problems (Schnelle & Reuben, 1999). The *American Therapeutic Recreation Association's (ATRA) Dementia Practice Guidelines for Treating Difficult Behaviors* (Buettner & Fitzsimmons, 2003) offers an example of this evidence-based approach. However, this message of efficient treatment may be incongruous with the promotion of leisure and quality of life. Pedlar and colleagues (2001) explain:

> Focusing on treatment-outcomes has tended to diminish many of the beneficial characteristics of leisure (Hemingway, 1986; Lahey, 1996; Mobily, 1996; Sylvester, 1998). This result is because leisure experience involves spontaneity and internal motivation. As such, leisure is essentially person focused (Coleman & Iso-Ahola, 1993). However, if [residents'] activities are prescribed and they are uninterested in engaging in them, as is all too often the case when the treatment-outcomes approach is followed, it is unlikely that leisure will be experienced. (p. 16)

Again, there are two streams of thought—one that promotes rights, respect, being treated as a unique individual, and quality of life, the other

driving standardized assessments, efficient treatments, consistent practices, increased monitoring, and enforcement. It may be argued that not only does the latter stream shift our attention back to quality of care and away from quality of life, but it also has the potential to *harm* long-term care residents. Years ago, a surprising article that is seldom cited in the field of recreation and leisure studies was published in the *Journal of Elder Abuse and Neglect*: "Therapeutic Recreation for the Institutionalized Elderly: Choice or Abuse" (Hall & Bocksnick, 1995). How could therapeutic recreation ever be construed as abuse? The researchers explained how recreation therapists' well-intended but paternalistic agendas led to the dynamic of restricted choice among residents (i.e., abuse). Through the execution of the recreation therapists' agendas, the residents' behaviors were "externally controlled and their needs for self-determination, control and autonomy regarding program participation were undermined" (p. 49).

It is important to consider how often the agendas of well-intended professionals are expressed at the expense of leisure and the risk of restricted choice. According to Sylvester (1987), "Leisure activity is the celebration of freedom at its crowning point" (p. 81). Advocates of culture change support this view and urge that in addition to planned activities, opportunities for meaningful engagement and spontaneity—quality experiences—in long-term care should also be available around the clock (Pioneer Network, 2010). According to *Gentlecare* author Moyra Jones (1999), meaningful activities are preferably self-motivated, provide a sense of joy and purpose, and are free from stress. Activities with characteristics such as these promote the *experience* of leisure.

The experience of leisure activities within long-term care stands in marked contrast to the experience of diversional or therapeutically structured activities. One just needs to look at a typical activity calendar in any long-term care setting to get a sense of the activities provided throughout the day. Diversional activities—the traditional fun and games at the core of many activity programs—provide superficial, temporary, and short-lived pleasures with little active engagement by residents (Buettner & Martin, 1995; Ragheb, 1996). Although there may certainly be a time and place for diversional activities, such as bingo, their overall contributions to quality of life are likely minimal and most certainly depend on what is meaningful to the residents.

Photo courtesy of Corrie Bradley.

Residents find creative ways to have fun.

A number of studies identify residents' preference for flexible, unstructured activities over more traditional, structured activity programs. For example, Kovach and Henschel (1996) studied the participation and behavior of long-term care residents with dementia during various therapeutic activities led by activity therapists with two different facilitation styles: structured and unstructured. They found that when the activity therapist used a mellow, less structured approach, the individual agendas of the residents were more likely to be expressed. Though the less structured approach was associated with more dozing, distraction, and at times disengagement, it was also associated with "more spontaneous self-expression—more revealing and releasing of self" (p. 40), which is a hallmark of leisure experiences. Similarly, Voelkl and Nicholson (1992) report that residents perceived a high level of pleasure and choice while engaged in unstructured activities, the most popular being visiting with family, friends, and other residents; helping or assisting other residents; and, of course, eating. In fact, the typical activities of older adults generally are not counted among the most valued pursuits of the leisure industry (Neumayer, Gattuso, Saw, & Jelinek,

1998). With this in mind, recreation and leisure professionals need to think more creatively about what leisure can mean and take on less formal roles to meet participants' quality-of-life needs.

One of the ways that recreation and leisure professionals working in long-term care can take on less formal roles in the promotion of meaningful leisure experiences and the enhancement of quality of life is to begin with the initial encounter between a professional and a resident traditionally known as the *assessment*. Perhaps one of the best examples of a less formal and more person-centered assessment comes from an action research project by Pedlar and colleagues (2001). In this study, a group of recreation therapists aimed to understand the assessment process from two perspectives, that of the resident and of the therapist. They wanted to explore the ways in which the assessment process supported or thwarted a person-centered approach to service delivery. Through the use of self-reflective practice, observations, and resident interviews, the therapist-researchers determined that their original assessment tool, a standardized leisure inventory designed to determine leisure interests and strengths, stifled the flow of conversation and involved terminology that was unfamiliar to the residents. Many aspects of the assessment were found to be "confusing, time-consuming and inappropriate" (p. 21), resulting in a disjointed discussion and unnatural exchange. Their findings also revealed an "unproductive focus on [residents'] past leisure interests" (p. 22), and following the assessment process, most residents still did not understand the role of the recreation therapist.

For the therapist-researchers, this action research project provided an opportunity to step back and examine their practice. Recognizing the disconnect that took place between themselves and the residents in the assessment process, they developed a person-centered Personal Leisure Profile to replace the previous assessment tool. The profile poses five simple questions (Pedlar et al., 2001, p. 27):

1. What do you enjoy? (past and present leisure interests)

2. What about that do you enjoy? (characteristics of pursuits that are enjoyed)

3. Recently, what has brought enjoyment or happiness to your day? (current leisure status)

4. What is stopping you from enjoying _____ (or some of those activities)? (barriers)

5. Is there something that you have always wanted to do? (dreams)

These questions offer an assessment style that is flexible, natural, relevant, and individualized. Moving away from a focus on activities, it allows residents to identify the range of ways they experience enjoyment in life. In addition to the Personal Leisure Profile, the therapist-researchers also created the following protocols for their recreation therapy department (Pedlar et al., 2001, pp. 25-27):

1. Be truly present with individuals by listening, accepting, and empathizing with their reality.

2. Use understandable language that is familiar to the individual.

3. Ensure the individual understands the purpose of therapist questions and actions.

4. Contribute personal experiences and ideas to the exchange of information.

5. Eliminate assessment tools in the first exchange and focus on individuals' current leisure interests.

6. Provide real and meaningful opportunities for choice.

Reflection and Practice

Think about the previous six questions in relation to your own life. What things would you want a recreation professional to know about you to ensure that you lived a meaningful life in long-term care? What brings you enjoyment? What kinds of experiences would you want to enjoy if you were living in a long-term care setting? Think about using these questions to interview an older adult in your life. How might you use what you learn from the questions to support the person in having a fulfilling and meaningful leisure lifestyle?

Once we understand the meaning of leisure from the resident's perspective and the types of experiences important to the resident and we work with them to facilitate meaningful experiences, how will we know our efforts are making a difference? Within a culture change initiative focused more on person- and relationship-centered care and partnership approaches, how we document and evaluate success also changes. Rather than focusing on the number of residents who attended an activity, the number of programs offered, and whether or not we are achieving outcomes determined by the recreation professional, the focus is on the process and documenting how we are working to facilitate meaningful experiences. What becomes important is recognizing those indicators in the moment that suggest residents might be experiencing something meaningful to them. These indicators can include a verbal response made by a resident as well as other indicators such as facial expressions and body language (e.g., muscle relaxation, smiling or laughing, humming, connecting with others such as through touch). So, if we return to the experiences identified by Dupuis and colleagues (2010) as meaningful to people living with dementia—being oneself, having fun, making a difference, seeking freedom, being with others, finding balance, and growing and developing—success would be found in the ways we were able to help residents experience these.

Being the best professional we can be requires a commitment to **self-reflective practice**. Self-reflective practice involves regular critical reflection on our professional judgments, assumptions, and actions and the impacts these have on others. It takes great courage and openness to engage in the process of self-reflection, but much can be gained from critically reflecting on both the positive and negative experiences we have and learning from them in order to identify ways to improve our practice (Miller & Pedlar, 2006; Mitchell, Jonas-Simpson, & Dupuis, 2006; Schön, 1983). When reflection guides practice, we continually ask ourselves (Mitchell et al., 2006):

- What happened today that I reacted well to?
- What happened today that I could have reacted better to?
- What judgments did I make in that situation?
- What have I learned from the experience?
- What could I do to improve the situation next time?

Through reflection, a practitioner "can criticize the tacit understandings that have grown up around the repetitive experiences of a specialized practice, and can make new sense of the situations of uncertainty or uniqueness which he [or she] may allow [him- or herself] to practice" (Schön, 1983, p. 61). Schön's self-reflective practice moves us away from the science of technical rationality and positivism and "recognizes that there simply is no one-size-fits-all solution, especially in those disciplines where we are constantly dealing with the unknown, the uncertain, and the unstable" (p. 35), such as in long-term care. Self-reflective practice links our thoughts and actions. It encourages us to engage in a more flexible and present practice, responding as we reflect on the situation at that moment.

Schön advocated for practitioners to cultivate the capacity for reflection in action and reflection on action. **Reflection in action** is sometimes described as thinking on your feet, and it involves looking to our experiences and linking them to our emotions (Schön, 1983). It entails building new understandings to inform our actions in the situation as it is unfolding. On the other hand, **reflection on action** is experienced after the encounter. The act of reflecting on action enables us to explore why we acted as we did, what was happening in a situation, and how our judgments affected the outcome. In doing so, we develop a set of reflective questions and personal ideas about our interactions and practice.

As leisure professionals strive to enhance the quality of life of older adults living in long-term care settings, they may reflect on action by asking questions such as the following:

- How am I supporting residents in living meaningful lives with meaningful experiences within both the LTCH and the community?
- How have I demonstrated my commitment to support resident choice?
- What am I doing to create a safe and supportive environment for all residents?
- How am I recognizing and supporting each resident's strengths and abilities?
- What am I doing to mobilize and nurture strong relationships and partnerships?
- What more can I do to promote opportunities for self-expression?
- How am I supporting family and staff well-being through leisure experiences and opportunities?
- How am I assisting residents in identifying and achieving their aspirations?

What reflective questions can you add to this list that might be important for you to ask as a recreation professional?

Conclusion

Although total-institution and biomedical approaches in long-term care continue, recreation and leisure professionals working in long-term care are encouraged to embrace the values and principles of the culture change movement that elevates living as the number one priority in long-term care. We can still provide excellent health care without making it the central focus. Shifting our attention from quality of care to quality of life carries the potential to make long-term care settings places to thrive and flourish rather than places where we go to die.

Leisure is one of the strongest contributors of quality of life for older adults living in long-term care. But, in order to support quality of life, we must be mindful and reflective about the differences between leisure activities and the leisure experience, doing all that we can do to provide opportunities for the latter. By working in authentic partnerships with residents, family members of residents, and other professionals, we can all engage in a process of critical reflection and dialogue to better understand what brings meaning to life for long-term care residents, family members, and staff and to develop creative strategies to support and facilitate quality leisure experiences for all. Recreation and leisure professionals have a vital role to play in the momentum and success of the culture change movement and the enhancement of quality of life, for one of the primary characteristics of long-term care is free time. What will become of that time? Will it be filled with diversional activities designed to distract and structured activities (interventions) designed to treat problems, or will it be filled with opportunities for life-enriching leisure experiences? What would you want?

KEY TERMS

biomedical model of care—Focuses on physical needs and the clinical treatment of symptoms and signs of disease by medical professionals, who are viewed as the experts (Wade & Halligan, 2004).

closed environments—Those environments that limit residents' opportunities for a range of experiences, for choice and control in daily life, and for involvement in decision making about care.

culture change—The process of reexamining the values, beliefs, attitudes, behaviors, and approaches embedded within an organization in order to develop and implement fundamental reforms within the culture (Rahman & Schnelle, 2008).

long-term care—Encompasses a range of medical, social, personal, and specialized housing services needed by people who require support with activities of daily living (U.S. Senate Special Committee on Aging, 2000).

partnership approach—Values the perspectives of all in the care context and actively incorporates all voices in decision making (Adams & Clarke, 1999).

person-centered approach—Holistic approach to care that places the person, not the disease, at the center of all care decisions and, focusing on the person's abilities, allows for choice and involvement in decision making (Kitwood, 1997).

quality of life—The subjective experience that life is good, meaningful, and satisfying (Sylvester, Voelkl, & Ellis, 2001).

reflection in action—Reflection that happens during an encounter that requires quick critical thinking as a situation is unfolding (Schön, 1983).

reflection on action—Reflection that happens after an encounter that enables further exploration of the situation in order to determine how we might act differently in similar situations in the future (Schön, 1983).

relationship-centered care—Recognizes that quality care depends on strong relationships among all those involved in the care context, including the resident, family members, and staff members at all levels, and focuses on building and maintaining trusting relationships (Nolan et al., 2004).

self-reflective practice—Involves regular critical reflection on professional judgments, assumptions, and actions and the effects these have on others (Schön, 1983).

senses framework—Experiences and interactions necessary for all to feel in the care context in order to build strong relationships, enhance care experiences, and ensure quality of life for all (Nolan et al., 2002, 2003).

total institutions—Places where all aspects of daily life are conducted within one place, such as a long-term care facility, with limited or no access to the world outside its walls (Goffman, 1961).

REVIEW AND DISCUSSION QUESTIONS

1. Reflect on the changes to Grace's life since her move to long-term care. What has remained the same? What is different? How would you work to enhance Grace's quality of life through leisure?

2. What are the professional implications of using the various care approaches within long-term care? What would need to change in LTCHs in order to adopt each of the philosophies?

3. How would you involve residents and family members in the planning of leisure opportunities?

4. How can staff and family members take a more active role in the leisure lifestyle of the residents?

5. What are some of the challenges of working in long-term care? What are the rewards of working in those settings?

LEARNING ACTIVITIES

1. Reflect on what leisure means to you and compare that meaning with how a grandparent experiences leisure. Are there similarities in the description? Are there any differences?

2. Use the Internet and other sources to research specific models of care used in long-term care, including the Eden Alternative, the Pioneer Network, Gentlecare, the family model of care, the Best Friends approach, and the Greenhouse Project, and consider their

philosophies in relation to the three approaches to care outlined in this chapter.

3. Reflect on the four approaches to care described in this chapter, from the traditional biomedical to the authentic partnership approach. Which approach speaks the most to you and what you value? How would the approach you adopt affect how you provide recreation and leisure in long-term care settings?

4. Arrange a tour of a long-term care setting in your community and meet with the therapeutic recreation practitioner to discuss his or her experience working in long-term care.

5. Consider the questions posed in the section on self-reflective practice. What judgments, behaviors, and learnings influenced your interactions today?

CRITICAL-THINKING ACTIVITIES

1. Reflecting on the four elements of person-centered care, how does a person-centered philosophy change how we deliver recreation and leisure services in LTCHs? How would a person-centered approach to recreation and leisure differ from a biomedical approach? How would you ensure a person-centered approach when working with Grace?

2. How do a relationship-centered philosophy and the senses framework change how we approach the delivery of recreation and leisure in LTCHs? If you adopted a relationship-centered approach, how would you use recreation and leisure to nurture relationship building among residents, family members, and staff alike?

3. How might you use an authentic partnership approach in planning and delivering recreation and leisure services in LTCHs? How would you ensure that the voices of residents, family members, and staff at all levels were incorporated in decision making? How might Grace's experience in the LTCH change if she were viewed as a partner in the home rather than simply a recipient of care?

SUGGESTED READING

Adams, T., & Clarke, C.L. (1999). *Dementia care: Developing partnerships in practice.* Edinburgh: Harcourt.

Froggatt, K., Davies, S., & Meyer, J. (2009). Understanding care homes: A research and development perspective. London: Jessica Kingsley.

Jones, M. (1999). *Gentlecare: Changing the experience of Alzheimer's disease in a positive way.* Point Roberts, WA: Hartley & Marks.

Kitwood, T. (1997). *Dementia reconsidered: The person comes first.* Buckingham, UK: Open University Press.

Miller, B., & Pedlar, A. (2006). Self-reflective practice in therapeutic recreation: Celebrating the authenticity and humanism of our practice. *Therapeutic Recreation Ontario Research Annual, 4,* 34-43.

Nolan, K., Davies, S., & Grant, G. (Eds.). (2002). *Working with older people and their families.* Buckingham, UK: Open University Press.

Thomas, W.H. (2004). *What are old people for? How elders will save the world.* Acton, MA: VanderWyk & Burnham.

Thomas, W.H. (1994). *The Eden Alternative: Nature, hope and nursing homes.* Columbia, MO: University of Missouri Press.

Weiner, A., & Ronch, J. (Eds.). (2003). *Culture change in long-term care.* Binghamton, NY: Hawthorn Social Work Practice Press.

REFERENCES

Adams, T. (2005). From person-centred care to relationship-centred care. *Generations Review, 15,* 4-7.

Adams, T., & Clarke, C.L. (1999). *Dementia care: Developing partnerships in practice.* Edinburgh, UK: Harcourt.

Antonelli, E., Rubini, V., & Fassone, C. (2000). The self-concept in institutionalized and non-institutionalized elderly people. *Journal of Environmental Psychology, 20,* 151-164.

Banerjee, A. (2009). Long-term care in Canada: An overview. In P. Armstrong, M. Boscoe, B. Clow, K. Grant, A. Haworth-Brockman, B. Jackson, A. Pederson, M. Seeley, & J. Springer (Eds.), *A place to call home: Long-term care in Canada.* (pp. 29-57). Halifax, NS: Fernwood.

Bond, J., & Corner, L. (2001). Researching dementia: Are there unique methodological challenges for health services research? *Ageing and Society, 21,* 95-116.

Boothman, S., & Savell, K. (2004). Development, reliability, and validity of the Measureable Assessment in Recreation for Resident-Centered Care (MARRCC). *Therapeutic Recreation Journal, 38*(4), 382-393.

Brill, P.A., Jensen, R.L., Koltyn, K.F., Morgan, L.A., Morrow, J.R., Keller, M.J., & Jackson, A.W. (1998). The feasibility of conducting a group-based progressive strength training program in residents of a multi-level care facility. *Activities, Adaptation & Aging, 22*(4), 53-63.

Brooker, D. (2007). *Person centred dementia care: Making services better.* London: Jessica Kingsley.

Buettner, L., & Fitzsimmons, S. (2003). *Dementia practice guidelines for recreational therapy: Treatment of disturbing behaviors.* Alexandria, VA: American Therapeutic Recreation Association.

Buettner, L., & Martin, S.L. (1995). *Therapeutic recreation in the nursing home.* State College: Venture.

Clark, P.G. (2002). Values and voices in teaching gerontology and geriatrics. *Gerontologist, 42,* 297-303.

de Medeiros, K. (2009, November). *Finding the person in person-centered dementia care: Using multiple perspectives to better inform care.* Paper presented at the Gerontological Society of America Conference, Atlanta.

Dröes, R., Boelens-Van Der Knoop, E., Bos, J., Meihuizen, L., Ettema, T.P., Gerritsen, D.L., Hoogeveen, F., De Lange, J., & Schölzel-Dorenbos, C. (2006). Quality of life in dementia in perspective: An exploratory study of variations in opinions among people with dementia and their professional caregivers, and in literature. *Dementia, 5*(4), 533-558.

Dupuis, S.L. (2006). Leisure and ageing well. In E.L. Jackson (Ed.), *Leisure and quality of life: Impacts on social, economic and cultural development* (pp. 91-107). Hangzhou, China: Zhejiang University Press.

Dupuis, S.L. (2008). Leisure and ageing well. *World Leisure Journal, 50,* 91-107.

Dupuis, S.L. (2010). A planning framework for improving the lives of persons with Alzheimer's disease and related dementias and their families: Implications for social policy, leisure policy and practice. In H. Mair, S.M. Arai, & D.G. Reid (Eds.), *Decentring work: Critical perspectives on leisure, social policy and human development* (pp. 91-117). Calgary, AB: Calgary University Press.

Dupuis, S.L., Gillies, J., Carson, J., Whyte, C., Genoe, R., Loiselle, L., & Sadler, L. (in press). Moving beyond patient and client approaches: Mobilizing authentic partnerships in dementia care. Manuscript submitted for publication. (*Dementia*).

Dupuis, S., Gillies, J., Mantle, A., Loiselle, L., & Sadler, L. (2008). *Creating partnerships in dementia care: A Changing Melody Toolkit.* Waterloo, ON: MAREP, University of Waterloo.

Dupuis, S., Smale, B., & Wiersma, E. (2005). Creating open environments in long-term care settings: An examination of influencing factors. *Therapeutic Recreation Journal, 39,* 277-298.

Dupuis, S.L., Whyte, C., Carson, J., Sadler, L., & Meschino, L. (2010, July). *Liberating leisure from therapy.* Paper presented at the Leisure Studies Association (LSA) Annual Conference, Leeds, UK.

Edelman, P., Fulton, B.R., Kuhn, D., & Chang, C.H. (2005). A comparison of three methods of measuring dementia specific quality of life: Perspectives of residents, staff, and observers. [Special issue]. *Gerontologist, 45*(1), 27-36.

Eliopoulos, C. (2010). Honouring the whole person: The culture change movement shines new light on holistic long-term care. *Advance for Long-Term Care Management.* Retrieved from http://long-term-care.advanceweb.com/Editorial/Content/PrintFriendly.aspx?CC=190721.

Estes, C.L., & Binney, E.A. (1989). The biomedicalization of aging: Dangers and dilemmas. *Gerontologist, 29,* 587-596.

Ettema, T.P., Dröes, R., de Lange, J., Mellenbergh, G.J., & Ribbe, M.W. (2005). A review of quality of life instruments used in dementia. *Quality of Life Research, 14*(3), 675-686.

Goffman, E. (1961). *Asylums: Essays on the social situation of mental patients and other inmates.* Garden City, NY: Anchor Books.

Hall, B.L., & Bocksnick, J.G. (1995). Therapeutic recreation for the institutionalized elderly: Choice or abuse. *Journal of Elder Abuse & Neglect, 7*(4), 49-60.

Hormuth, S.E. (1990). *The ecology of self: Relocation and self-concept change.* Cambridge, UK: Cambridge University Press.

Henderson, K.A. (2008). Expanding the meanings of leisure in a both/and world. *Loisir et Société/Society and Leisure, 31*(1), 15-30.

Hollander, M.J. (2002). The continuum of care: An integrated system of service delivery. In M. Stephenson & E. Sawyer (Eds.), *Continuing the care: An integrated system of service delivery* (pp. 57-70). Ottawa: CHA Press.

Hooyman, N.R., & Kiyak, H.A. (2008). *Social gerontology: A multidisciplinary perspective* (8th ed.). San Francisco: Pearson.

Hughes, J.C., Bamford, C., & May, C. (2008). Types of centredness in health care: Themes and concepts. *Medicine, Health Care and Philosophy, 11,* 455-463.

Jenkins, K., Pienta, A., & Horgas, A. (2002). Activity and health-related quality of life in continuing care retirement communities. *Research on Aging, 24*(1), 124-149.

Jonas-Simpson, C., & Mitchell, G.J. (2005). Giving voice to expressions of quality of life for persons living with dementia through story, music and art. *Alzheimer's Care Quarterly, 6*(1), 52-61.

Jones, M. (1999). *Gentlecare: Changing the experience of Alzheimer's disease in a positive way.* Point Roberts, WA: Hartley & Marks.

Kane, R.A. (2001). Long-term care and a good quality of life: Bringing them closer together. *Gerontologist, 41,* 293-304.

Kane, R.A. (2003). Definition, measurement, and correlates of quality of life in nursing homes: Toward a reasonable practice, research, and policy agenda. *Gerontologist, 43*(Special Issue II), 28-36.

Kane, R.L., Kane, R.A., Bershadsky, B., Degenholtz, H., Kling, K., Totten, A., Jung, K. (2005). Proxy sources for information on nursing home residents' quality of life. *Journal of Gerontology, 60B*(6), S318-S325.

Kitwood, T. (1997). *Dementia reconsidered: The person comes first.* Buckingham, UK: Open University Press.

Koren, M.J. (2010). Person-centered care for nursing home residents: The culture-change movement. *Health Affairs, 29,* 312-317.

Kovach, C.R., & Henschel, H. (1996). Behavior and participation during therapeutic activities on special care units. *Activities, Adaptation & Aging, 20*(4), 35-45.

Lawton, M.P. (1997). Measures of quality of life and subjective well-being. *Generations, 21,* 45-47.

Lee, Y., Datillo, J., & Howard, D. (1994). The complex and dynamic nature of leisure experience. *Journal of Leisure Research, 26*(3), 195.

Lloyd, K.M., & Auld, C.J. (2002). The role of leisure in determining quality of life: Issues of content and measurement. *Social Indicators Research, 57,* 43-71.

Logsdon, R.G., Gibbons, L.E., McCurry, S.M., & Teri, L. (1999). Quality of life in Alzheimer's disease: Patient and caregiver reports. *Journal of Mental Health and Aging, 5*(1), 21-32.

Marin, B., Leichsenring, K., Rodrigues, R., & Huber, M. (2009). *Who cares? Care coordination and cooperation to enhance quality of elderly care in the European Union.* Vienna: European Centre for Social Welfare Policy and Research.

Marshall, M.J., & Hutchinson, S.A. (2001). A critique of research on the use of activities with persons with Alzheimer's disease: A systematic literature review. *Journal of Advanced Nursing, 35*(4), 488-496.

McCormack, B. (2004). Person-centredness in gerontological nursing: An overview of the literature. *Journal of Clinical Nursing, 13,* 31-38.

McNown Johnson, M., & Rhodes, R. (2007). Institutionalization: A theory of human behavior and the social environment. *Advances in Social Work, 8,* 219-236.

Miller, B., & Pedlar, A. (2006). Self-reflective practice in therapeutic recreation: Celebrating the authenticity and humanism of our practice. *TRO Research Annual, 4,* 34-43.

Mitchell, G., Jonas-Simpson, C., & Dupuis, S.L. (2006). *I'm still here: A teaching-learning guide to understanding living with dementia through the medium of the arts.* Waterloo, ON: MAREP, University of Waterloo.

Neumayer, R., Gattuso, S., Saw, C., & Jelinek, H. (1998). Programming home-based activities for people with dementia: Benefits and constraints. *Journal of Leisurability, 25*(4), 29-39.

Nolan, M.R., Davies, S., Brown, J., Keady, J., & Nolan, J. (2004). Beyond person-centered care: A new vision of gerontological nursing. *International Journal of Older People Nursing, 13*(3a), 45-53.

Nolan, M., Davies, S., & Grant, G. (2002). Introduction: The changing face of health and social care. In M. Nolan, S. Davies, & G. Grant (Eds.), *Working with older people and their families* (pp. 4-18). Buckingham, UK: Open University Press.

Nolan, M.R., Lundh, U., Grant, G., & Keady, J. (2003). *Partnerships in family care.* Buckingham: Open University Press.

Nolan, M., Ryan, T., Enderby, P., & Reid, D. (2002). Towards a more inclusive vision of dementia care practice and research. *Dementia, 1*(2), 193-211.

Omnibus Budget Reconciliation Act of 1987 (OBRA), Pub.L. 100-203, 101 Stat. 1330 (1987).

Ontario Ministry of Health and Long-Term Care. (2010). *Long Term Care Homes Act, 2007.* Ontario, Canada: Author. Retrieved from www.e-laws.gov.on.ca/html/source/regs/english/2010/elaws_src_regs_r10079_e.htm#BK78.

Parse, R.R. (1996). Quality of life for persons living with Alzheimer's disease: The human becoming perspective. *Nursing Science Quarterly, 9*(3), 126-133.

Pedlar, A., Hornibrook, T., & Haasen, B. (2001). Patient-focused care: Theory and practice. *Therapeutic Recreation Journal, 35*(1), 15-30.

Pioneer Network. (2010). *Culture change.* Retrieved from www.pioneernetwork.net.

Pitters, S. (2002). Long-term care facilities. In P. Armstrong, M. Boscoe, B. Clow, K. Grant, A. Haworth-Brockman, B. Jackson, A. Pederson, M. Seeley, & J. Springer (Eds.), *A place to call home: Long-term care in Canada.* (pp. 163-202). Halifax, NS: Fernwood.

Ragheb, M.G. (1996). The search for meaning in leisure pursuits: Review, conceptualization and a need for a psychometric development. *Leisure Studies, 15,* 245-258.

Ragsdale, V., & McDougall, Jr., G.J. (2008). The changing face of long-term care: Looking at the past decade. *Issues in Mental Health Nursing, 29,* 992-1001.

Rahman, A.N., & Schnelle, J.F. (2008). The nursing home culture-change movement: Recent past, present, and future directions for research. *Gerontologist, 48,* 142-148.

Renwick, R., & Brown, I. (1996). The Centre for Health Promotion conceptual approach to quality of life: Being, belonging, and becoming. In R. Renwick, I. Brown, & M. Nagler (Eds.), *Quality of life in health promotion and rehabilitation: Conceptual approaches, issues and applications* (pp. 75-86). Thousand Oaks, CA: Sage.

Rogers, C. (1956). On becoming a person: Some hypotheses regarding the facilitation of personal growth. *Pastoral Psychology, 7,* 9-13.

Rogers, C. (1961). *On becoming a person.* Boston: Houghton Mifflin.

Ryan, T., Nolan, M., Reid, D., & Enderby, P (2008). Using the senses framework to achieve relationship-centred dementia care services: A case example. *Dementia, 7,* 71-93.

Schnelle, J.F., & Reuben, D.B. (1999). Long-term care in the nursing home. In E. Calkins, C. Boult, E.H. Wagner, & J.T. Pacala (Eds.), *New ways to care for older people: Building systems based on evidence* (pp. 168-181). New York: Springer.

Schölzel-Dorenbos, C.J., Ettema, T.P., Bos, J., Boelens-van der Knoop, E., Gerritesen, D.L., Hoogeveen, F., de Lange, J., Meihuizen, L., & Dröes, R. (2007). Evaluating the outcome of interventions on quality of life in dementia: Selection of the appropriate scale. *International Journal of Geriatric Psychiatry, 22,* 511-519.

Schön, D. (1983). *The reflective practitioner: How professionals think in action.* Aldershot: Ashgate.

Sloane, P.D., Zimmerman, S., Williams, C.S., Reed, P.S., Gill, K.S., & Preisser, J.S. (2005). Evaluating the quality of life of long-term care residents with dementia. *Gerontologist, 45,* 37-49.

Statistics Canada. (2007). *A portrait of seniors in Canada 2006.* Ottawa: Ministry of Industry (Catalogue no. 89-519-XIE).

Sullivan, A.-M., Pedlar, A., & Miller, B. (2002). Experiencing leisure on a cognitive support unit. *Loisir et Société/ Society and Leisure, 25,* 443-471.

Sylvester, C. (1985). Freedom, leisure and therapeutic recreation: A philosophical view. *Therapeutic Recreation Journal, 19,* 6-13.

Sylvester, C. (1987). Therapeutic recreation and the end of leisure. *Philosophy of Therapeutic Recreation, 1,* 76-89.

Sylvester, C., Voelkl, J.E., & Ellis, G.D. (2001). *Therapeutic recreation programming: Theory and practice.* State College, PA: Venture.

Teague, M.L., & MacNeil, R.D. (1992). *Aging and leisure: Vitality in later life.* Dubuque, IA: Brown & Benchmark.

Thomas, W.H. (1994). *The Eden Alternative: Nature, hope and nursing homes.* Sherburne, NY: Eden Alternative Foundation.

Thomas, W.H. (1996). *Life worth living: How someone you love can still enjoy life in a nursing home: The Eden Alternative in action.* Acton, MA: Vander Wyk and Burham.

Thorgrimson, L., Selwood, A., Spector, A., Royan, L., de Madariaga, L., Woods, R.T., & Orrell, M. (2003). Whose quality of life is it anyway? The validity and reliability of the Quality of Life–Alzheimer's Disease (QOL-AD) scale. *Alzheimer's Disease & Associated Disorders, 17*(4), 201-208.

Tomiak, M., Berthelot, J., & Mustard, A.C. 2000. Factors associated with nursing home entry for elders in Manitoba, Canada. *Journal of Gerontology, 55A*(5), M279-M287.

Train, G.H., Nurock, S.A., Manela, M., Kitchen, G., & Livingston, G.A. (2005). A qualitative study of the experiences of long-term care for residents with dementia, their relatives and staff. *Aging & Mental Health, 9,* 119-128.

Tresolini, C.P., & the Pew-Fetzer Task Force. (1994). *Health professions education and relationship-centered care.* San Francisco: Pew Health Professions Commission.

Trottier, H., Martel, L., Houle, C., Berthelot, J., & Légaré, J. (2000). Living at home or in an institution: What makes the difference for seniors? *Health Reports, 11*(4), 49-61.

United States Senate Special Committee on Aging. (2000, February). *Developments in aging: 1997 and 1998* (Vol. 1, Report 106-229). Washington, DC: Author.

van der Roest, H.G., Meiland, F.J., Maroccini, R., Comijis, H.C., Jonker, C., & Dröes, R. (2007). Subjective needs of people with dementia: A review of the literature. *International Psychogeriatrics, 19*(3), 559-592.

Voelkl, J.E., Battisto, D.G., Carson, J., & McGuire, F.A. (2004). A family model of care: Creating life enriching environments in nursing homes. *World Leisure, 3,* 18-29.

Voelkl, J.E., Galecki, A.T., & Fries, B.E. (1996). Nursing home residents with severe cognitive impairments: Predictors of participation in activity groups. *Therapeutic Recreation Journal, 30*(1), 27-40.

Voelkl, J.E., & Nicholson, L.A. (1992). Perceptions of daily life among residents of a long-term care facility. *Activities, Adaptation & Aging, 16*(4), 99-114.

Wade, D., & Halligan, P. (2004). Do biomedical models of illness make for good healthcare systems? *British Medical Journal, 329,* 1398-1401.

Whitehouse, P.J., & Rabins, P.V. (1992). Quality of life and dementia. *Alzheimer's Disease and Associated Disorders, 6*(3), 135-137.

CHAPTER 13

Bridging Community and Long-Term Care Settings

Elaine Wiersma ■ Stephanie Chesser

After reading this chapter, you will be able to

- understand and propose a definition of *community*,
- understand the transition process from community settings to long-term care settings for older adults in a Canadian context,
- challenge traditional views of long-term care facilities as institutions,
- explore the long-term care setting as a community, and
- explore how health care professionals can support older adults as they transition from community settings into long-term care settings.

LEARNING OBJECTIVES

Long-term care facilities have typically been viewed as total institutions (Goffman, 1961) with the assumption that residents have limited access to the community; in fact, the total institution is often contrasted with the community. The transition for older people, then, into a long-term care facility can be particularly traumatic and leave them separated from family, friends, and community. Viewing the long-term care facility as a community itself enhances the permeability of the institution so that the long-term care facility is part of the greater community surrounding it (Rowles, Concotelli, & High, 1996).

Definition of Concepts

Before we can discuss bridging community and long-term care settings, definitions of key concepts would be helpful, in particular *long-term care* and *community*. Typically when we talk about long-term care homes, we assume that people living in these homes are moved from their community. In this way, long-term care settings are often contrasted with community, where community is thought of as a place or neighborhood and long-term care settings are segregated from this place. As described by Dupuis, Whyte, and Carson in chapter 12, long-term care settings are seen as closed environments from the community.

Because of a lack of common history and language, long-term care currently can mean many things across Canada and the United States (Banerjee, 2009). **Long-term care** refers to ongoing, indefinite care for people who can no longer care for themselves (Banerjee, 2009). **Long-term care homes (LTCHs)**, then, refer to what were commonly known as *nursing homes* (Smith, 2004). In Ontario, the Ministry of Health and Long-Term Care (MOHLTC) has deliberately changed the name of *nursing homes* and *homes for the aged* in new legislation to long-term care homes (MOHLTC, 2009a). Thus, publicly subsidized institutional facilities designed to care for seniors are referred to as *long-term care homes* (LTCHs). In the United States, LTCHs are referred to as *nursing homes* or *skilled nursing facilities*. Because this article is written from a Canadian perspective, we will be referring to facilities as LTCHs.

As described in chapter 12, the nursing home or LTCH has often been likened to Goffman's (1961) description of total institutions (Dupuis, Smale, & Wiersma, 2005). Goffman describes a **total institution** as "a place of residence and work where a large number of like-situated individuals,

cut off from the wider society for an appreciable period of time, together lead an enclosed, formally administered way of life" (p. xiii), which includes institutions established to care for people who are seen as incapable. Goffman defines four characteristics of total institutions. First, all aspects of life are conducted in the same place. Second, all daily activity is conducted in the company of others who are all treated alike. Third, all activities of the day are rigidly scheduled. And finally, the activities are all designed to fulfill the official aims of the institution. In this way, LTCHs are segregated from the community settings in which they are located.

The notion of **community** can be viewed in a variety of ways. Often, community is viewed as a geographic location, whether it is a neighborhood, area, or city. Community can also refer to groups of which we are a part. Finally, community can refer to a broader sense of connectedness: "Communities are natural human associations based on the ties of relationship and shared experiences in which we mutually provide meaning in our lives, meet needs, and accomplish interpersonal goals" (Brueggeman, 2001, p. 114). Another definition of community lends more of a group focus to the broader concept.

> A community is a group of people who are socially interdependent, who participate together in discussion and decision making, and who share certain practices that both define community and are nurtured by it. Such a community is not always quickly formed. It almost always has a history and so is also a community of memory, defined in part by its past and its memory of the past. (Bellah, Madsen, Sullivan, Swidler, & Tipton, 1985, p. 333)

From these definitions, three main concepts can be derived that can be attributed to the definition of community: social networks, role identity, and sharing. **Social networks** have been defined by Powers (1995) as "complex sets of interpersonal ties that in personal networks connect network members to a focal individual and to each other" (p. 184). Social networks can also include services and organizations that residents are a part of or connected to.

Role identities are an important concept with regard to community. "A role is a comprehensive pattern of behaviours and attitudes constituting a strategy for coping with a recurrent set of situations" (Mahoney, 1994, p. 135). Another definition of a role is the following: "[A role] is also defined as behaviour associated with positions within the organisation of a group, and comes from particular relationships between individuals" (Levin, 2000, p. 171). Essentially, roles are defined by one's social networks. Roles for older adults in North America have been defined as "sets of expectations that members of our society have about the capabilities, interests, and behaviours of older persons" (Mahoney, 1994, p. 136). The negative valuations of these roles can include loss of competence, disability, reduced ability to learn and change, dependence, and poverty, among many others.

The third concept of community, **sharing**, involves the sharing of experiences, history, and goals (Bellah et al., 1985). Experiences are shared when people have opportunities to participate in life together. Past experiences can be defined as a shared history, which does not always have to be a personal history but can also be a community or cultural history. Sharing goals indicates the common desire to attain specific objectives. These goals may be personal ones that are similar to those of other individuals, or they may be communal goals for a specific group or community. In order to share any of these three things—experiences, history, or goals—people must have access to the community in which this sharing takes place.

Transition From Community Settings to Long-Term Care Settings

Medical technology has advanced to the point that people can recover from surgery, obtain medical treatments, receive palliative care, and live out their older years in the comfort of their homes. Indeed, home care remains a popular option for older adults; the familiar environment at home can allow for greater independence and psychological comfort as well as an increased quality of life (Canadian Research Network for Care in the Community, 2006). In Canada, provincial and territorial health authorities have been given the task of assessing eligibility for medical and support services received at home, referred to as *home and community care*, or HACC (Banerjee, 2009; CCAC, 2006). Generally speaking, HACC services are aimed at rehabilitation and end-of-life care or are provided to people waiting for entry into LTCHs (CCAC, 2006; MOHLTC, 2009a). Since 1996, HACC in Ontario has been overseen by Community Care Access Centres (CCACs) that receive funding via Local Health Integration Networks (LHINs) through the MOHLTC (Kerzner, 2004).

Due to the fact that CCACs are covered under the Ontario government's 1994 Long-Term Care Act and governed by the federal Canada Health Act (CHA) of 1984, they are required to provide medically necessary support services free of charge to eligible people receiving care at home (Baranek, Deber, & Williams, 2004; Kerzner, 2004). These services can include nursing services, physical or occupational therapy, speech language therapy, and personal support such as assistance with toileting or bathing (CCAC, 2006). The Long-Term Care Act does not, however, require CCACs to financially cover services that address many of the tasks necessary to live independently in a home environment (e.g., cooking, cleaning, laundry, home repairs, snow shoveling, banking, grocery shopping). Historically, assistance with these tasks would have come from the children of older adults; however, recent evidence suggests that elderly people today have fewer children and are more likely to have children living farther away than in previous generations (Armstrong et al., 2009). As a result, older adults are often forced to rely on extended family, friends, volunteers, or hired service providers to help manage household tasks (Baranek et al., 2004).

Although HACC can help older adults to age in place, the progression of certain medical conditions (e.g., arthritis, emphysema, heart failure, dementia) or the demands involved with taking care of a home can necessitate a move into long-term care. For older adults, entry into an LTCH can be self-motivated, but it often occurs at the urging of family members or medical professionals concerned about the person's ability to manage health issues or to live independently (Eckert, Carder, Morgan, Frankowski, & Roth, 2009). In a study by Tracy and DeYoung (2004), one resident discussed how his family's fears influenced his decision to move into long-term care: "I'll either drive [my family] nuts thinking I'm going to fall or do something like that or come here and relieve their minds. That's why I'm here" (p. 29).

When an older person first relocates into an LTCH, a transition period begins that may be characterized by stress, disorganization, and adaptation (Dobbs, 2004; Heliker & Scholler-Jaquish, 2006; Tracy & DeYoung, 2004). Heliker and Scholler-Jaquish (2006) found that the transition into residential long-term care for older adults takes place in phases over the first few months following admission. Older adults were found to initially deal with feelings of homelessness as they grieved the loss of their home. The authors describe how the concept of home can be constructed; for many, home is a place where family and friends gather, a space that helps to reinforce or mirror who a person is in addition to the person's sense of cultural identity within a larger community. Gubrium (1993) echoes this concept: "Meaningful relationships with friends and family and personal possessions constitute a considerable amount of what home means to people" (pp. 55-56). A move into long-term care removes this personal and cultural mirror and can leave older adults with feelings of loss and isolation (Heliker & Scholler-Jaquish, 2006).

Following this initial homeless phase, residents were found to transition into a stage where they learned the ropes of residing in LTCH (Heliker & Scholler-Jaquish, 2006) and became socialized into the environment (Wiersma, 2007; Wiersma

& Dupuis, 2010). This process involved learning how to maneuver in an unfamiliar space, becoming oriented with residents and staff, and learning the rules and routines that often govern life within long-term care. Transitioning into a structured environment managed through regulation and routine can be particularly difficult for people who have been accustomed to living independently and can leave residents feeling confined or like prisoners (Wiersma, 2007, 2008a).

Porter and Clinton (1992) found that LTCH residents had a number of adjustment approaches, or ways they saw as getting used to long-term care. To these residents, "getting used to it" simply meant living in the facility while time passed. Some residents tried to fit in by purposefully meshing with the circumstances of LTCH life, while others tried to fit in by not fitting in. Residents expressed

Long-Term Care Homes and Their Communities

A Case Study of One Rural Community

Birchwood Grove* is a community of approximately 2,500 residents in northern Ontario located approximately 400 kilometers from the nearest major city and a number of kilometers off a major highway. Founded as a mining and forestry town many years ago, Birchwood Grove is still home to many of the town's original residents.

The hospital serves as a community center. Many auxiliary health services are located here. In addition, a gift shop inside the main entrance is known as a great place to buy gifts, and local handiwork is displayed and sold here. A sizeable group of volunteers run the gift shop and volunteer in various aspects of the hospital. When community members visit a patient in the hospital, they often visit more than one person since they typically know other patients and residents. Staff at the hospital know patients, visitors, and families.

A small, long-term care wing has been incorporated into the hospital and serves as the town's only residential LTCH. Most of the long-term care residents are also long-time residents of the town and were familiar with the facility prior to admission. Many also report having once owned homes only a few blocks away and having been acquainted with hospital staff through the community. As a result, residents report a relatively easy transition from community living into long-term care.

The hospital is located next to Birchwood Grove's seniors' apartments and is just a short walk from the main shopping district; thus, visits to the long-term care wing by town residents are convenient and common. Indeed, many residents are visited daily by family and friends coming to chat about town news, assemble a puzzle in the game room, or have a meal in the hospital cafeteria, which is known for having some of the best food in town. The residents are talked about in the community since many visitors know a number of residents and can report on their conditions and health to others in the community. Volunteer drivers also assist in transporting some of the more mobile residents to town events, meetings of the local seniors' center, and religious services. Overall, the long-term care residents in Birchwood Grove appear to be well integrated into community life and are able to maintain relationships both within the facility and with the larger Birchwood Grove community.

*Not its real name.

that they gave the transitioning process their best effort, as they would in other circumstances of their lives.

The final stage of adjusting to life in long-term care, occurring approximately two to three months following admission, was characterized by residents claiming a place and creating a neighborhood within long-term care (Heliker & Scholler-Jaquish, 2006). This neighborhood provided a place where new memories, new social networks, and new neighbors could be made. Wilson (1997) found a similar transition stage, termed the *initial acceptance phase*, which was characterized by a focus beyond self, a sense of well-being, the development of new social networks, and taking control of one's situation. Wilson found that older adults whose admission into long-term care was planned reached this acceptance stage earlier than older adults whose admission was unplanned.

Concepts of Community in Long-Term Care Settings

Throughout this section, we discuss building community on two levels. First, we discuss the **internal community**, that is, the LTCH as a community. Issues surrounding residents' involvement in their own communities (i.e., LTCHs) are addressed. Building community at the second level refers to the external community. This **external community** is defined in two ways: the geographical area in which the LTCH is located, and the sense of community associated with the residents, families, and staff of the facility. Conceptualizing community as it relates to LTCHs is discussed through the three characteristics of community described earlier, that is, sharing, social networks, and role identity.

As discussed earlier, most LTCHs would be considered total institutions (Dupuis et al., 2005; Goffman, 1961); however, this does not necessarily have to be the case. Rowles et al. (1996) suggest

> that separation does not have to be an underlying motif of nursing home life, that it is possible for many residents to preserve their ongoing involvement within the larger community and, more important, to retain their self-identity and a continuity with their pasts. One of the key mechanisms through which this integration is maintained is a high level of permeability of the institution, manifest in easy and ongoing exchanges of resources, people, and information between the facility and the community in which it is located. (p. 189)

There are many ways to create a sense of community within the facility or to sustain integration into the larger community. Using the three characteristics of community (social networks, role identity, and sharing), we explore the notion of bridging community and long-term care settings, using leisure as a particular framework. First, we explore the idea of sharing and the context of leisure as the opportunity for sharing. Then we explore social networks and relationships and role identities.

Sharing and Leisure in Long-Term Care Settings

The first component of community is the notion of sharing. Although we will be discussing various types of leisure activities, we see sharing as the fundamental component of leisure activities in LTCHs. Sharing must occur in order for people to participate in leisure activities together, because leisure in LTCHs is typically provided as group activities and thus is based on the sharing of an activity. As illustrated by a number of studies, sharing in leisure activities can create a sense of community within the LTCH (Sullivan, Pedlar, & Miller, 2002; Wiersma & Pedlar, 2008).

Leisure in LTCHs can be categorized in several ways. In chapter 12, recreation and leisure provision in long-term care is discussed from a traditional approach with the goal of moving toward a partner approach. Most typically, recreation programs are provided by recreation staff who have some level of training or background in providing recreation programs. Recreation programs can be grouped into categories, as described by Dupuis et al. (2005). In-house recreation programs are provided purely for entertainment and to enrich the lives of residents; they are provided in the facility by facility staff. In-house therapeutic recreation programs are one-to-one or small-group programs focusing on specific aspects of a resident's well-being and are provided by a trained professional. In-house community recreation programs are initiatives designed to bring community groups and programs into the facility. Finally, community-outreach recreation programs are opportunities for residents to participate in recreation programs in the community. In-house recreation programs and in-house therapeutic recreation programs can both be grouped together under in-house programs, and in-house community programs and community-outreach recreation programs can be grouped together as community-access programs (Dupuis et al., 2005).

In a national survey of facilities in Canada, Dupuis et al. (2005) found that in-house recreation programs were the most common type of program offered to residents (72% of all recreation program offerings), while community-access recreation programs only made up 28.6% of program offerings and were offered significantly less frequently than in-house programs. The more residents there were in a facility, the higher the percentage of community-access programs offered. In addition, the higher the number of recreation volunteers, the higher the percentage of community-access recreation programs being offered. Recreation staff perceived benefits to residents participating in community-access programs, most of which related to continuity benefits, such as enabling residents to feel connected to the community, enabling maintenance of valued community ties, providing a greater opportunity to maintain independence, and helping residents feel they could still contribute to their community. The most significant constraints to offering community-access programs are related to residents' functioning abilities, accessibility constraints in the community, and staff resources. Even if recreation staff perceived positive benefits to community-access programs, the constraints, particularly resident-focused constraints, were still significant, and positive perceptions had no impact on the frequency or diversity of community-access programs offered.

Wiersma and Dupuis (2002) also explored residents' perceptions of community-access programs to gain a further understanding of residents' experiences in these programs. Specifically, they examined how residents think about community involvement, the reasons for participating in community-outreach recreation programs, and possible constraints to participation in community-outreach programs. Six residents from a small long-term care facility in southern Ontario volunteered to participate in in-depth, semistructured interviews. It became evident early on in the project that although not all residents participated in formal community opportunities offered by the facility's recreation department, residents often participated in informal community involvement initiated by themselves or by family and friends. Thus, the residents described a number of alternative ways they remained connected to their communities and defined community involvement in various ways.

Recognizing the alternative ways that residents thought about and attempted to maintain community involvement, three overarching themes emerged that reflected the meaning of community involvement and the challenges of that involvement for these residents: change in the nature of community involvement, value attached to community involvement, and challenges to present community involvement. First, participants talked about their past community involvement primarily in terms of volunteering opportunities they had participated in. Nonetheless, present community involvement had changed significantly for these residents and now was described as recreation programs offered by the recreation services department within the facility, outings with family and friends, and even simply getting off the floor and visiting the main lobby of the facility. Some residents chose to participate in informal community opportunities, while others chose more structured avenues. Much importance was placed on community involvement and being part of the world outside the institution.

Four values were identified when participants described community involvement in this study: connection with the past, desire for change, social interaction, and personal rewards. First, residents described a connection with the past through visits to their homes or to a family member's residence as well as continued involvement in the community. Second, they described the importance of change, particularly change of scenery. Third, social interaction as a part of community involvement was also important to the residents. Contact with others outside the facility as well as the maintenance of family relationships were important as connections with the outside world can provide opportunities for valued social interactions. The final value concerned personal rewards, which included demonstration of continued competence and independence and opportunity for stimulation.

Four challenges to community involvement that affected either the residents' ability to participate or their experience were also emphasized by the participants: concerns related to illness or disability, facility policies, issues related to support, and negative attitudes toward other residents. Participants cited a number of experiences where they were unable to participate or the experience had changed due to their own health status. In addition, the policies of the facility often prevented participants from engaging in community leisure opportunities as much as they would like. Some examples cited were quarantines due to influenza outbreaks and the requirements for appropriate supervision when out of the facility. Although residents placed a high importance on community access and participation, many of the constraints to accessing the community hindered participation.

Sharing, then, as a concept of community can occur within the context of leisure opportunities. In particular, the ways that institutions are structured and how leisure opportunities are offered can ensure a sense of community within the facility and integration with the community outside.

Caring for Seniors in Africa

Benjamin Mireku

I am a citizen of Ghana, West Africa, and have lived in Africa most of my life. I have also traveled to some countries on the African continent. This puts me in a good position to give a vivid account of how the African culture treats seniors. I must first emphasize that there are 54 independent countries in Africa with individual cultures and practices, but many of these practices overlap. One such practice is the value of seniors. In African cultures, the older you are, the more respect you are accorded. Seniors are a source of inspiration, wisdom, and experience. They are sometimes called the *reference book* and if someone has a dilemma, the seniors are consulted for direction.

Seniors have therefore remained an integral unit of the community in a continent that has always practiced an extended family system. They are actually the heads of such families, and it is therefore not surprising to see kings, chiefs, queen mothers, and other vital positions in African society being occupied by seniors. Almost all traditional courts, which handle everything from minor to very difficult litigation, are constituted by seniors because society sees them as a source of reference and wisdom. The values and culture of each tribe or traditional area are passed on to the young ones by the elderly. It is therefore common to see the elderly surrounded by children for storytelling. There is a saying in the Akan language that translates into English as, "A family without a senior is an empty family." In addition, in Ghana, for instance, once one becomes a senior (65+), one qualifies for free health care. The national health insurance scheme registers all seniors without taking any premium and the insurance benefit covers all hospital care, including prescription drugs.

I must admit that these roles and value placed on seniors in African society are gradually changing due to so-called modernization. For instance, women who acted as caregivers for this important group are gradually moving out of home, becoming educated, and gaining full-time employment. It is now being said that the African society is forgetting how to treat its seniors. Some nursing homes have started to emerge in some countries, but these facilities are not fully being used because we have still not come to that point. Presently, families are chastised by society for taking seniors to any such environment and are viewed as neglecting their family. This is causing problems because, as stated earlier, the caregivers are out of home, and children are being enrolled in schools more than before. Seniors are therefore left in the house alone during the day, although in the evenings, the whole family gets together. This has raised a lot of debate as to whether nursing homes should be encouraged to concentrate on the care of seniors. Urban areas are caught up in this debate more than rural villages; taking care of seniors and the major roles they play in the African society is still present in many rural areas.

Thus, seniors are an important part of the community in most parts of Africa. They naturally command a high level of respect that is not necessarily tied to how wealthy they are (even though it sometimes influences their image). As long as a senior is morally upright, is healthy, and gives advice and direction to young people, that senior is guaranteed a comfortable life. Africa still values the extended-family system, and the roles of seniors in this society are still very relevant. Seniors will always form an integral component of African society, and I believe they will continue to be used as a point of reference for decision making.

Recreation programs such as community-access programs are ways in which integration with the outside community can be facilitated as the walls of the institution become permeable. "The easy flow of people and communication back and forth between [the facility] and the community contributes to a sense that the boundary between inside and outside, although physically apparent, is both socially and psychologically blurred" (Rowles et al., 1996, p. 197). Residents, then, have a chance to share opportunities with others in the facility, but they also have opportunities to share leisure activities and interact with others outside the facility.

Social Networks and Relationships in Long-Term Care Settings

Though much has been written about social isolation and loneliness in long-term care (e.g., Slama & Bergman-Evans, 2000; Thomas, 1996), few researchers have examined social interactions specifically in long-term care settings (Applegate & Morse, 1994; Golander, 1995; Powers, 1995, 1996). Social networks in long-term care facilities consist of a number of networks: Institution-centered networks comprise mainly people within the institution, small cluster networks consist of close groups of residents, kin-centered networks are composed mainly of family members and relatives, and balanced networks contain a wide range of contacts including residents, staff, family, and outside friends and acquaintances (Powers, 1995, 1996). Thus, social networks can consist of other residents, staff, family members, and outside acquaintances.

Social networks change upon admission to LTCHs (Powers, 1995, 1996). When older people are admitted to LTCHs, the transition is often accompanied by the loss of a spouse or partner or changes in the relationship with a spouse or partner (Wiersma, 2007, 2008a). Relationships with friends and community members also change as people lose touch with the outside community (Powers, 1995, 1996). Admission to LTCHs is premised on loss—loss of functional and cognitive abilities, loss of relationships, and loss of home and possessions (Wiersma, 2008b). Examining specific types of relationships can help further illuminate the nature of relationships in LTCHs.

The relationships between staff and residents can be complicated. Staff play a significant role in socializing residents into the LTCH environment (Wiersma, 2007) and can use their hierarchical

power to coerce residents into conforming to the expectations of the LTCH (Foner, 1995; Wiersma, 2007). Applegate and Morse (1994) found that resident–staff interactions were predominantly associated with care activities and were characterized by indifference, where residents appreciated the staff only as long as their own care needs were met and staff viewed themselves only in the context of their roles as caregivers. Residents viewed their relationships with staff members as a master–servant relationship and as a means of getting something done. The staff treated the residents as objects; they did not demonstrate kindness, compassion, and understanding but saw them as tasks to be completed as quickly as possible. However, researchers have also found that staff can view residents as friends or family. When interactions between residents and staff were personalized, residents appreciated staff and perceived them to be more than workers responsible for their care, while staff attempted to view the residents in a broader social context beyond their identity as residents in an institution (Applegate & Morse, 1994; Wiersma & Pedlar, 2008). Thus, as evidenced by the literature, relationships with staff can range from impersonal to closely personal.

Relationships between residents can also be complicated. Applegate and Morse (1994) found that residents related to each other as objects, strangers, or friends. When residents interacted with each other as objects, they regarded other residents without consideration for their humanness or frailties and treated them as if they were objects with no redeeming qualities. This was most evident in interactions between residents without cognitive impairments toward residents with such impairments. When residents interacted with each other as strangers, they were indifferent to those who shared the facility with them and did not acknowledge others near them. When residents interacted as friends, they demonstrated a genuine interest in other residents and recognized their individuality, although this occurred infrequently. Hubbard, Tester, and Downs (2003) found that humor and flirtation were common between residents in long-term care settings, and although some residents did not like each other, not every relationship was antagonistic.

Families are also an important part of residents' social networks. Researchers have found that the longer a person resides within an LTCH, the less frequently the family visits, although many residents have stated that they would like to see friends and family more often (Bitzan & Kruzich, 1990). In particular, relationships between families and staff in long-term care are important to strong social networks, because families will feel more welcome in the facility when they have positive relationships with LTCH staff. The importance of families to social networks should ensure that LTCH staff support and maintain these relationships in as many ways as possible.

Creating a sense of community in LTCHs involves supporting and maintaining relationships that are fulfilling for residents. There are many ways in which this can be accomplished. Although the literature has typically not examined leisure and recreation in LTCHs, we do know a little about how leisure can contribute to a sense of community. Leisure activities in LTCHs are typically offered in group settings. Because of this group nature, leisure has great potential to increase a sense of community through the establishment of social networks and enhanced relationships.

Sullivan et al. (2002) explored the lived experience of residents and practitioners providing leisure services on a cognitive-support unit of an LTCH. They found that in leisure settings, enlivening relationships could be described as the way relationships developed. Feelings of enjoyment, socializing, making a contribution, and being involved in meaningful activity all were part of enlivening relationships. Being with the person also characterized the relationships between residents and therapeutic recreation practitioners. Being with the person meant that the practitioners embraced the unique identities of each resident and responded accordingly. Numerous types of interactions characterized these relationships in leisure settings, including flattery, language, humor, nonverbal communication, and the hostess–guest relationship. Close relationships between practitioners and residents and among residents themselves developed in leisure settings, creating a sense of community. Residents participated in these relationships

John Birdsall/PA Photo

Creating a sense of community in LTCHs involves supporting and maintaining relationships that are fulfilling for residents.

with reciprocity and delighted in complimenting, flirting with, and flattering the practitioners and other residents.

Rowles and colleagues (1996) discussed how the nursing home they examined was integrated into the community because of the small, rural, close-knit nature of the community. There were numerous kinship links between staff and residents, and "because of such linkages, staff often are viewed by residents through an interpersonal kinship lens that transcends the formal professional relationship characteristic of many nursing homes" (Rowles et al., 1996, p. 193). Families visit the facility often, staff frequently visit the facility outside of working hours, and strong social relationships carry over from relationships existing before residents were admitted to the LTCH.

Wiersma and Pedlar (2008) explored the nature of relationships in alternative dementia care environments. The experiences of older adults with dementia were explored while they were in an LTCH and while they were at a summer camp. In the LTCH, which was a secure unit, relationships with staff were functional and task oriented, and residents appeared less likely to reveal deeper personal feelings or aspects of the self. In the leisure setting at a summer camp, relationships between staff and residents became positive and supportive. Residents and staff were seen as equal at the camp; staff did not wear uniforms or name tags and there were no defined roles or job descriptions. Residents from the secure unit interacted with residents from other units and were not segregated because of their cognitive status. Relationships between staff and residents became more reciprocal and open, with more conversation being initiated by residents than was observed in the LTCH. Staff described the residents as being able to be themselves. As evidenced by this work, the change to a more open environment (i.e., the camp setting) had a significant positive influence on resident and staff relationships. Thus, leisure opportunities can build a sense of community and strengthen relationships.

As mentioned earlier, Wiersma and Dupuis (2002) also explored the meanings of leisure opportunities in the community. Social opportunities as part of community involvement were seen to be very important to LTCH residents. Contact with others was an important connection with the outside world because residents felt they still had some involvement in and sense of belonging to the outside world. Since conversation was often difficult with other residents in the facility, participating in leisure activities with people from the outside or going out of the facility to participate allowed residents to maintain social connections and talk to a variety of people. One type of activity that was important to the participants was the opportunity to go home with one's spouse, partner, or children for the day. Participating in activities such as the family meal and interaction with other family members was important and residents were able to feel like they were still a part of their families. Other activities that enabled opportunities for social contact with people outside the facility included shopping trips, going out for dinner, and visiting friends. Participating in in-house community programs and community-access programs, as well as visiting with community members in the facility, provided opportunities for valued social interactions.

Leisure opportunities thus demonstrate the opportunity to strengthen relationships and social networks, creating a sense of community in terms of shared experience and social networks. Residents are able to continue to be part of family activities and other community activities, to maintain social connections with community members, and to feel connected to the community beyond the facility. The permeability of the walls of the institution, allowing residents out into the community and inviting the community, family, and friends into the facility, helps build and strengthen these social networks and relationships. The loss of relationships that can accompany admission to an LTCH can be mitigated by enabling and supporting residents to maintain relationships outside the facility.

Role Identities in Long-Term Care Settings

Typically, residents living in LTCHs are seen as bed-and-body work, so to speak (Gubrium, 1975; Paterniti, 2000, 2003), and are often identified as tasks (Diamond, 1992). Because LTCHs are primarily focused on accomplishing tasks related to the physical care of residents, the psychological and social dimensions of life in long-term care are often ignored (Diamond, 1992). Consequently, residents can become institutional bodies, seen only as tasks and as physical bodies to be cared for rather than as individuals with identities and histories (Wiersma, 2007). Indeed, residents have been seen as having little to contribute once they enter an LTCH (Wiersma, 2003). One study found that staff members used various ways to make residents aware of the focus on their bodies and of the expectations for care of the body within institutional routines (Wiersma, 2007). A paradox existed in that bodies were considered of utmost importance in certain contexts, such as risk management. Yet in other contexts, such as personal care, bodies were placed at the discretion of staff and care was often delayed because of staff schedules. Although body care was important, staff schedules and routines were much more important than the body. In this way, although the body was still in focus, it was part of the day-to-day routines and structure of the institution, and interactions between residents and staff were centered on the body (Wiersma, 2007).

One of the things that leisure can give people is a role identity, particularly when they may have lost theirs or have a negative one. *Identity* refers to "public and shared aspects of individuals. Identity establishes what and where the person is within social structures, thereby linking self to social structure. . . . Identity defines a person as a social object locked into group memberships and social relationships" (Kelly & Field, 1996, p. 245; Kelly, 1992). Though the LTCH structures residents' identities as bodies (Wiersma, 2007) and as bed-and-body work (Gubrium, 1975; Paterniti, 2000, 2003), leisure can give the opportunity for people to associate with a valued identity and claim or reclaim a role identity (Haggard & Williams, 1992). People can desire the leisure identity images associated with their activity and choose activities that are aligned with their sense of self (Haggard & Williams, 1992; Pedlar, Dupuis, & Gilbert, 1996). Thus, leisure activities in LTCHs can provide opportunities for residents to redefine the role of being a body, the primary role assigned to them (Wiersma, 2007). Through social networks, relationships, and social interactions, residents can present a different self-identity than the one assigned by the institution (Paterniti, 2000). Paterniti (2003) found that residents did not solely define themselves by institutional terms, and casual sociability was one way of framing who they were on their own terms: "Storytelling thus allowed the residents to transcend the institutional rhythms surrounding their daily lives" (p. 68).

Leisure can also help people residing in institutions to regain valued roles they may have lost because of institutionalization. Pedlar, Dupuis, and Gilbert (1996) examined this phenomenon in an action research project focusing on one participant, Eric, and the experience of integrating him into community leisure activities. At the time of the study, Eric resided in a nursing home, and leisure opportunities were provided for him within the facility. The researchers interviewed and observed Eric in integrated community recreation over 10 months. Three patterns emerged through the process of integrating Eric into a community woodworking program: (1) identifying common enthusiasms in leisure, (2) having an opportunity to contribute, and (3) demonstrating capabilities. Eric had been interested in woodworking throughout his life and identified with others in the program who shared this interest. Because of Eric's competence in woodworking, other participants in the program began to ask him for advice on their work, giving him an opportunity to contribute. As well, Eric was able to demonstrate and was recognized for his capabilities. Throughout this integration process, Eric was able to resume a valued role that he had lost upon institutionalization. As evidenced in this study, leisure can enable people to resume role identities.

Wiersma and Dupuis' (2002) study examining residents' perceptions of community-access programs found that residents obtained personal rewards from participating in community-access programs. The personal rewards centered on continued competence and independence. Residents were able to demonstrate that they were not solely dependent and defined as a body by institutional structures as they reclaimed an identity where they were competent, involved, and independent.

As discussed, there are various ways that leisure and recreation can create a sense of community within the facility and bridge the gap between the outside community and the institution. The opportunities to create permeable boundaries through recreation and leisure activities are limitless and can be provided from the inside out (community outreach) and from the outside in (community access) (Rowles et al., 1996). Although challenges exist to creating permeable boundaries, recreation therapists and practitioners should strive to ensure that these goals are achieved through leisure activities. Ideally, LTCHs can become part of the community, as in the case study of Mountain View (Rowles et al., 1996), where a sense of community ownership pervaded people's images of the LTCH. The benefits to residents have been demonstrated through the literature (Dupuis et al., 2005; Pedlar et al., 1996; Wiersma & Dupuis, 2002), and a sense of community within the facility and integration with the greater community can be achieved, helping to ease the transition for residents and ultimately enhancing quality of life.

Creating Community in Practice

Health care providers, particularly therapeutic recreation practitioners, can play a significant role in creating and maintaining a sense of community. In this section we propose various ways that practitioners can build community in the LTCH.

Sharing

- Provide residents with the opportunity to participate in community activities. For example, take residents to a nearby park in the summertime.
- Plan outings to local restaurants. Invite families to join.
- Plan outings to the local pub. Start a men's group and a women's group and have get-togethers at the pub.
- Plan programs in the facility that involve both staff and residents. For example, when planning a birthday party, celebrate birthdays of both staff and residents.
- Plan events that celebrate a common history, such as a special historical event of the community.

Social Networks

- Plan activities that focus on building social networks and relationships within the facility. For example, have a ladies' tea or start a men's group.
- In your interactions with residents, involve other residents and facilitate the conversation between residents rather than just between yourself and the resident.
- Facilitate a visit between two residents by bringing one to the other's room or to a sitting area.
- Plan special events for families and friends, such as dinners.
- Provide space for families and friends to visit with residents.
- Provide outdoor spaces for families and friends to visit with residents.
- Provide resources and guides for families and friends about various activities they can participate in with residents.
- Help residents visit family members' houses, such as by arranging transportation or ensur-

ing that the necessary support is available for families.

Role Identity

- Find out the past activities that residents participated in and find opportunities for them to continue to participate in these activities.
- Have residents be history experts for a local school class.
- Have residents document the history of the community and share their memories with the town or city.
- Relate to the residents based on what they have done and who they are rather than what care they need.
- Document the history of the residents together and share it with the staff.
- Find opportunities for residents to volunteer in the community.

Conclusion

We have attempted in this chapter to demonstrate that community is not contradictory to LTCHs and that LTCHs do not have to be isolated from the greater community. Indeed, we challenge the notion of community as a geographic place and suggest alternative definitions—those of sharing, social networks, and role identity. In this way, LTCHs are not solely seen as institutions but instead as vibrant places that can develop a strong sense of community within and be integrated with the greater community. Thus, similar to the ideas of Rowles et al. (1996), we see community being built from the inside out and the outside in.

As demonstrated by research, residents in LTCHs wish to be part of their communities and to stay involved in community activities. Because of the ways that LTCHs have been structured, particularly in Ontario, and because of the ideas associated with LTCHs (i.e., closed institutions), residents have not always been supported in their desire to be part of their communities. Recreation and leisure programs can play a significant role in developing a sense of community within the facility as well as allowing residents to remain integrated with the world outside the facility. It is our hope that this chapter will inspire community integration of LTCH residents and challenge practitioners to support residents in being involved in community activities and creating a sense of community within the facility.

KEY TERMS

community—Refers to geographic location, groups of which one is a part, or a sense of connectedness.

external community—The geographical area in which the LTCH is located and the sense of community associated with residents, staff, and families.

internal community—The LTCH as a community.

long-term care—Ongoing, indefinite care for people who can no longer care for themselves.

long-term care homes (LTCHs)—Institutional facilities designed to care for seniors; also referred to as *nursing homes, skilled nursing facilities,* or *long-term care facilities.*

role identities—Social meaning of one's position within a group and social relationships, defining a person as a social object.

sharing—Common experiences, history, and goals that contribute to a sense of community.

social networks—Interpersonal ties that connect people to each other, services, and organizations.

total institution—A place of residence where people lead an enclosed way of life, removed from wider society, with little or no control over the administration of the institution.

REVIEW AND DISCUSSION QUESTIONS

1. Community was defined in different ways in this chapter. What definition of community do you feel is the most appropriate for LTCHs?
2. How can the concepts of community make the transition easier or less stressful for seniors coming to live in an LTCH?
3. What kinds of leisure and recreation activities can enhance a sense of community?
4. Brainstorm other ideas that TR practitioners can use to enhance a sense of community in the LTCH.

LEARNING ACTIVITIES

1. Think about the leisure activities that you are involved in and the people that you participate in leisure with. What do you share together? How does sharing enhance a sense of belonging and community?
2. Draw your social networks on a piece of paper. Draw a small circle and put yourself inside. Draw another larger circle around the smaller circle. In this circle, write close friends and family. Draw another larger circle around these two circles and write in friends and acquaintances. Highlight in yellow the people you have close relationships with, and use green for people you have a more distant relationship with. Outside the largest circle, put institutions, organizations, and activities that you are involved with. What does your diagram look like? Now imagine you were a resident in an LTCH and do the same activity. What would your social networks look like?
3. Who are you? Name as many things that describe you as you can, such as "I am a runner" or "I am a mother." What does this say about your role identities? What role identities do you think LTCH residents have? What identities would they have if they were integrated into the world outside the facility? What identities would they have if community were created within their LTCH?
4. Brainstorm ways that therapeutic recreation practitioners can enhance a sense of community in LTCHs.

CRITICAL-THINKING ACTIVITIES

1. When you think of the concept of community, what does it mean to you?
2. How do you think residents in LTCHs should be involved in the greater community?
3. What responsibility do LTCHs and their staff have to facilitate residents' involvement in the community?
4. In what ways can a sense of community within the LTCH be enhanced?
5. What challenges exist to creating a sense of community within an LTCH and to integrating the LTCH into the greater community? How can these challenges be mitigated?

SUGGESTED READING

Dupuis, S.L., Smale, B.J., & Wiersma, E.C. (2005). Creating open environments in long-term care settings: An examination of influencing factors. *Therapeutic Recreation Journal, 39*(4), 277-298.

Gubrium, J.F. (1993). *Speaking of life: Horizons of meaning for nursing home residents.* Hawthorne, NY: Aldine de Gruyter.

Pedlar, A., Dupuis, S., & Gilbert, A. (1996). Resumption of role status through leisure in later life. *Leisure Sciences, 18,* 259-276.

Rowles, G.D., Concotelli, J.A., & High, D.M. (1996). Community integration of a rural nursing home. *Journal of Applied Gerontology, 15*(2), 188-201.

Sullivan, A., Pedlar, A., & Miller, B. (2002). Experiencing leisure on a cognitive support unit. *Society and Leisure, 25*(2), 443-471.

Wiersma, E.C. (2008). The experiences of place: Veterans with dementia making meaning of their environments. *Health and Place, 14*(4), 779-794.

Wiersma, E.C., & Pedlar, A. (2008). The nature of relationships in alternative dementia care environments. *Canadian Journal on Aging, 27*(1), 101-108.

REFERENCES

Applegate, M., & Morse, J.M. (1994). Personal privacy and interactional patterns in a nursing home. *Journal of Aging Studies, 8*(4), 413-434.

Armstrong, P., Banerjee, A., Szebehely, M., Armstrong, H., Daly, T., Lafrance, S. (2009). *They deserve better: The long-term care experience in Canada and Scandinavia.* Ottawa: Canadian Centre for Policy Alternative.

Banerjee, A. (2009). Long-term care in Canada: An overview. In P. Armstrong, M. Boscoe, B. Clow, K. Grant, M. Haworth-Brockman, B. Jackson, A. Pederson, M. Seeley, & J. Springer (Eds.), *A place to call home: Long-term care in Canada* (pp. 29-57). Black Point, NS: Fernwood.

Baranek, P., Deber, R., & Williams, A.P. (2004). *Almost home: Reforming home and community care in Ontario.* Toronto: University of Toronto Press.

Bellah, R.N., Madsen, R., Sullivan, W.M., Swidler, A., & Tipton, M. (1985). *Habits of the heart: Individualism and commitment in American life.* New York: Harper & Row.

Bitzan, J.E., & Kruzich, J.M. (1990). Interpersonal relationships of nursing home residents. *Gerontologist, 30*(3), 385-390.

Brueggemann, W.G. (2001). *The practice of macro social work* (2nd ed.). Belmont, CA: Brooks/Thomson Learning.

Canada Research Network for Care in the Community. (2006). In-focus fact sheet: Community support services. Retrieved from www.ryerson.ca/.../factsheets/.../InFocus-CommunitySupportServicesfinal.pdf.

CCAC Client Services Policy Manual. (2006). Eligibility criteria for CCAC services. Retrieved from http://www.health.gov.on.ca/english/providers/pub/manuals/ccac/ccac_3.pdf.

Diamond, T. (1992). *Making gray gold: Narratives of nursing home care.* Chicago: University of Chicago Press.

Dobbs, D. (2004). The adjustment to a new home. *Journal of Housing for the Elderly, 18*(1), 51-71.

Dupuis, S.L., Smale, B.J., & Wiersma, E.C. (2005). Creating open environments in long-term care settings: An examination of influencing factors. *Therapeutic Recreation Journal, 39*(4), 277-298.

Eckert, J.K., Carder, P., Morgan, L., Frankowski, A.C., & Roth, E.G. (2009). *Inside assisted living: The search for home.* Baltimore: Johns Hopkins University Press.

Foner, N. (1995). *The caregiving dilemma: Work in an American nursing home.* Berkeley, CA: University of California Press.

Goffman, E. (1961). *Asylums.* New York: Anchor Books/Doubleday.

Golander, H. (1995). Rituals of temporality: The social construction of time in a nursing ward. *Journal of Aging Studies, 9*(2), 119-135.

Gubrium, J.F. (1975). *Living and dying at Murray Manor.* New York: St. Martin's Press.

Gubrium, J.F. (1993). *Speaking of life: Horizons of meaning for nursing home residents.* Hawthorne, NY: Aldine de Gruyter.

Haggard, L.M., & Williams, D.R. (1992). Identity affirmations through leisure activities: Leisure symbols of self. *Journal of Leisure Research, 24*(1), 1-18.

Heliker, P., Scholler-Jaquish, A. (2006). Transition of new residents: Basing practice on residents' perspective. *Journal of Gerontological Nursing, 32*(9), 34-42.

Hubbard, G., Tester, S., & Downs, M.G. (2003). Meaningful social interactions between older people in institutional care settings. *Ageing and Society, 23,* 99-114.

Kelly, M. (1992). Self, identity, and radical surgery. *Sociology of Health and Illness, 14,* 390-415.

Kelly, M.P., & Field, D. (1996). Medical sociology, chronic illness and the body. *Sociology of Health and Illness, 18*(2), 241-257.

Kerzner, L. (2004). Home care services: Provided through Community Care Access Centres (CCASs). Retrieved from www.archdisabilitylaw.ca/ARCH/liveaccess/.../05_homeCare.pdf.

Levin, C. (2000). Social functioning. In R.L. Kane & R.A. Kane (Eds.), *Assessing older persons: Measures, meaning, and practical applications* (pp. 170-199). New York: Oxford University Press.

Mahoney, A.R. (1994). Change in the older-person role: An application of Turner's process role and model of role change. *Journal of Aging Studies, 8*(2), 133-148.

Ministry of Health and Long-Term Care (MOHLTC). (2009a). Notice of the proposed initial draft regulation Long-Term Care Homes Act, 2007. Retrieved from http://health.gov.on.ca/english/public/legislation/ltc_homes/pdf/ltcha_draft_reg2.pdf.

Paterniti, D.A. (2000). The micropolitics of identity making in adverse circumstance: A study of identity making in a total institution. *Journal of Contemporary Ethnography, 29*(1), 93-119.

Paterniti, D.A. (2003). Claiming identity in a nursing home. In J.A. Holstein & J.F. Gubrium (Eds.), *Ways of aging* (pp. 58-74). Malden, MA: Blackwell.

Pedlar, A., Dupuis, S., & Gilbert, A. (1996). Resumption of role status through leisure in later life. *Leisure Sciences, 18*, 259-276.

Porter, E.J., & Clinton, J.F. (1992). Adjusting to the nursing home. *Western Journal of Nursing Research, 14*(4), 464-481.

Powers, B.A. (1995). From the inside out: The world of the institutionalized elderly. In J.N. Henderson & M.D. Vesperi (Eds.), *The culture of long-term care: Nursing home ethnography* (pp. 179-196). Westport, CT: Bergin & Garvey.

Powers, B.A. (1996). Relationships among older women living in a nursing home. *Journal of Women & Aging, 8*(3/4), 179-198.

Rowles, G.D., Concotelli, J.A., & High, D.M. (1996). Community integration of a rural nursing home. *Journal of Applied Gerontology, 15*(2), 188-201.

Slama, C.A., & Bergman-Evans, B. (2000). A troubling triangle: An exploration of loneliness, helplessness, and boredom of residents of a veterans' home. *Journal of Psychosocial Nursing, 38*(12), 36-43.

Smith, M. (2004). Commitment to care: A plan for long-term care in Ontario. Ministry of Health and Long-Term Care. Retrieved from www.health.gov.on.ca/english/public/pub/ministry_reports/ltc_04/mohltc_report04.pdf.

Sullivan, A., Pedlar, A., & Miller, B. (2002). Experiencing leisure on a cognitive support unit. *Society and Leisure, 25*(2), 443-471.

Thomas, W.H. (1996). *Life worth living: The Eden Alternative in action.* Acton, MA: VanderWyk & Burnham.

Tracy, P., & DeYoung, S. (2004). Moving to an assisted living facility: Exploring the transitional experience for elderly individuals. *Journal of Gerontological Nursing, 30*(10), 26-33.

Wiersma, E.C. (2003). *Making meaning: Place and the experiences of individuals living with dementia.* Unpublished master's thesis, University of Waterloo, Waterloo, Ontario.

Wiersma, E.C. (2007). *Making institutional bodies: Socialization into the nursing home.* Unpublished doctoral dissertation, University of Waterloo, Waterloo, Ontario.

Wiersma, E.C. (2008a). The experiences of place: Veterans with dementia making meaning of their environments. *Health and Place, 14*(4), 779-794.

Wiersma, E.C. (2008b). Dismantling of the self: Loss and grief in admission to long-term care. *Senior Care Canada, 10*(3), 12-15.

Wiersma, E., & Dupuis, S.L. (2002). A qualitative analysis of the meaning of community involvement for older adults living in long-term care facilities. In E.L. Jackson (Ed.), *Celebrating the past and the future of Canadian leisure studies: Book of Abstracts, CCLR 10* (pp. 348-351). Edmonton, Alberta: Canadian Association for Leisure Studies.

Wiersma, E.C., & Dupuis, S.L. (2010). Becoming institutional bodies: Socialization into a long-term care home. *Journal of Aging Studies, 24*(4), 278-291.

Wiersma, E.C., & Pedlar, A. (2008). The nature of relationships in alternative dementia care environments. *Canadian Journal on Aging, 27*(1), 101-108.

Wilson, S.A. (1997). The transition to nursing home life: A comparison of planned and unplanned admissions. *Journal of Advanced Nursing, 26*, 864-871.

Epilogue

As the demographics of both developed and developing countries change and populations age, what does the future hold for scholars and practitioners who are interested in leisure and aging? The chapters in this text illustrate the complexity of the intersection of leisure and aging. The text has examined the physical, social, spiritual, psychological, and service-delivery components of enhancing the leisure of people who are aging. Scholars from around the world, including Canada, the United States, Israel, New Zealand, and Australia, have discussed how leisure benefits the well-being of aging populations. The text has provided an understanding of how theory can be used to frame service delivery as well as opportunities for critical reflections of how terms such as *aging* and *leisure* are socially constructed and reflect the society that is defining them.

Current Understanding

Historically the dominant discourse in the aging literature has been based on negative stereotypes of older adults. Dionigi and Horten (chapter 3) stated that most knowledge about older adults is based on widespread stereotypes and myths. But due to economic and demographic changes, new perspectives on aging are emerging (Bloom & Canning, 2006; MacNeil & Gould, chapter 1; Kohlbacher & Cornelius, 2008; SEN@ER, 2005). The changing discourse on how societies perceive aging is starting to encompass new roles for older adults, including athlete, world traveler, community volunteer, and more. The pervasive view that old age is one homogenous life stage characterized by mental and physical decline is being challenged by the use of new theories such as poststructuralism and by the baby boom generation as they transition into late adulthood. One example of these new perspectives is found in emerging policy directions, such as the Silver Economy Network of European Regions (SEN@ER).

The SEN@ER has recognized that the current aging of its member countries will influence how societies define aging. This network views population aging not as a threat but as a challenge to encourage older adults to continue working (www.silvereconomy-europe.org). This reflects a shift from a negative stereotype of aging to one that views aging from a positive perspective. This is due to the shifting understanding of the baby boomers, who are the largest cohort today and will affect developed countries for the next 20 years. The question for many governments faced with a declining workforce is, how can they encourage people to remain engaged in the labor force rather than encouraging them to seek early retirement?

Working from the idea of changes in the world's population, the following questions could potentially frame leisure and aging research in the future:

- What do older people think about the elimination of mandatory retirement in Western society?
- How will Western societies react to eliminating mandatory retirement or changing the retirement age such as in France in 2010? How will this changing perspective influence government policies, communities, and individual perspectives of work, leisure, aging, and well-being? How will this changing expectation influence the next generation of older adults? The millennium generation (1982 to 2000) will begin turning 65 in 2047. What will be this generation's perspective of aging, leisure, and well-being?
- How will the migration of people from developing nations to developed nations affect how the term *leisure* is defined?
- How is the term *aging* defined in developing nations?
- How is the term *leisure* defined in developing nations?

■ How will the shift of economic power to the emerging economies of Asia and Latin America affect attitudes toward leisure and retirement in these countries?

As we experience global changes in the demographics of developed and developing nations during the next 40 years, how can scholars of leisure and aging frame their research to understand the effects of these changes? Bronfenbrenner's (1979) ecological model was used by a variety of authors (see chapters 3 and 5) to understand the construction of the leisure and aging experience while taking into account the interaction of gender, culture, and government policy. Bronfenbrenner's model is similar to a Russian doll, with each layer nestled within the layers of influence from the macro system (government policies) to the micro system (individual). These layers influence people's opportunities within the society they reside in (see chapter 5).

Shifting Understanding of Leisure, Aging, and Well-Being

The authors in this text have provided insights into the meaning of leisure and aging within the classic and current literature. The authors acknowledge that the opportunities engaged in by older adults will be influenced by the person's culture and gender as well as how the researchers have operationalized these terms in their studies. Do researchers perpetuate ageism by how they define the concepts *aging* or *leisure* in their research? Do the theories perpetuate the role expectations of people who are aging? Are researchers segregating people by age versus what the person is interested in across the life course? How have the theories and tools used in research shaped our understanding of the leisure activities older people participate in? Are our insights into leisure and aging limited by the research methodology used in the studies, such as cross-sectional versus longitudinal? Smale and Gillies (chapter 4) provided insight into how research may shape our understanding of leisure and aging.

Scholars in the text have discussed older adults' participation in community and their transition into long-term care. These insights enable you to understand how participation in leisure influences well-being. In the studies cited in these chapters, how did the researchers define *leisure* and *aging* and how did their definitions influence the results? Did the older populations that participated in these studies reflect the diversity of aging people within a global society or just Western societies? What populations have been underrepresented in studies of older adults? Could researchers have perpetuated stereotypes of aging by the theory and method they used in their studies? What areas have not been examined as extensively as others in the literature on leisure and aging?

This text sets the framework for continued discussions based on the questions raised by the contributing scholars in enhancing the understanding of the intersection of leisure and aging in research. The cohort of older adults in the year 2065 will be composed of the millennium generation. How will this cohort influence what we understand about leisure across the life course? How will government policy influence how the terms *leisure* and *aging* are defined during the next 50 years? You will either perpetuate stereotypes of aging or provide new insights to the literature on leisure and aging related to your experiences. The text provides the framework for you to move the practice and research agenda for leisure and aging forward.

How will your perception of who is older influence the type of services provided to the baby boomers? What services will the millennium generation expect as they enter late adulthood? How will services for an aging population change due to the demographic shifts occurring in developed nations? The chapters in this text have challenged you to be a critical thinker in regard to research as well as in regard to how you will provide services for a changing population of aging adults. How will you develop services for people who are older? Will you use the dominant theories in provision of services, or will you use gap analysis (Davis, Misra, & Van Auken, 2002) or relationship marketing (Gummesson, 2002, 2004) to understand how people engage in leisure consumption?

This text has provided critical-thinking activities throughout the chapters to give you the opportunity to reflect on how you think about leisure and aging. Your insights based upon the systematic process provided in each of the chapters will frame how you provide leisure services to meet the needs of the changing demographics of the global population.

REFERENCES

Bloom, D.E., & Canning, D. (2006). *Global demography: Fact, force and future.* The WDA-HSG Discussion Paper Series on Demographic Issues, No. 2006/1, World Demographic Association. Retrieved from www.wdaforum. org/images/stories/diskussionspapiere/WDA-HSG-DP2006-1_Bloom_Canning.pdf.

Bronfenbrenner, U. (1979). *The ecology of human development.* Cambridge, MA: Harvard University Press.

Davis, R., Misra, S., & Van Auken, S. (2002). A gap analysis approach to marketing curriculum assessment: A study of skills and knowledge. *Journal of Marketing Education, 24,* 218-224.

Gummesson, E. (2002). Relationship marketing and a new economy. In W.J. Glynn &J.G. Barnes (Eds.), *Understanding services management* (pp. 244-268). New York: Wiley.

Gummesson, E. (2004) Return on relationships (ROR): The value of relationship marketing and CRM in business-to-business contexts. *Journal of Business & Industrial Marketing, 19*(2), 136.

Kohlbacher, F., & Cornelius, H. (Eds.). (2008). *The Silver Market Phenomenon.* Berlin: Springer.

Silver Economy Network of European Regions (SEN@ER). (2005). Policy documents. Retrieved from www.silvereconomy-europe.org/EC_policies/eu-policy_en.htm.

Index

Note: Page numbers followed by an italicized *f* or *t* refer to the figure or table on that page, respectively.

About the Editors

Heather J. Gibson, PhD, is an associate professor in the department of tourism, recreation, and sport management at the University of Florida and an associate director of the Center for Tourism Research and Development. She graduated from Brighton Polytechnic in the UK with a bachelor's degree in physical education with a specialization in sport sociology. This focus on the sociology of sport and leisure led her to the University of Connecticut, where she earned her master's and PhD and was introduced to tourism as a field of study. Currently, Dr. Gibson teaches classes in leisure theory, tourism, and research methods. She also leads study abroad programs to Australia, New Zealand, and Fiji. She was selected as the Distinguished International Educator for her college in 2004 and 2010. Her research interests include leisure and tourism in later life, female travelers, sport tourism with a particular focus on sport-related travel in later life and small-scale events, and perceived risk in travel. Dr. Gibson has published over 40 peer-reviewed articles in scholarly journals, and she edited the top-selling book *Sport Tourism: Concepts and Theories.* She is an associate editor for *Leisure Sciences*; North American regional editor for *Leisure Studies*; and an editorial board member for the *Journal of Sport Management, Journal of Sport and Tourism,* and *World Leisure Journal.* She is ad hoc reviewer for countless journals, including the *Journal of Leisure Research*, *Annals of Tourism Research,* and *Tourism Management.*

Jerome F. Singleton, PhD, CTRS is a professor in the recreation and leisure studies department in the School of Health and Human Performance at Dalhousie University. He is also cross-appointed to the Schools of Nursing, Sociology and Anthropology, and Business Administration at Dalhousie. Dr. Singleton's research is focused on leisure and aging. He earned his bachelor's degree with honors in recreation from the University of Waterloo and then completed his master's of science degree in recreation at Pennsylvania State University and his PhD in leisure studies at the University of Maryland. He also completed the academic requirements for a doctorate certificate in gerontology at the University of Maryland. Currently Dr. Singleton teaches courses in the area of therapeutic recreation and aging, therapeutic recreation techniques, and introduction to recreation and leisure and aging at Dalhousie University. He was made a fellow of the World Demographic

Association in 2006 and was named Canadian Therapeutic Recreation Association Professional of the Year in 2007. He was recognized by the Recreation and Leisure Studies program at the University of Waterloo as a Distinguished Alumnus in 2008 and is also the founding member of the Leisure and Aging Research Group, which was established in 2008. Dr. Singleton received the Dr. Gonzaga da Gama Memorial Award from the Canadian Therapeutic Recreation Association in 2011 and was made a fellow of the Academy of Leisure Science by the Society of Parks and Recreation educators in 2011. Dr. Singleton is currently a research associate with the Dalhousie European Center of Excellence. Dr. Singleton has advised 25 graduate students who have investigated questions related to leisure and aging and has published over 80 journal articles during his career and made presentations locally, nationally, and internationally. He has served on the editorial boards for the *Therapeutic Recreation Journal*; *American Therapeutic Recreation Annual*; *Topics in Geriatric Rehabilitation*; and the *Journal of Recreation and Society in Africa, Asia and Latin America*. He has also reviewed articles for *Loisir*, *Leisure Sciences*, and *Topics in Geriatric Rehabilitation*.

About the Contributors

Carissa Bakker has a master of arts in recreation and leisure studies from the University of Waterloo. Her area of research is in Aboriginal youth and recreation participation.

Jennifer Carson, PhD, is a doctoral candidate in the aging, health and well-being collaborative PhD program, at the University of Waterloo, Canada. Professionally, Jennifer has worked in long-term care and assisted-living settings as a certified therapeutic recreation specialist, program director, quality of life consultant, and general manager. Her current research aims to foster culture change in long-term care settings through the use of critical participatory action research and other participatory approaches.

Stephanie Chesser is a second-year PhD student in the department of recreation and leisure studies at the University of Waterloo. Her academic background includes a BScH (biology) from Queen's University and a master of public health degree and diploma in health services and policy research from Lakehead University. Stephanie's research interests relate to feminist explorations of gender, family, and aging using qualitative methodologies.

Rylee A. Dionigi is associate head of the school of human movement studies at Charles Sturt University, Australia. She has published in the fields of sport sociology, aging and physical activity, exercise psychology, and leisure studies. Dr. Dionigi has expertise in qualitative research methods and extensive knowledge on the older athlete. Her book, *Competing for Life: Older People, Sport and Ageing* (2008), is the first published research monograph to present extensive empirical qualitative data on the personal and cultural meanings of competitive sports participation in later life.

Sherry L. Dupuis, PhD, is a professor in the department of recreation and leisure studies and the director of the Murray Alzheimer Research and Education Program (MAREP) at the University of Waterloo, Canada. Her research focuses on facilitating culture change in long-term care broadly and dementia care more specifically through the active and meaningful involvement in decision making by persons with dementia, family members, and staff at all levels working collaboratively. She is also exploring the use of alternative representations of research such as research-based drama in challenging assumptions and triggering personal and social change.

Julie Freelove-Charton received her PhD in health behavior from the Arnold School of Public Health at the University of South Carolina, and holds a master's degree in kinesiology and a professional certificate in gerontology. She is a senior research associate at the Center for Behavioral Epidemiology and Community Health at the Graduate School of Public Health at San Diego State University. For over two decades, she has worked to help older adults increase their motivation to live a more physically active and healthy lifestyle. Her research focuses on the role of physical activity for disease management and prevention, and the development and implementation of community-based behavior change interventions. Her current program examines the use of group-travel to increase physical activity, brain health, and social support in underserved older adults.

Rebecca Genoe, PhD, is an assistant professor in the faculty of kinesiology and health studies at the University of Regina. She earned her PhD in recreation and leisure studies at the University of Waterloo, specializing in aging, health, and well-being. Rebecca's research focuses on meanings and experiences of leisure in later life, particularly for persons living with chronic illness.

Jennifer Gillies, PhD, is a postdoctoral fellow with the Murray Alzheimer Research and Education Program (MAREP) at the University of Waterloo. Jennifer's academic background includes a PhD in recreation and leisure studies from the University of Waterloo, a BA and MA in recreation and leisure studies from the University of Waterloo, and a second MA in critical disability studies from York University. Jennifer's research explores issues of accessibility, inclusion, and human rights for persons with disabilities and illnesses. She has experience utilizing various qualitative research methods including participatory action research, appreciative inquiry, and creative analytic practice.

Richard Gitelson, PhD, received his graduate certificate in gerontology from Arizona State University in 2000. He has conducted research on aging and healthy behavior for the past 13 years, focusing on the Arizona Senior Olympics, the National Senior Games, senior centers, and retirement communities. His involvement in aging research projects was recognized by the National Communication Association in 2003 and by the National Institute of Senior Centers in 2002 with their National Award for Research. Dr. Gitelson has made numerous presentations at the Gerontological Society of America and American Society on Aging annual conferences and written extensively on leisure and aging.

David Gould is the associate director for student development in the University of Iowa's college of liberal arts and sciences. He also holds a faculty position in the department of health and human physiology. His courses explore the cultural importance of leisure and play. In 2007 he won an award for outstanding teaching at the university. He was a nominee for the 2008 President and Provost Award for Teaching Excellence, and for the Lola Lopes Award for Undergraduate Student Advocacy in both 2009 and 2010. In 2010 and 2011, graduating seniors at the University of Iowa recognized him as one of the top faculty and staff members who had a positive effect on their lives.

Bevan C. Grant is a professor in the department of sport and leisure studies at the University of Waikato, New Zealand. His widely published research primarily explores the meanings older people attach to their day-to-day experiences, particularly in regards to active leisure and quality of life. This includes examining the interaction between research, policy, and community initiatives. He is an active member of NZ Gerontology Association, NZ Recreation Association, and Age Concern. His favorite leisure pursuits are cycling and trying to outwit an elusive trout in a slow flowing stream in clean, green New Zealand.

Paul Heintzman is an associate professor of leisure studies at the University of Ottawa where he completed his undergraduate degree. Before completing his PhD in recreation and leisure studies at the University of Waterloo, he was a recreation practitioner for 12 years in various positions across Canada. He has also been a professor at Acadia and Brock universities. In 2003 he received the Society of Park and Recreation Educator's Innovation in Teaching Award for the experiential exercises he developed to teach about leisure and spirituality. His areas of research include leisure and spirituality, philosophy and ethics of leisure, and recreation and the environment.

Sean Horton is an associate professor in kinesiology at the University of Windsor. His research interests lie primarily in the area of skill acquisition and expert performance, both in young athletes and as individuals age. His most recent work has focused on older adults and the extent to which high levels of performance can be maintained into the latter stages of life.

Erica Hummel recently completed her MA in tourism policy and planning at the University of Waterloo. Her research is in the area of recreation and leisure of marginalized groups and her masters investigated the motivations of sexual minority adults for vacationing at a sexual minority-focused seasonal home campground.

Megan C. Janke, PhD, CTRS, is an assistant professor of gerontology at the University of South Florida Polytechnic. She received her PhD in child and family development with an emphasis in aging from the University of Georgia. In addition, she earned her

BS and MS degrees in parks and recreation management with a concentration in therapeutic recreation. She is a certified therapeutic recreation specialist (CTRS) and has experience working with older adults in physical rehabilitation, long-term care, and community settings.

Douglas Kleiber is a professor in the recreation and leisure studies program at the University of Georgia, with courtesy appointments in the department of psychology and the Institute of Gerontology. He has degrees in psychology and educational psychology from Cornell University and the University of Texas, respectively. He is a past president of the Academy of Leisure Sciences and, with Gordon Walker and Roger Mannell, the author of *Leisure Experience and Human Development: A Social Psychology of Leisure.* He has also written numerous articles and book chapters on the significance of leisure in adjusting to negative life events and other developmental transitions.

Mary Ann Kluge, PhD, is a tenured associate professor at the Beth-El College of Nursing and Health Sciences at the University of Colorado, Colorado Springs (UCCS) where she teaches undergraduate and graduate courses in health and wellness promotion. Dr. Kluge has extensive experience working with people of all ages and ability levels but for the past 15 years, she has focused on older adult fitness, wellness, and sports participation. Her research, writing, and public speaking is primarily on how to best support older adults' discovery and maintenance of a physically active self through the later years. Her research method of choice is qualitative inquiry.

Richard MacNeil has been a professor at the University of Iowa since 1975. His primary teaching responsibilities are in the fields of therapeutic recreation and gerontology. He has served the university in a wide variety of capacities including departmental chair and coordinator of the university's aging studies program. MacNeil is the co-author of three books and has published over 50 papers in the fields of therapeutic recreation and aging studies. He has received the National Therapeutic Recreation Society's Professional Research Award (1993), Presidential Award (1994), and the Meritorious Service Award (1995).

Roger C. Mannell, PhD, is a psychologist and professor of leisure and health studies and gerontology at the University of Waterloo and director of the Royal Bank of Canada Retirement Research Centre. His research on determinants of leisure and lifestyle choices and their influence on health and successful aging has been funded by various organizations including the Social Science and Humanities Research Council of Canada. Roger is an elected fellow and past president of the Academy of Leisure Sciences and recipient of the Allen V. Sapora Research Award and National Parks and Recreation Association's Theodore and Franklin Roosevelt Research Excellence Award.

Steven E. Mock is an assistant professor in the department of recreation and leisure studies and the school of public health and health systems at the University of Waterloo. Dr. Mock's research is in the area of life span development with a focus on the social nature of coping and decision making, coping with stigmatized identities, and leisure as a coping resource.

Galit Nimrod, PhD, Fulbright scholar, is a senior lecturer at the department of communication studies and a research fellow at the Center for Multidisciplinary Research in Aging at Ben-Gurion University of the Negev, Israel. She studies psychological and sociological aspects of leisure among populations with special needs such as older adults and people with disabilities. Within this area, she focuses on several subjects, including leisure and later life transitions (such as retirement, widowhood, and health decline), innovation in leisure, and new media as leisure activity and their functions for individuals and various social groups.

Erin Patriquin studied health sciences and leisure studies at the University of Ottawa. She graduated cum laude with an Honours BA with a specialization in leisure studies. Her areas of focus include leisure for specialized population, tourism, and environmental leisure.

Ian Patterson, PhD, is an associate professor in the school of tourism at the University of Queensland, Australia. He teaches courses in leisure, tourism, and sport management, and has published over 60 peer reviewed scholarly articles and 17 book chapters. He has also successfully supervised 11 PhD thesis completions. He is primarily interested in researching the leisure, tourism, and event experiences of baby boomers and older people. In 2006 he wrote the textbook titled *Growing Older: Tourism and Leisure Behaviour of Older Adults* with CABI Publishing House. He is currently an editor of the journal, *Annals of Leisure Research.*

Shane Pegg, PhD, MBA, is a senior lecturer with the school of tourism in the faculty of business, economics, and law at The University of Queensland, Australia. He has an active and ongoing involvement in research and consultancy projects related to the effective management of sport and tourism services, experience management, and volunteerism. Shane has published over 50 refereed papers and 15 book chapters related to the field. Recent projects he has been involved in have included an assessment of participant engagement in the Australian University Games, an exploration of the visitor experience at the Shanghai World Expo, and the perception of hotel managers toward issues pertaining to accessible tourism.

Susan M. Shaw is professor emeritus at the University of Waterloo, Ontario, Canada. She is past president of the Academy of Leisure Sciences and the Canadian Association for Leisure Studies. Her research publications, which include *Both Gains and Gaps: Feminist Perspectives on Women's Leisure* (co-author) and *A Handbook of Leisure Studies* (co-editor), have focused on leisure and gender; the intersection of work, family, and leisure; and the implications of leisure for social and cultural change.

Bryan Smale, PhD, is a professor in the department of recreation and leisure studies, and director of the *Canadian Index of Wellbeing*, both in the faculty of applied health sciences at the University of Waterloo. He is cross-appointed to the department of geography and environmental management, and is a research faculty associate in the Murray Alzheimer Research and Education Program (MAREP) and the Social Innovation Generation (SiG). His research focuses on the role of leisure in the health and well-being of individuals and communities, the spatial distribution and analysis of leisure, time use allocation, social indicators research, innovative applications of multiple research methods, and multivariate statistical techniques and applications.

Ryan Snelgrove is a CIHR postdoctoral fellow in population intervention for chronic disease prevention at the University of Waterloo. His research focuses on the personal and social factors that contribute to health and well-being for youth, and the management of the built environment as a way of increasing overall health. Ryan's recent research examines the personal and social experience of living with a chronic illness in adolescence and emerging adulthood. He completed his doctoral work at the University of Waterloo in recreation and leisure studies.

Colleen Whyte, PhD, is a doctoral candidate in the department of recreation and leisure studies at the University of Waterloo and a lecturer in the department of recreation and leisure studies at Brock University, Canada. Her research is examining meanings and experiences of community for residents living in long-term care homes, how a sense of community changes with the transition to a long-term care setting, and the role of leisure in maintaining a sense of community for residents.

Elaine Wiersma is an associate professor in the department of health sciences, faculty of health and behavioural sciences, at Lakehead University in Thunder Bay, Ontario, Canada. Her work has spanned community and long-term care sectors, using qualitative and participatory methodologies to examine the social dimensions of aging and dementia. Currently, her work is focusing on the development of self-management in dementia and exploring the context of aging and dementia in rural northern communities in Ontario.